MW00717625

JAVA Database Programming with JDBC

2nd Edition

JAVA Database Programming with JDBC

2nd Edition

Pratik Patel
Karl Moss

CORIOLIS GROUP BOOKS

an International Thomson Publishing company I(T)P®

Albany, NY • Belmont, CA • Bonn • Boston • Cincinnati • Detroit • Johannesburg • London
Madrid • Melbourne • Mexico City • New York • Paris • Singapore • Tokyo • Toronto • Washington

PUBLISHER	KEITH WEISKAMP
PROJECT EDITOR	MICHELLE STROUP
PRODUCTION PROJECT COORDINATOR	MICHAEL PEEL
COVER ARTIST	GARY SMITH
COVER DESIGN	SQUARE ONE DESIGN
INTERIOR DESIGN	NICOLE COLÓN
COMPOSITOR	PROIMAGE
COPYEDITOR	MARISA PÉNA, BONNIE TRENGA
PROOFREADER	ERIC KINGSBURY
INDEXER	LAURA LAWRIE
CD-ROM DEVELOPMENT	ROBERT CLARFIELD

Visual Developer Java Database Programming with JDBC, 2nd Edition
ISBN: 1-57610-159-2
Copyright © 1997 by The Coriolis Group, Inc.

The Coriolis Group, Inc.
An International Thomson Publishing Company
14455 N. Hayden Road, Suite 220
Scottsdale, Arizona 85260

602/483-0192
FAX 602/483-0193
http://www.coriolis.com

Printed in the United States of America
10 9 8 7 6 5 4 3 2

CONTENTS

Acknowledgments

First and foremost, thanks to Krishna, Mom and Dad for their continuous support in life. The folks at MetaLAB UNC deserve tons of credit for supporting the crazy ideas I get: Mark, Donald, Uzoma, Charlie, Kelly, Michael, Lane, Simon, Bascha, and last but not least, Paul Jones.

The Medical Informatics group for their challenges and thoughts: Joe, Gary, Marc, Guy, Matt, Bob, Dr. Loonsk and Dr. Downs. The 'fellas' Vij, Shru, Rish, and Mehul for putting up with my rants and raves. Thanks to CNS for looking out for me.

Certainly the groovy people at Coriolis who made this book into a winner the first time around, and will make it a superstar this time. My editor Michelle was a joy to work with, and Keith Weiskamp is the publisher that listens.
—*Pratik R. Patel*

There are many people who have influenced my contributions to this book. First I would like to mention John Goodson at Intersolv. John's knowledge of ODBC, SQL, and database middleware is unparalleled in the industry. John gave me the opportunity to develop Intersolv's JDBC products, and I thank him. I would also like to thank Pratik Patel for giving me the opportunity to contribute my ideas and effort to this book. To Vallory, Jillian, and Austin for allowing Dad to encroach on their computer and playtime, I can finally say that I'm finished. We're going to Disney World! And finally, thanks to my wife, Shanna, who was always there with support and encouragement.
—*Karl Moss*

INTRODUCTION

Welcome to the future of database connectivity. The Java Database Connectivity (JDBC) specification is a new basis for developers to interface with data sources. The structure of the JDBC is designed to allow developers to program for a standard interface, and let the low-level JDBC driver for different databases deal with the connection and querying of the databases; hence, the developer does not need to worry about dealing with different SQL flavors for each database. The JDBC is also very flexible—a developer doesn't necessarily lose features specific to the target database. Best of all, the JDBC is based on the Java language!

This is the second edition of this book. We had great success with the first edition, and decided to do a second edition because we wanted to update the book for the revised JDBC specification. We also wanted to show you how to utilize the JDBC with some of the other hot APIs coming out for Java, like the Servlet API and the Java Beans specification. We've also added two additional chapters based on the feedback we received from readers on the Internet.

Getting Software

The software that you'll need to get started with the JDBC is readily available on the Web. The JDBC drivers that you will need to connect to your databases are currently available for most popular databases from a variety of software vendors. The basic package you'll need is the JDBC API, which consists of the core classes of the JDBC. If you don't already have a Java development kit, such as Javasoft's JDK, you'll need that as well. The JDBC is actually part of the standard JDK version 1.1.1! At the time this manuscript was finished, the examples in the book were tested with the JavaSoft JDK, Symantec Cafe, and Microsoft J++. You can get the JavaSoft JDK at **www.javasoft.com**.

The JDBC API, and the ODBC driver for JDBC (that's right, you can use the JDBC with your current ODBC drivers!) commonly referred to as the JDBC-ODBC bridge can be downloaded at the JDBC Web site at **splash.javasoft.com/jdbc**. You'll also find the documentation for the JDBC API at this Web site. If you want to see some of the original JDBC specification, this can be downloaded from the JDBC Web site as well. The java.sql.* package in the standard JDK 1.1.1 (or later) is the JDBC—the documentation is also part of the standard package.

Overview Of Chapters

Chapter 1, *JDBC: Databases, The Java Way!*, begins with a high-level introduction to the JDBC. You'll see how modular JDBC drivers fit into the development cycle, as well as where ODBC fits into the JDBC's overall structure.

Chapter 2, *SQL 101: An Introduction To SQL*, takes a quick stroll through SQL, the language of databases. This chapter is a primer on SQL, and is useful if you need to brush up on your data-speak. It provides a basis of reference for some of the SQL queries performed in the JDBC programs in the book.

Chapter 3, *Using JDBC Drivers*, shows you how to install JDBC drivers, as well as how to handle the installation of the JDBC API base classes. A "quick start" section also prepares you for what's ahead by giving you a simple, but complete JDBC program.

Chapter 4, *The Interactive SQL Query Applet*, takes you head first into the JDBC by presenting a complete Java applet that uses the JDBC. The applet allows a user to enter SQL queries and run them against a database, and to show the results.

Chapter 5, *Middleware*, details three-tier database systems. A three-tier system is developed in this chapter to give you an idea of the functionality possible with these types of "indirect" database access. The full source code for the developed application server and the client are presented, as well as a sample applet that uses the client to query and obtain results from a database.

Chapter 6, *Choosing the Right JDBC Driver*, looks at the four basic types of JDBC drivers. The disadvantages and advantages of the different types, as well as other issues specifically about drivers, is discussed.

Chapter 7, *Writing Database Drivers*, takes you into the heart of the JDBC with a thorough discussion of the programming details of JDBC drivers. You'll even see an actual JDBC driver produced, as our SimpleText JDBC driver is hammered out during the chapter. The full source code for this driver is presented in Appendix B, while the intricacies of writing a JDBC driver are explained in detail in Chapter 7.

Chapter 8, *Accessing ODBC Services*, takes a look at the JDBC-ODBC bridge in detail. Limitations of the bridge, as well as a complete listing of the features of ODBC available in the JDBC, are presented.

Chapter 9, *SQL Datatypes In Java*, shows you how to map SQL datatypes into Java, and provides a discussion of some of the special classes available in the JDBC API that facilitate the exchange of data between your Java program and the database.

Chapter 10, *Java and Database Security*, reflects on the security consideration you need to ponder before you put your JDBC programs into production. The issue of "applet trusting," and more, is covered in this chapter.

Chapter 11, *Deploying Data-Aware Applets*, will help you consider the issues for deploying your JDBC-aware Java applet. We'll look at topics related specifically to Internet and intranet deployment.

Chapter 12, *The Multimedia JDBC Application: Icon Store*, expands on the discussion in Chapter 7 into the realm of multimedia. Streams that contain binary data, such as images, are the focus of this chapter. We'll show you how to store and retrieve binary data from a database, using the methods available in the JDBC.

Chapter 13, *Working With Query Results*, provides a pathway for using results fetched from a SQL query. The complete cycle of querying a database, formatting the results, and displaying or printing them in nice graphs is presented with complete source code. A bar graph and pie chart are dynamically created in an applet using data from a query.

Chapter 14, *Server-Side Databases: Servlets And JDBC*, looks at how to program servlets that are data-aware. We quickly cover the Servlet API so that we can develop a project that utilizes JDBC to access a database. Web pages are dynamically produced by the servlet from information in a database. Processing HTML forms in the servlet is covered as well.

Chapter 15, *Building Data-Aware Components Using Java Beans*, explores the Java Beans component specification. You'll learn all about Java Beans as you create several simple beans. Using the JDBC, we'll step through an example bean that accesses a database. Java Beans allows you to create reusable components in Java, so it's something you definitely want to read about.

Chapter 16, *The JDBC API*, provides you with a reference for all of the methods, variables, classes, exceptions, and interfaces that are the JDBC.

Part 1

GETTING STARTED WITH JDBC

JDBC DATABASES THE JAVA WAY

1

T he Internet has spurred the invention of several new technologies in client/server computing—the most recent of which is Java. Java is two-dimensional: it's a programming language and also a client/server system in which programs are automatically downloaded and run on the local, or client, machine. The wide acceptance of Java has prompted its quick development. Java includes Java compilers, interpreters, tools, libraries, and integrated development environments (IDEs). JavaSoft is leading the way in the development of libraries to extend the functionality and usability of Java as a serious platform for creating applications. One of these libraries, called Application Programming Interfaces (APIs), is the Java Database Connectivity API, or JDBC. Its primary purpose is to use the Java language to intimately tie connectivity to databases.

We'll discuss the reasoning behind the JDBC in this chapter, as well as the design of the JDBC and its associated API. The Internet, or better yet, the technologies used in the operation of the Internet, is tied into the design of the JDBC. The other dominant design basis for the JDBC is the database standard known as SQL. Hence, the JDBC is a fusion of three discrete computer areas: Java, Internet technology, and SQL. With the

3

growing implementation of these Internet technologies in "closed" networks, called *intranets*, the time is right for the development of Java-based enterprise APIs. In this book, Intranet and Internet are both used to describe the software technology behind a network such as the World Wide Web.

What Is The JDBC?

JDBC stands for Java Database Connectivity. But besides a nifty acronym, what *is* this JDBC? It refers to several things, depending on its context:

- It's a specification for using data sources in Java applets and applications.

- It's an API for using low-level JDBC drivers.

- It's an API for creating the low-level JDBC drivers, which do the actual connecting/transacting with data sources.

- It's based on the X/Open SQL Call Level Interface (CLI) that defines how client/server interactions are implemented for database systems.

Confused yet? It's really quite simple: The JDBC defines every aspect of making data-aware Java applications and applets. The low-level JDBC drivers perform the database-specific translation to the high-level JDBC interface. The developer uses this interface so he doesn't need to worry about the database-specific syntax when connecting to and querying different databases. The JDBC is a package, much like other Java packages such as java.awt. It is currently a part of the standard Java Developer's Kit (JDK) distribution. It's also included in the standard part of the general Java API as the java.sql package. Soon it will also become a standard package in Java-enabled Web browsers, though there is no definite time frame for this inclusion. The exciting aspect of the JDBC is that the drivers necessary for connection to their respective databases do not require the client to pre-install anything: A JDBC driver can be downloaded along with an applet!

The JDBC project was started in January of 1996, and the specification was frozen in June of 1996. JavaSoft sought the input of industry database vendors so that the JDBC would be as widely accepted as possible when it was ready for release. And, as you can see from this list of vendors who have already endorsed the JDBC, it's sure to be widely accepted by the software industry (this is only a partial list):

- Borland International, Inc.

- IBM

- Informix Software, Inc.

- Intersolv

- Oracle Corporation

- SAS Institute, Inc.

- SCO

- Sybase, Inc.

- Symantec

- Visigenic Software, Inc.

The JDBC is heavily based on the ANSI SQL-92 standard, which specifies that a JDBC driver should be SQL-92 entry-level compliant to be considered a 100 percent JDBC-compliant driver. This is not to say that a JDBC driver has to be written for a SQL-92 database; a JDBC driver can be written for a legacy database system and still function perfectly. As a matter of fact, the simple JDBC driver developed in Chapter 7 uses delimited text files to store table data. Even though the driver does not implement every single SQL-92 function, it is still a JDBC driver. This flexibility will be a major selling point for developers who are bound to legacy database systems, but who still want to extend their client applications.

The JDBC Structure

As I mentioned earlier, the JDBC is both a programming language and a client/server system. The purpose for this two-dimensional design is to separate the low-level programming from the high-level application interface. The low-level programming is facilitated by the JDBC driver. JDBC drivers are quite flexible; they can be local data sources or remote database servers. The implementation of the actual connection to the data source/database is left entirely to the JDBC driver. So the idea behind the JDBC driver is that database vendors and third-party software vendors can supply pre-built drivers for connecting to different databases.

The structure of the JDBC includes these key concepts:

- The goal of a DBMS-independent interface, a "generic SQL database access framework," and a uniform interface to different data sources.

- The programmer writes only *one* database interface; using JDBC, the program can access any data source without the need to change code.

Figure 1.1 shows the architecture of the JDBC. The **DriverManager** class is used to open a connection to a database via a JDBC driver, which must register with the **DriverManager** before the connection can be formed. When a connection is attempted, the **DriverManager** chooses from a given list of available drivers to suit the explicit type of database connection. After a connection is formed, the calls to query and fetch results are made directly with the JDBC driver. The JDBC driver must implement the classes to process these functions for the specific database, but the rigid specification of the JDBC ensures that the drivers will perform as expected. Essentially, the developer who has JDBC drivers for a certain database does not need to worry about changing the code for the Java program if a different type of database is used (assuming that the JDBC driver for the other database is available). This is especially useful in the scenario of distributed databases.

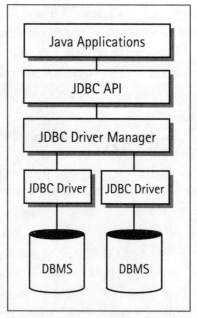

Figure 1.1
The architecture of the JDBC.

The JDBC uses a URL syntax for specifying a database. For example, a connection to a mysql database, which was used to develop some of the Java applets in this book, is:

```
jdbc:mysql://president:3333/newswire
```

This statement specifies the transport to use—jdbc, the database type—mysql; the server name; the port—3333; and the database to connect to—newswire. We'll discuss specifying a database more thoroughly in Chapter 3.

The data types in SQL are mapped into native Java types whenever possible. When a native type is not present in Java, a class is available for retrieving data of that type. Consider, for example, the **Date** type in the JDBC. A developer can assign a date field in a database to a JDBC **Date** class, after which the developer can use the methods in the **Date** class to display or perform operations. The JDBC also includes support for binary large objects, or BLOB data types; you can retrieve and store images, sound, documents, and other binary data in a database with the JDBC. In Chapter 9, we'll cover the SQL data types and their mapping into Java/JDBC.

ODBC's Part In The JDBC

The JDBC and ODBC share a common parent: Both are based on the same X/Open call-level interface for SQL. Though there are JDBC drivers emerging for many databases, you can write database-aware Java programs using existing ODBC drivers. In fact, JavaSoft and Intersolv have written a JDBC driver—the JDBC-ODBC bridge—that allows developers to use existing ODBC drivers in Java programs. Figure 1.2 shows the place of the JDBC-ODBC bridge in the overall architecture of the JDBC. However, because the bridge must make native method calls to do the translation from ODBC to JDBC, the JDBC-ODBC bridge requires pre-installation on the client machine, or wherever the Java program is actually running. Pre-installation is also required for JDBC drivers that use native methods. Only drivers that are 100 percent Java JDBC drivers can be downloaded across a network with a Java applet, thus requiring no pre-installation of the driver.

ODBC drivers function in the same manner as "true" JDBC drivers. In fact, the JDBC-ODBC bridge is actually a sophisticated JDBC driver that does low-level translation to and from ODBC. When the JDBC driver for a certain

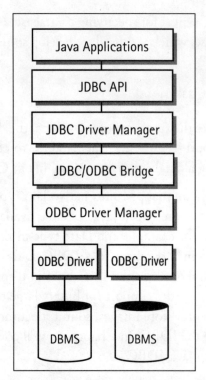

Figure 1.2
The JDBC-ODBC Bridge in the overall architecture of the JDBC.

database becomes available, you can easily switch from the ODBC driver to the new JDBC driver with few, if any, changes to the code of the Java program.

Summary

The JDBC is not only a specification for using data sources in Java applets and applications, but it also allows you to create and use low-level drivers to connect and "talk" with data sources. You have now explored the JDBC architecture and seen how the ODBC fits into the picture. The important concept to remember about the JDBC is that the modular design of the JDBC interface allows you to change between drivers, hence databases, without recoding your Java programs.

In the next chapter, we'll take a step back to give you a quick primer on SQL, one of the pillars of the JDBC. If you are already familiar with SQL-92, feel free to skip the chapter. However, the chapter may help clarify the SQL queries performed in the sample JDBC programs we develop in this book.

SQL 101: An Introduction To SQL

2

SQL—the language of database. This chapter's primary purpose is to serve as a primer on this data sublanguage. Although it would be impossible for me to cover the intricacies of SQL in just one chapter, I do intend to give you a solid introduction that we'll build on in this book. Because the JDBC requires that drivers support the ANSI SQL-92 standard to be JDBC compliant, this chapter is based on that standard. SQL-92, which I'll refer to as SQL, is modeled after database management proposed in 1970 by Dr. E.F. Codd. Over time, SQL evolved into the full-featured language it is today, and it continues to evolve with our ever-changing needs.

A JDBC driver doesn't absolutely *have* to be SQL-92 compliant. The JDBC specification states the following: "In order to pass JDBC compliance tests and to be called 'JDBC compliant,' we require that a driver support at least ANSI SQL-92 Entry Level." This requirement is clearly not possible with drivers for legacy database management systems (DBMSes). The driver in these cases will not implement all of the functions of a "compliant" driver. In Chapter 7, *Writing JDBC Drivers*, we develop the basics of a JDBC driver that implements only some of the features of SQL—but it is a JDBC driver nonetheless.

We'll start our exploration of SQL by discussing the relational model, the basis for SQL. Then we'll cover the essentials of building data tables using SQL. Finally, we'll go into the manipulation and extraction of the data from a datasource.

The Relational Model And SQL

Although SQL is based on the relational model, it is not a rigid implementation of it. In this section, we'll discuss the relational model as it pertains to SQL so we do not obfuscate our discussion of this standard, which is central to the JDBC specification. As part of its specification, the SQL-92 standard includes the definition of data types. We'll cover these data types, and how to map to Java, in Chapter 9, *SQL Data Types In Java*.

Understanding The Basics

The basic units in SQL are tables, columns, and rows. So where does the "relational" model fit into the SQL units? Strictly speaking, in terms of the relational model, the "relation" is mapped in the table: It provides a way to relate the data contained within the table in a simple manner. A column represents a data element present in a table, while a row represents an instance of a record, or entry, in a table. Each row contains one specific value for each of the columns (a value can be blank or undefined and still be considered valid). The table can be visualized—you guessed it—as a matrix, with the columns as the vertical fields and the horizontal fields as the rows. Figure 2.1 shows an example table that can be used to store information about a company's employees.

Before we push on, there are some syntax rules you need to be aware of:

- SQL is not whitespace sensitive. Carriage returns, tabs, and spaces don't have any special meaning when executing queries. Keywords and tokens are delimited by commas, when applicable, and parentheses are used for grouping.

- When performing multiple queries at one time, you must use semicolons to separate distinct queries.

- Queries are *not* case sensitive.

Employee Number	Last Name	First Name	Function
00031	Patel	Pratik	Author
00032	Moss	Karl	Author
00022	Weiskamp	Keith	Developmental
00075	Pronk	Ron	Editing

Figure 2.1
An SQL Table.

Case Sensitivity

A word of caution: While the keywords are not case sensitive, the string values that are stored as data in a table do preserve case. Keep this in mind when doing string comparisons in queries.

Putting It Into Perspective: Schema And Catalog

Though you can stick all of your data into a single table, it isn't logical to do this all the time. For example, in our EMPLOYEE table shown previously, we could add information about company departments; however, the purpose of the EMPLOYEE table is to store data on the employees. The solution is for us to create another table, called DEPARTMENT, which will contain information about the specific departments in the company. To associate an employee with a department, we can simply add a column to the EMPLOYEE table that contains the department name or number. Now that we have employees and departments neatly contained, we can add another table, called PROJECT, to keep track of the projects each employee is involved in. Figure 2.2 shows our tables.

Now that you understand how to logically separate your data, it's time to take our model one step higher and introduce you to the schema/catalog relationship. The *schema* is a higher-level container that is defined as a collection of zero or more tables, where a table belongs to exactly one schema. In the same way, a *catalog* can contain zero or more schemas. This abstract is a necessary part of a robust relational database management system (RDBMS). The primary reason is access control: It facilitates who can read a table, who can change a table, and

EMPLOYEE Table

Employee Number	Last Name	First Name	Function	Department
00031	Patel	Pratik	Author	0379
00032	Moss	Karl	Author	0379

DEPARTMENT Table

Department Number	Department Head (Employee)	Location
0379	00022	Scottsdale
0480	00075	Scottsdale

PROJECTS Table

Number	Title	Type	Leader
0798	JDBC Book	Book	00022

Figure 2.2
The EMPLOYEE, DEPARTMENT, and PROJECT tables track employees by department and project.

even who can create or destroy tables. Figure 2.3 demonstrates this point nicely. Here we have added another table, called CONFIDENTIAL. It contains the home address, home phone number, and salary of each employee. This information needs to belong in a separate schema so that only payroll can access the data, while those in marketing can get the necessary data to do their job.

Introducing Keys

As you can see in the previous example, we have purposely set up the three tables to link to one another. The EMPLOYEE table contains a column that has the department number that the employee belongs in. This department number also appears in the DEPARTMENT table, which describes each department in the company. The EMPLOYEE and CONFIDENTIAL tables are related, but we still need to add one corresponding entry (row) in one table for each entry in the other, the distinction coming from the employee's number.

The link we have set up—employee number and department number—can be thought of as a *key*. A key is used to identify information within a table. Each

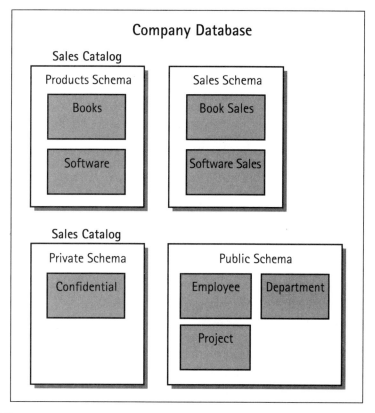

Figure 2.3
The table, schema, and catalog relationship allow you to limit access to confidential information.

individual employee or department should have a unique key to aid in various functions performed on the tables. In keeping with the relational model, the key is supposed to be unique within the table: No other entry in the table may have the same primary key.

A single column is sometimes enough to uniquely identify a row or entry. However, a combination of rows can be used to compose a *primary key*. For example, we might want to just use the combination of the title and city location of a department to comprise the primary key. In SQL, columns defined as primary keys must be defined. They cannot be "undefined" (also known as NULL).

Using Multiple Tables And Foreign Keys

As we have shown, it's best to split data into tables so that the data contained within a table is logically associated. Often, the data will logically belong in more than one table, as in the case of the employee number in the EMPLOYEE and CONFIDENTIAL tables. We can further define that if a row in one table exists, a corresponding row must exist in another related table; that is, we can say that if there is an entry in the EMPLOYEE table, there must be a corresponding entry in the CONFIDENTIAL table. We can solidify this association with the use of *foreign keys*, where a specific column in the dependent table matches a column in a "parent" table. In essence, we are linking a "virtual" column in one table to a "real" column in another table. In our example database, we link the CONFIDENTIAL table's employee number column to the employee number column in the EMPLOYEE table. We are also specifying that the employee number is a key in the CONFIDEN-TIAL table (hence the term, foreign key). A composite primary key can contain a foreign key if necessary.

We can create a logical structure to our data using the concept of a foreign key. However, in preparation, you'll have to put quite a bit of thought into creating your set of tables. An efficient and planned structure to the data, by way of the tables and keys, requires good knowledge of the data that is to be modeled. Unfortunately, a full discussion on the techniques of the subject is beyond the scope of this book. There are several different ways to efficiently model data. Figure 2.4 shows a preliminary plan of the database we have created. The SQL queries we perform in the examples of this book are not very complex, so the information outlined in this section should suffice to convey a basic understanding of the example databases created throughout the following chapters.

Data Definition Language

Now that we have outlined the basic foundation of SQL, let's write some code to implement our database. The formal name for the language components used to create tables is Data Definition Language, or DDL. The DDL is also used to create tables and perform a variety of other functions, such as adding and deleting rows (entries) from a table, and adding and deleting columns from a table. I'll show you some of these along the way.

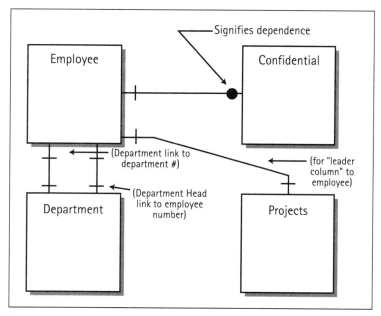

Figure 2.4
E-R diagram if relationships between tables.

Declaring Domains

One of the handy shortcuts that the DDL offers is a way to create predefined data objects. Though we haven't really talked about the data types available in SQL, you can probably guess the common ones like integer, character, decimal (floating point), date, and so on. Domains allow you to declare a data type of specific length and then give the declared type a name. This can come in handy if you have numerous data columns that are of the same data type and characteristics. Here's the SQL statement you use to declare a domain:

```
CREATE DOMAIN EMP_NUMBER AS CHAR(5)
```

Smart Domain Declaration Habits

When you are actually creating or altering tables, this domain can be used instead of specifying **CHAR(20)** each time. There are a number of reasons why this is good practice. Notice that we chose to make **EMP_NUMBER** a domain. This is a column that appears in several tables.

If we mistakenly use the wrong type or length in one of the table definitions where we have employee numbers, it could cause havoc when running SQL queries. You'll have to keep reading to find out the other reason.

Performing Checks

Predefining a data object is also useful for making sure that a certain entry in a column matches the data we expect to find there. For example, our *empno* field should contain a number. If it doesn't, performing a *check* of that data will alert us to the error. These checks can exist in the actual table definition, but it's efficient to localize a check in a domain. Hence, we can add a check to our employee number domain:

```
CREATE DOMAIN EMP_NUMBER AS CHAR(5) CHECK (VALUE IS NOT NULL);
```

Now our domain automatically checks for any null entries in columns defined as **EMP_NUMBER**. This statement avoids problems that crop up from non-existent entries, as well as allows us to catch any rogue SQL queries that add an incorrect entry (those that do not set the employee number) to the table.

Creating Tables

Creating a table in SQL is really pretty easy. The one thing you need to keep in mind is that you should define the referenced table—in this case, EMPLOYEE—before defining the referencing table, CONFIDENTIAL. The following code creates the EMPLOYEE table, shown in Figure 2.2:

```
CREATE TABLE EMPLOYEE
(
empno        CHAR(5) PRIMARY KEY,
lastname     VARCHAR(20) NOT NULL,
firstname    VARCHAR(20) NOT NULL,
function     VARCHAR(20) NOT NULL,
department   VARCHAR(20)
);
```

We also could have easily incorporated the domain that we defined earlier into the creation of the table, as shown here:

```
CREATE DOMAIN EMP_NUMBER AS CHAR(5) CHECK (VALUE IS NOT NULL);

CREATE TABLE EMPLOYEE
(
empno          EMP_NUMBER PRIMARY KEY,
lastname       VARCHAR(20) NOT NULL,
firstname      VARCHAR(20) NOT NULL,
function       VARCHAR(20) NOT NULL,
department     VARCHAR(20)
);
```

I can hear you now, "What's this **VARCHAR** data type?" SQL has two defined string types: **CHAR** and **VARCHAR**. The RDBMS allocates exactly the amount of space you specify when you use a **CHAR** data type. When you set an entry that is defined as a **CHAR(N)** to a string smaller than the size of **N**, the remaining number of characters is set to be blank. On the other hand, **VARCHAR** simply stores the exact string entered. The size you have specified is strictly a limit on how big the entered value can be.

We also see the **NOT NULL** directive again, which institutes the check on the specific column entry. We discussed primary and foreign keys earlier, now let's see how we actually implement them. Note that you should define the referenced table before defining the referencing table.

It's time to create the CONFIDENTIAL table. This table uses the *empno* attribute of the EMPLOYEE table as its primary key, via the **REFERENCES** keyword:

```
CREATE DOMAIN EMP_NUMBER AS CHAR(5) CHECK (VALUE IS NOT NULL);

CREATE TABLE CONFIDENTIAL
(
empno          EMP_NUMBER PRIMARY KEY,
homeaddress    VARCHAR(50),
homephone      VARCHAR(12),
salary         DECIMAL,
FOREIGN KEY ( empno ) REFERENCES EMPLOYEE ( empno )
)
```

We have linked the empno field in the CONFIDENTIAL table to the empno field in the EMPLOYEE table. The fact that we used the same name, "empno," is a matter of choice rather than a matter of syntax. We could have named the empno field whatever we wanted in the CONFIDENTIAL table, but we would need to change the first field referred to in the **FOREIGN KEY** declaration accordingly.

Manipulating Tables

Database management often requires you to make minor modifications to tables. However, careful planning can help you keep these alterations to a minimum. Let's begin by dropping, or removing, a table from a database:

```
DROP TABLE EMPLOYEE;
```

This is all we have to do to remove the EMPLOYEE table from our database. However, if the table is referenced by another table, as is the case with the CONFIDENTIAL table, a RDBMS may not allow this operation to occur. In this situation, you would have to drop any referencing tables first, and then rebuild them without the referencing.

Altering a table definition is as straightforward as removing a table. To remove a column from a table, issue a command like this:

```
ALTER TABLE EMPLOYEE
DROP firstname;
```

Of course, if this column is part of the table's key, you won't be able to remove it. Also, if another table references the column, or there is another column in any table that is dependent on this column, the operation is not allowed.

To add a column to a table, run a query like this:

```
ALTER TABLE CONFIDENTIAL
ADD dateofbirth DATE NOT NULL;
```

You can also make multiple "alterations" at one time with the **ALTER** clause.

Data Maintenance Language

The subset of commands for adding, removing, and changing the data contained in tables is the Data Maintenance Language (DML). As pointed out earlier, the data is manifest in the form of rows. So, basically, DML performs row-based operations. Let's see how this works by inserting an entry (row) in the EMPLOYEE table:

```
INSERT INTO EMPLOYEE
VALUES (
'00201',
'Pratik',
'Patel',
'Author',
''
);
```

Here we have inserted the appropriate information *in the correct order* into the EMPLOYEE table. To be safe, you can specify which field each of the listed tokens goes into:

```
INSERT INTO EMPLOYEE (empno, lastname, firstname, function, department)
VALUES (
'00201', 'Pratik', 'Patel',  'Author', ''
);
```

If you don't want to add all the fields in the row, you can specify only the fields you wish to add:

```
INSERT INTO EMPLOYEE (empno, lastname, firstname, function)
VALUES (
'00201', 'Pratik', 'Patel',  'Author'
);
```

As you can see, I chose not to add anything in the department field. Note that if a field's check constraint is not met, or a table check is not met, an error will occur. For example, if we did not add something under the firstname field, an error would have been returned because we defined the table's firstname column check as NOT NULL. We did not set up a check for the department field, so the previous command would not produce an error.

To delete a table's contents without removing the table completely, you can run a command like this:

```
DELETE FROM EMPLOYEE;
```

This statement will wipe the table clean, leaving no data in any of the columns, and, essentially, deleting all of the rows in the table. Deleting a single entry requires that you specify some criteria for deletion:

```
DELETE FROM EMPLOYEE
WHERE empno='00201';
```

You can delete multiple rows with this type of operation, as well. If the **WHERE** clause matches more than one row, all of the rows will be deleted. You can also delete multiple entries by using the **SELECT** command in the **WHERE** clause; we will get to the **SELECT** command in the next section.

If you really want to get fancy, you can use one statement to delete the same row from more than one table:

```
DELETE FROM EMPLOYEE, CONFIDENTIAL
WHERE empno='00201';
```

The final command I want to cover in this section is **UPDATE**. This command allows you to change one or more existing fields in a row. Here is a simple example of how to change the firstname field in the EMPLOYEE table:

```
UPDATE EMPLOYEE
SET firstname = 'PR'
WHERE empno='00201';
```

We can set more than one field, if we wish, by adding more expressions, separated by commas, like this:

```
UPDATE EMPLOYEE
SET firstname='PR', function='Writer'
WHERE empno='00201';
```

As you'll see in the next section, the **WHERE** clause can take the form of a SELECT query so that you can change multiple rows according to certain criteria.

Data Query Language

You've learned how to create your tables and add data to them, now we'll see how to retrieve data from them. The SQL commands that you use to retrieve data from a table are part of the Data Query Language (DQL). DQL's primary command is **SELECT**, but there are a host of predicates you can use to enhance the **SELECT** command's flexibility and specificity. Often, the key to understanding the process of querying is to think in terms of mathematical sets. SQL, like all fourth-generation languages, is designed to pose the question, "What do I want?" as opposed to other computer languages, like Java and C++, which pose the question, "How do I do it?"

Let's look at a set representation of our example database as shown back in Figure 2.3. When making queries, you'll want to ask these questions:

- Where is the data located in terms of the table?

- What are the references?

- How can I use them to specify what I want?

Mastering SQL querying is not an easy task, but if you have the proper mindset, it can be intuitive and efficient, thanks to the relational model upon which SQL is based.

The syntax of the **SELECT** statement is shown here:

```
SELECT column_names
FROM table_names
WHERE predicates
```

Let's take a look at the various functions of the **SELECT** command. To retrieve a complete table, run this query:

```
SELECT * FROM EMPLOYEE;
```

To get a list of employees in the Editorial department, run this query:

```
SELECT * FROM EMPLOYEE
WHERE department = 'Editorial';
```

To sort the list based on the employees' last names, use the **ORDER BY** directive:

```
SELECT * FROM EMPLOYEE
WHERE department= 'Editorial'
ORDER BY lastname;
```

To get this ordered list but only see the employee number, enter the following statements:

```
SELECT empno FROM EMPLOYEE
WHERE department = 'Editorial'
ORDER BY lastname;
```

To get a list of users with the name Pratik Patel, you would enter:

```
SELECT * FROM EMPLOYEE
WHERE (firstname='Pratik') AND (lastname='Patel');
```

What if we want to show two tables at once? No problem, as shown here:

```
SELECT EMPLOYEE.*, CONFIDENTIAL.*
FROM EMPLOYEE, CONFIDENTIAL;
```

Here's a more challenging query: Show the salary for employees in the Editorial department. According to our tables, the salary information is in the CONFI-DENTIAL table, and the department in which an employee belongs is in the EMPLOYEE table. How do we associate a comparison in one table to another? Since we used the reference of the employee number in the CONFIDENTIAL table from the EMPLOYEE table, we can specify the employees that match a specified department, and then use the resulting employee number to retrieve the salary information from the CONFIDENTIAL table:

```
SELECT c.salary
FROM EMPLOYEE as e, CONFIDENTIAL as c
WHERE e.department = 'Editorial'
          AND c.empno = e.empno;
```

We have declared something like a variable using the **as** keyword. We can now reference the specific fields in the table using a ".", just like an object. Let's begin by determining which people in the entire company are making more than $25,000:

```
SELECT salary
FROM CONFIDENTIAL
WHERE salary > 25000;
```

Now let's see who in the Editorial department is making more than $25,000:

```
SELECT c.salary
FROM EMPLOYEE as e, CONFIDENTIAL as c
WHERE e.department = 'Editorial'
         AND c.empno = e.empno
         AND c.salary > 25000;
```

You can perform a number of other functions in SQL, including averages. Here's how to get the average salary of the people in the Editorial department:

```
SELECT AVG (c.salary)
FROM EMPLOYEE as e, CONFIDENTIAL as c
WHERE e.department = 'Editorial'
         AND c.empno = e.empno;
```

Of course, the possibilities with SQL exceed the relatively few examples shown in this chapter. Because this book's goal is to introduce the JDBC specifically, I didn't use complex examples.

That completes our discussion on SQL. If you are interested in learning more about SQL, I recommend that you check out our book's Web site (**www .coriolis.com/jdbc-book**), where I have posted a list of recommended books on SQL and distributed databases.

Coming Up Next

The next chapter begins our journey into JDBC. I'll show you how to use JDBC drivers for connecting to data sources. Then we'll cover installing drivers, as well as the proper way to use drivers that are dynamically fetched with an applet. Finally, we'll discuss the security restrictions of using directly downloaded drivers as opposed to locally installed drivers.

USING JDBC 3
DRIVERS

As a developer who's using the JDBC, one of the first things you need to understand is how to use JDBC drivers and the JDBC API to connect to a data source. This chapter outlines the steps necessary for you to begin that process. We'll be covering the details of getting JDBC drivers to work, as well as the driver registration process we touched on in Chapter 1. We'll also take some time to explore JavaSoft's JDBC-ODBC bridge, which allows your Java programs to use ODBC drivers to call ODBC data sources.

Before our discussion gets underway though, I need to point out a few things about JDBC drivers. First, no drivers are packaged with the JDBC API; you must get them yourself from software vendors. Check out this book's Web site (**www.coriolis.com/jdbc-book**) for links to demo versions of drivers for your favorite database server, as well as for free JDBC drivers available on the Internet. There are also some JDBC drivers on the CD-ROM enclosed with this book. Second, if you want to use ODBC, don't forget that you'll also need ODBC drivers. If you don't have a database server but want to use JDBC, don't despair: You can use the ODBC drivers packaged with Microsoft Access. Using the JDBC-ODBC bridge, you can write Java applications that can interact with an Access database. The bridge is now included in the standard Java Development Kit (JDK) available from JavaSoft, version 1.1.1 or greater.

Unfortunately, applets enforce a security restriction that does not allow access to the local disk, so ODBC drivers might *not* work in the applet context (inside a Web browser). A future release of the JDK may change or relax this security restriction. A workaround for Java-enabled Web browsers is in development, and by the time you read this, it may very well be possible to use the JDBC-ODBC bridge in a Web browser. Using ODBC drivers in Java programs also requires pre-installation of the ODBC drivers and the JDBC-ODBC bridge on the client machine. In contrast, both JDBC drivers that are 100 percent Java class files and the calling applet's class file can be downloaded dynamically over the network. We'll provide a more thorough discussion of this point in Chapter 6.

Quick Start Guide

So you're a regular Java hacker, and you've already figured out how to install the JDBC API package. Now you want to jump right into it. This section will outline the four steps for running your first query and getting the results. Chapter 4 provides more details on these steps. Figure 3.1 is a diagram relating the four classes that you'll call on in your JDBC Java program, and it is the skeleton around which you can build database-aware Java programs. The diagram does not list all of the methods available in the respective classes. See Chapter 16, the JDBC API reference, for the complete class and method list.

Listing 3.1, below, is a very simple JDBC application that follows these four steps. It runs a query and gets one row from the returned result. If you don't understand everything going on here, don't worry—it's all explained in detail in Chapter 4.

LISTING 3.1   EXAMPLE JDBC APPLICATION.

```
import java.net.URL;
import java.sql.*;

class Select {
  public static void main(String argv[]) {
    try {
      Class.forName("gwe.sql.gweMysqlDriver")
      String url = " jdbc:mysql://president:3333/usersDB ";
      Connection con = DriverManager.getConnection(url, "prpatel",
                                                        "mypass");

      Statement stmt = con.createStatement();
      ResultSet rs = stmt.executeQuery("SELECT * FROM Users");
```

```
    System.out.println("Got results:");
    while(rs.next()) {

    String UID= rs.getString(1);
    String Password= rs.getString(2);
    String Last= rs.getString(3);
    String First= rs.getString(4);
    String OfficeID= rs.getString(5);

    System.out.print(UID +" "+ Password+"
    "+Last+" "+First+" "+OfficeID );
    System.out.print("\n");
    }
    stmt.close();
    con.close();
  }
  catch( Exception e ) {
    e.printStackTrace();

  }
 }
}
```

WHICH VERSION OF JAVA ARE YOU RUNNING?

If you're still developing for JDK version 1.0.2, you will need to read the sections entitled *Installing java.sql.** and *Installing The JDBC-ODBC Bridge.* If you're using version 1.1.1 or greater, you don't need to worry about installing either one of these packages: They are already part of the standard JDK. The JDBC-ODBC bridge is accessed as sun.jdbc.odbc.JdbcOdbcDriver.

Keep in mind that most Web browsers as of this writing support Java version 1.0.2. This means that you'll have to run your applets using the Appletviewer or rename and recompile the java.sql.* package, reflecting this change in the JDBC driver you're using. Microsoft offers a package to upgrade Internet Explorer to the new version of Java.

If you're already using Java 1.1 or greater, you don't need to worry about this. You will have to keep in mind that applets you create with this version will not work properly unless the Web browser is running a JVM that supports this new version of Java. You can always use the HotJava browser from JavaSoft to test applets based in the new Java specification while you wait for the other browsers to catch up to the new standard.

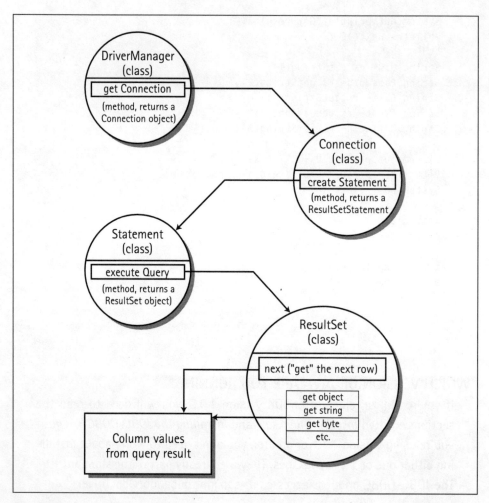

Figure 3.1
An overview of the process.

Installing java.sql.*

You don't need to read this section if you're using the new version of Java (version 1.1 or greater). If you're still developing with version 1.0.2, then this section applies. Consult the sidebar *Which Version of Java Are You Running?* for more information.

The java.sql.* package contains the JDBC base API classes. These classes are supposed to be in the normal java.* hierarchy that is distributed as part of the Java API (which includes the java.awt, java.io, and java.lang packages).

Currently, the JDBC API is distributed with the JDK, but versions of Java before 1.1.1 do not have the JDBC classes included. The java.sql.* package will also be included in the future APIs of popular Java-enabled Web browsers.

However, you don't have to wait for the release of this updated software. You can grab the JDBC API classes from the JavaSoft Web site at **http:// splash.java.com/jdbc**. As I was writing this chapter, the classes were stored in a file named "jdbc.122.tar.Z". By the time you read this chapter, however, the file name may be slightly different. Once you have your software, simply follow the easy instructions below to install the API classes in the proper place on your computer's hard disk. The following method allows you to compile and run Java applications *and* applets (using the Appletviewer) that use the JDBC:

1. Download the JDBC API package from the JavaSoft Web site, or make a copy of the file from the CD-ROM enclosed with this book.

2. On your hard drive, locate the directory that stores the Java API packages. (On my PC, the directory is C:\JAVA\SRC, and on my Sun box, the directory is \usr\local\java\src.) You do not need to install the JDBC API package in the same directory as the rest of the Java API. However, I strongly recommend that you do, because, as I mentioned earlier, the JDBC API is now a standard part of the Java API distribution and is packaged in the Java API hierarchy.

3. Unpack the JDBC API classes using one of the following methods (for Unix-based machines or PCs), substituting the location where you down-loaded the JDBC class file and the location where you want to install the JDBC classes:

Unix Procedure:

- To unpack the file, enter *prompt> uncompress \home\prpatel\ jdbc.122.tar.Z.*

- To create a jdbc directory with the classes and their source in separate directories, enter *prompt> tar xvf \home\prpatel\jdbc.122.tar.Z.*

- To install the JDBC classes, enter *prompt> cd \usr\local\java\src,* then enter *prompt> mv \home\prpatel\jdbc\classes\java,* and finally, enter *prompt> mv \home\prpatel\jdbc\src\java.*

Windows 95 Procedure:

- Using a Windows 95 ZIP utility such as WinZip, uncompress and untar the file. Be sure the file name ends with *.tar* when you uncompress the file so that utilities will recognize the file. Untar the file to a temporary folder.

- Copy the java folder from the JDBC\CLASSES directory (from the temp directory where you untarred the downloaded file) to the C:\JAVA\SRC directory.

- Copy the java folder from the JDBC\SRC directory to C:\JAVA\SRC.

4. Set the CLASSPATH to point to c:/usr/local/java/src (for Unix-based machines) or C:\JAVA\SRC (for PCs). Again, remember to substitute your location if this is not where you installed the downloaded file.

Save The API Documentation

The only item left from the JDBC package you downloaded is the API documentation, which is in the jdbc\html directory that was created when you uncompressed the downloaded file. You may want to save the API documentation somewhere for reference. You can view the file using a Web browser. You can also download this documentation by itself from the JDBC home page.

I must stress that you should make sure that you have the CLASSPATH set properly. The package will be called in the following way in your Java program:

```
import java.sql.*
```

You need to point the CLASSPATH at the *parent* of the java directory you copied in Step 2, which is why we set the CLASSPATH in Step 3. The package is contained in the java/sql/ folder, which is exactly as it should be according to the calling code snippet.

Registering And Calling JDBC Drivers

Now that we've installed the JDBC classes, let's cover how you load a JDBC driver. Note that you must import the java.sql.* into your Java program if you want to use a JDBC driver. These JDBC base classes contain the necessary elements for properly instantiating JDBC drivers, and they serve as the "middle-man" between you and the low-level code in the JDBC driver. The JDBC API provides you with an easy-to-use interface for interacting with data sources, independent of the driver you are using. The following sections cover three ways to tell the JDBC's **DriverManager** to load a JDBC driver.

The sql.drivers Property

When you want to identify a list of drivers that can be loaded with the **DriverManager**, you can set the sql.drivers system property. Because this is a system property, it can be set at the command line using the -D option:

```
java -Dsql.drivers= gwe.sql.gweMysqlDriver classname
```

If there is more than one driver to include, just separate them using colons. If you do include more than one driver in this list, the **DriverManager** will look at each driver once the connection is created and decide which one matches the JDBC URL supplied in the **Connection** class' instantiation. (I'll provide more detail on the JDBC URL and the **Connection** class later on in Chapter 4.) You'll use the first driver specified in the URL that is a successful candidate for establishing the connection. This is handy in case there are several JDBC drivers that may be used to connect to a database. You'll probably know beforehand which driver you plan to utilize, so the above discussion is some-what inessential.

There's Always A Class For A Name

You can explicitly load a driver using the standard **Class.forName** method. This technique is a more direct way of instantiating the driver class that you want to use in the Java program. To load the MySQL JDBC driver, insert this line into your code:

```
Class.forName("gwe.sql.gweMysqlDriver ");
```

This method tries first to load the gwe/sql/gweMysqlDriver from the local CLASSPATH, then the driver using the same class loader as the Java program—the applet class loader, which is stored on the network.

Just Do It

Another approach is what I call the "quick and dirty" way of loading a JDBC driver. In this case, you simply instantiate the driver's class. Of course, I don't advise you to take this route because the driver may not properly register with the JDBC **DriverManager**. The code for this technique, however, is quite simple and worth mentioning:

```
new gwe.sql.gweMysqlDriver ;
```

Again, if this code is in the applet context, it will first try to find this driver in the local CLASSPATH, then it will try to load it from the network.

JDBC URL And The Connection

The format for specifying a data source is an extended Universal Resource Locator (URL). The JDBC URL structure is broadly defined as follows

```
jdbc:<subprotocol>:<subname>
```

where *jdbc* is the standard base, *subprotocol* is the particular data source type, and *subname* is an additional specification that the subprotocol can use. The subname is based solely on the subprotocol. The subprotocol (which can be "odbc," "oracle," etc.) is used by the JDBC drivers to identify themselves and then to connect to that specific subprotocol. The subprotocol is also used by the **DriverManager** to match the proper driver to a specific subprotocol. The subname can contain additional information used by the satisfying subprotocol such as the driver, the location of the data source, as well as a port number or catalog. Again, this is dependent on the subprotocol's JDBC driver. JavaSoft suggests that a network name follow the URL syntax:

```
jdbc:<subprotocol>://hostname:port/subsubname
```

The MySQL JDBC driver we use in this book follows this syntax. Here's the URL you will see in some of the example code:

```
jdbc:mysql://president:3333/databasename
```

The **DriverManager.getConnection** method in the JDBC API uses this URL when attempting to start a connection. Remember that a valid driver must be registered with the JDBC **DriverManager** before attempting to create this connection (as I discussed earlier in the *Registering And Calling JDBC Drivers* section). The **DriverManager.getConnection** method can be passed in a **Property** object where the keys "user," "password," and even "server" are set accordingly. The direct way of using the **getConnection** method involves passing these attributes in the constructor. The following is an example of how to create a **Connection** object from the **DriverManager.getConnection** method. This method returns a **Connection** object that is to be assigned to an instantiated **Connection** class:

```
String url=" jdbc:mysql://president:3333/databasename";
Name = "pratik";
password = "";
Connection con;
con = DriverManager.getConnection(url, Name, password);
//Remember to register the driver before doing this!
```

Chapter 4 shows a complete example of how to use the **DriverManager** and **Connection** classes, as well as how to execute queries against the database server and get the results.

Using ODBC Drivers

In an effort to close the gap between existing ODBC drivers for data sources and the emerging pure Java JDBC drivers, JavaSoft and Intersolv released the JDBC-ODBC bridge. Note that there is a Java interface (hidden as a JDBC driver called JdbcOdbcDriver and found in the sun/jdbc/odbc/ directory below) that does the necessary JDBC-to-ODBC translation with the native method library that is part of the JDBC-ODBC bridge package. Although Chapter 8 covers the inner workings of the bridge, I would like to show you how to install it here. Once the bridge is set up, the JDBC handles access to the ODBC data sources just like access to normal JDBC drivers. In essence, you can use the same Java code with either JDBC drivers or ODBC drivers that use the bridge— all you have to do is change the JDBC URL to reflect a different driver.

Installing The JDBC-ODBC Bridge

You don't need to read this section if you're using the new version of Java (version 1.1 or greater). If you're still developing with version 1.0.2, this section applies. Consult the sidebar titled *Which Version of Java Are You Running?* for more information. The JDBC-ODBC bridge is now a standard part of the Java Developer's Kit, for version 1.1 or greater.

There are three steps to installing the JDBC-ODBC bridge. You'll need to get the package first. Look on the CD-ROM enclosed with this book, or grab the latest version from JavaSoft's Web site at **http://splash.javasoft.com/jdbc**.

1. Uncompress the package.

2. Move the jdbc directory (located in the jdbc-odbc/classes directory) into a directory listed in your CLASSPATH, or move it to your regular Java API tree.

3. Move JdbcOdbc.dll into your java/bin directory to make sure that the system and Java executables can find the file. You can also:

Unix Procedure:

- Add the path location of the JdbcOdbc.dll to your LD_LIBRARY_ PATH, or move the DLL into a directory covered by this environment variable.

Windows 95 Procedure:

- Move the DLL into the \WINDOWS\SYSTEM directory.

Setting Up ODBC Drivers

The data sources for the ODBC driver and the drivers themselves must be configured before you can run Java programs that access them. Consult your platform documentation and ODBC server's documentation for specific information.

One of the great features of the bridge is that it allows you to use existing data sources to start developing database-aware Java applications. And with Access, you don't even need a database server! In Chapter 5, I present the full source code for writing an application server that can use the JDBC-ODBC bridge, the Access ODBC drivers that come with Access 95, and an Access database to develop Java applets that can interact with a database without having a database server.

To set up an Access database for ODBC, follow these steps (I'm assuming you are using Windows 95):

1. Make sure you have the Access 95 ODBC drivers installed. You can install them from the Access install program.

2. Select Start Menu|Settings|Control Panels.

3. Click on 32-bit ODBC.

4. Click on the Add button and choose the Access Driver.

5. Type in a Data Source Name and Description (anything you like).

6. In the Database area, click on Select.

7. Select the Access database file; a sample database is located in MSOffice\ACCESS\Samples (if you installed it during the Access installation). However, you can specify any Access database you want.

8. You may want to click on the Advanced button and set the Username and Password. Click on OK and then on Close to complete the configuration.

That is all you need to do to set up the ODBC data source. Now you can write Java applications to interact with the data source on the machine in which you performed the configuration; the ODBC driver is not directly accessible over the network. You can access the data source by using the name you supplied in Step 5. For example, the URL would be something like

```
jdbc:odbc:DataSourceName
```

and the statement

```
Class.forName("sun.jdbc.odbc.JdbcOdbcDriver")
```

would load the JDBC-ODBC bridge.

Because of the security manager's restrictions for applets, it won't allow you to load the bridge directly. If you're running a Java application, you'll have no problems. If you're developing a Java applet, you'll see a security exception raised that won't allow your applet to continue. To get around this, you can test your applet that uses the JDBC-ODBC bridge by executing it like this:

```
java java.applet.AppletViewer IQ.html
```

Don't forget that because you're accessing a local ODBC data source when you use the JDBC-ODBC driver, you can't readily deploy this applet over the network. Each client machine must have the ODBC data source configured properly. If you don't have access to a database server that has a 100 percent Java driver, the JDBC-ODBC bridge can be a great way to start programming JDBC applets. You can simply set up an ODBC data source that points to an Access database (you need the Access ODBC driver, of course) and then use the JDBC-ODBC bridge to hit the Access database. We cover this more in Chapter 8. If you have a database server that has a JDBC driver, you'll want to use it, if possible, to write your JDBC applets and applications.

Coming Up Next

The next chapter works through a complete example of using a JDBC driver. I use the MySQL driver to query a MySQL database server over the network. The JDBC driver can easily be changed to use an ODBC driver or another JDBC driver to connect to a different data source, if necessary.

THE INTERACTIVE SQL QUERY APPLET

4

Now that you have seen how to use JDBC drivers, it's time to create an applet that uses the API. In this chapter, we jump into the JDBC with an example applet that is used to connect to a database and run some queries. Our Interactive Query applet will accomplish a number of tasks. It will:

- Connect to a database server, using a JDBC driver

- Wait for a user to enter an SQL query for the database server to process

- Display the results of the query in another text area

Of course, before we can get to the programming details of the applet, we need to take a step back, review the basics, and put together a plan. I know—plans take time to develop, and you want to get into the good stuff right away. But trust me, we'll be saving ourselves a lot of trouble later on by figuring out just the right way to get where we want.

Your First JDBC Applet

Our first step in creating a quality applet is understanding exactly what we need to do. This section covers some applet basics, at a high level. We'll begin by discussing the functionality of the Interactive Query applet, and then we'll explore how to fit the data-aware components contained in the JDBC into the Java applet model. As I said before, every great program starts with a well thought-out plan, so we'll work through the steps to create one. If you are familiar with Java, take the time to at least review this section before moving on to *Getting A Handle On The JDBC Essentials*. However, if you are unsure about what an applet really is and why it's different from a generic application, you will want to read this section all the way through.

The Blueprint

The applet structure has a well-defined flow, and is an event-driven development. Let's begin by defining what we want the SQL query applet to do at a high level. First, we want to connect to a database, which requires some user input: the database we want to connect to, a user name, and, possibly, a password. Next, we want to let the user enter an SQL query, which will then be executed on the connected data source. Finally, we need to retrieve and display the results of the query. We'll make this applet as simple as possible (for now), so that you understand the details of using the JDBC API and have a firm grasp of the foundations of making database-aware Java applets.

Our next task is to fill in some of the technical details of our plan. The absolute first thing we need to do, besides setting up the constructors for the various objects we use, is design and lay out the user interface. We aren't quite to that phase yet (remember, we're still in the planning phase), so we'll defer the design details for a later section of this chapter, *The Look Of The Applet*.

We need to get some preliminary input from the user; we need to have some event handlers to signal to the applet that the user has entered some information that needs to be processed, like the SQL query. Finally, we need to clean up when the applet is terminated, like closing the connection to the data source.

Figure 4.1 shows the flow diagram for the applet. As you can see, we do most of our real work in the **Select** method. The dispatcher is the event handler method, **mouseClicked**(). We use several global objects so that we don't have to pass around globally used objects (and the data contained within). This approach also adds to the overall efficiency; the code shows how to deal with some of the events directly in the event handler.

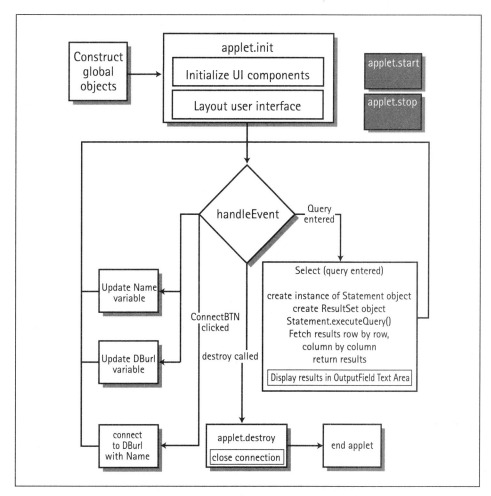

Figure 4.1
Flow diagram of the Interactive Query applet.

THE APPLET "FOUR-STEP"

As indicated in Figure 4.2, Java applets have a life cycle of four steps: initialization, execution, termination, and clean up. It's often unnecessary to implement all four, but we can use them to our advantage to make our database-aware applet more robust. Why does an applet have this flow? Applets run inside a Java Virtual Machine (JVM), or Java interpreter, like the one embedded within a Java-enabled Web browser. The interpreter handles the allocation of memory and resources for the applet; therefore, the applet must live within the context of the JVM. This is a pre-defined specification of the Java environment,

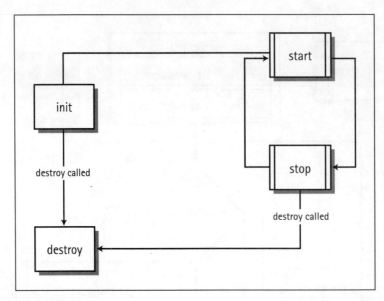

Figure 4.2
An applet's life cycle.

designed to control the applet's behavior. Note that Java applications do not follow this life cycle as they are not bound to run in the context of Java applets. Here's a synopsis of what the four methods, or steps, which can be overridden, do in the context of Java applets:

- **init**—This method is called when you first start the applet. It is only called once, and is where you should initialize objects (via construction or assignment). It is also a good place to set up the user interface.

- **start**—Once the applet has been initialized, this method is called to begin the execution of the applet. If you are using threads, this is the ideal place to begin threads that you create to use in the applet. This method is called when the Web browser (or Appletviewer) becomes *active,* that is, when the user brings up the window or focuses attention to the window.

- **stop**—This method is called when the applet window (which can be within a Web browser) becomes *inactive.* For instance, making the Web browser an icon calls this method. This can be used to suspend the execution of the applet when the user's attention is somewhere else.

- **destroy**—This method is called before the applet is wiped from memory and its resources returned to the operating system. This is a great place to flush buffers and close connections, and generally clean house.

As I said earlier, you don't need to have all four steps in your applet. For instance, our simple applet doesn't need the **start** and **stop** methods. Because we aren't running animation or other CPU-consuming process continuously, we aren't stealing any precious system cycles. Besides, if you are connected to a database across the Internet and execute a query that requires both processing time and time to download results, you may want to check your email instead of staring at the computer while the applet is working. These methods are meant to be overridden, as there is a minimal "default" for each method; the default depends on the intended function of each method.

EVENTS TO WATCH FOR

The flow chart shown back in Figure 4.1 shows some of the events we want to process. In this applet, we are only looking for mouse clicks on buttons. We override the **mouseClicked** method to allow us to program for these events. We use the target property of the **MouseEvent** object, which is passed into the event handler, to look for a specific object. Then, we can look for more specific events. Listing 4.1 contains a code snippet showing how we deal with the user clicking the Connect button.

EVENT HANDLING IN THE NEW JAVA 1.1

Event handling in Java has changed quite a bit from the 1.0.2 standard. See the bonus chapter in the back of this book for more information on JDK 1.1.1 event handling.

LISTING 4.1 TRAPPING FOR THE ENTER KEY EVENT IN A SPECIFIC OBJECT.

```
if (mEvt.getComponent() == ConnectBtn) {
    Name=NameField.getText();
    url=DBurl.getText();
    Passwd = PassField.getText();
}
```

The object **mEvt** is the local instantiation of the **MouseEvent** parameter that is part of the **MouseListener** interface, as we'll see later in the complete source code listing. We use the **getComponent** property to see in which object the event occurred. Then, we get the fields' information and stick it into our variables for later use.

EVENT HANDLERS

The applet has to be implemented as a **MouseListener** for us to be able to use the **mouseClicked** method:

```
public class IQ extends java.applet.Applet implements MouseListener {
```

In the new event handling model, we must either use interfaces like **Mouse Listener**, or use inner classes. There is no longer a generic **handleEvent** method that we can use to trap all events. We have to use a specific interface, and override its specific methods. In this example, we only use mouse clicks to signal the program that we're ready to do something, so we only need to override the **mouseClicked**, **mouseEntered**, **mouseExited**, **mousePressed**, and **mouseReleased** methods, which are part of the **MouseListener** interface. If you needed to watch for key strokes, you would implement the applet as a **KeyListener** interface, and override its methods, like **keyPressed**. You could implement the applet as a **MouseListener** and **KeyListener** if you needed to trap both types of events.

The other necessary step to make the new event handling model work is registering listeners. In our example applet, we need to *register* the two buttons that we use for letting the applet know that something needs to be done. We register the button with the listener interface by doing this:

```
QueryBtn.addMouseListener(this);
```

This lets the **MouseListener** interface we used in this applet know that it needs to process events that happen in this specific object. This new event handling model requires more coding, but it is very efficient. Before, all events happening in all AWT components were watching for events and passing them to the generic event handlers. This meant that anything the user did within the applet (mouse moving, key presses, and so on) generated some kind of event. The new model will surely help improve the speed of Java applets. See the bonus chapter in the back of this book for more information on the new event model for a thorough discussion of how events work in the new Java environment.

FINISHING UP

One of Java's great strengths lies in its ability to automatically allocate and de-allocate memory for objects created in the program, so the programmer doesn't have to. We primarily use the **destroy** method to close the database connection that we open in the applet. The JDBC driver that we used to connect to the data source is alerted that the program is exiting, so it can gracefully close the connection and flush input and output buffers.

Getting A Handle On The JDBC Essentials: The Complete Applet Source Code

Okay, enough talk, let's get busy! Listings 4.2 through 4.9 show the complete source code. Listing 4.10 shows the HTML file that we use to call our applet. I bet you're not too keen on entering all that code. But wait! There's no need to type it all in, just pull out the CD-ROM enclosed with this book and load the source into your favorite editor or IDE. Don't forget, though, that you need to have the JDBC driver for the database, and you may need your CLASSPATH set so that the applet can find the driver. If you're planning on loading the driver as a class along with the applet, make sure you put the driver in the same place as the applet. Refer back to Chapter 3 if you have trouble getting the applet to run and you keep getting the Can't Find A Driver or Class Not Found error.

 ### Source Code On The CD-ROM

There's no need to type in the source code because the Interactive Query applet can be found on the CD-ROM enclosed with this book, as is all source code in this book.

The Look Of The Applet

As we promised earlier, we're going to cover the details of user interface design and layout. Listing 4.2 covers the initialization of the user interface, as well as the normal "preliminaries" associated with Java programs. To help you along, we've included some comments to elaborate on the fine points that will help you to understand what's going on and what we are doing.

LISTING 4.2   SETTING UP THE OBJECTS.

```
import java.net.URL;
import java.awt.*;
import java.applet.Applet;
// These are standard issue with applets, we need the net.URL
// class because the database identifier is a glorified URL.

import java.sql.*;
// These are the packages needed to load the JDBC kernel,
// known as the DriverManager.
import gwe.sql.*;
// This the JDBC driver I used for MySQL. It's also included on
// the CD-ROM.
import java.awt.event.*;
// This is the new event handling class we need.

public class IQ extends java.applet.Applet implements MouseListener {
// This is the constructor for the base applet. Remember that the applet
// name must match the file name the applet is stored in—this applet
// should be saved in a file called "IQ.java". Also, we're using
// the MouseListener Interface for trapping mouse clicks.

// Below we create the objects we plan to use in the applet.
   Button ConnectBtn = new Button("Connect to Database");
   Button QueryBtn = new Button("Execute Query");

   TextField QueryField = new TextField(40);
   TextArea OutputField = new TextArea(10,75);
   TextField NameField = new TextField(40);
   TextField PassField = new TextField(40);
   TextField DBurl = new TextField(40);
   String url = "";
   String Name = "";
   String Passwd = "";
   Connection con;
// The Connection object is part of the JDBC API, and is
// the primary way of tying the JDBC's function to the applet.
```

GridBagLayout: It's Easier Than It Seems!

In Listing 4.2, we set up the objects we'll be using in the user interface. We loaded the necessary classes and the specific driver we will use in the applet. In

Listing 4.3, we go through the **init** phase of the applet, where we set up the user interface. We use **GridBagLayout**, a Java layout manager, to position the components in the applet window. **GridBagLayout** is flexible and offers us a quick way of producing an attractive interface.

LISTING 4.3   SETTING UP THE USER INTERFACE.

```
public void init() {
  QueryField.setEditable(true);
  OutputField.setEditable(false);
  NameField.setEditable(true);
  DBurl.setEditable(true);
// We want to set the individual TextArea and TextField to be
// editable so the user can edit the OutputField, where we plan
// on showing the results of the query.

 GridBagLayout gridbag = new GridBagLayout();
 GridBagConstraints Con = new GridBagConstraints();
// Create a new instance of GridBagLayout and the complementary
// GridBagConstraints.

 setLayout(gridbag);
// Set the layout of the applet to the gridbag that we created above.

 setFont(new Font("Helvetica", Font.PLAIN, 12));
 setBackground(Color.gray);
// Set the font and color of the applet.

 Con.weightx=1.0;
 Con.weighty=0.0;
 Con.anchor = GridBagConstraints.CENTER;
 Con.fill = GridBagConstraints.NONE;
 Con.gridwidth = GridBagConstraints.REMAINDER;
```

This code requires some explanation. The **weightx** and **weighty** properties determine how the space in the respective direction is distributed. If either weight property is set to 0, the default, any extra space is distributed around the outside of the components in the corresponding direction. The components are also centered automatically in that direction. If either weight property is set to 1, any extra space is distributed within the spaces between components in the corresponding direction. Hence, in setting the **weightx=1**, we have told the **GridBagLayout** manager to position the components on each row so that extra space is added equally between the components on that row. However, the rows of components are vertically "clumped" together because the **weighty** property is set to 0.0. Later on, we'll change **weighty** to 1 so that the large **TextArea** (the OutputField) takes up all of the space available. Take a look at Figure 4.3, shown at the end of the chapter, to see what we mean.

We also set the anchor property to tell the **GridBagLayout** to position the components in the center, relative to each other. The **fill** property is set to NONE so that the components are not stretched to fill empty space. You will find this technique to be useful when you want a large graphics area (the Canvas) to take up any empty space available around it, respective to the other components. The **gridwidth** is set to REMAINDER to signal that any component assigned the **GridBagConstraint Con** takes up the rest of the space on a row. Similarly, we can set **gridheight** to REMAINDER so that a component assigned this constraint takes up the remaining vertical space. The last detail associated with **GridBagLayout** involves assigning the properties to the component. This is done via the **setConstraints** method in **GridBagLayout**.

Listing 4.4 shows how we do this. Notice that we assign properties for the **TextArea**, but not for the **Labels**. Because we're positioning the **Labels** on the correct side of the screen (the default), there is no need to assign constraints. You can set more properties with **GridBagLayout**, but it's beyond the scope of this book.

LISTING 4.4 ASSIGNING PROPERTIES TO COMPONENTS.

```
add(new Label("Name"));
gridbag.setConstraints(NameField, Con);
add(NameField);
add(new Label("Password"));
gridbag.setConstraints(PassField, Con);
add(PassField);

// Note that we did not setConstraints for the Label. The
// GridBagLayout manager assumes they carry the default
// constraints. The NameField is assigned to be the last
// component on its row via the constraints Con, then added
// to the user interface.

add(new Label("Database URL"));
gridbag.setConstraints(DBurl, Con);
add(DBurl);
```

```
  gridbag.setConstraints(ConnectBtn, Con);
  add(ConnectBtn);
// Here, we only want the ConnectBtn button on a row, by itself,
// so we set the constraints, and add it.

 ConnectBtn.addMouseListener(this);
// Here is where we "register" the ConnectBtn with the
// MouseListener interface.

  add(new Label("SQL Query"));
  gridbag.setConstraints(QueryField, Con);
  add(QueryField);

  gridbag.setConstraints(QueryBtn, Con);
  add(QueryBtn);
  QueryBtn.addMouseListener(this);

  Label result_label = new Label("Result");
  result_label.setFont(new Font("Helvetica", Font.PLAIN, 16));
  result_label.setForeground(Color.blue);
  gridbag.setConstraints(result_label, Con);
  Con.weighty=1.0;
  add(result_label);
// Above we add a label on its own line. We also set the colors for it.

  gridbag.setConstraints(OutputField, Con);
  OutputField.setForeground(Color.white);
  OutputField.setBackground(Color.black);
  add(OutputField);
// This is what we were talking about before. We want the large
// OutputField to take up as much of the remaining space as possible,
// so we set the weighty=1 at this point. This sets the field apart
// from the previously added components, and gives it more room to exist.

 setVisible(true);
   } //init
```

We've added everything to the user interface, so let's show it! We also don't need to do anything else as far as preparation, so that ends the **init** method of our applet. We can now move on to handling events.

Handling Events

We want to watch for two events when our applet is running: the user clicking on either the **QueryBtn** or the **ConnectBtn**. Earlier in the chapter, we saw how to watch for events, but now we get to see what we do once the event is trapped, as Listing 4.5 shows. The event handling code is contained in the **mouseClicked** method for this specific applet.

LISTING 4.5   HANDLING EVENTS.

```
public void mouseClicked(MouseEvent mEvt) {

    if (mEvt.getComponent() == QueryBtn) {
      System.out.println(QueryField.getText());
      OutputField.setText(Select(QueryField.getText()));
    // Get the contents of the QueryField, and pass them to the
    // Select method that is defined in Listing 4.7. The Select
    // method executes the entered query, and returns the results.
    // These results are shown in the OutputField using the
    // setText method.
    }
```

Opening The Connection

Our next step is to connect to the database that will process the user's query, as Listing 4.6 shows.

LISTING 4.6   OPENING A DATABASE CONNECTION.

```
if (mEvt.getComponent() == ConnectBtn) {
// If the user clicks the Connect button, connect to the database
// specified in the url TextField and the user name specified in the
// NameField TextArea, using the password in the PassField field.
  Name=NameField.getText();
      url=DBurl.getText();
      Passwd = PassField.getText();
      // Set the global Name variable to the contents in the NameField.
      // Do the same thing for the JDBC URL and Password fields.

    try {
       Class.forName("gwe.sql.gweMysqlDriver");
// This creates a new instance of the Driver we want to use. There are a
// number of ways to specify which driver you want to use, and there is
// even a way to let the JDBC DriverManager choose which driver it thinks
// it needs to connect to the data source.
con = DriverManager.getConnection(url, Name, Passwd);
// Actually make the connection. Use the entered URL and the
// entered user name and password when making the connection.
       ConnectBtn.setLabel("Reconnect to Database");
       // Finally, change what the ConnectBtn to show "Reconnect
       // to Database".
```

```
      }
    catch(Exception e) {
      e.printStackTrace();
      OutputField.setText(e.getMessage());
    }
// The creation of the connection throws an exception if there was a
// problem connecting using the specified parameters. We have to
// enclose the getConnection method in a try-catch block to catch
// any exceptions that may be thrown. If there is a problem and an
// exception thrown, print it out to the console, and to the
// OutputField.


  }
} // end mouseClicked

  // We must override that method because we implemented this applet as a
  // MouseListener. To avoid doing this, we could do an abstract
  // implement of this applet.
  public void mouseEntered (MouseEvent mEvt) { }
  public void mouseExited (MouseEvent mEvt) { }
  public void mousePressed (MouseEvent mEvt) { }
  public void mouseReleased (MouseEvent mEvt) { }
```

No Guts, No Glory: Executing Queries And Processing Results

Now that we have opened the connection to the data source (Listing 4.6), it's time to set up the mechanism for executing queries and getting the results, as Listings 4.7 and 4.8 show. The parameter that we need in this method is a string containing the SQL query the user entered into the QueryField. We will return the results of the query as a string because we only want to pipe all of the results into the OutputField **TextArea**. We cast all of the returned results into a string; however, if the database contains binary data, we could get some weird output, or the program could even break. When we tested the applet, the data source we queried contained numbers and strings only. In Chapter 9, I'll show you how to deal with different data types in the ANSI SQL-2 specification, upon which the JDBC data types are based.

LISTING 4.7   EXECUTING A STATEMENT.

```
public String Select(String QueryLine) {
// This is the method we called in Listing 4.5.
// We return a String, and use a String parameter
// for the entered query.
```

```
    String Output="";
    int columns;
    int pos;
      try {
// Several of the following methods can throw exceptions if there
// was a problem with the query, or if the connection breaks, or if
// we improperly try to retrieve results.

        Statement stmt = con.createStatement();
// First, we instantiate a Statement class that is required to execute
// the query. The Connection class returns a Statement object in its
// createStatement method, which links the opened connection to the
// passed-back Statement object. This is how the stmt instance is linked
// to the actual connection to the data source.

        ResultSet rs = stmt.executeQuery(QueryLine);
// The ResultSet in turn is linked to the connection to the data source
// via the Statement class. The Statement class contains the executeQuery
// method, which returns a ResultSet class. This is analogous to a pointer
// that can be used to retrieve the results from the JDBC connection.

        columns=(rs.getMetaData()).getColumnCount();
// Here we use the getMetaData method in the result set to return a
// MetaData object. The MetaData object contains a getColumnCount method
// that we use to determine how many columns of data are present in the
// result. We set this equal to an integer variable.
```

LISTING 4.8   GETTING THE RESULT AND METADATA INFORMATION.

```
        while(rs.next()) {
// Now, we use the next method of the ResultSet instance rs to fetch
// each row, one by one. There are more optimized ways of doing this—
// namely using the inputStream feature of the JDBC driver. I show you
// an example of this in Chapter 9.

        for( pos=1; pos<=columns; pos++) {
// Now let's get each column in the row (each cell), one by one.

        Output+=rs.getString(pos)+" ";
// Here we've used the general method for getting a result. The
// getString method will attempt to cast the result in the form
// of a String. We simply get each "cell" and add a space to it,
// then append it onto the Output variable.

        }
// End for loop (end looping through the columns for a specific row).
```

```
        Output+="\n";
// For each row that we fetch, we need to add a carriage return
// so that the next fetched row starts on the next line.


        }
// End while loop (end fetching rows when no more rows are left).

        stmt.close();
// Clean up, close the stmt, in effect, close the input-output query
// connection streams, but stay connected to the data source.
    }
    catch(Exception e) {
      e.printStackTrace();
      Output=e.getMessage();
    }
// We have to catch any exceptions that were thrown while we were
// querying or retrieving the data. Print the exception to the console
// and return it so it can be shown to the user in the applet.

return Output;
// Before exiting, return the result that we got.
  }
```

Wrapping It Up

The last part of the applet, which Listing 4.9 shows, involves terminating the connection to the data source. This is done in the **destroy** method of the applet. We have to catch an exception, if one occurs, while the **close** method is called on the connection.

LISTING 4.9   TERMINATING THE CONNECTION.

```
public void destroy() {

  try {con.close();}
  catch(Exception e) {
     e.printStackTrace();
    System.out.println(e.getMessage());
    }
 } // end destroy
} // end applet IQ
```

The HTML File That Calls The Applet

We need to call this applet from an HTML file, which Listing 4.10 shows. We don't pass in any properties, but we could easily include a default data source URL and user name that the applet would read before initializing the user interface, and then set the appropriate **TextField** to show these defaults. Note that we set the width and height carefully in the <APPLET> tag to make sure that our applet's user interface has enough room to be properly laid out.

LISTING 4.10   HTML CODE TO CALL THE INTERACTIVE
                QUERY APPLET.

```
<HTML>
<HEAD>
<TITLE>JDBC Client Applet - Interactive SQL Command Util</TITLE>
</HEAD>
<BODY>
<H1>Interactive JDBC SQL Query Applet</H1>
<hr>

<applet code=IQ.class width=450 height=350>
</applet>

<hr>
</BODY>
</HTML>
```

The Final Product

Figure 4.3 shows a screen shot of the completed applet, and Figure 4.4 shows the applet running. Not too shabby for our first try. We've covered a lot of ground in creating this applet, so let's take some time to recap the important details. We learned how to:

• Open a connection to a data source

• Connect a **Statement** object to the data source via the connection

• Execute a query

• Get MetaData information about the result of the query

- Use the MetaData information to properly get the results row by row, column by column

- Close the connection

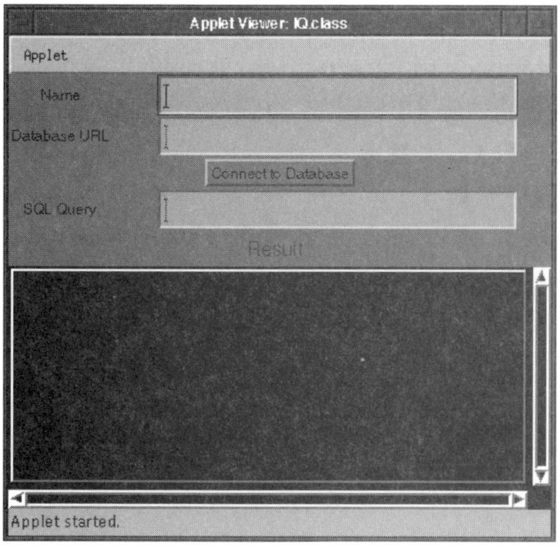

Figure 4.3
Screen shot of our example applet.

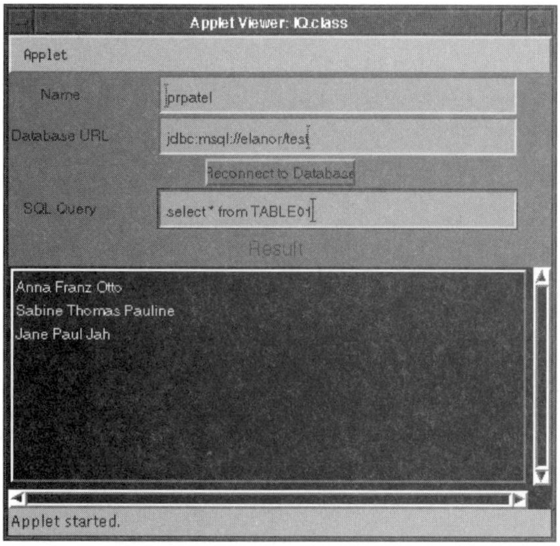

Figure 4.4
Screen shot of our example applet running a query.

To use the applet, you can load the HTML file in a Java-enabled Web browser, or you can start the applet from the command line:

```
bash$ appletviewer IQ.html &
```

Don't forget, if you have problems finding the class file or the driver, set the CLASSPATH. Refer back to Chapter 3 for more help on this topic.

Coming Up Next

In the next chapter, we'll explore middleware. We'll have a look at what middleware means and the advantages it can offer. We'll also develop a middleware server in Java, using JDBC, of course!

Part

2

JDBC DRIVERS

MIDDLEWARE 5

The JDBC specification says that the JDBC API should serve as a platform for building so-called "three-tier" client/server systems, often called *middleware*. As you might imagine, these systems have three components: the client, the server, and the application server. Figure 5.1 shows the structure of a three-tier system.

In this chapter, I'll provide you with the code necessary to implement a simple application server of your own. We'll also build a client for our home-grown application server. But before we get to the code, we need to discuss why we would want to go to such lengths to build a three-tier system instead of allowing direct database access.

Several middleware solutions based on the JDBC are already available, and although you may ultimately decide to buy one from a vendor instead of coding one yourself, it's important you learn the issues involved with middleware. Knowing the advantages and disadvantages of inserting a middle tier to a system can help you decide if you need one. There are also a few middleware products included on the CD-ROM enclosed with this book: the IDS server and the Weblogic server.

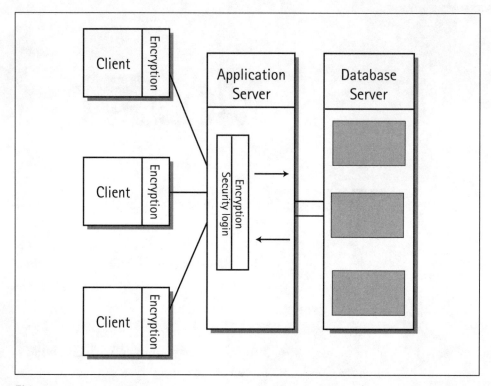

Figure 5.1
Middleware architecture.

Connectivity Issues Involved With Database Access

Let's begin by examining some database scalability issues that you are likely to encounter. The Internet and large intranet scenarios pose interesting dilemmas for databases that serve a large number of users:

- **Concurrency**—Suppose a user receives some data from the database server, and while the user is looking at it, the data on the database server changes in some way. For the user to see the updated material, both the database server and the client must be able to handle the change. While some database servers can handle the necessary coding (and the increased load on the server) for updating, some cannot.

- **Legacy Databases**—Some legacy database systems may not support simultaneous connections, or even direct connections that use TCP/IP.

- **Security**—Most database servers do not support encrypted connections, which means that certain transactions, such as the login using a password, will not be secure. Over the Internet, such a lack of security is a major hole.

- **Simultaneous Connections**—Database servers have a limit on the number of active connections. Unfortunately, it is easy to exceed this predefined limit on the Internet.

Advantages Of Middleware

Let's now have a look at how a middle tier can both address the issues presented in the previous section and add extra capability to a client/server system:

- **Concurrency**—You can program the application server to handle concurrency issues by off-loading the task from the database server. Of course, you would also need to program the clients to respond to update broadcasts. You can implement concurrency checking entirely on the application server, if necessary. This process involves checking to see if a specific data object a client requested has changed since the current request, asking the client to update the previously retrieved data, and alerting the user.

- **Legacy Databases**—Databases that operate on older network protocols can be piped through an application server running on a machine that can communicate with the database server, as well as with remote Internet clients. You can use a JDBC driver that can speak to a non-networked legacy database to provide Internet access to its data. You can even use an ODBC driver, courtesy of the JDBC-ODBC bridge. The application server can reside on the same machine as the non-networked database, and provide network access using a client that communicates to the application server.

- **Security**—You can program or obtain an application server that supports a secure connection to the remote clients. If you keep the local connection between the database server and the application server restricted to each other, you can create a fairly secure system. In this type of setup, your database server can only talk to the application server, which greatly limits the threat of someone connecting directly to the database server and causing damage. However, you must be sure that there are no loopholes in your application server.

- **Simultaneous Connections**—The application server, in theory, can maintain only one active connection to the database server. On the other hand, it can allow as many connections to itself from clients as it wants. In practice, however, significant speed problems will arise as more users attempt to use one connection. Managing a number of fixed connections to the database server is possible, though, so this speed degradation is not noticeable.

Disadvantages Of Middleware

Of course, middleware has its own pitfalls. Let's take a brief look at some disadvantages you may encounter if you choose to implement an application server:

- **Speed**—As I've hinted, decreased speed is the main drawback to running an application server, especially if the application server is running on a slow machine. If the application server does not run on the same machine as the database server, communication may be even slower as the two communicate with each other.

- **Security**—If your application server is not properly secured, additional security holes could easily crop up. For example, a rogue user could break into the application server and then break into the database server using the application server's functions. Again, you must take great care to ensure that unauthorized access to the database server via the application server is not possible.

- **Reliability**—Adding an application server to the system introduces potential problems that may not be present in a two-tier system, in which the clients are communicating directly with the database server. In essence, you are adding another place where a hacker could break into your system, so adding a middle layer must be done carefully.

The Application Server: A Complete Example With Code

I've shown you the advantages and disadvantages of implementing an application server; it's up to you to weigh these points and other related factors when it comes time to decide what to do on your own system. Let's look at a fully functional application server. The application server shown in Listing 5.1 uses

JDBC to interact with data sources, so you could use any JDBC driver. I used the MySQL driver in this example, but you can easily modify the code to use the JDBC-ODBC bridge, and then use the ODBC drivers for Access 97 to allow applets to query an Access 97 database. (This is an interesting scenario, because Access does not provide direct network connectivity in the form of a true "database server.") This application server is truly multithreaded—it spawns each client connection into its own thread. Each client connection also makes a new instance of the JDBC driver, so each client has its own virtual connection to the data source via the application server.

The application server allows only two real functions:

• Connect to a predefined data source

• Make Select queries against the data source

The query is processed against the data source, and the result is piped directly back to the client in pre-formatted text. You can easily extend this approach so that a ResultSet can be encapsulated and sent unprocessed to the client by using the upcoming remote objects specification from JavaSoft. For the purposes of this example, I won't make it too elaborate; instead, I just send over the results in a delimited String format. The client is not a true JDBC client in that it does not implement a JDBC driver; it uses the two functions defined earlier to make queries. The results can be parsed by the applet calling the client, but for the purposes of this simple example, we'll just show them to the user (you'll see this when we show the code for the client).

You can find the source file for Listing 5.1 on the CD-ROM enclosed with this book or on the book's Web site at **www.coriolis.com/jdbc-book**. Figure 5.2 shows the application server's window.

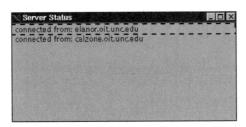

Figure 5.2
The application server console.

Listing 5.1   Application server.

```java
import java.util.*;
import java.sql.*;
import gwe.sql.*;
// Remember that we are using the JDBC driver on the _server_ to
// connect to a data source, so we need the JDBC API classes!


public class ApplicationServer extends Thread {
    public final static int DEFAULT_PORT = 6001;
    protected int port;
    protected ServerSocket server_port;
    protected ThreadGroup CurrentConnections;
    protected List connection_list;
    protected Vector connections;
    protected ConnectionWatcher watcher;
    public Frame f;
  // We plan on showing the connections to the server,
  // so we need a frame.

   // Exit with an error message if there's an exception.
   public static void fail(Exception e, String msg) {
       System.err.println(msg + ": " +  e);
       System.exit(1);
   }

// Create a ServerSocket to listen for connections and start its
// thread.
        public ApplicationServer(int port) {
        // Create our server thread with a name.
        super("Server");
        if (port == 0) port = DEFAULT_PORT;
        this.port = port;
        try { server_port = new ServerSocket(port); }
        catch (IOException e) {fail(e, "Exception creating
                                      server socket");}
        // Create a threadgroup for our connections.
        CurrentConnections = new ThreadGroup("Server Connections");

        // Create a window to display our connections in.
        f = new Frame("Server Status");
        connection_list = new List();
        f.add("Center", connection_list);
        f.setSize(400, 200);
        f.setVisible(true);
```

```java
        // Initialize a vector to store our connections in.
        connections = new Vector();
    // Create a ConnectionWatcher thread to wait for other
    // threads to die and to perform clean-up.

        watcher = new ConnectionWatcher(this);
            // Start the server listening for connections.
        this.start();
    }


  public void run() {
    // This is where new connections are listened for.
    try {
          while(true) {
                Socket client_socket = server_port.accept();
 ServerConnection c = new ServerConnection(client_socket,
                                    CurrentConnections, 3, watcher);
            // Prevent simultaneous access.
            synchronized (connections) {
             connections.addElement(c);
             connection_list.addItem(c.getInfo());
             }
             }
       }
     catch (IOException e)
        {fail(e, "Exception while listening for connections");}
     f.dispose();
     System.exit(0);
    }

    // Start the server up, get a port number if specified.
    public static void main(String[] args) {
        int port = 0;
        if (args.length == 1) {
         try {port = Integer.parseInt(args[0]);}
         catch (NumberFormatException e) {port = 0;}
        }
        new ApplicationServer(port);
    }
}


// This class is the thread that handles all communication with
// a client. It also notifies the ConnectionWatcher when the
// connection is dropped.
class ServerConnection extends Thread {
    static int numberOfConnections = 0;
```

```
      protected Socket client;
      protected ConnectionWatcher watcher;
      protected BufferedReader in;
      protected InputStreamReader inReader;
      protected PrintWriter out;
   Connection con;

      // Initialize the streams and start the thread.
      public ServerConnection(Socket client_socket, ThreadGroup
                                        CurrentConnections,
            int priority, ConnectionWatcher watcher) {
         // Give the thread a group, a name, and a priority.
         super(CurrentConnections, "Connection number" +
                                        numberOfConnections++);
         this.setPriority(priority);
         // We'll need this data later, so store it in local objects.
         client = client_socket;
         this.watcher = watcher;

         // Create the streams.
         try {
            inReader = new
                    InputStreamReader(client.getInputStream());
            in = new BufferedReader(inReader);
            out = new PrintWriter(client.getOutputStream());
         }
         catch (IOException e) {
          try {client.close();} catch (IOException e2) {
            System.err.println("Exception while getting
                          socket streams: " + e);
            return;}
         }
         // And start the thread up.
         this.start();
      }


// This is where the real "functionality" of the server takes place.
// This is where the input and output is done to the client.
   public void run() {
      String inline;

      try {
      // Loop forever, or until the connection is broken!
         while(true) {
            // Read in a line.
            inline="";
            inline = in.readLine();
            if (inline == null) break;
```

```
                   // If the client has broken connection, get out of
                   // the loop.

                   inline=inline.trim();
                    // Get rid of leading and trailing white space.

                   // These are the two functions implemented, connect
                   // and query. The client sends one of these commands,
                   // and if it's query ("S"), then the server expects the
                   // next line sent to be the query.

               switch(inline.toCharArray()[0]) {
                   case 'L': out.println("Connected to datasource");
                           out.println("DONE");
                           out.flush();
                           ConnectToDatasource("jdbc:mysql://president/
                                                       newswire",
           "wireuser", "cancan");
                           break;
               // See this method next...it starts up the driver and
               // connects to the data source.
                   case 'S': out.println("Run query: send SQL Query");
                           out.println("DONE");
                           out.flush();
                           inline = in.readLine();
           // This line gets the query sent here, runs it against
           // the connected data source, and returns the results in
           // formatted text.
                           inline=inline.trim();
                           out.println(RunQuery(inline));
   // RunQuery is the method that runs the passed-in
   // query using the initialized driver and connection.
                               out.println("DONE");
                               out.flush();
                           break;
                   default: out.println("ERROR - Invalid Request");
                           out.println("DONE");
                   }
                           out.flush();
               }
           }
       catch (IOException e) {}

// If the client broke off the connection, notify the
// ConnectionWatcher (watcher), which will close the connection.
```

```
        finally {
         try {client.close();}
         catch (IOException e2) {
            synchronized (watcher) {watcher.notify();}
              }
          }
    }


// This sends info back to the connection starter so that it can
// be displayed in the frame.
    public String getInfo() {
       return (inline+" connected from: "
                + client.getInetAddress().getHostName());
    }


  // DB-specific stuff follows!
private void ConnectToDatasource(String url, String Name, String Pass) {
try {
     Class.forName("gwe.sql.gweMysqlDriver");
     con = DriverManager.getConnection(url, Name, Pass);
// Create an instance of the driver and connect to the DB server.
    }
    catch( Exception e ) {
       e.printStackTrace(); System.out.println(e.getMessage());
    }
}


private String RunQuery(String QueryLine) {
// Run the passed-in query and return the Stringified results.
   String Output="";
   int columns;
   int pos;
   try {

     Statement stmt = con.createStatement();
     ResultSet rs = stmt.executeQuery(QueryLine);
     columns=(rs.getMetaData()).getColumnCount();

       while(rs.next()) {

        for( pos=1; pos<=columns; pos++) {

          Output+=rs.getString(pos)+" ";
        }
        Output+="\n";

       }
     stmt.close();
```

```
      //  con.close();
    }
    catch( Exception e ) {
      e.printStackTrace();
      Output=e.getMessage();
    }
    return Output;
  }
  // end DB-specific stuff

} // end class Connection

// This class cleans up closed connections and updates the displayed
// list of connected clients.
class ConnectionWatcher extends Thread {
    protected ApplicationServer server;
    protected ConnectionWatcher(ApplicationServer s) {
        super(s.CurrentConnections, "ConnectionWatcher");
        server = s;
        this.start();
    }

    public synchronized void run() {
        while(true) {
          try {this.wait(10000);}
            catch (InterruptedException e){
                System.out.println("Caught an Interrupted
                                            Exception");
                }
                // Prevent simultaneous access.
            synchronized(server.connections) {
                // Loop through the connections.
                for(int i = 0; i < server.connections.size(); i++) {
                    ServerConnection c;
               c = (ServerConnection)server.connections.elementAt(i);
                    // If the connection thread isn't alive anymore,
                    // remove it from the Vector and List.
                    if (!c.isAlive()) {
                        server.connections.removeElementAt(i);
                     server.connection_list.delItem(i);
                        i-;
                    }
                }
            }
        }
    }
```

The Client: A Complete Example With Code

Now that we have the server code, let's look at the client class, which Listing 5.2 shows. This client class is not self-standing; we'll need an applet to call this class and make use of the methods we define in it. Listing 5.3 shows the code for a sample applet that calls this client class. Note that the client is specially coded to communicate with the application server in Listing 5.1, and that it does not require the Web browser on which it is run to have the JDBC API classes. For our simple example, we don't need to implement all of the functionality that is demanded of a JDBC driver, so I didn't write a driver. A JDBC driver that can talk to our application server would not be difficult to write at this point, however, because we have a simple "command set" and simple functionality. Figure 5.3 shows the client applet in Listing 5.3, which uses the **Dbclient** class.

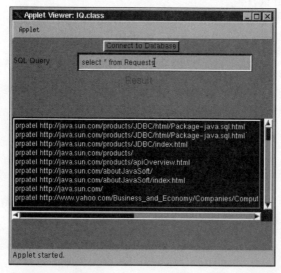

Figure 5.3
Sample applet that uses our client.

LISTING 5.2   CLIENT CLASS.

```java
import java.io.*;
import java.net.*;
import java.applet.*;
import java.awt.event.*;

public class DBClient {
public Socket socket;
public PrintWriter out;
public String Name;
public Reader reader;

public DBClient (String ServerName, int ServerPort) {
  try {
// We put the reading of the inputStream from the application
// server in its own thread, Reader.
        socket = new Socket(ServerName, ServerPort);
    reader = new Reader(this);
              out = new PrintWriter(socket.getOutputStream());
                    }
    catch (IOException e) {System.err.println(e);}
}

public String ProcessCommand(String InLine) {
System.out.println("FROM DBCLIENT:"+InLine);
  out.println(InLine);

  out.flush();
// Tell the reader we've sent some data/command.
  synchronized(reader){reader.notify();reader.notifyOn=false;}
  while(true) {
// We have to wait until the Reader has finished reading, so we set
// this notifyOn flag in the Reader when it has finished reading.

    if (reader.notifyOn) {break;}
  }

// Return the results of the command/query.
  return(reader.getResult());
}
}

class  Reader extends Thread {
// This class reads data in from the application server.
protected DBClient client;
public String Result="original";
public  boolean notifyOn=true;
```

```
public        String line;
protected BufferedReader in;
protected InputStreamReader inReader;

public Reader(DBClient c) {
  super("DBclient Reader");
  this.client = c;
  this.start();
}

public synchronized void run() {

  try {
    inReader = new
           InputStreamReader(client.socket.getInputStream());
    in = new BufferedReader(inReader);
    while(true) {
// We start reading when we are notified from the main thread
// and we stop when we have finished reading the stream for
// this command/query.
      try {if (notifyOn) {this.wait(); notifyOn=false; Result="";}}
      catch (InterruptedException e){
                  System.out.println("Caught an Interrupted Exception");
      }
      // prevent simultaneous access
      line = in.readLine();
      if (line.equalsIgnoreCase("DONE")) {
       notifyOn=true;
      } else
       {
       if (line == null) {
         System.out.println("Server closed connection.");
         break;
       } // if NOT null
       else {Result+=line+"\n";}
       System.out.println("Read from server: "+Result);
       } // if NOT done
    } //while loop
  }
  catch (IOException e) {System.out.println("Reader: " + e);}
  finally {
    try {if (in != null) in.close();}
    catch (IOException e) {
      System.exit(0);
    }
  }
}
```

```
public String getResult() {
  return (Result);
  }
}
```

You need to instantiate the client class in a Java program, and the connection needs to be started before you can make any queries. If you remember our Interactive Query applet from Chapter 4, the sample applet in Listing 5.3 will certainly look familiar to you.

LISTING 5.3 APPLET TO CALL OUR CLIENT CLASS.

```
import java.net.URL;
import java.awt.*;
import java.applet.Applet;
import DBClient;

public class IQ extends java.applet.Applet {
Button ConnectBtn = new Button("Connect to Database");
        Button QueryBtn = new Button("Query Database");
        protected DBClient DataConnection;

  TextField QueryField = new TextField(40);
  TextArea OutputField = new TextArea(10,75);


public void init() {
  QueryField.setEditable(true);
  OutputField.setEditable(false);
  DataConnection = new DBClient(getDocumentBase().getHost(), 6001);

 GridBagLayout gridbag = new GridBagLayout();
 GridBagConstraints Con = new GridBagConstraints();
 setLayout(gridbag);
 setFont(new Font("Helvetica", Font.PLAIN, 12));
 setBackground(Color.gray);
 Con.weightx=1.0;
 Con.weighty=0.0;
 Con.anchor = GridBagConstraints.CENTER;
 Con.fill = GridBagConstraints.NONE;
 Con.gridwidth = GridBagConstraints.REMAINDER;

  gridbag.setConstraints(ConnectBtn, Con);
  add(ConnectBtn);
      ConnectBtn.addMouseListener(this);
```

```
    add(new Label("SQL Query"));
    gridbag.setConstraints(QueryField, Con);
    add(QueryField);

    gridbag.setConstraints(QueryBtn, Con);
    add(QueryBtn);
    QueryBtn.addMouseListener(this);

    Label result_label = new Label("Result");
    result_label.setFont(new Font("Helvetica", Font.PLAIN, 16));
    result_label.setForeground(Color.blue);
    gridbag.setConstraints(result_label, Con);
    Con.weighty=1.0;
    add(result_label);

    gridbag.setConstraints(OutputField, Con);
    OutputField.setForeground(Color.white);
    OutputField.setBackground(Color.black);
    add(OutputField);



setVisible(true);
    } // init


public void mouseClicked( MouseEvent mEvt ) {

    if (mEvt.getComponent() == QueryBtn) {
// When a user enters a query and hits "return," we send the
// query to be processed and get the results to show in the
// OutputField.
     DataConnection.ProcessCommand("S");
    OutputField.setText(DataConnection.ProcessCommand(
                            QueryField.getText()));
    }

    if (mEvt.getComponent() == ConnectBtn) {
// This is the first command the application server expects,
// so connect to the data source.
        OutputField.setText(DataConnection.ProcessCommand("L"));
    }
  }


// We must override these methods because we implemented this
// applet as a MouseListener. To avoid doing this, we could do
// an abstract implement of this applet.
```

```
public void mouseEntered (MouseEvent mEvt ) { }
public void mouseExited (MouseEvent mEvt ) { }
public void mousePressed (MouseEvent mEvt ) { }
public void mouseReleased (MouseEvent mEvt ) { }

}
```

You'll need a Web page to call this applet from:

```
<HTML>
<HEAD>
<TITLE>
JDBC Client Applet - Interactive SQL Command Util via
application server
</TITLE>
</HEAD>
<BODY>
<H1>Interactive JDBC SQL command interpreter via
 application server</H1>
<hr>
<applet code=IQ.class width=450 height=350>
</applet>
<hr>
</BODY>
</HTML>
```

Coming Up Next

In this chapter, we took a brief look at middleware. You saw the advantages and disadvantages of implementing a three-tier system, and we created a simple application server and a client server that you can easily extend to fit your needs.

The next chapter looks at the different types of JDBC drivers. Drivers that use middleware are actually type 3 drivers, as you'll see in the next chapter. We'll look at the advantages and disadvantages of each type of driver so you have an idea of what is the best solution for you.

CHOOSING THE RIGHT JDBC DRIVER

6

This chapter takes a look at the four different types of JDBC drivers. These drivers vary in the way they interact with Java and in their network capability. A third party can develop JDBC drivers, much like ODBC drivers; a JDBC driver may not necessarily be developed by the actual database vendor. For instance, there is a JDBC driver for Microsoft SQL Server that Microsoft did not develop.

Driver Categories

Let's look at the four driver types defined by the JDBC specification. Each type has pros and cons, as we'll see in the next section. Drivers in each category exist for several databases. Type 1 JDBC drivers consist of only one Java driver: the JDBC-ODBC bridge. It is unique in comparison to the other drivers, which are more open in nature and are not bound to ODBC. Type 2, 3, and 4 drivers can connect to databases without having to go through ODBC.

Type 1

This driver is also known as the JDBC-ODBC bridge. We discuss the JDBC-ODBC bridge in great detail in Chapter 8. This driver is also included in the standard JDK 1.1 distribution. It is accessible as the sun.jdbc.odbc.JdbcOdbc Driver. This requires that ODBC be installed on the machine on which the Java applications accessing the JDBC-ODBC driver are executed. Additionally, this driver uses native methods, meaning that there are certain security restrictions when using it. For example, most Web browsers can't use the bridge because the security manager that is built into the browser's JVM won't allow an applet to call native methods. There are patches that allow Netscape browsers to use the bridge, but because Microsoft Internet Explorer doesn't support the same native methods interface as defined by the Sun specification, Internet Explorer won't run Java applets that use the JDBC-ODBC bridge.

The JDBC-ODBC bridge also requires ODBC drivers for connecting to a specific database. These ODBC drivers must also be installed on the client machine. Overall, this type of driver is not very flexible and can't be deployed over the network. If you have existing drivers for ODBC and you can't find a JDBC driver for a specific database, this is a viable option.

Type 2

This driver uses native method calls to a database's client library to make the data connection. This was a popular interim solution, because client libraries for databases generally come with the database software. Vendors write a JDBC driver that translates from the JDBC API to the specific client library. This type of driver also has certain restrictions. It uses native methods so the driver and the native executables must be pre-installed on the client machines.

Type 3

This driver is pure Java, with no native method binding, and it can be deployed with a Java applet with no pre-installation. This driver uses a proprietary protocol for connecting to a middleware server. The middleware server then takes the JDBC API calls from the Java client using its type 3 driver and converts them to DBMS-specific calls. The JDBC driver talks indirectly to the database server via a middleware server that is required to be running on a machine.

Type 4

This driver allows your Java applet to connect directly to a database server. It does not use native methods and is 100 percent Java. Hence, you can send it to a Web browser over the network along with a Java applet. The JDBC driver translates to the specific database protocol and allows direct querying of the database.

Assessing Differences Between Types

You may be asking why it's so important to know the type of driver you're using in your Java programs. Many issues surround the four driver types—sometimes they enhance the speed or flexibility; sometimes they do the opposite. We mentioned a few pros and cons to each type in the definitions. Now let's take a closer look.

100 Percent Java Means Portability

The biggest advantage of type 3 and type 4 drivers is that they are truly portable. Just like Java applets are portable between different operating systems and platforms, the JDBC driver, which is written purely in Java, inherits this advantage. This means you only need to write a driver once if you're in the business of writing your own JDBC driver. For developers who are just using a driver supplied by someone else, it means they only need to write the JDBC applets and applications in Java once—they can then run on any platform that supports Java.

The other big (possibly bigger) advantage to using a type 3 or type 4 driver is that the drivers do not need pre-installation on client machines. When someone loads a Java applet that uses the JDBC, if the driver is type 3 or 4, it will be downloaded just like the regular applet class files. The driver is essentially loaded dynamically over the network. A type 1 or type 2 driver needs to have certain software pre-installed and configured on each client machine, which can take time (and money). Additionally, if the driver needs updating, it has to be re-installed. If you're using a type 3 or type 4 JDBC driver, you can simply update the driver on the Web site from which you are serving the driver, and you're ready to go. When the user returns to run your data-aware Java applet, the Web browser will get the new JDBC driver.

Middleware Means Flexibility

Why bother with middleware, or a type 3 driver, when you can connect directly to the database using a type 4 driver? Well, there are several reasons, the most important being that it's inherently more secure, and you can build a more secure framework around a three-tier system. When you use a type 3 driver, you are using a three-tier system: the client, the middleware server, and the actual database. FYI, a two-tier system is manifested as a type 4 driver.

SECURITY

A type 3 driver can implement a secure connection to the middleware server. Indeed, many type 3 drivers available today, along with their corresponding middleware servers, implement encrypted connections. When the type 3 driver connects to the middleware server with which it was designed to interface, it can use SSL or some other secure method for transferring data. Hence, someone sniffing around the network won't be able to readily pull passwords or see the data being passed from the middleware server to the Java clients. If you plan on deploying your Java applet over the Internet and are concerned that sensitive data needs to remain secure, you should make sure that the JDBC driver you are using supports secure connections. This can involve a type 3 driver that uses something like SSL when talking to the middleware server, or a type 4 driver that supports secure connections directly to the database server.

CACHING

The database server you are using may only support a few simultaneous connections. This can be a problem if you plan on using a type 2 or type 4 driver that connects directly to the database server. If you know that there are only going to be a few people using your Java/JDBC applet, this may not be a problem. However, if you plan on deploying your applet on the Internet or large intranet, people may not be able to connect if the number of open connections has been exhausted on the database server.

Middleware servers can manage a set number of connections to the database server so that you can have many more connections on the client side. Along with mapping a few connections to many, the middleware server can cache common SQL queries so that you don't need to query the database server repeatedly for the same information. The mapping from the client to the server side that the middleware server incorporates can also hold session information so that this important feature is not lost. Some middleware servers, though, do not ensure a state-oriented connection from the client to the database server. This can be a problem if you plan on using the rollback features that JDBC API supports (assuming the database supports rollback).

CONNECTION CONTROL

The additional security feature that the middleware server can implement is restricted access, based on IP address and other characteristics. You can also put access control lists on the middleware server; the middleware server has the list of passwords and login IDs instead of the database server. The middleware server will control what database tables and permissions a specific user ID has. Most middleware servers support this type of security scheme, which is very useful when you have a large number of users who will be connecting via your Java/JDBC applet.

Direct Connection Means Speed

We've been talking about how great a middleware server can be, but there is one underlying problem: speed. Because you've added an extra layer between the client and the database server, you've also added another possible bottleneck. Not to mention that you need to run another piece of software. For some users, the features that a middleware server gives you are not necessary. For example, if you are developing a Java applet that handles the company payroll where the data is stored in a database server, a type 4 direct connection driver would be the optimal solution, if only three or four people use it. Frequent queries and updates benefit from the direct connection in more ways than speed. Rollbacks are also possible using a type 4 driver (assuming the database server supports it).

If you are transferring large amounts of data between the client and the database server, a direct connection JDBC (type 4) is likely the optimal solution. This goes almost without saying, but you may only realize it if you are retrieving images from a multimedia database. Type 3 drivers with the middleware layer have an extra layer where the data must be transferred through, so it is inherently less efficient.

Type 1: What Is It Good For?

By now you're asking yourself why anyone even uses a type 1 driver. There are two good reasons for using this driver—it's quick and cheap. In the introduction, we said that you could use Access as the database for your JDBC applets. This is where the JDBC-ODBC bridge, or type 1 driver, comes in. You can set up a local data source in ODBC that uses Access as the database. You can then write a Java program that uses the JDBC-ODBC driver included in the JDK 1.1. You don't need a database server in this configuration and there is no additional software to install if you have already installed Access. It's very handy, especially when prototyping a new Java program. When you're ready to move from Access to a real database server, you simply change your code to reflect that you're using a new JDBC driver, and the location of the database server along with the username and password for connecting to the database. These changes involve a few lines of code.

A type 1 driver is also handy because it is self-contained. If you're using a local database, running Access on the same machine, for example, then you can prototype without being connected to the network. This means you can develop Java/JDBC programs on your laptop, at the office or on the road, without having to go over the network to hit a database. You can distribute or show demos for your Java/JDBC program using this configuration as well.

Moving On

We've looked at the available JDBC drivers. We've also discussed the advantages and drawbacks of each. Finding the right driver for your needs is not necessarily a trivial task, especially if you have to consider many of the issues we've raised here. Look around and see what's out there, and try out a driver before buying it if possible. Currently, type 4 drivers for Sybase and Oracle are being distributed for free as part of the standard development libraries that come with the database software. These drivers are developed by Sybase and Oracle, respectively, for connecting specifically to their database servers.

Coming Up Next

In the next chapter, we dive into the heart of the JDBC with a step-by-step tutorial on how to develop a JDBC driver of your own. If you're not interested in developing your own driver, feel free to skip the next chapter. It might be interesting reading, however, because it discusses many of the internal details of the JDBC.

7

WRITING DATABASE DRIVERS

W e've covered a lot of territory so far in this book. Now we can put some of your newly gained knowledge to use. In this chapter, we will explore what it takes to develop a JDBC driver. In doing so, we will also touch on some of the finer points of the JDBC specification. Throughout this chapter, I will use excerpts from the SimpleText JDBC driver that is included on the CD-ROM. This driver allows you to manipulate simple text files; you will be able to create and drop files, as well as insert and select data within a file. The SimpleText driver is not fully JDBC-compliant, but it provides a solid starting point for developing a driver. We'll cover what the JDBC components provide, how to implement the JDBC API interfaces, how to write native code to bridge to an existing non-Java API, some finer points of driver writing, and the major JDBC API interfaces that must be implemented.

The JDBC Driver Project: SimpleText

The SimpleText JDBC driver is just that: a JDBC driver that manipulates simple text files, with a few added twists. It is not a full-blown relational database system, so I do not recommend attempting to use it as one. If you are looking for a good way to prototype a system, or need a very lightweight database system to drive a simplistic application or applet, then SimpleText is for you. More importantly, the SimpleText driver can serve as a starting point for your own JDBC driver. Feel free to take the source code and use it for whatever purpose you deem necessary; just be sure to preserve the original copyright text. Before continuing, let's take a look at the SimpleText driver specifications.

SimpleText SQL Grammar

The SimpleText JDBC driver supports only very specific SQL grammar. This is one reason that the driver is not JDBC compliant; a JDBC-compliant driver must support ANSI92 entry-level SQL grammar. The following SQL statements define the base SimpleText grammar:

- *create-table-statement* ::= CREATE TABLE *table-name*
  (column-element [, column-element]...)

- *drop-table-statement* ::= DROP TABLE *table-name*

- *insert-statement* ::= INSERT INTO *table-name*
  [(column-identifier [, column-identifier]...)] VALUES
  (insert-value [, insert-value]...)

- *select-statement* ::= SELECT *select-list* FROM *table-name* [WHERE *search-condition*]

The following elements are used in these SQL statements:

- *column-element* ::= *column-identifier data-type*

- *column-identifier* ::= *user-defined-name*

- *comparison-operator* ::= < | > | = | <>

- *data-type* ::= VARCHAR | NUMBER | BINARY

- *dynamic-parameter* ::= ?

- *insert-value* ::= *dynamic-parameter* | *literal*

- *search-condition* ::= *column-identifier comparison-operator literal*

- *select-list* ::= * | *column-identifier* [, *column-identifier*]...

- *table-name* ::= *user-defined-name*

- *user-defined-name* ::= *letter* [*digit* | *letter*]

What all this grammar means is that the SimpleText driver supports a **CRE-ATE TABLE** statement, a **DROP TABLE** statement, an **INSERT** statement (with parameters), and a very simple **SELECT** statement (with a **WHERE** clause). It may not seem like much, but this grammar is the foundation that will allow us to create a table, insert some data, and select it back.

SimpleText File Format

The format of the files used by the SimpleText driver is, of course, very simple. The first line contains a signature, followed by each one of the column names (and optional data types). Any subsequent lines in the text file are assumed to be comma-separated data. There is no size limit to the text file, but the larger the file, the longer it takes to retrieve data (the entire file is read when selecting data; there is no index support). The data file extension is hard-coded to be .SDF (Simple Data File). For example, the statement

```
CREATE TABLE TEST (COL1 VARCHAR, COL2 NUMBER, COL3 BINARY)
```

creates a file named TEST.SDF, with the following initial data (just the signature line):

```
.SDFCOL1,#COL2,@COL3
```

Note that none of the SQL grammar is case sensitive. The .SDF is the file signature (this is how the SimpleText driver validates whether the text file can be used), followed by a comma-separated list of column names. The first character of the column name can specify the data type of the column. A column name starting with a # indicates a numeric column, while a column name starting with an @ indicates a binary column. What's that? Binary data in a text file? Well, not quite. A binary column actually contains an offset pointer into a sister file. This file, with an extension of .SBF (Simple Binary File), contains any binary data for columns in the text file, as well as the length of the data (maximum length of 1048576 bytes). Any other column name is considered to be character data (with a maximum length of 5120 bytes). The following statement shows how data is inserted into the TEST table:

```
INSERT INTO TEST VALUES ('FOO', 123, '0123456789ABCDEF')
```

After the **INSERT**, TEST.SDF will contain the following data:

```
.SDFCOL1,#COL2,@COL3
FOO,123,0
```

COL3 contains an offset of zero since this is the first row in the file. This is the offset from within the TEST.SBF table in which the binary data resides. Starting at the given offset, the first four bytes will be the length indicator, followed by the actual binary data that was inserted. Note that any character or binary data must be enclosed in single quotation marks.

We'll be looking at plenty of code from the SimpleText driver throughout this chapter. But first, let's start by exploring what is provided by the JDBC developer's kit.

The DriverManager

The JDBC **DriverManager** is a static class that provides services to connect to JDBC drivers. The **DriverManager** is provided by JavaSoft and does not require the driver developer to perform any implementation. Its main purpose is to assist in loading and initializing a requested JDBC driver. Other than using the **DriverManager** to register a JDBC driver (**registerDriver**) to make itself known and to provide the logging facility (which is covered in detail later in this chapter), a driver does not interface with the **DriverManager**. In fact, once a JDBC driver is loaded, the **DriverManager** drops out of the picture altogether, and the application or applet interfaces with the driver directly.

JDBC Exception Types

JDBC provides special types of exceptions to be used by a driver: **SQLException**, **SQLWarning**, and **DataTruncation**. The **SQLException** class is the foundation for the other types of JDBC exceptions, and it extends **java.lang.Exception**. When created, an **SQLException** can have three pieces of information: a **String** describing the error, a **String** containing the XOPEN SQLstate (as described in the XOPEN SQL specification), and an **int** containing an additional vendor or database-specific error code. Also note that **SQLExceptions** can be chained together: that is, multiple **SQLExceptions** can be thrown for a single operation. The following code shows how an **SQLException** is thrown:

```
//- - - - - - - - - - - - - - - - - - - - - - -
// fooBar
// Demonstrates how to throw an SQLException
//- - - - - - - - - - - - - - - - - - - - - - -
public void fooBar()
    throws SQLException
{
    throw new SQLException("I just threw an SQLException");
}
```

Here's how you call **fooBar** and catch the **SQLException**:

```
try {
    fooBar();
}
catch (SQLException ex) {

    // If an SQLException is thrown, we'll end up here. Output the error
    // message, SQLstate, and vendor code.
    System.out.println("A SQLException was caught!");
    System.out.println("Message: " + ex.getMessage());
    System.out.println("SQLState: " + ex.getSQLState());
    System.out.println("Vendor Code: " + ex.getErrorCode());
}
```

An **SQLWarning** is similar to, but extends, an **SQLException**. The main difference is in semantics. If an **SQLException** is thrown, it is considered to be a
critical error—one that needs attention. If an **SQLWarning** is thrown, it is considered to be a non-critical error—a warning or informational message. For this
reason, JDBC treats **SQLWarnings** much differently than **SQLExceptions**.
SQLExceptions are thrown just like any other type of exception; **SQLWarnings**
are not thrown, but put on a list of warnings on an owning object type—
for instance, **Connection**, **Statement**, or **ResultSet**, which we'll cover later.
Because they are put on a list, it is up to the application to poll for warnings
after the completion of an operation. Listing 7.1 shows a method that accepts
an **SQLWarning** and places it on a list.

LISTING 7.1   PLACING AN SQLWARNING ON A LIST.

```
//- - - - - - - - - - - - - - - - - - - - - - - - - - - - - - - -
// setWarning
// Sets the given SQLWarning in the warning chain. If null, the
// chain is reset. The local attribute, lastWarning, is used
// as the head of the chain.
//- - - - - - - - - - - - - - - - - - - - - - - - - - - - - - - -
```

```
protected void setWarning(
    SQLWarning warning)
{
    // A null warning can be used to clear the warning stack
    if (warning == null) {
        lastWarning = null;
    }
    else {
        // Set the head of the chain. We'll use this to walk through the
        // chain to find the end.
        SQLWarning chain = lastWarning;

        // Find the end of the chain. When the current warning does
        // not have a next pointer, it must be the end of the chain.
        while (chain.getNextWarning() != null) {
            chain = chain.getNextWarning();
        }

        // We're at the end of the chain. Add the new warning
        chain.setNextWarning(warning);
    }
}
```

Listing 7.2 uses this method to create two **SQLWarnings** and chain them together.

LISTING 7.2   CHAINING SQLWARNINGS TOGETHER.

```
//- - - - - - - - - - - - - - - - - - - - - - - - - -
// fooBar
// Do nothing but put two SQLWarnings on our local
// warning stack (lastWarning).
//- - - - - - - - - - - - - - - - - - - - - - - - - -
protected void fooBar()
{
    // First step should always be to clear the stack. If a warning
    // is lingering, it will be discarded. It is up to the application to
    // check and clear the stack.
    setWarning(null);

    // Now create our warnings
    setWarning(new SQLWarning("Warning 1"));
    setWarning(new SQLWarning("Warning 2"));
}
```

Now we'll call the method that puts two **SQLWarnings** on our warning stack, then poll for the warning using the JDBC method **getWarnings**, as shown in Listing 7.3.

LISTING 7.3   POLLING FOR WARNINGS.

```
// Call fooBar to create a warning chain
fooBar();

// Now, poll for the warning chain. We'll simply dump any warning
// messages to standard output.
SQLWarning chain = getWarnings();

if (chain != null) {
    System.out.println("Warning(s):");

    // Display the chain until no more entries exist
    while (chain != null) {
        System.out.println("Message: " + chain.getMessage());

        // Advance to the next warning in the chain. null will be
        // returned if no more entries exist.
        chain = chain.getNextWarning();
    }
}
```

DataTruncation objects work in the same manner as **SQLWarnings**. A **DataTruncation** object indicates that a data value that was being read or written was truncated, resulting in a loss of data. The **DataTruncation** class has attributes that can be set to specify the column or parameter number, whether a truncation occurred on a read or a write, the size of the data that should have been transferred, and the number of bytes that were actually transferred. We can modify our code from Listing 7.2 to include the handling of **DataTruncation** objects, as shown in Listing 7.4.

LISTING 7.4   CREATING DATATRUNCATION WARNINGS.

```
//- - - - - - - - - - - - - - - - - - - - - - - - - -
// fooBar
// Do nothing but put two SQLWarnings on our local
// warning stack (lastWarning) and a DataTruncation
// warning.
//- - - - - - - - - - - - - - - - - - - - - - - - - -
protected void fooBar()
{
```

```
// First step should always be to clear the stack. If a warning
// is lingering, it will be discarded. It is up to the application to
// check and clear the stack.
setWarning(null);

// Now create our warnings
setWarning(new SQLWarning("Warning 1"));
setWarning(new SQLWarning("Warning 2"));

// And create a DataTruncation indicating that a truncation
// occurred on column 1, 1000 bytes were requested to
// read, and only 999 bytes were read.
setWarning(new DataTruncation(1, false, true, 1000, 999);
}
```

Listing 7.5 shows the modified code to handle the **DataTruncation**.

LISTING 7.5   PROCESSING DATATRUNCATION WARNINGS.

```
// Call fooBar to create a warning chain
fooBar();

// Now, poll for the warning chain. We'll simply dump any warning
// messages to standard output.
SQLWarning chain = getWarnings();

if (chain != null) {
    System.out.println("Warning(s):");

    // Display the chain until no more entries exist
    while (chain != null) {
        // The only way we can tell if this warning is a DataTruncation
        // is to attempt to cast it. This may fail, indicating that
        // it is just an SQLWarning.
        try {
            DataTruncation trunc = (DataTruncation) chain;
            System.out.println("Data Truncation on column: " +
                trunc.getIndex());
        }
        catch (Exception ex) {
            System.out.println("Message: " + chain.getMessage());
        }

        // Advance to the next warning in the chain. Null will be
        // returned if no more entries exist.
        chain = chain.getNextWarning();
    }
}
```

JDBC Data Types

The JDBC specification provides definitions for all of the SQL data types that can be supported by a JDBC driver. Only a few of these data types may be natively supported by a given database system, which is why data coercion becomes such a vital service (we'll discuss data coercion a little later in this chapter). The data types are defined in **Types.class**:

```
public class Types
{
    public final static int BIT = -7;
    public final static int TINYINT = -6;
    public final static int SMALLINT = 5;
    public final static int INTEGER = 4;
    public final static int BIGINT = -5;
    public final static int FLOAT = 6;
    public final static int REAL = 7;
    public final static int DOUBLE = 8;
    public final static int NUMERIC = 2;
    public final static int DECIMAL = 3;
    public final static int CHAR = 1;
    public final static int VARCHAR = 12;
    public final static int LONGVARCHAR = -1;
    public final static int DATE = 91;
    public final static int TIME = 92;
    public final static int TIMESTAMP = 93;
    public final static int BINARY = -2;
    public final static int VARBINARY = -3;
    public final static int LONGVARBINARY = -4;
    public final static int OTHER = 1111;
}
```

At a minimum, a JDBC driver must support one (if not all) of the character data types (**CHAR, VARCHAR,** and **LONGVARCHAR**). A driver may also support driver-specific data types (**OTHER**), which can only be accessed in a JDBC application as an **Object**. In other words, you can get data as some type of object and put it back into a database as that same type of object, but the application has no idea what type of data is actually contained within. Let's take a closer look at each of the data types.

Character Data: CHAR, VARCHAR, And LONGVARCHAR

CHAR, VARCHAR, and LONGVARCHAR data types are used to express character data. These data types are represented in JDBC as Java **String** objects. Data of type **CHAR** is represented as a fixed-length **String** and may include some padding spaces to ensure that it is the proper length. If data is being written to a database, the driver must ensure that the data is properly padded. Data of type **VARCHAR** is represented as a variable-length **String** and is trimmed to the actual length of the data. **LONGVARCHAR** data can be either a variable-length **String** or returned by the driver as a Java **InputStream**, allowing the data to be read in chunks of whatever size the application desires.

Exact Numeric Data: NUMERIC And DECIMAL

The **NUMERIC** and **DECIMAL** data types are used to express signed, exact numeric values with a fixed number of decimal places. These data types are often used to represent currency values. **NUMERIC** and **DECIMAL** data are both represented in JDBC as **BigDecimal** objects.

Binary Data: BINARY, VARBINARY, And LONGVARBINARY

The **BINARY**, **VARBINARY**, and **LONGVARBINARY** data types are used to express binary (non-character) data. These data types are represented in JDBC as Java byte arrays. Data of type **BINARY** is represented as a fixed-length byte array, and it may include some padding zeros to ensure that it is the proper length. If data is being written to a database, the driver must ensure that the data is properly padded. Data of type **VARBINARY** is represented as a variable-length byte array, and it is trimmed to the actual length of the data. **LONGVARBINARY** data can either be a variable-length byte array or returned by the driver as a Java **InputStream**, allowing the data to be read in chunks of whatever size the application desires.

Boolean Data: BIT

The **BIT** data type is used to represent a boolean value—either true or false—and is represented in JDBC as a **boolean** object or **boolean** data type.

Integer Data: TINYINT, SMALLINT, INTEGER, And BIGINT

The TINYINT, SMALLINT, INTEGER, and BIGINT data types are used to represent signed integer data. Data of type TINYINT is represented in JDBC as a Java *byte* data type (1 byte), with a minimum value of -128 and a maximum value of 127. Data of type SMALLINT is represented in JDBC as a Java *short* data type (2 bytes), with a minimum value of -32,768 and a maximum value of 32,767. Data of type INTEGER is represented as a Java *int* data type (4 bytes), with a minimum value of -2,147,483,648 and a maximum value of 2,147,483,647. Data of type BIGINT is represented as a Java *long* data type (8 bytes), with a minimum value of -9,223,372,036,854,775,808 and a maximum value of 9,223,372,036,854,775,807.

Floating-Point Data: REAL, FLOAT, And DOUBLE

The REAL, FLOAT, and DOUBLE data types are used to represent signed, approximate values. Data of type REAL supports seven digits of mantissa precision, and it is represented as a Java *float* data type. Data types FLOAT and DOUBLE support 15 digits of mantissa precision, and they are represented as Java *double* data types.

Time Data: DATE, TIME, And TIMESTAMP

The DATE, TIME, and TIMESTAMP data types are used to represent dates and times. Data of type DATE supports specification of the month, day, and year, and is represented as a JDBC **Date** object. Data of type TIME supports specification of the hour, minutes, seconds, and milliseconds, and is represented as a JDBC **Time** object. Data of type TIMESTAMP supports specification of the month, day, year, hour, minutes, seconds, and milliseconds, and is represented as a JDBC **Timestamp** object. The **Date**, **Time**, and **Timestamp** objects, which we'll get into a bit later, are new with JDBC.

Be Aware Of Date Limitations

One important note about **Date** and **Timestamp** objects: The Java calendar starts at January 1, 1970, which means that you cannot represent dates prior to 1970.

New Data Classes

The JDBC API introduced several new data classes. These classes were developed to solve specific data-representation problems like how to accurately represent fixed-precision numeric values (such as currency values) for **NUMERIC** and **DECIMAL** data types, and how to represent time data for **DATE**, **TIME**, and **TIMESTAMP** data types.

BigDecimal

The **BigDecimal** class was introduced to represent signed, exact numeric values with a fixed number of decimal places. This class is ideal for representing monetary values, allowing accurate arithmetic operations and comparisons.

Date

The **Date** class is used to represent dates in the ANSI SQL format YYYY-MM-DD, where YYYY is a four-digit year, MM is a two-digit month, and DD is a two-digit day. The JDBC **Date** class extends the existing **java.util.Date** class (setting the hour, minutes, and seconds to zero) and, most importantly, adds two methods to convert strings into dates, and vice versa:

```
// Create a Date object with a date of June 30th, 1996
Date d = Date.valueOf("1996-06-30");

// Print the date
System.out.println("Date=" + d.toString());

// Same thing, without leading zeros
Date d2 = Date.valueOf("1996-6-30");
System.out.println("Date=" + d2.toString());
```

The **Date** class also serves very well in validating date values. If an invalid date string is passed to the **valueOf** method, a **java.lang.IllegalArgument-Exception** is thrown:

```
String s;

// Get the date from the user
...
// Validate the date
try {
```

```
    Date d = Date.valueOf(s);
}
catch (java.lang.IllegalArgumentException ex) {
    // Invalid date, notify the application
…
}
```

Time

The **Time** class is used to represent times in the ANSI SQL format HH:MM:SS, where HH is a two-digit hour, MM is a two-digit minute, and SS is a two-digit second. The JDBC **Time** class extends the existing **java.util.Date** class (setting the year, month, and day to zero) and, most importantly, adds two methods to convert strings into times, and vice versa:

```
// Create a Time object with a time of 2:30:08 pm
Time t = Time.valueOf("14:30:08");

// Print the time
System.out.println("Time=" + t.toString());

// Same thing, without leading zeros
Time t2 = Time.valueOf("14:30:8");
System.out.println("Time=" + t2.toString());
```

The **Time** class also serves very well in validating time values. If an invalid time string is passed to the **valueOf** method, a **java.lang.IllegalArgument-Exception** is thrown:

```
String s;

// Get the time from the user
.

.

.

// Validate the time
try {
    Time t = Time.valueOf(s);
}
catch (java.lang.IllegalArgumentException ex) {
    // Invalid time, notify the application
    .

    .

    .
}
```

Timestamp

The **Timestamp** class is used to represent a combination of date and time values in the ANSI SQL format YYYY-MM-DD HH:MM:SS.F..., where YYYY is a four-digit year, MM is a two-digit month, DD is a two-digit day, HH is a two-digit hour, MM is a two-digit minute, SS is a two-digit second, and F is an optional fractional second up to nine digits in length. The JDBC **Timestamp** class extends the existing **java.util.Date** class (adding the fraction seconds) and, most importantly, adds two methods to convert strings into timestamps, and vice versa:

```
// Create a Timestamp object with a date of 1996-06-30 and a time of
// 2:30:08 pm.
Timestamp t = Timestamp.valueOf("1996-06-30 14:30:08");

// Print the timestamp
System.out.println("Timestamp=" + t.toString());

// Same thing, without leading zeros
Timestamp t2 = Timestamp.valueOf("1996-6-30 14:30:8");
System.out.println("Timestamp=" + t2.toString());
```

The **Timestamp** class also serves very well in validating timestamp values. If an invalid time string is passed to the **valueOf** method, a **java.lang.IllegalArgumentException** is thrown:

```
String s;

// Get the timestamp from the user
...
// Validate the timestamp
try {
    Timestamp t = Timestamp.valueOf(s);
}
catch (java.lang.IllegalArgumentException ex) {
    // Invalid timestamp, notify the application
    ...
}
```

As is the case with the **Date** class, the Java date epoch is January 1, 1970; therefore, you cannot represent any date values prior to January 1, 1970 with a **Timestamp** object.

Native Drivers: You're Not From Around Here, Are Ya?

Before you begin to implement a JDBC driver, the first question that you must answer is: Will this driver be written completely in Java, or will it contain native (machine dependent) code? You may be forced to use native code because many major database systems—such as Oracle, Sybase, and SQLServer—do not provide Java client software. In this case, you will need to write a small library containing C code to bridge Java and the database client API (the JDBC to ODBC Bridge is a perfect example). The obvious drawback is that the JDBC driver is not portable and cannot be automatically downloaded by today's browsers.

If a native bridge is required for your JDBC driver, you should keep a few things in mind. First, do as little as possible in the C bridge code; you will want to keep the bridge as small as possible, ideally creating just a Java wrapper around the C API. Most importantly, avoid the temptation to perform memory management in C (for example, malloc). This is best left in Java code, since the Java Virtual Machine so nicely takes care of garbage collection. Secondly, keep all of the native method declarations in one Java class. By doing so, all of the bridge routines will be localized and much easier to maintain. Finally, don't make any assumptions about data representation. An integer value may be 2 bytes on one system and 4 bytes on another. If you are planning to port the native bridge code to a different system (which is highly likely), you should provide native methods that provide the size and interpretation of data.

Listing 7.6 illustrates these suggestions. This module contains all of the native method declarations, as well as the code to load our library. The library will be loaded when the class is instantiated.

LISTING 7.6   JAVA NATIVE METHODS.

```
//- - - - - - - - - - - - - - - - - - - - - - - - - - - -
// MyBridge.java
//
// Sample code to demonstrate the use of native methods
//- - - - - - - - - - - - - - - - - - - - - - - - - - - -
package jdbc.test;

import java.sql.*;
```

```
public class MyBridge
    extends Object
{
    //- - - - - - - - - - - - - - - - - - - - - - - - - - - - - -
    // Constructor
    // Attempt to load our library. If it can't be loaded, an
    // SQLException will be thrown.
    //- - - - - - - - - - - - - - - - - - - - - - - - - - - - - -
    public MyBridge()
        throws SQLException
    {
        try {

            // Attempt to load our library. For Win95/NT, this will
            // be myBridge.dll. For Unix systems, this will be
            // libmyBridge.so.
            System.loadLibrary("myBridge");
        }
        catch (UnsatisfiedLinkError e) {
            throw new SQLException("Unable to load myBridge library");
        }
    }


    //- - - - - - - - - - - - -
    // Native method declarations
    //- - - - - - - - - - - - -

    // Get the size of an int
    public native int getINTSize();

    // Given a byte array, convert it to an integer value
    public native int getINTValue(byte intValue[]);

    // Call some C function that does something with a String, and
    // returns an integer value.
    public native void callSomeFunction(String stringValue, byte
    intValue[]);
}
```

Once this module has been compiled (javac), a Java-generated header file and C
file must be created:

```
javah jdbc.test.MyBridge
javah -stubs jdbc.test.MyBridge
```

These files provide the mechanism for the Java and C worlds to communicate with each other. Listing 7.7 shows the generated header file (jdbc_test_My Bridge.h, in this case), which will be included in our C bridge code.

LISTING 7.7   MACHINE-GENERATED HEADER FILE FOR NATIVE METHODS.

```
/* DO NOT EDIT THIS FILE - it is machine-generated */
#include <native.h>
/* Header for class jdbc_test_MyBridge */

#ifndef _Included_jdbc_test_MyBridge
#define _Included_jdbc_test_MyBridge

typedef struct Classjdbc_test_MyBridge {
    char PAD; /* ANSI C requires structures to have at least one member */
} Classjdbc_test_MyBridge;
HandleTo(jdbc_test_MyBridge);

#ifdef __cplusplus
extern "C" {
#endif
__declspec(dllexport) long jdbc_test_MyBridge_getINTSize(struct
Hjdbc_test_MyBridge *);
__declspec(dllexport) long jdbc_test_MyBridge_getINTValue(struct
Hjdbc_test_MyBridge *,HArrayOfByte *);
struct Hjava_lang_String;
__declspec(dllexport) void jdbc_test_MyBridge_callSomeFunction(struct
Hjdbc_test_MyBridge *,struct Hjava_lang_String *,HArrayOfByte *);
#ifdef __cplusplus
}
#endif
#endif
```

The generated C file (shown in Listing 7.8) must be compiled and linked with the bridge.

LISTING 7.8   MACHINE-GENERATED C FILE FOR NATIVE METHODS.

```
/* DO NOT EDIT THIS FILE - it is machine-generated */
#include <StubPreamble.h>

/* Stubs for class jdbc/test/MyBridge */
/* SYMBOL: "jdbc/test/MyBridge/getINTSize()I",
Java_jdbc_test_MyBridge_getINTSize_stub */
__declspec(dllexport) stack_item *Java_jdbc_test_MyBridge_getINTSize_stub(
        stack_item *_P_,struct execenv *_EE_) {
```

```
    extern long jdbc_test_MyBridge_getINTSize(void *);
    _P_[0].i = jdbc_test_MyBridge_getINTSize(_P_[0].p);
    return _P_ + 1;
    }
    /* SYMBOL: "jdbc/test/MyBridge/getINTValue([B)I",
    Java_jdbc_test_MyBridge_getINTValue_stub */
    __declspec(dllexport) stack_item
    *Java_jdbc_test_MyBridge_getINTValue_stub(stack_item *_P_,struct
    execenv *_EE_) {
    extern long jdbc_test_MyBridge_getINTValue(void *,void *);
        _P_[0].i = jdbc_test_MyBridge_getINTValue(_P_[0].p,((_P_[1].p)));
        return _P_ + 1;
}
/* SYMBOL: "jdbc/test/MyBridge/callSomeFunction(Ljava/lang/String;[B)V",
Java_jdbc_test_MyBridge_callSomeFunction_stub */
__declspec(dllexport) stack_item
*Java_jdbc_test_MyBridge_callSomeFunction_stub(stack_item *_P_,struct
execenv *_EE_) {
        extern void jdbc_test_MyBridge_callSomeFunction(void *,void *,void
        *);
        (void) jdbc_test_MyBridge_callSomeFunction(_P_[0].p,((_P_[1].p)),
        ((_P_[2].p)));return _P_;
}
```

The bridge code is shown in Listing 7.9. The function prototypes were taken
from the generated header file.

LISTING 7.9   BRIDGE CODE.

```
//- - - - - - - - - - - - - - - - - - - - - - - -
// MyBridge.c
//
// Sample code to demonstrate the use of native methods
//- - - - - - - - - - - - - - - - - - - - - - - -
#include <stdio.h>
#include <ctype.h>
#include <string.h>

// Java internal header files
#include "StubPreamble.h"
#include "javaString.h"

// Our header file generated by JAVAH
#include "jdbc_test_MyBridge.h"
```

```
//- - - - - - - - - - - - -
// getINTSize
// Return the size of an int
//- - - - - - - - - - - - - -
long jdbc_test_MyBridge_getINTSize(
    struct Hjdbc_test_MyBridge *caller)
{
    return sizeof(int);
}


//- - - - - - - - - - - - - - - - - - - - - - - -
// getINTValue
// Given a buffer, return the value as an int
//- - - - - - - - - - - - - - - - - - - - - - - -
long jdbc_test_MyBridge_getINTValue(
    struct Hjdbc_test_MyBridge *caller,
    HArrayOfByte *buf)
{
    // Cast our array of bytes to an integer pointer
    int* pInt = (int*) unhand (buf)->body;

    // Return the value
    return (long) *pInt;
}


//- - - - - - - - - - - - - - - - - - - - - - - - - - - - - - - -
// callSomeFunction
// Call some function that takes a String and an int pointer as arguments
//- - - - - - - - - - - - - - - - - - - - - - - - - - - - - - - -
void jdbc_test_MyBridge_callSomeFunction(
    struct Hjdbc_test_MyBridge *caller,
    struct Hjava_lang_String *stringValue,
    HArrayOfByte *buf)
{
    // Cast the string into a char pointer
    char* pString = (char*) makeCString (stringValue);

    // Cast our array of bytes to an integer pointer
    int* pInt = (int*) unhand (buf)->body;

    // This fictitious function will print the string, then return the
    // length of the string in the int pointer.
    printf("String value=%s\n", pString);
    *pInt = strlen(pString);
}
```

Now, create a library (DLL or Shared Object) by compiling this module and linking it with the **jdbc_test_MyDriver** compiled object and the one required Java library, **javai.lib.** Here's the command line I used to build it for Win95/NT:

```
cl -DWIN32 mybridge.c jdbc_test_mybridge.c -FeMyBridge.dll -MD -LD
  javai.lib
```

Now we can use our native bridge, as shown in Listing 7.10.

LISTING 7.10   IMPLEMENTING THE BRIDGE.

```
import jdbc.test.*;
import java.sql.*;

class Test {

    public static void main (String args[]) {

        MyBridge myBridge = null;
        boolean loaded = false;

        try {

            // Create a new bridge object. If it is unable to load our
            // native library, an SQLException will be thrown.
            myBridge = new MyBridge();
            loaded = true;
        }
        catch (SQLException ex) {
            System.out.println("SQLException: " + ex.getMessage());
        }

        // If the bridge was loaded, use the native methods
        if (loaded) {

            // Allocate storage for an int
            byte intValue[] = new byte[myBridge.getINTSize()];

            // Call the bridge to perform some function with a string,
            // returning a value in the int buffer.
            myBridge.callSomeFunction("Hello, World.", intValue);

            // Get the value out of the buffer.
            int n = myBridge.getINTValue(intValue);
```

```
            System.out.println("INT value=" + n);
        }
    }
}
```

Listing 7.10 produces the following output:

```
String value=Hello, World.
INT value=13
```

As you can see, using native methods is very straightforward. Developing a JDBC driver using a native bridge is a natural progression for existing database systems that provide a C API. The real power and ultimate solution, though, is to develop non-native JDBC drivers—those consisting of 100 percent Java code.

Implementing Interfaces

The JDBC API specification provides a series of *interfaces* that must be implemented by the JDBC driver developer. An interface declaration creates a new reference type consisting of constants and abstract methods. An interface cannot contain any implementations—that is, executable code. What does all of this mean? The JDBC API specification dictates the methods and method interfaces for the API, and a driver must fully implement these interfaces. A JDBC application makes method calls to the JDBC interface, not a specific driver. Because all JDBC drivers must implement the same interface, they are interchangeable.

There are a few rules that you must follow when implementing interfaces. First, you must implement the interface exactly as specified. This includes the name, return value, parameters, and **throws** clause. Secondly, you must be sure to implement all interfaces as **public** methods. Remember, this is the interface that other classes will see; if it isn't **public**, it can't be seen. Finally, all methods in the interface must be implemented. If you forget, the Java compiler will kindly remind you.

Take a look at Listing 7.11 for an example of how interfaces are used. The code defines an interface, implements the interface, and then uses the interface.

LISTING 7.11   WORKING WITH INTERFACES.

```java
//- - - - - - - - - - - - - - - - - - - - - - - - -
// MyInterface.java
//
// Sample code to demonstrate the use of interfaces
//- - - - - - - - - - - - - - - - - - - - - - - - -
package jdbc.test;

public interface MyInterface
{
    //- - - - - - - - - - - - - - - - - -
    // Define 3 methods in this interface
    //- - - - - - - - - - - - - - - - - -
    void method1();
    int method2(int x);
    String method3(String y);
}
//- - - - - - - - - - - - - - - - - - - - - - - - -
// MyImplementation.java
//
// Sample code to demonstrate the use of interfaces
//- - - - - - - - - - - - - - - - - - - - - - - - -

package jdbc.test;

public class MyImplementation
    implements jdbc.test.MyInterface
{
    //- - - - - - - - - - - - - - - - - - - - - -
    // Implement the 3 methods in the interface
    //- - - - - - - - - - - - - - - - - - - - - -
    public void method1()
    {
    }

    public int method2(int x)
    {
        return addOne(x);
    }

    public String method3(String y)
    {
        return y;
    }
```

```
    //- - - - - - - - - - - - - - - - - - - - - - - - - - - - - -
    // Note that you are free to add methods and attributes to this
    // new class that were not in the interface, but they cannot be
    // seen from the interface.
    //- - - - - - - - - - - - - - - - - - - - - - - - - - - - - -
    protected int addOne(int x)
    {
        return x + 1;
    }
}
//- - - - - - - - - - - - - - - - - - - - - - - - - - -
// TestInterface.java
//
// Sample code to demonstrate the use of interfaces
//- - - - - - - - - - - - - - - - - - - - - - - - - - -
import jdbc.test.*;

class TestInterface {

    public static void main (String args[])
    {
        // Create a new MyImplementation object. We are assigning the
        // new object to a MyInterface variable, thus we will only be
        // able to use the interface methods.
        MyInterface myInterface = new MyImplementation();

        // Call the methods
        myInterface.method1();
        int x = myInterface.method2(1);
        String y = myInterface.method3("Hello, World.");

    }
}
```

As you can see, implementing interfaces is easy. We'll go into more detail with the major JDBC interfaces later in this chapter. But first, we need to cover some basic foundations that should be a part of every good JDBC driver.

Tracing

One detail that is often overlooked by software developers is providing a facility to enable debugging. The JDBC API provides methods to enable and disable tracing, but it is ultimately up to the driver developer to provide tracing information in the driver. It becomes even more critical to provide a detailed level of tracing when you consider the possible widespread distribution of your driver. People from all over the world may be using your software, and they will expect a certain level of support if problems arise. For this reason, I consider it a must to trace all of the JDBC API method calls (so that a problem can be recreated using the output from a trace).

Turning On Tracing

The **DriverManager** provides a method to set the tracing **PrintStream** to be used for all of the drivers—not only those that are currently active, but any drivers that are subsequently loaded. Note that if two applications are using JDBC, and both have turned tracing on, the **PrintStream** that is set last will be shared by both applications. The following code snippet shows how to turn tracing on, sending any trace messages to a local file:

```
try {
    // Create a new OuputStream using a file. This may fail if the
    // calling application/applet does not have the proper security
    // to write to a local disk.
    java.io.OutputStream outFile = new
    java.io.FileOutputStream("jdbc.out");

    // Create a PrintStream object using our newly created OuputStream
    // object. The second parameter indicates to flush all output with
    // each write. This ensures that all trace information gets written
    // into the file.
    java.io.PrintStream outStream = new java.io.PrintStream(outFile,
    true);

    // Enable the JDBC tracing, using the PrintStream
    DriverManager.setLogStream(outStream);
}
catch (Exception ex) {
    // Something failed during enabling JDBC tracing. Notify the
    // application that tracing is not available.
    .
    .
    .
}
```

Using this code, a new file named jdbc.out will be created (if an existing file already exists, it will be overwritten), and any tracing information will be saved in the file.

Writing Tracing Information

The **DriverManager** also provides a method to write information to the tracing **OutputStream**. The **println** method will first check to ensure that a trace **OutputStream** has been registered, and if so, the **println** method of the **OutputStream** will be called. Here's an example of writing trace information:

```
// Send some information to the JDBC trace OutputStream
String a = "The quick brown fox ";
String b = "jumped over the ";
String c = "lazy dog";

DriverManager.println("Trace=" + a + b + c);
```

In this example, a **String** message, "Trace=The quick brown fox jumped over the lazy dog", will be constructed. The message will be provided as a parameter to the **DriverManager.println** method, and the message will be written to the **OutputStream** being used for tracing (if one has been registered).

Some of the JDBC components also provide tracing information. The **DriverManager** object traces most of its method calls. **SQLException** also sends trace information whenever an exception is thrown. If you were to use the previous code example and enable tracing to a file, the following example output would be created when attempting to connect to the SimpleText driver:

```
DriverManager.initialize: jdbc.drivers = null
JDBC DriverManager initialized
registerDriver:
driver[className=jdbc.SimpleText.SimpleTextDriver,context=null,
jdbc.SimpleText.SimpleTextDriver@1393860]
DriverManager.getConnection("jdbc:SimpleText")
trying
driver[className=jdbc.SimpleText.SimpleTextDriver,context=null,
jdbc.SimpleText.SimpleTextDriver@1393860]
driver[className=jdbc.SimpleText.SimpleTextDriver,context=null,j
dbc.SimpleText.SimpleTextDriver@1393860]
```

Checking For Tracing

I have found it quite useful for both the application and the driver to be able to test for the presence of a tracing **PrintStream**. The JDBC API provides us with a method to determine if tracing is enabled, as shown here:

```
//- - - - - - - - - - - - - - - - - - - - - - - - - - - - -
// traceOn
// Returns true if tracing (logging) is currently enabled
//- - - - - - - - - - - - - - - - - - - - - - - - - - - - -
public static boolean traceOn()
{
    // If the DriverManager log stream is not null, tracing
    // must be currently enabled.
    return (DriverManager.getLogStream() != null);
}
```

From an application, you can use this method to check if tracing has been previously enabled before blindly setting it:

```
// Before setting tracing on, check to make sure that tracing is not
// already turned on. If it is, notify the application.
if (traceOn()) {
    // Issue a warning that tracing is already enabled
    ...
}
```

From the driver, I use this method to check for tracing before attempting to send information to the **PrintStream**. In the example where we traced the message text of "Trace=The quick brown fox jumped over the lazy dog", a lot had to happen before the message was sent to the **DriverManager.println** method. All of the given **String** objects had to be concatenated, and a new **String** had to be constructed. That's a lot of overhead to go through before even making the **println** call, especially if tracing is not enabled (which will probably be the majority of the time). So, for performance reasons, I prefer to ensure that tracing has been enabled before assembling my trace message:

```
// Send some information to the JDBC trace OutputStream
String a = "The quick brown fox ";
String b = "jumped over the ";
String c = "lazy dog";

// Make sure tracing has been enabled
if (traceOn()) {
    DriverManager.println("Trace=" + a + b + c);
}
```

Data Coercion

At the heart of every JDBC driver is data. That is the whole purpose of the driver: providing data. Not only providing it, but providing it in a requested format. This is what data coercion is all about—converting data from one format to another. As Figure 7.1 shows, JDBC specifies the necessary conversions.

In order to provide reliable data coercion, a data wrapper class should be used. This class contains a data value in some known format and provides methods to convert it to a specific type. As an example, I have included the **CommonValue** class from the SimpleText driver in Listing 7.12. This class has several over-loaded constructors that accept different types of data values. The data value is

	TINYINT	SMALLINT	INTEGER	BIGINT	REAL	FLOAT	DOUBLE	DECIMAL	NUMERIC	BIT	CHAR	VARCHAR	LONGVARCHAR	BINARY	VARBINARY	LONGVARBINARY	DATE	TIME	TIMESTAMP
TINYINT	●	○	○	○	○	○	○	○	○	○	○	○	○						
SMALLINT	○	●	○	○	○	○	○	○	○	○	○	○	○						
INTEGER	○	○	●	○	○	○	○	○	○	○	○	○	○						
BIGINT	○	○	○	●	○	○	○	○	○	○	○	○	○						
REAL	○	○	○	○	●	○	○	○	○	○	○	○	○						
FLOAT	○	○	○	○	○	●	○	○	○	○	○	○	○						
DOUBLE	○	○	○	○	○	○	●	○	○	○	○	○	○						
DECIMAL	○	○	○	○	○	○	○	●	○	○	○	○	○						
NUMERIC	○	○	○	○	○	○	○	○	●	○	○	○	○						
BIT	○	○	○	○	○	○	○	○	○	●	○	○	○						
CHAR	○	○	○	○	○	○	○	○	○	○	●	○	○	○	○	○	○	○	○
VARCHAR	○	○	○	○	○	○	○	○	○	○	○	●	○	○	○	○	○	○	○
LONGVARCHAR	○	○	○	○	○	○	○	○	○	○	○	○	●	○	○	○	○	○	○
BINARY											○	○	○	●	○	○			
VARBINARY											○	○	○	○	●	○			
LONGVARBINARY											○	○	○	○	○	●			
DATE											○	○	○				●		○
TIME											○	○	○					●	○
TIMESTAMP											○	○	○				○	○	●

Figure 7.1
JDBC data conversion table.

stored within the class, along with the type of data (**String, Integer**, etc.). A series of methods are then provided to get the data in different formats. This class greatly reduces the burden to the JDBC driver developer, and can serve as a fundamental class for any number of drivers.

LISTING 7.12   THE COMMONVALUE CLASS.

```
package jdbc.SimpleText;

import java.sql.*;

public class CommonValue
    extends         Object
{
    //- - - - - - - -
    // Constructors
    //- - - - - - - -
    public CommonValue()
    {
        data = null;
    }

    public CommonValue(String s)
    {
        data = (Object) s;
        internalType = Types.VARCHAR;
    }

    public CommonValue(int i)
    {
        data = (Object) new Integer(i);
        internalType = Types.INTEGER;
    }

    public CommonValue(Integer i)
    {
        data = (Object) i;
        internalType = Types.INTEGER;
    }

    public CommonValue(byte b[])
    {
        data = (Object) b;
        internalType = Types.VARBINARY;
    }
```

```
//- - - - - - - - - - - - - - - - -
// isNull
// Returns true if the value is null
//- - - - - - - - - - - - - - - - -
public boolean isNull()
{
    return (data == null);
}


//- - - - - -
// getMethods
//- - - - - -

// Attempt to convert the data into a String. All data types
// should be able to be converted.
public String getString()
    throws SQLException
{
    String s;

    // A null value always returns null
    if (data == null) {
        return null;
    }

    switch(internalType) {

    case Types.VARCHAR:
        s = (String) data;
        break;

    case Types.INTEGER:
        s = ((Integer) data).toString();
        break;

    case Types.VARBINARY:
        {
            // Convert a byte array into a String of hex digits
            byte b[] = (byte[]) data;
            int len = b.length;
            String digits = "0123456789ABCDEF";
            char c[] = new char[len * 2];

            for (int i = 0; i < len; i++) {
                c[i * 2] = digits.charAt((b[i] >> 4) & 0x0F);
                c[(i * 2) + 1] = digits.charAt(b[i] & 0x0F);
```

```
                }
                s = new String(c);
            }
            break;

        default:
            throw new SQLException("Unable to convert data type to
              String: " +
                                    internalType);
        }

        return s;
    }

    // Attempt to convert the data into an int
    public int getInt()
        throws SQLException
    {
        int i = 0;

        // A null value always returns zero
        if (data == null) {
            return 0;
        }

        switch(internalType) {

        case Types.VARCHAR:
            i = (Integer.valueOf((String) data)).intValue();
            break;

        case Types.INTEGER:
            i = ((Integer) data).intValue();
            break;

        default:
            throw new SQLException("Unable to convert data type to
              String: " +
                                    internalType);
        }

        return i;
    }

    // Attempt to convert the data into a byte array
    public byte[] getBytes()
        throws SQLException
```

```
{
    byte b[] = null;

    // A null value always returns null
    if (data == null) {
        return null;
    }

    switch(internalType) {

    case Types.VARCHAR:
        {
            // Convert the String into a byte array. The String must
            // contain an even number of hex digits.
            String s = ((String) data).toUpperCase();
            String digits = "0123456789ABCDEF";
            int len = s.length();
            int index;

            if ((len % 2) != 0) {
                throw new SQLException(
                        "Data must have an even number of hex
                            digits");
            }

            b = new byte[len / 2];

            for (int i = 0; i < (len / 2); i++) {
                index = digits.indexOf(s.charAt(i * 2));

                if (index < 0) {
                    throw new SQLException("Invalid hex digit");
                }

                b[i] = (byte) (index << 4);
                index = digits.indexOf(s.charAt((i * 2) + 1));

                if (index < 0) {
                    throw new SQLException("Invalid hex digit");
                }
                b[i] += (byte) index;
            }
        }
        break;

    case Types.VARBINARY:
        b = (byte[]) data;
        break;
```

```
        default:
            throw new SQLException("Unable to convert data type to
            byte[]: " +
                                internalType);
        }
        return b;
    }


    protected Object data;
    protected int internalType;
}
```

Note that the SimpleText driver supports only character, integer, and binary data; thus, **CommonValue** only accepts these data types and only attempts to convert data to these same types. A more robust driver would need to further implement this class to include more (if not all) data types.

Escape Clauses

Another consideration to keep in mind when implementing a JDBC driver is processing escape clauses. Escape clauses are used as extensions to SQL and provide a method to perform DBMS-specific extensions, which are interoperable among DBMSes. The JDBC driver must accept escape clauses and expand them into the native DBMS format before processing the SQL statement. While this sounds simple enough on the surface, this process may turn out to be an enormous task. If you are developing a driver that uses an existing DBMS, and the JDBC driver simply passes SQL statements to the DBMS, you may have to develop a parser to scan for escape clauses.

The following types of SQL extensions are defined:

- Date, time, and timestamp data
- Scalar functions, such as numeric, string, and data type conversion
- LIKE predicate escape characters
- Outer joins
- Procedures

The JDBC specification does not directly address escape clauses; they are inherited from the ODBC specification. The syntax defined by ODBC uses the escape clause provided by the X/OPEN and SQL Access Group SQL CAE specification (1992). The general syntax for an escape clause is:

```
{escape}
```

We'll cover the specific syntax for each type of escape clause in the following sections.

Date, Time, And Timestamp

The **date**, **time**, and **timestamp** escape clauses allow an application to specify date, time, and timestamp data in a uniform manner, without concern to the native DBMS format (for which the JDBC driver is responsible). The syntax for each (respectively) is

```
{d 'value'}
{t 'value'}
{ts 'value'}
```

where **d** indicates that **value** is a date in the format YYYY-MM-DD, **t** indicates that **value** is a time in the format HH:MM:SS, and **ts** indicates that **value** is a timestamp in the format YYYY-MM-DD HH:MM:SS[.F...]. The following SQL statements illustrate the use of each:

```
UPDATE EMPLOYEE SET HIREDATE={d '1992-04-01'}
UPDATE EMPLOYEE SET LAST_IN={ts '1996-07-03 08:00:00'}
UPDATE EMPLOYEE SET BREAK_DUE={t '10:00:00'}
```

Scalar Functions

The five types of scalar functions—string, numeric, time and date, system, and data type conversion—all use the syntax

```
{fn scalar-function}
```

To determine what type of string functions a JDBC driver supports, an application can use the **DatabaseMetaData** method **getStringFunctions**. This method returns a comma-separated list of string functions, possibly containing **ASCII**, **CHAR**, **CONCAT**, **DIFFERENCE**, **INSERT**, **LCASE**, **LEFT**, **LENGTH**, **LOCATE**, **LTRIM**, **REPEAT**, **REPLACE**, **RIGHT**, **RTRIM**, **SOUNDEX**, **SPACE**, **SUBSTRING**, and/or **UCASE**.

To determine what type of numeric functions a JDBC driver supports, an application can use the **DatabaseMetaData** method **getNumericFunctions**. This method returns a comma-separated list of numeric functions, possibly containing **ABS, ACOS, ASIN, ATAN, ATAN2, CEILING, COS, COT, DEGREES, EXP, FLOOR, LOG, LOG10, MOD, PI, POWER, RADIANS, RAND, ROUND, SIGN, SIN, SQRT, TAN,** and/or **TRUNCATE.**

To determine what type of system functions a JDBC driver supports, an application can use the **DatabaseMetaData** method **getSystemFunctions**. This method returns a comma-separated list of system functions, possibly containing **DATABASE, IFNULL,** and/or **USER.**

To determine what type of time and date functions a JDBC driver supports, an application can use the **DatabaseMetaData** method **getTimeDateFunctions**. This method returns a comma-separated list of time and date functions, possibly containing **CURDATE, CURTIME, DAYNAME, DAYOFMONTH, DAYOFWEEK, DAYOFYEAR, HOUR, MINUTE, MONTH, MONTH NAME, NOW, QUARTER, SECOND, TIMESTAMPADD, TIME STAMPDIFF, WEEK,** and/or **YEAR.**

To determine what type of explicit data type conversions a JDBC driver supports, an application can use the **DatabaseMetaData** method **supportsConvert**. This method has two parameters: a *from* SQL data type and a *to* SQL data type. If the explicit data conversion between the two SQL types is supported, the method returns **true.** The syntax for the **CONVERT** function is

```
{fn CONVERT(value, data_type)}
```

where **value** is a column name, the result of another scalar function, or a literal, and **data_type** is one of the JDBC SQL types listed in the **Types** class.

LIKE Predicate Escape Characters

In a **LIKE** predicate, the % (percent character) matches zero or more of any character, and the _ (underscore character) matches any one character. In some instances, an SQL query may have the need to search for one of these special matching characters. In such cases, you can use the % and _ characters as literals in a **LIKE** predicate by preceding them with an escape character. The

DatabaseMetaData method **getSearch-StringEscape** returns the default escape character (which for most DBMSes will be the backslash character (\)). To override the escape character, use the following syntax:

```
{escape 'escape-character'}
```

The following SQL statement uses the **LIKE** predicate escape clause to search for any columns that start with the % character:

```
SELECT * FROM EMPLOYEE WHERE NAME LIKE '\%' {escape '\'}
```

Outer Joins

JDBC supports the ANSI SQL-92 **LEFT OUTER JOIN** syntax. The escape clause syntax is

```
{oj outer-join}
```

where **outer-join** is the table-reference **LEFT OUTER JOIN** {table-reference | outer-join} **ON** search-condition.

Procedures

A JDBC application can call a procedure in place of an SQL statement. The escape clause used for calling a procedure is

```
{[?=] call procedure-name[(param[, param]...)]}
```

where **procedure-name** specifies the name of a procedure stored on the data source, and **param** specifies procedure parameters. A procedure can have zero or more parameters and may return a value.

The JDBC Interfaces

Now let's take a look at each of the JDBC interfaces, which are shown in Figure 7.2. We'll go over the major aspects of each interface and use code examples from our SimpleText project whenever applicable. You should understand the JDBC API specification before attempting to create a JDBC driver; this section is meant to enhance the specification, not to replace it.

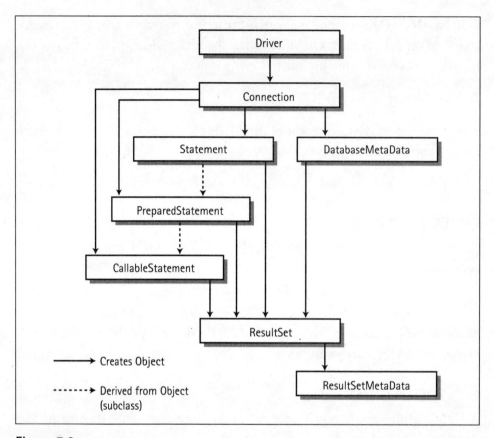

Figure 7.2
The JDBC interfaces.

Driver

The **Driver** class is the entry point for all JDBC drivers. From here, a connection to the database can be made in order to perform work. This class is intentionally very small; the intent is that JDBC drivers can be pre-registered with the system, enabling the **DriverManager** to select an appropriate driver given only a *URL* (Universal Resource Locator). The only way to determine which driver can service the given URL is to load the **Driver** class and let each driver respond via the **acceptsURL** method. To keep the amount of time required to find an appropriate driver to a minimum, each **Driver** class should be as small as possible so it can be loaded quickly.

REGISTER THYSELF

The first thing a driver should do is register itself with the **DriverManager**. The reason is simple: You need to tell the **DriverManager** that you exist; otherwise you may not be loaded. The following code illustrates one way of loading a JDBC driver:

```
java.sql.Driver d = (java.sql.Driver)
    Class.forName ("jdbc.SimpleText.SimpleTextDriver").newInstance();

Connection con = DriverManager.getConnection("jdbc:SimpleText", "", "");
```

The class loader will create a new instance of the SimpleText JDBC driver. The application then asks the **DriverManager** to create a connection using the given URL. If the SimpleText driver does not register itself, the **DriverManager** will not attempt to load it, which will result in a nasty "No capable driver" error.

The best place to register a driver is in the **Driver** constructor:

```
public SimpleTextDriver()
    throws SQLException
{
    // Attempt to register this driver with the JDBC DriverManager.
    // If it fails, an exception will be thrown.
    DriverManager.registerDriver(this);
}
```

URL PROCESSING

As I mentioned a moment ago, the **acceptsURL** method informs the **DriverManager** whether a given URL is supported by the driver. The general format for a JDBC URL is

```
jdbc:subprotocol:subname
```

where **subprotocol** is the particular database connectivity mechanism supported (note that this mechanism may be supported by multiple drivers) and the **subname** is defined by the JDBC driver. For example, the format for the JDBC-ODBC Bridge URL is

```
jdbc:odbc:data source name
```

Thus, if an application requests a JDBC driver to service the URL of

`jdbc:odbc:foobar`

the only driver that will respond that the URL is supported is the JDBC-ODBC Bridge; all others will ignore the request.

Listing 7.13 shows the **acceptsURL** method for the SimpleText driver. The SimpleText driver will accept the following URL syntax:

`jdbc:SimpleText`

Note that no subname is required; if a subname is provided, it will be ignored.

LISTING 7.13   THE ACCEPTSURL METHOD.

```
//- - - - - - - - - - - - - - - - - - - - - - - - - - - - - - - -
// acceptsURL - JDBC API
//
// Returns true if the driver thinks that it can open a connection to the
// given URL. Typically, drivers will return true if they understand the
// subprotocol specified in the URL, and false if they don't.
//
//    url        The URL of the database.
//
// Returns true if this driver can connect to the given URL.
//- - - - - - - - - - - - - - - - - - - - - - - - - - - - - - - -
public boolean acceptsURL(
    String url)
    throws SQLException
{
    if (traceOn()) {
        trace("@acceptsURL (url=" + url + ")");
    }

    boolean rc = false;

    // Get the subname from the URL. If the URL is not valid for
    // this driver, a null will be returned.
    if (getSubname(url) != null) {
        rc = true;
    }
    if (traceOn()) {
        trace(" " + rc);
    }
    return rc;
}
```

```
//- - - - - - - - - - - - - - - - - - - - - - - - - - - - - - - - -
// getSubname
// Given a URL, return the subname. Returns null if the protocol is
// not "jdbc" or the subprotocol is not "simpletext".
//- - - - - - - - - - - - - - - - - - - - - - - - - - - - - - - - -
public String getSubname(
    String url)
{
    String subname = null;
    String protocol = "JDBC";
    String subProtocol = "SIMPLETEXT";

    // Convert to uppercase and trim all leading and trailing
    // blanks.
    url = (url.toUpperCase()).trim();

    // Make sure the protocol is jdbc:
    if (url.startsWith(protocol)) {

        // Strip off the protocol
        url = url.substring (protocol.length());

        // Look for the colon
        if (url.startsWith(":")) {
            url = url.substring(1);

            // Check the subprotocol
            if (url.startsWith(subProtocol)) {

                // Strip off the subprotocol, leaving the subname
                url = url.substring(subProtocol.length());

                // Look for the colon that separates the subname
                // from the subprotocol (or the fact that there
                // is no subprotocol at all).
                if (url.startsWith(":")) {
                    subname = url.substring(subProtocol.length());
                }
                else if (url.length() == 0) {
                    subname = "";
                }
            }
        }
    }
    return subname;
}
```

PROPERTIES

Connecting to a JDBC driver with only a URL specification is great, but the vast majority of the time, a driver will require additional information in order to properly connect to a database. The JDBC specification has addressed this issue with the **getPropertyInfo** method. Once a **Driver** has been instantiated, an application can use this method to find out which required and optional properties can be used to connect to the database. You may be tempted to require the application to embed properties within the URL subname, but by returning them from the **getPropertyInfo** method, you can identify the properties at runtime, giving a much more robust solution. Listing 7.14 shows an application that loads the SimpleText driver and gets the property information.

LISTING 7.14   USING THE GETPROPERTYINFO METHOD TO IDENTIFY PROPERTIES AT RUNTIME.

```
import java.sql.*;

class PropertyTest {

    public static void main(String args[])
    {
        try {

            // Quick way to create a driver object
            java.sql.Driver d = new jdbc.SimpleText.SimpleTextDriver();

            String url = "jdbc:SimpleText";

            // Make sure we have the proper URL
            if (!d.acceptsURL(url)) {
                throw new SQLException("Unknown URL: " + url);
            }

            // Setup a Properties object. This should contain an entry
            // for all known properties to this point. Properties that
            // have already been specified in the Properties object will
            // not be returned by getPropertyInfo.
            java.util.Properties props = new java.util.Properties();

            // Get the property information
            DriverPropertyInfo info[] = d.getPropertyInfo(url, props);
```

```
            // Just dump them out
            System.out.println("Number of properties: " + info.length);

            for (int i=0; i < info.length; i++) {
                System.out.println("\nProperty " + (i + 1));
                System.out.println("Name:        " + info[i].name);
                System.out.println("Description: " +
                  info[i].description);
                System.out.println("Required:    " + info[i].required);
                System.out.println("Value:       " + info[i].value);
                System.out.println("Choices:     " + info[i].choices);
            }

        }
        catch (SQLException ex) {
            System.out.println ("\nSQLException(s) caught\n");

            // Remember that SQLExceptions may be chained together
            while (ex != null) {
                System.out.println("SQLState: " + ex.getSQLState());
                System.out.println("Message:  " + ex.getMessage());
                System.out.println ("");
                ex = ex.getNextException ();
            }
        }
    }
}
```

Listing 7.14 produces the following output:

```
Number of properties: 1

Property 1
Name:        Directory
Description: Initial text file directory
Required:    false
Value:       null
Choices:     null
```

It doesn't take a lot of imagination to envision an application or applet that gathers the property information and prompts the user in order to connect to the database. The actual code to implement the **getPropertyInfo** method for the SimpleText driver is very simple, as shown in Listing 7.15.

LISTING 7.15 IMPLEMENTING THE GETPROPERTYINFO METHOD.

```
//- - - - - - - - - - - - - - - - - - - - - - - - - - - - - - - - - -
// getPropertyInfo - JDBC API
//
// The getPropertyInfo method is intended to allow a generic GUI tool to
// discover what properties it should prompt a human for in order to get
// enough information to connect to a database. Note that depending on
// the values the human has supplied so far, additional values may become
// necessary, so it may be necessary to iterate though several calls
// to getPropertyInfo.
//
//  url     The URL of the database to connect to.
//
//  info    A proposed list of tag/value pairs that will be sent on
//          connect open.
//
// Returns an array of DriverPropertyInfo objects describing possible
// properties. This array may be an empty array if no properties are
// required.
//- - - - - - - - - - - - - - - - - - - - - - - - - - - - - - - - - -

public DriverPropertyInfo[] getPropertyInfo(
    String url,
    java.util.Properties info)
    throws SQLException
{

    DriverPropertyInfo prop[];

    // Only one property required for the SimpleText driver, the
    // directory. Check the property list coming in. If the
    // directory is specified, return an empty list.
    if (info.getProperty("Directory") == null) {

        // Set up the DriverPropertyInfo entry
        prop = new DriverPropertyInfo[1];
        prop[0] = new DriverPropertyInfo("Directory", null);
        prop[0].description = "Initial text file directory";
        prop[0].required = false;

    }
    else {
        // Create an empty list
        prop = new DriverPropertyInfo[0];
    }

    return prop;
}
```

LET'S GET CONNECTED

Now that we can identify a driver to provide services for a given URL and get a list of the required and optional parameters necessary, it's time to establish a connection to the database. The **connect** method does just that (as shown in Listing 7.16) by taking a URL and connection property list and attempting to make a connection to the database. The first thing that **connect** should do is verify the URL (by making a call to **acceptsURL**). If the URL is not supported by the driver, a null value will be returned. This is the only reason that a null value should be returned. Any other errors during the **connect** should throw an **SQLException**.

LISTING 7.16 CONNECTING TO THE DATABASE.

```
//- - - - - - - - - - - - - - - - - - - - - - - - - - - - - - - - - - - -
// connect - JDBC API
//
// Try to make a database connection to the given URL.
// The driver should return "null" if it realizes it is the wrong kind
// of driver to connect to the given URL. This will be common, as when
// the JDBC driver manager is asked to connect to a given URL, it passes
// the URL to each loaded driver in turn.
//
// The driver should raise an SQLException if it is the right driver to
// connect to the given URL, but has trouble connecting to the database.
//
// The java.util.Properties argument can be used to pass arbitrary
// string tag/value pairs as connection arguments.
// Normally, at least "user" and "password" properties should be
// included in the Properties.
//
//   url    The URL of the database to connect to.
//
//   info   A list of arbitrary string tag/value pairs as connection
//          arguments; normally, at least a "user" and "password"
//          property should be included.
//
// Returns a Connection to the URL.
//- - - - - - - - - - - - - - - - - - - - - - - - - - - - - - - - - - - -
public Connection connect(
    String url,
    java.util.Properties info)
    throws SQLException
{
```

```
        if (traceOn()) {
            trace("@connect (url=" + url + ")");
        }

        // Ensure that we can understand the given URL
        if (!acceptsURL(url)) {
            return null;
        }

        // For typical JDBC drivers, it would be appropriate to check
        // for a secure environment before connecting, and deny access
        // to the driver if it is deemed to be unsecure. For the
        // SimpleText driver, if the environment is not secure, we will
        // turn it into a read-only driver.

        // Create a new SimpleTextConnection object
        SimpleTextConnection con = new SimpleTextConnection();

        // Initialize the new object. This is where all of the
        // connection work is done.
        con.initialize(this, info);

        return con;
}
```

As you can see, there isn't a lot going on here for the SimpleText driver; remember that we need to keep the size of the **Driver** class implementation as small as possible. To aid in this, all of the code required to perform the database connection resides in the **Connection** class, which we'll discuss next.

Connection

The **Connection** class represents a session with the data source. Using this class, you can create **Statement** objects to execute SQL statements and gather database statistics. Depending upon the database that you are using, multiple connections may be allowed for each driver.

For the SimpleText driver, we don't need to do anything more than actually connect to the database. In fact, there really isn't a database at all—just a bunch of text files. For typical database drivers, some type of connection context will be established, and default information will be set and gathered. During the SimpleText connection initialization, all that we need to do is check for a read-only condition (which can only occur within untrusted applets) and any properties that are supplied by the application, as shown in Listing 7.17.

LISTING 7.17   SIMPLETEXT CONNECTION INITIALIZATION.

```java
public void initialize(
    Driver driver,
    java.util.Properties info)
    throws SQLException
{
    // Save the owning driver object
    ownerDriver = driver;

    // Get the security manager and see if we can write to a file.
    // If no security manager is present, assume that we are a trusted
    // application and have read/write privileges.
    canWrite = false;

    SecurityManager securityManager = System.getSecurityManager ();

    if (securityManager != null) {
        try {
            // Use some arbitrary file to check for file write privileges
            securityManager.checkWrite ("SimpleText_Foo");

            // Flag is set if no exception is thrown
            canWrite = true;
        }

        // If we can't write, an exception is thrown. We'll catch
        // it and do nothing.
        catch (SecurityException ex) {
        }
    }
    else {
        canWrite = true;
    }

    // Set our initial read-only flag
    setReadOnly(!canWrite);

    // Get the directory. It will either be supplied in the property
    // list, or we'll use our current default.
    String s = info.getProperty("Directory");

    if (s == null) {
        s = System.getProperty("user.dir");
    }

    setCatalog(s);
}
```

CREATING STATEMENTS

From the **Connection** object, an application can create three types of **Statement** objects. The base **Statement** object is used for executing SQL statements directly. The **PreparedStatement** object (which extends **Statement**) is used for pre-compiling SQL statements that may contain input parameters. The **CallableStatement** object (which extends **PreparedStatement**) is used to execute stored procedures that may contain both input and output parameters.

For the SimpleText driver, the **createStatement** method does nothing more than create a new **Statement** object. For most database systems, some type of statement context, or handle, will be created. One thing to note whenever an object is created in a JDBC driver: Save a reference to the owning object because you will need to obtain information (such as the connection context from within a **Statement** object) from the owning object.

Consider the **createStatement** method within the **Connection** class:

```
public Statement createStatement()
    throws SQLException
{
    if (traceOn()) {
        trace("Creating new SimpleTextStatement");
    }

    // Create a new Statement object
    SimpleTextStatement stmt = new SimpleTextStatement();

    // Initialize the statement
    stmt.initialize(this);

    return stmt;
}
```

Now consider the corresponding **initialize** method in the **Statement** class:

```
public void initialize(
    SimpleTextConnection con)
    throws SQLException
{
    // Save the owning connection object
    ownerConnection = con;
}
```

Which module will you compile first? You can't compile the **Connection** class until the **Statement** class has been compiled, and you can't compile the **Statement** class until the **Connection** class has been compiled. This is a circular dependency. Of course, the Java compiler does allow multiple files to be compiled at once, but some build environments do not support building multiple Java files at the same time. I have solved this problem in the SimpleText driver by defining some simple interface classes. In this way, the **Statement** class knows only about the general interface of the **Connection** class; the implementation of the interface does not need to be present. Our modified **initialize** method looks like this:

```
public void initialize(
    SimpleTextIConnection con)
    throws SQLException
{
    // Save the owning connection object
    ownerConnection = con;
}
```

Note that the only difference is the introduction of a new class, **Simple TextIConnection**, which replaces **SimpleTextConnection**. I have chosen to preface the JDBC class name with an "I" to signify an interface. Here's the interface class:

```
public interface SimpleTextIConnection
    extends java.sql.Connection
{
    String[] parseSQL(String sql);
    Hashtable getTables(String directory, String table);
    Hashtable getColumns(String directory, String table);
    String getDirectory(String directory);
}
```

Note that our interface class extends the JDBC class, and our **Connection** class implements this new interface. This allows us to compile the interface first, then the **Statement**, followed by the **Connection**. Say goodbye to your circular dependency woes.

Now, back to the **Statement** objects. The **prepareStatement** and **prepareCall** methods of the **Connection** object both require an SQL statement to be provided. This SQL statement should be pre-compiled and stored with the

Statement object. If any errors are present in the SQL statement, an exception should be raised, and the **Statement** object should not be created.

TELL ME ABOUT YOURSELF

One of the most powerful aspects of the JDBC specification (which was inherited from **X/Open**) is the ability for introspection. This is the process of asking a driver for information about what is supported, how it behaves, and what type of information exists in the database. The **getMetaData** method creates a **DatabaseMetaData** object that provides us with this wealth of information.

DatabaseMetaData

With more than 130 methods, the **DatabaseMetaData** class is by far the largest. It supplies information about what is supported and how things are supported. It also supplies catalog information such as listing tables, columns, indexes, procedures, and so on. Because the JDBC API specification does an adequate job of explaining the methods contained in this class, and most of them are quite straightforward, we'll just take a look at how the SimpleText driver implements the **getTables** catalog method. But first, let's review the basic steps needed to implement each of the catalog methods (that is, those methods that return a **ResultSet**):

1.   Create the result columns, which includes the column name, type, and other information about each of the columns. You should perform this step regardless of whether the database supports a given catalog function (such as stored procedures). I believe that it is much better to return an empty result set with only the column information than to raise an exception indicating that the database does not support the function. The JDBC specification does not currently address this issue, so it is open for interpretation.

2.   Retrieve the catalog information from the database.

3.   Perform any filtering necessary. The application may have specified the return of only a subset of the catalog information. You may need to filter the information in the JDBC driver if the database system doesn't.

4.   Sort the result data per the JDBC API specification. If you are lucky, the database you are using will sort the data in the proper sequence. Most

likely, it will not. In this case, you will need to ensure that the data is returned in the proper order.

5.   Return a **ResultSet** containing the requested information.

The SimpleText **getTables** method will return a list of all of the text files in the catalog (directory) given. If no catalog is supplied, the **getTables** method will use the default directory . Note that the SimpleText driver does not perform all of the steps shown previously; it does not provide any filtering, nor does it sort the data in the proper sequence. You are more than welcome to add this functionality. In fact, I encourage it. One note about column information: I prefer to use a **Hashtable** containing the column number as the key, and a class containing all of the information about the column as the data value. So, for all **ResultSets** that are generated, I create a **Hashtable** of column information that is then used by the **ResultSet** object and the **ResultSetMetaData** object to describe each column. Listing 7.18 shows the **SimpleTextColumn** class that is used to hold this information for each column.

LISTING 7.18   THE SIMPLETEXTCOLUMN CLASS.

```
package jdbc.SimpleText;

public class SimpleTextColumn
    extends         Object
{
    //- - - - - - -
    // Constructor
    //- - - - - - -
    public SimpleTextColumn(
        String name,
        int type,
        int precision)
    {
        this.name = name;
        this.type = type;
        this.precision = precision;
    }

    public SimpleTextColumn(
        String name,
        int type)
    {
```

```
        this.name = name;
        this.type = type;
        this.precision = 0;
    }

    public SimpleTextColumn(
        String name)
    {
        this.name = name;
        this.type = 0;
        this.precision = 0;
    }

    public String name;
    public int type;
    public int precision;
    public boolean searchable;
    public int colNo;
    public int displaySize;
    public String typeName;
}
```

Note that I have used several constructors to set up various default information and that all of the attributes are **public**. To follow object-oriented design, I should have provided a **get** and **set** method to encapsulate each attribute, but I chose to let each consumer of this object access them directly. Listing 7.19 shows the code for the **getTables** method.

LISTING 7.19   THE GETTABLES METHOD.

```
//- - - - - - - - - - - - - - - - - - - - - - - - - - - - - - - - -
// getTables - JDBC API
// Get a description of tables available in a catalog
//
// Only table descriptions matching the catalog, schema, table
// name, and type criteria are returned. They are ordered by
// TABLE_TYPE, TABLE_SCHEM, and TABLE_NAME.
//
// Each table description has the following columns:
//
//    (1) TABLE_CAT      String => table catalog (may be null)
//    (2) TABLE_SCHEM    String => table schema (may be null)
//    (3) TABLE_NAME     String => table name
//    (4) TABLE_TYPE     String => table type
//            Typical types are "TABLE", "VIEW", "SYSTEM TABLE",
//            "GLOBAL TEMPORARY", "LOCAL TEMPORARY", "ALIAS", "SYNONYM"
```

```
//     (5) REMARKS        String => explanatory comment on the table
//
// Note: Some databases may not return information for all tables.
//
//   catalog           A catalog name; "" retrieves those without a catalog.
//   schemaPattern     A schema name pattern; "" retrieves those without
//                       a schema.
//   tableNamePattern  A table name pattern.
//   types             A list of table types to include; null returns all
//                       types.
//
// Returns a ResultSet. Each row is a table description.
//- - - - - - - - - - - - - - - - - - - - - - - - - - - - - - - - - - -
public ResultSet getTables(
    String catalog,
    String schemaPattern,
    String tableNamePattern,
    String types[])
    throws SQLException
{

    if (traceOn()) {
        trace("@getTables(" + catalog + ", " + schemaPattern +
                ", " + tableNamePattern + ")");
    }

    // Create a statement object
    SimpleTextStatement stmt =
                (SimpleTextStatement) ownerConnection.createStatement();

    // Create a Hashtable for all of the columns
    Hashtable columns = new Hashtable();

    add(columns, 1, "TABLE_CAT", Types.VARCHAR);
    add(columns, 2, "TABLE_SCHEM", Types.VARCHAR);
    add(columns, 3, "TABLE_NAME", Types.VARCHAR);
    add(columns, 4, "TABLE_TYPE", Types.VARCHAR);
    add(columns, 5, "REMARKS", Types.VARCHAR);

    // Create an empty Hashtable for the rows
    Hashtable rows = new Hashtable();

    // If any of the parameters will return an empty result set, do so
    boolean willBeEmpty = false;

    // If table types are specified, make sure that 'TABLE' is
    // included. If not, no rows will be returned.
```

```
    if (types != null) {
        willBeEmpty = true;
        for (int ii = 0; ii < types.length; ii++) {
            if (types[ii].equalsIgnoreCase("TABLE")) {
                willBeEmpty = false;
                break;
            }
        }
    }

    if (!willBeEmpty) {

        // Get a Hashtable with all tables
        Hashtable tables = ownerConnection.getTables(
                ownerConnection.getDirectory(catalog),
                tableNamePattern);

        Hashtable singleRow;
        SimpleTextTable table;

        // Create a row for each table in the Hashtable
        for (int i = 0; i < tables.size(); i++) {
            table = (SimpleTextTable) tables.get(new Integer(i));

            // Create a new Hashtable for a single row
            singleRow = new Hashtable();

            // Build the row
            singleRow.put(new Integer(1), new CommonValue(table.dir));
            singleRow.put(new Integer(3), new CommonValue(table.name));
            singleRow.put(new Integer(4), new CommonValue("TABLE"));

            // Add it to the row list
            rows.put(new Integer(i + 1), singleRow);
        }
    }

    // Create the ResultSet object and return it
    SimpleTextResultSet rs = new SimpleTextResultSet();

    rs.initialize(stmt, columns, rows);

    return rs;
}
```

Let's take a closer look at what's going on here. The first thing we do is create a **Statement** object to "fake out" the **ResultSet** object that we will be creating to return back to the application. The **ResultSet** object is dependant upon a **Statement** object, so we'll give it one. The next thing we do is create all of the column information. Note that all of the required columns are given in the JDBC API specification. The **add** method simply adds a **SimpleTextColumn** object to the **Hashtable** of columns:

```
protected void add(
    Hashtable h,
    int col,
    String name,
    int type)
{
    h.put(new Integer(col), new SimpleTextColumn(name,type));
}
```

Next, we create another **Hashtable** to hold all of the data for all of the catalog rows. The **Hashtable** contains an entry for each row of data. The entry contains the key, which is the row number, and the data value, which is yet another **Hashtable** whose key is the column number and whose data value is a **CommonValue** object containing the actual data. Remember that the **CommonValue** class provides us with the mechanism to store data and coerce it as requested by the application. If a column is null, we simply don't store any information in the **Hashtable** for that column number.

After a sanity check to ensure that we really need to look for the catalog information, we get a list of all of the tables. The **getTables** method in the **Connection** class provides us with a list of all of the SimpleText data files:

```
public Hashtable getTables(
    String dir,
    String table)
{
    Hashtable list = new Hashtable();

    // Create a FilenameFilter object. This object will only allow
    // files with the .SDF extension to be seen.
    FilenameFilter filter = new SimpleTextEndsWith(
            SimpleTextDefine.DATA_FILE_EXT);
```

```
File file = new File(dir);

if (file.isDirectory()) {

    // List all of the files in the directory with the .SDF extension
    String entries[] = file.list(filter);
    SimpleTextTable tableEntry;

    // Create a SimpleTextTable entry for each, and put in
    // the Hashtable.
    for (int i = 0; i < entries.length; i++) {

        // A complete driver needs to further filter the table
        // name here.
        tableEntry = new SimpleTextTable(dir, entries[i]);
            list.put(new Integer(i), tableEntry);
    }
}

return list;
}
```

Again, I use a **Hashtable** for each table (or file in our case) that is found. By now, you will have realized that I really like using **Hashtables**; they can grow in size dynamically and provide quick access to data. And because a **Hashtable** stores data as an abstract **Object**, I can store whatever is necessary. In this case, each **Hashtable** entry for a table contains a SimpleTextTable object:

```
public class SimpleTextTable
    extends         Object
{
    //- - - - - - -
    // Constructor
    //- - - - - - -
    public SimpleTextTable(
        String dir,
        String file)
    {
        this.dir = dir;
        this.file = file;

        // If the file name has the .SDF extension, get rid of it
        if (file.endsWith(SimpleTextDefine.DATA_FILE_EXT)) {
            name = file.substring(0, file.length() -
                    SimpleTextDefine.DATA_FILE_EXT.length());
        }
```

```
        else {
            name = file;
        }
    }

    public String dir;
    public String file;
    public String name;
}
```

Notice that the constructor strips the file extension from the given file name, creating the table name.

Now, back to the **getTables** method for **DatabaseMetaData**. Once a list of all of the tables has been retrieved, the **Hashtable** used for storing all of the rows is generated. If you want to add additional filtering, this is the place that it should be done. Finally, a new **ResultSet** object is created and initialized. One of the constructors for the **ResultSet** class accepts two **Hashtables**: one for the column information (**SimpleTextColumn** objects) and the other for row data (**CommonValue** objects). We'll see later how these are handled by the **ResultSet** class. For now, just note that it can handle both in-memory results (in the form of a **Hashtable**) and results read directly from the data file.

Statement

The **Statement** class contains methods to execute SQL statements directly against the database and to obtain the results. A **Statement** object is created using the **createStatement** method from the **Connection** object. The three methods used to execute SQL statements—**executeUpdate**, **executeQuery**, and **execute**—are used in Listing 7.20. In actuality, you only need to worry about implementing the **execute** method; the other methods use it to perform their work. In fact, the code provided in the SimpleText driver should be identical for all JDBC drivers.

LISTING 7.20   EXECUTING SQL STATEMENTS.

```
//- - - - - - - - - - - - - - - - - - - - - - - - - - - - - -
// executeQuery - JDBC API
// Execute an SQL statement that returns a single ResultSet.
//
//    sql    Typically this is a static SQL SELECT statement.
//
```

```
// Returns the table of data produced by the SQL statement.
//- - - - - - - - - - - - - - - - - - - - - - - - - - - - -
public ResultSet executeQuery(
    String sql)
    throws SQLException
{
    if (traceOn()) {
        trace("@executeQuery(" + sql + ")");
    }

    java.sql.ResultSet rs = null;

    // Execute the query. If execute returns true, then a result set
    // exists.
    if (execute(sql)) {
        rs = getResultSet();
    }
    else {          // If the statement does not create a ResultSet, the
                    // specification indicates that an SQLException should
                    // be raised.
        throw new SQLException("Statement did not create a ResultSet");
    }
    return rs;
}


//- - - - - - - - - - - - - - - - - - - - - - - - - - - - - - -
// executeUpdate - JDBC API
// Execute an SQL INSERT, UPDATE, or DELETE statement. In addition,
// SQL statements that return nothing, such as SQL DDL statements,
// can be executed.
//
//    sql    an SQL INSERT, UPDATE, or DELETE statement, or an SQL
//           statement that returns nothing.
//
// Returns either the row count for INSERT, UPDATE, or DELETE; or 0
// for SQL statements that return nothing.
//- - - - - - - - - - - - - - - - - - - - - - - - - - - - - - -
public int executeUpdate(
    String sql)
    throws SQLException
{
    if (traceOn()) {
        trace("@executeUpdate(" + sql + ")");
    }

    int count = -1;
```

```
    // Execute the query. If execute returns false, then an update
    // count exists.
    if (execute(sql) == false) {
        count = getUpdateCount();
    }
    else {
        // If the statement does not create an update count, the
        // specification indicates that an SQLException should be raised.
        throw new SQLException("Statement did not create an update
          count");
    }

    return count;
}
```

As you can see, **executeQuery** and **executeUpdate** are simply helper methods for an application; they are built exclusively upon other methods within the class. The **execute** method accepts an SQL statement as its only parameter, and will be implemented differently, depending upon the underlying database system. For the SimpleText driver, the SQL statement will be parsed, prepared, and executed. Note that parameter markers are not allowed when executing an SQL statement directly. If the SQL statement created results containing columnar data, **execute** will return true; if the statement created a count of rows affected, **execute** will return false. If **execute** returns true, the application then uses **getResultSet** to return the current result information; otherwise, **getUpdate Count** will return the number of rows affected.

WARNINGS

As opposed to **SQLException**, which indicates a critical error, an **SQLWarning** can be issued to provide additional information to the application. Even though **SQLWarning** is derived from **SQLException**, warnings are not thrown. Instead, if a warning is issued, it is placed on a warning stack with the **Statement** object (the same holds true for the **Connection** and **ResultSet** objects). The application must then check for warnings after every operation using the **getWarnings** method. At first, this may seem a bit cumbersome, but when you consider the alternative of wrapping **try..catch** statements around each operation, this seems like a better solution. Note also that warnings can be chained together, just like **SQLExceptions** (for more information on chaining, see the *JDBC Exception Types* section earlier in this chapter).

Two (Or More) For The Price Of One

Some database systems allow SQL statements that return multiple results (columnar data or an update count) to be executed. If you are unfortunate enough to be developing a JDBC driver using one of these database systems, take heart. The JDBC specification does address this issue. The **getMoreResults** method is intended to move through the results. Figuring out when you have reached the end of the results, however, is a bit convoluted. To do so, you first call **getMoreResults**. If it returns true, there is another **ResultSet** present and you can use **getResultSet** to retrieve it. If **getMoreResults** returns false, you have either reached the end of the results, or an update count exists; you must call **getUpdateCount** to determine which situation exists. If **getUpdateCount** returns -1, you have reached the end of the results; otherwise, it will return the number of rows affected by the statement.

The SimpleText driver does not support multiple result sets, so I don't have any example code to present to you. The only DBMS that I am aware of that supports this is Sybase. Because there are already multiple JDBC drivers available for Sybase (one of which I developed), I doubt you will have to be concerned with **getMoreResults**. Consider yourself lucky.

PreparedStatement

The **PreparedStatement** is used for pre-compiling an SQL statement, typically in conjunction with parameters, and can be efficiently executed multiple times with just a change in a parameter value; the SQL statement does not have to be parsed and compiled each time. Because the **PreparedStatement** class extends the **Statement** class, you will have already implemented a majority of the methods. The **executeQuery**, **executeUpdate**, and **execute** methods are very similar to the **Statement** methods of the same name, but they do not take an SQL statement as a parameter. The SQL statement for the **PreparedStatement** was provided when the object was created with the **prepareStatement** method from the **Connection** object. One danger to note here: Because **PreparedStatement** is derived from the **Statement** class, all of the methods in **Statement** are also in **PreparedStatement**. The three execute methods from the **Statement** class that accept SQL statements are not valid for the **PreparedStatement** class. To prevent an application from invoking these methods, the driver should also implement them in **PreparedStatement**, as shown here:

```
// The overloaded executeQuery on the Statement object (which we
// extend) is not valid for PreparedStatement or CallableStatement
// objects.
public ResultSet executeQuery(
    String sql)
    throws SQLException
{
    throw new SQLException("Method is not valid");
}

// The overloaded executeUpdate on the Statement object (which we
// extend) is not valid for PreparedStatement or CallableStatement
// objects.
public int executeUpdate(
    String sql)
    throws SQLException
{
    throw new SQLException("Method is not valid");
}

// The overloaded execute on the Statement object (which we
// extend) is not valid for PreparedStatement or CallableStatement
// objects.
public boolean execute(
    String sql)
    throws SQLException
{
    throw new SQLException("Method is not valid");
}
```

SETTING PARAMETER VALUES

The **PreparedStatement** class introduces a series of *set* methods to set the value of a specified parameter. Consider the following SQL statement:

```
INSERT INTO FOO VALUES (?, ?, ?)
```

If this statement was used in creating a **PreparedStatement** object, you would need to set the value of each parameter before executing it. In the SimpleText driver, parameter values are kept in a **Hashtable**. The **Hashtable** contains the parameter number as the key and a **CommonValue** object as the data object. By using a **CommonValue** object, the application can set the parameter using any one of the supported data types, and we can coerce the data into the format that we need in order to bind the parameter. Here's the code for the **setString** method:

```
public void setString(
    int parameterIndex,
    String x)
    throws SQLException
{
    // Validate the parameter index
    verify(parameterIndex);

    // Put the parameter into the boundParams Hashtable
    boundParams.put(new Integer(parameterIndex), x);
}
```

The **verify** method validates that the given parameter index is valid for the current prepared statement and also clears any previously bound value for that parameter index:

```
protected void verify(
    int parameterIndex)
    throws SQLException
{
    clearWarnings();

    // The paramCount was set when the statement was prepared
    if ((parameterIndex <= 0) ||
        (parameterIndex > paramCount)) {
        throw new SQLException("Invalid parameter number: " +
                                parameterIndex);
    }

    // If the parameter has already been set, clear it
    if (boundParams.get(new Integer(parameterIndex)) != null) {
        boundParams.remove(new Integer(parameterIndex));
    }
}
```

Because the **CommonValue** class does not yet support all of the JDBC data types, not all of the set methods have been implemented in the SimpleText driver. You can see, however, how easy it would be to fully implement these methods once **CommonValue** supported all of the necessary data coercion.

What Is It?

Another way to set parameter values is by using the **setObject** method. This method can easily be built upon the other set methods. Of interest here is the ability for an application to set an **Object** without giving the JDBC driver the type of driver being set. The SimpleText driver implements a simple method to determine the type of object, given only the object itself:

```
protected int getObjectType(
    Object x)
    throws SQLException
{

    // Determine the data type of the Object by attempting to cast
    // the object. An exception will be thrown if an invalid casting
    // is attempted.
    try {
        if ((String) x != null) {
            return Types.VARCHAR;
        }
    }
    catch (Exception ex) {
    }

    try {
        if ((Integer) x != null) {
            return Types.INTEGER;
        }
    }
    catch (Exception ex) {
    }

    try {
        if ((byte[]) x != null) {
            return Types.VARBINARY;
        }
    }
    catch (Exception ex) {
    }

    throw new SQLException("Unknown object type");
}
```

SETTING INPUTSTREAMS

As we'll see with **ResultSet** later, using **InputStreams** is the best way to work with long data (blobs). There are two ways to treat **InputStreams** when using them as input parameters: Read the entire **InputStream** when the parameter is set and treat it as a large data object, or defer the read until the statement is executed and read it in chunks at a time. The latter approach is the preferred method because the contents of an **InputStream** may be too large to fit into memory. Here's what the SimpleText driver does with **InputStreams**:

```java
public void setBinaryStream(
    int parameterIndex,
    java.io.InputStream x,
    int length)
    throws SQLException
{
    // Validate the parameter index
    verify(parameterIndex);

    // Read in the entire InputStream all at once. A better way of
    // handling this would be to defer the read until execute time,
    // and only read in chunks at a time.
    byte b[] = new byte[length];

    try {
        x.read(b);
    }
    catch (Exception ex) {
        throw new SQLException("Unable to read InputStream: " +
                                ex.getMessage());
    }

    // Set the data as a byte array
    setBytes(parameterIndex, b);
}
```

But wait, this isn't the preferred way! You're right, it isn't. The SimpleText driver simply reads in the entire **InputStream** and then sets the parameter as a byte array. I'll leave it up to you to modify the driver to defer the read until execute time.

ResultSet

The **ResultSet** class provides methods to access data generated by a table query. This includes a series of **get** methods that retrieve data in any one of the JDBC SQL type formats, either by column number or by column name. When the issue of providing **get** methods by name was first introduced by JavaSoft, some disgruntled programmers argued that they were not necessary; if an application wanted to get data in this manner, then the application could provide a routine to cross reference the column name to a column number. Unfortunately, JavaSoft chose to keep these methods in the API and provide the implementation of the cross-reference method in an appendix. Because it is part of the API, all drivers must implement the methods. Implementing the methods is not all that difficult, but it is tedious and adds overhead to the driver. The driver simply takes the column name that is given, gets the corresponding column number for the column name, and invokes the same **get** method using the column number:

```
public String getString(
    String columnName)
    throws SQLException
{
    return getString(findColumn(columnName));
}
```

And here's the **findColumn** routine:

```
public int findColumn(
    String columnName)
    throws SQLException
{
    // Make a mapping cache if we don't already have one
    if (md == null) {
        md = getMetaData();
        s2c = new Hashtable();
    }

    // Look for the mapping in our cache
    Integer x = (Integer) s2c.get(columnName);

    if (x != null) {
        return (x.intValue());
    }

    // OK, we'll have to use metadata
    for (int i = 1; i < = md.getColumnCount(); i++) {
        if (md.getColumnName(i).equalsIgnoreCase(columnName)) {

            // Success! Add an entry to the cache
            s2c.put(columnName, new Integer(i));
            return (i);
        }
    }
```

```
        throw new SQLException("Column name not found: " + columnName,
                        "S0022");
}
```

This method uses a **Hashtable** to cache the column number and column names.

IT'S YOUR WAY, RIGHT AWAY

An application can request column data in any one of the supported JDBC data types. As we have discussed before, the driver should coerce the data into the proper format. The SimpleText driver accomplishes this by using a **CommonValue** object for all data values. Therefore, the data can be served in any format, stored as a **CommonValue** object, and the application can request it in any other supported format. Let's take a look at the **getString** method:

```java
public String getString(
    int columnIndex)
    throws SQLException
{
    // Verify the column and get the absolute column number for the
    // table.
    int colNo = verify(columnIndex);

    String s = null;

    if (inMemoryRows != null) {
        s = (getColumn(rowNum, columnIndex)).getString();
    }
    else {
        CommonValue value = getValue(colNo);

        if (value != null) {
            s = value.getString();
        }
    }

    if (s == null) {
        lastNull = true;
    }

    return s;
}
```

The method starts out by verifying that the given column number is valid. If it is not, an exception is thrown. Some other types of initialization are also performed. Remember that all **ResultSet** objects are provided with a **Hashtable** of **SimpleTextColumn** objects describing each column:

```
protected int verify(
    int column)
    throws SQLException
{
    clearWarnings();
    lastNull = false;

    SimpleTextColumn col = (SimpleTextColumn) inMemoryColumns.get(
                                    new Integer(column));

    if (col == null) {
        throw new SQLException("Invalid column number: " + column);
    }
    return col.colNo;
}
```

Next, if the row data is stored in an in-memory **Hashtable** (as with the **DatabaseMetaData** catalog methods), the data is retrieved from the **Hashtable**. Otherwise, the driver gets the data from the data file. In both instances, the data is retrieved as a **CommonValue** object, and the **getString** method is used to format the data into the requested data type. Null values are handled specially; the JDBC API has a **wasNull** method that will return true if the last column that was retrieved was null:

```
public boolean wasNull()
    throws SQLException
{
    return lastNull;
}
```

The SimpleText driver also supports **InputStreams**. In our case, the **SimpleTextInputStream** class is just a wrapper around a **CommonValue** object. Thus, if an application requests the data for a column as an **InputStream**, the SimpleText driver will get the data as a **CommonValue** object (as it always does) and create an **InputStream** that fetches the data from the **CommonValue**.

The **getMetaData** method returns a **ResultSetMetaData** object, which is our last class to cover.

ResultSetMetaData

The **ResultSetMetaData** class provides methods that describe each one of the columns in a result set. This includes the column count, column attributes, and the column name. **ResultSetMetaData** will typically be the smallest class in a JDBC driver and is usually very straightforward to implement. For the SimpleText driver, all of the necessary information is retrieved from the **Hashtable** of column information that is required for all result sets. Thus, to retrieve the column name:

```
public String getColumnLabel(
    int column)
    throws SQLException
{
    // Use the column name
    return getColumnName(column);
}

protected SimpleTextColumn getColumn(
    int col)
    throws SQLException
{
    SimpleTextColumn column = (SimpleTextColumn)
                    inMemoryColumns.get(new Integer(col));

    if (column == null) {
        throw new SQLException("Invalid column number: " + col);
    }

    return column;
}
```

Coming Up Next

We have covered a lot of material in this chapter, including the JDBC **DriverManager** and the services that it provides, implementing Java interfaces, creating native JDBC drivers, tracing, data coercion, escape sequence processing, and each one of the major JDBC interfaces. This information, in conjunction with the SimpleText driver, should help you create your own JDBC driver without too much difficulty.

In the next chapter, we'll explore the bridge between ODBC and JDBC. You'll see how easy it is to use existing ODBC drivers with JDBC, and learn some of the fine points of the relation, similarity, and difference between the two database connectivity standards.

ACCESSING ODBC SERVICES

8

One of JavaSoft's first tasks when developing the JDBC API was to get it into the hands of developers. Defining the API specification was a major step, but JDBC drivers must be implemented in order to actually access data. Because ODBC has already established itself as an industry standard, what better way to make JDBC usable by a large community of developers than to provide a JDBC driver that uses ODBC? JavaSoft turned to INTERSOLV to provide resources to develop a bridge between the two, and the resulting JDBC driver—the Bridge—is now included with the Java Developer's Kit.

The Bridge works great, but there are some things you need to understand before you can implement it properly. In this chapter, we'll cover the requirements for using the Bridge, the limitations of the Bridge, and the most elegant way to make a connection to a JDBC URL. I'll also provide you with a list of each JDBC method and the corresponding ODBC call (broken down by the type of call).

Bridge Requirements

One thing to note about the JDBC-ODBC bridge is that it contains a very thin layer of native code. This library's sole purpose is to accept an ODBC call from Java, execute that call, and return any results back to the driver. There is no other magic happening within this library; all processing, including memory management, is contained within the Java side of the Bridge. Unfortunately, this means that there is a library containing C code that must be ported to each of the operating systems that the Bridge will execute on. This is obviously not an ideal situation, and invalidates one of Java's major advantages—portability. So, instead of being able to download Java class files and execute on the fly, you must first install and configure additional software in order to use the Bridge. Here's a short checklist of required components:

- The Java Developer's Kit
- The JDBC Interface classes (java.sql.*)
- The JDBC-ODBC bridge classes (sun.jdbc.odbc.*)
- An ODBC Driver Manager (such as the one provided by Microsoft for Win95/NT); do not confuse this with the JDBC **DriverManager** class
- Any ODBC drivers to be used from the Bridge (from vendors such as INTERSOLV, Microsoft, and Visigenic)

Before actually attempting to use the Bridge, save yourself lots of head-aches—be sure to test the ODBC drivers that you will be using. I have pursued countless reported problems that ended up being nothing more than an ODBC configuration issue. Make sure you set up your data sources properly, and then test them to make sure you can connect and perform work. You can accomplish this by either using an existing tool (such as Microsoft's ODBC Test) or by writing your own sample ODBC application. Most vendors include sample source code to create an ODBC application, and Microsoft provides a tool named Gator (a.k.a ODBCTE32.EXE), which can fully exercise ODBC data sources on Win95/NT.

The Bridge Is Great, But...

All looks good for the Bridge; it gives you access to any ODBC data source, and it's *free*! But wait, there are a few limitations that you need to know before you start.

First, as I mentioned before, a lot of software must be installed and configured on each system that will be using the Bridge. In today's environment, this feat cannot be accomplished automatically. Unfortunately, this task can be a major limitation, not only in getting the software installed and configured properly, but ODBC drivers may not be readily available (or may be quite costly) for your operating system.

Second, understand the limitations of the ODBC driver that you will be using. If the ODBC driver can't do it, neither can the Bridge. The Bridge is not going to add any value to the ODBC driver that you are using other than allowing you to use it via JDBC. One of the most frequently asked questions I hear is: "If I use the Bridge, can I access my data over the Internet?" If the ODBC driver that you are using can, the Bridge can; if it can't, neither can the Bridge.

Third, keep in mind the quality of the ODBC driver. In order for the Bridge to properly use an ODBC driver, it must conform to ODBC 2.0 or higher. Also, if there are bugs in the ODBC driver, they will surely be present when you use it from JDBC.

Finally, there are Java security considerations. From the JDBC API specification, all JDBC drivers must follow the standard security model, most importantly:

- JDBC should not allow untrusted applets access to local database data.

- An untrusted applet will normally only be allowed to open a database connection back to the server from which it was downloaded.

For trusted applets and any type of application, the Bridge can be used in any fashion to connect to any data source. For untrusted applets, the prognosis is bleak. Untrusted applets can only access databases on the server from which they were downloaded. Normally, the Java Security Manager will prohibit a TCP connection from being made to an unauthorized hostname; that is, if the TCP connection is being made from within the Java Virtual Machine (JVM). In the case of the Bridge, this connection would be made from within the ODBC driver, outside the control of the JVM (also called being outside of the sandbox). If the Bridge could determine the hostname that it will be connected to, a call to the Java Security Manager could easily check to ensure that a connection is allowed. Unfortunately, it is not always possible to determine the hostname for a given ODBC data source name. For this reason, the Bridge always assumes the worst. An untrusted applet is not allowed to access any ODBC data source. This means that if you can't convince the Internet browser in use that an applet is trusted, you can't use the Bridge from that applet.

Using The Bridge From An Applet

There are two major obstacles to overcome in order to get an applet to use the Bridge:

- The applet must be trusted (because of the use of native code).

- The browser in use must be able support the same native function call interface as the Bridge.

The first part is easy. One type of trusted applet is one that is loaded locally from the client. If you placed applet code on your client and are now explicitly loading it, you must trust the code. The opposite is true for an applet that is downloaded from a remote server; it's being downloaded from a source that you have no control over, so Java isn't going to trust it (thus it won't be allowed to execute native code). If you are using the AppletViewer that is installed with the JDK, it can only load applets from the local client (no downloading), so all applets are considered trusted. In the future, browsers such as Netscape will support things like signed applets, which contain a signature identifying the applet's origin and guaranteeing that it is safe to use (trusted). But until browsers support these types of features, you will be relegated to loading the applet from your client.

The second part isn't so easy. Prior to JDK 1.1, the way that the Java Virtual Machine interfaced with C functions wasn't dictated in the JDK specification. Because of the lack of specification, everyone came up with their own way to interface to native methods. To you and me, this means that a native library that works with the JavaSoft VM won't necessarily work with the VM from Netscape or Microsoft. In fact, this is exactly the case at the time of this writing. JDK 1.1 will prove to solve this problem because it now contains the JNI (Java Native Interface) specification, which will force all Java VM vendors into alignment. Until that happens, though, the Bridge library that is supplied with the JDK (JdbcOdbc) will only work with VMs by JavaSoft (like AppletViewer). But wait—if you are using Netscape Navigator 3.0 (or higher), there is hope! INTERSOLV provides a library that conforms to the Netscape JRI (Java Runtime Interface), which will allow you to use the Bridge. This library (Netscape_JdbcOdbc) is also included on the CD-ROM enclosed with this book. Remember, even if you are using the special Netscape library with your applet, the applet must be trusted. At the time of this writing, the only way to accomplish this is to load the applet locally from the client.

The ODBC URL

To make a connection to a JDBC driver, you must supply a URL. The general structure of the JDBC URL is

```
jdbc:<subzprotocol>:<subname>
```

where **subprotocol** is the kind of database connectivity being requested, and **subname** provides additional information for the subprotocol. For the Bridge, the specific URL structure is

```
jdbc:odbc:<ODBC datasource name>[;attribute-name=attribute-value]...
```

The Bridge can only provide services for URLs that have a subprotocol of **odbc**. If a different subprz Bridge will simply tell the JDBC **DriverManager** that it has no idea what the URL means, and that it can't support it by returning **false** from the **Driver.acceptsURL** method. The **subname** specifies the ODBC data source name to use, followed by any additional connection string attributes. Here's a code snippet that you can use to connect to an ODBC data source named *Accounting*, with a user name of *dept12* and a password of *Julie*:

```
// Create a new instance of the JDBC-ODBC bridge.

new jdbc.odbc.JdbcOdbcDriver();

// The JDBC-ODBC bridge will have registered itself with the JDBC
// DriverManager. We can now let the DriverManager choose the right
// driver to connect to the given URL.

Connection con = DriverManager.getConnection("jdbc:odbc:Accounting",
  "dept12", "Julie");
```

An alternative way of connecting to this same data source would be to pass the user name and password as connection string attributes:

```
Connection con = DriverManager.getConnection("jdbc:odbc:Accounting;UID=
  dept12;PWD=Julie");
```

A third, more effective way of connecting would be to use a **java.util.Properties** object. **DriverManager.getConnection** is overloaded to support three versions of the interface:

```
public static synchronized Connection getConnection(String url, String
  user, String password) throws SQLException;
public static synchronized Connection getConnection(String url);
public static synchronized Connection getConnection(String url,
  java.util.Properties info);
```

The third method listed here is by far the most elegant way of connecting to any JDBC driver. An intelligent Java application or applet will use **Driver.getPropertyInfo** (which was covered in Chapter 7) to get a list of all of the required and optional properties for the driver. The Java program can then prompt the user for this information, and then create a **java.util.Properties** object that contains an element for each of the driver properties to be used for the JDBC connection. Instead of creating one string with all of the properties concatenated together, each property is set individually. The following code shows how to setup the **java.util.Properties** object:

```
// Create the Properties object.

java.util.Properties prop = new java.util.Properties();

// Populate the Properties object with each property to be passed to the
// JDBC driver.

prop.put("UID", "dept12");
prop.put("PWD", "Julie");

Connection con = DriverManager.getConnection("jdbc:odbc:Accounting",
  prop);
```

JDBC To ODBC Calls:
A Roadmap

For all of you ODBC junkies, Tables 8.1 through 8.8 show each JDBC method and the corresponding ODBC call (only JDBC methods that actually make an ODBC call are included). I can hear you now: "But isn't this a closely guarded national secret? What if someone takes this information to write another Bridge?"

TABLE 8.1

DRIVER ODBC CALLS.

JDBC Interface Method	ODBC Call	Comments
connect	SQLDriverConnect	The Bridge creates a connection string using the java.util. Properties attribute given
getPropertyInfo	SQLBrowseConnect	Each property returned is converted into a DriverPropertyInfo object

First of all, the information provided here can be easily gathered by turning on the JDBC logging facility (**DriverManager.setLogStream**). The Bridge is nice enough to log every ODBC call as it is made, providing a log stream has been set via the **DriverManager** (all good JDBC drivers should provide adequate logging to aid in debugging). And second, the Bridge is free and distributed with the Java Developer's Kit. No one could possibly take this information to create a better Bridge at a lower price. It simply can't be done. I provide this information in an effort to help you better understand how the Bridge operates, and, if you are well versed in ODBC, to give you the direct correlation between the Bridge and ODBC. This should enable you to write advanced JDBC applications right off the starting line.

TABLE 8.2

CONNECTION ODBC CALLS.

JDBC Interface Method	ODBC Call	Comments
prepareStatement	SQLPrepare	Prepares the statement for use with IN parameters
prepareCall	SQLPrepare	Prepares the statement for use with IN and OUT parameters (JDBC has not defined the use of IN/OUT parameters together)
nativeSQL	SQLNativeSql	Converts the given SQL into native format, expanding escape sequences
setAutoCommit	SQLSetConnectOption	fOption = SQL_AUTOCOMMIT
getAutoCommit	SQLGetConnectOption	fOption = SQL_AUTOCOMMIT

(continued)

TABLE 8.2

CONNECTION **ODBC** CALLS (*CONTINUED*).

JDBC Interface Method	ODBC Call	Comments
commit	SQLTransact	fType = SQL_COMMIT
rollback	SQLTransact	fType = SQL_ROLLBACK
close	SQLFreeConnect	Frees the connection handle associated with the connection
setReadOnly	SQLSetConnectOption	fOption = SQL_ACCESS_MODE; this is only a hint to the ODBC driver; the underlying driver may not actually change its behavior
isReadOnly	SQLGetConnectOption	fOption = SQL_ACCESS_MODE
setCatalog	SQLSetConnectOption	fOption = SQL_CURRENT_ QUALIFIER
getCatalog	SQLGetInfo	fInfoType = SQL_DATABASE_NAME
setTransactionIsolation	SQLSetConnectOption	fOption = SQL_TXN_ISOLATION
getTransactionIsolation	SQLGetConnectOption	fOption = SQL_TXN_ISOLATION
setAutoClose		ODBC does not provide a method to modify this behavior
getAutoClose	SQLGetInfo	fInfoType = SQL_CURSOR_COMMIT_ BEHAVIOR and fInfoType = SQL_ CURSOR_ROLLBACK_BEHAVIOR; the Bridge makes both calls, and if either are true, then getAutoClose returns true

TABLE 8.3

DATABASEMETADATA **ODBC** CALLS.

JDBC Interface Method	ODBC Call	Comments
allProceduresAreCallable	SQLGetInfo	fInfoType = SQL_ACCESSABLE_ PROCEDURES
allTablesAreSelectable	SQLGetInfo	fInfoType = SQL_ACCESSABLE_ TABLES

(continued)

TABLE 8.3

DATABASEMETADATA **ODBC** CALLS (*CONTINUED*).

JDBC Interface Method	ODBC Call	Comments
getUserName	SQLGetInfo	fInfoType = SQL_USER_NAME
isReadOnly	SQLGetInfo	fInfoType = SQL_DATA_SOURCE_ READ_ONLY
nullsAreSortedHigh	SQLGetInfo	fInfoType = SQL_NULL_COLLATION; the result must be SQL_NC_HIGH
nullsAreSortedLow	SQLGetInfo	fInfoType = SQL_NULL_COLLATION; the result must be SQL_NC_LOW
nullsAreSortedAtStart	SQLGetInfo	fInfoType = SQL_NULL_COLLATION; the result must be SQL_NC_START
nullsAreSortedAtEnd	SQLGetInfo	fInfoType = SQL_NULL_COLLATION; the result must be SQL_NC_END
getDatabaseProductName	SQLGetInfo	fInfoType = SQL_DBMS_NAME
getDatabaseProductVersion	SQLGetInfo	fInfoType = SQL_DBMS_VER
usesLocalFiles	SQLGetInfo	fInfoType = SQL_FILE_USAGE; the result must be SQL_FILE_QUALIFIER
usesLocalFilePerTable	SQLGetInfo	fInfoType = SQL_FILE_USAGE; the result must be SQL_FILE_TABLE
supportsMixedCaseIdentifiers	SQLGetInfo	fInfoType = SQL_IDENTIFIER_CASE; the result must be SQL_IC_UPPER, SQL_IC_LOWER or SQL_IC_MIXED
storesUpperCaseIdentifiers	SQLGetInfo	fInfoType = SQL_IDENTIFIER_CASE, the result must be SQL_IC_UPPER
storesLowerCaseIdentifiers	SQLGetInfo	fInfoType = SQL_IDENTIFIER_CASE; the result must be SQL_IC_LOWER
storesMixedCaseIdentifiers	SQLGetInfo	fInfoType = SQL_IDENTIFIER_CASE; the result must be SQL_IC_MIXED
supportsMixedCaseQuoted Identifiers	SQLGetInfo	fInfoType = SQL_QUOTED_ IDENTIFIER_CASE; the result must be SQL_IC_UPPER, SQL_IC_LOWER, or SQL_IC_MIXED

(continued)

TABLE 8.3

DATABASEMETADATA **ODBC** CALLS (*CONTINUED*).

JDBC Interface Method	ODBC Call	Comments
storesUpperCaseQuoted Identifiers	SQLGetInfo	fInfoType = SQL_QUOTED_ IDENTIFIER_CASE; the result must be SQL_IC_UPPER
storesLowerCaseQuoted Identifiers	SQLGetInfo	fInfoType = SQL_QUOTED_ IDENTIFIER_CASE; the result must be SQL_IC_LOWER
storesMixedCaseQuoted Identifiers	SQLGetInfo	fInfoType = SQL_QUOTED_ IDENTIFIER_CASE; the result must be SQL_IC_MIXED
getIdentifierQuoteString	SQLGetInfo	fInfoType = SQL_IDENTIFIER_ QUOTE_CHAR
getSQLKeywords	SQLGetInfo	fInfoType = SQL_KEYWORDS
getNumericFunctions	SQLGetInfo	fInfoType = SQL_NUMERIC_ FUNCTIONS; the result is a bitmask enumerating the scalar numeric functions; this bitmask is used to create a comma-separated list of functions
getStringFunctions	SQLGetInfo	fInfoType = SQL_STRING_FUNCTIONS; the result is a bitmask enumerating the scalar string functions; this bitmask is used to create a comma-separated list of functions
getSystemFunctions	SQLGetInfo	fInfoType = SQL_SYSTEM_ FUNCTIONS; the result is a bitmask enumerating the scalar system functions; this bitmask is used to create a comma-separated list of functions
getTimeDateFunctions	SQLGetInfo	fInfoType = SQL_TIMEDATE_ FUNCTIONS; the result is a bitmask enumerating the scalar date and time functions; This bitmask is used to create a comma-separated list of functions

(continued)

TABLE 8.3

DATABASEMETADATA ODBC CALLS (*CONTINUED*).

JDBC Interface Method	ODBC Call	Comments
getSearchStringEscape	SQLGetInfo	fInfoType = SQL_SEARCH_PATTERN_ESCAPE
getExtraNameCharacters	SQLGetInfo	fInfoType = SQL_SPECIAL_CHARACTERS
supportsAlterTableWithAdd	SQLGetInfo	fInfoType = SQL_ALTER_TABLE; the Column result must have the SQL_AT_ADD_COLUMN bit set
supportsAlterTableWithDrop	SQLGetInfo	fInfoType = SQL_ALTER_TABLE; the Column result must have the SQL_AT_DROP_COLUMN bit set
supportsColumnAliasing	SQLGetInfo	fInfoType = SQL_COLUMN_ALIAS
nullPlusNonNullIsNull	SQLGetInfo	fInfoType = SQL_CONCAT_NULL_BEHAVIOR; the result must be SQL_CB_NULL
supportsConvert	SQLGetInfo	fInfoType = SQL_CONVERT_FUNCTIONS; the result must be SQL_FN_CVT_CONVERT
supportsTableCorrelationNames	SQLGetInfo	fInfoType = SQL_CORRELATION_NAME; the result must be SQL_CN_DIFFERENT or SQL_CN_ANY
supportsDifferentTable CorrelationNames	SQLGetInfo	fInfoType = SQL_CORRELATION_NAMES; the result must be SQL_CN_DIFFERENT
supportsExpressionsInOrderBy	SQLGetInfo	fInfoType = SQL_EXPRESSIONS_IN_ORDER_BY
supportsOrderByUnrelated	SQLGetInfo	fInfoType = SQL_ORDER_BY_COLUMNS_IN_SELECT
supportsGroupBy	SQLGetInfo	fInfoType = SQL_GROUP_BY; the result must not be SQL_GB_NOT_SUPPORTED
supportsGroupByUnrelated	SQLGetInfo	fInfoType = SQL_GROUP_BY; the result must be SQL_GB_NO_RELATION

(continued)

TABLE 8.3

DATABASEMETADATA ODBC CALLS (*CONTINUED*).

JDBC Interface Method	ODBC Call	Comments
upportsGroupByBeyondSelect	SQLGetInfo	fInfoType = SQL_GROUP_BY; the result must be SQL_GB_GROUP_BY_CONTAINS_SELECT
supportsLikeEscapeClause	SQLGetInfo	fInfoType = SQL_LIKE_ESCAPE_CLAUSE
supportsMultipleResultSets	SQLGetInfo	fInfoType = SQL_MULT_RESULT_SETS
supportsMultipleTransactions	SQLGetInfo	fInfoType = SQL_MULTIPLE_ACTIVE_TXN
supportsNonNullableColumns	SQLGetInfo	fInfoType = SQL_NON_NULLABLE_COLUMNS; the result must be SQL_NNC_NON_NULL
supportsMinimumSQLGrammar	SQLGetInfo	fInfoType = SQL_ODBC_SQL_CONFORMANCE; result must be SQL_OSC_MINIMUM, SQL_OSC_CORE, or SQL_OSC_EXTENDED
supportsCoreSQLGrammar	SQLGetInfo	fInfoType = SQL_ODBC_SQL_CONFORMANCE; the result must be SQL_OSC_CORE or SQL_OSC_EXTENDED
supportsExtendedSQLGrammar	SQLGetInfo	fInfoType = SQL_ODBC_SQL_CONFORMANCE; the result must be SQL_OSC_EXTENDED
supportsIntegrityEnhancement Facility	SQLGetInfo	fInfoType = SQL_ODBC_SQL_OPT_IEF
supportsOuterJoins	SQLGetInfo	fInfoType = SQL_OUTER_JOINS; the result must not be "N"
supportsFullOuterJoins	SQLGetInfo	fInfoType = SQL_OUTER_JOINS; the result must be "F"
supportsLimitedOuterJoins	SQLGetInfo	fInfoType = SQL_OUTER_JOINS; the result must be "P"
getSchemaTerm	SQLGetInfo	fInfoType = SQL_OWNER_TERM

(continued)

TABLE 8.3

DATABASEMETADATA ODBC CALLS (*CONTINUED*).

JDBC Interface Method	ODBC Call	Comments
getProcedureTerm	SQLGetInfo	fInfoType = SQL_PROCEDURE_TERM
getCatalogTerm	SQLGetInfo	fInfoType = SQL_QUALIFIER_TERM
isCatalogAtStart	SQLGetInfo	fInfoType = SQL_QUALIFIER_LOCATION; the result must be SQL_QL_START
getCatalogSeparator	SQLGetInfo	fInfoType = SQL_QUALIFIER_NAME_SEPARATOR
supportsSchemasInData	SQLGetInfo	fInfoType = SQL_OWNER_USAGE; the Manipulation result must have the SQL_OU_DML_STATEMENTS bit set
supportsSchemasInProcedure	SQLGetInfo	fInfoType = SQL_OWNER_USAGE; the Calls result must have the SQL_OU_PROCEDURE_INVOCATION bit set
supportsSchemasInTable	SQLGetInfo	fInfoType = SQL_OWNER_USAGE; the Definitions result must have the SQL_OU_TABLE_DEFINITION bit set
supportsSchemasInIndex	SQLGetInfo	fInfoType = SQL_OWNER_USAGE; the Definitions result must have the SQL_OU_INDEX_DEFINITION bit set
supportsSchemasInPrivilege	SQLGetInfo	fInfoType = SQL_OWNER_USAGE; the Definitions result must have the SQL_OU_PRIVILEGE_DEFINITION bit set
supportsCatalogsInData	SQLGetInfo	fInfoType = SQL_QUALIFIER_USAGE;Manipulation the result must have the SQL_QU_DML_STATEMENTS bit set
supportsCatalogsInProcedure	SQLGetInfo	fInfoType = SQL_QUALIFIER_USAGE; Calls the result must have the SQL_QU_PROCEDURE_INVOCATION bit set

(continued)

TABLE 8.3

DatabaseMetaData ODBC calls (*continued*).

JDBC Interface Method	ODBC Call	Comments
upportsCatalogsInTable	SQLGetInfo	fInfoType = SQL_QUALIFIER_USAGE; Definitions the result must have the SQL_QU_TABLE_DEFINITION bit set
supportsCatalogsInIndex	SQLGetInfo	fInfoType = SQL_QUALIFIER_USAGE; Definitions the result must have the SQL_QU_INDEX_DEFINITION bit set
supportsCatalogsInPrivilege	SQLGetInfo	fInfoType = SQL_QUALIFIER_USAGE; Definitions the result must have the SQL_QU_PRIVILEGE_DEFINITION bit set
supportsPositionedDelete	SQLGetInfo	fInfoType = SQL_POSITIONED_ STATEMENTS; the result must have the SQL_PS_POSITIONED_DELETE bit set
supportsPositionedUpdate	SQLGetInfo	fInfoType = SQL_POSITIONED_ STATEMENTS; the result must have the SQL_PS_POSITIONED_UPDATE bit set
supportsSelectForUpdate	SQLGetInfo	fInfoType = SQL_POSITIONED_ STATEMENTS; the result must have the SQL_PS_SELECT_FOR_UPDATE bit set
supportsStoredProcedures	SQLGetInfo	fInfoType = SQL_PROCEDURES
supportsSubqueriesIn	SQLGetInfo	fInfoType = SQL_SUBQUERIES; the Comparisons result must have the SQL_SQ_COMPARISON bit set
supportsSubqueriesInExists	SQLGetInfo	fInfoType = SQL_SUBQUERIES; the result must have the SQL_SQ_ EXISTS bit set
supportsSubqueriesInIns	SQLGetInfo	fInfoType = SQL_SUBQUERIES; the result must have the SQL_SQ_IN bit set
supportsSubqueriesIn	SQLGetInfo	fInfoType = SQL_SUBQUERIES; the Quantifieds result must have the SQL_SQ_QUANTIFIED bit set

(continued)

TABLE 8.3

DATABASEMETADATA ODBC CALLS (*CONTINUED*).

JDBC Interface Method	ODBC Call	Comments
supportsCorrelatedSubqueries	SQLGetInfo	fInfoType = SQL_SUBQUERIES; the result must have the SQL_SQ_ CORRELATED_SUBQUERIES bit set
supportsUnion	SQLGetInfo	fInfoType = SQL_UNION; the result must have the SQL_U_UNION bit set
supportsUnionAll	SQLGetInfo	fInfoType = SQL_UNION; the result must have the SQL_U_UNION_ALL bit set
supportsOpenCursorsAcross	SQLGetInfo	fInfoType = SQL_CURSOR_COMMIT_ Commit BEHAVIOR; the result must be SQL_CB_PRESERVE
supportsOpenCursorsAcross Rollback	SQLGetInfo	fInfoType = SQL_CURSOR_ ROLLBACK_BEHAVIOR; the result must be SQL_CB_PRESERVE
supportsOpenStatementsAcross Commit	SQLGetInfo	fInfoType = SQL_CURSOR_ COMMIT_BEHAVIOR; the result must be SQL_CB_PRESERVE or SQL_CB_CLOSE
supportsOpenStatementsAcross Rollback	SQLGetInfo	fInfoType = SQL_CURSOR_ ROLLBACK_BEHAVIOR; the result must be SQL_CB_PRESERVE or SQL_CB_CLOSE
getMaxBinaryLiteralLength	SQLGetInfo	fInfoType = SQL_MAX_BINARY_ LITERAL_LEN
getMaxCharLiteralLength	SQLGetInfo	fInfoType = SQL_MAX_CHAR_ LITERAL_LEN
getMaxColumnNameLength	SQLGetInfo	fInfoType = SQL_MAX_COLUMN_ NAME_LEN
getMaxColumnsInGroupBy	SQLGetInfo	fInfoType = SQL_MAX_COLUMNS_ IN_GROUP_BY
getMaxColumnsInIndex	SQLGetInfo	fInfoType = SQL_MAX_COLUMNS_ IN_INDEX
getMaxColumnsInOrderBy	SQLGetInfo	fInfoType = SQL_MAX_COLUMNS_ IN_ORDER_BY

(continued)

TABLE 8.3

DATABASEMETADATA ODBC CALLS (*CONTINUED*).

JDBC Interface Method	ODBC Call	Comments
getMaxColumnsInSelect	SQLGetInfo	fInfoType = SQL_MAX_COLUMNS_IN_SELECT
getMaxColumnsInTable	SQLGetInfo	fInfoType = SQL_MAX_COLUMNS_IN_TABLE
getMaxConnections	SQLGetInfo	fInfoType = SQL_ACTIVE_CONNECTIONS
getMaxCursorNameLength	SQLGetInfo	fInfoType = SQL_MAX_CURSOR_NAME_LEN
getMaxIndexLength	SQLGetInfo	fInfoType = SQL_MAX_INDEX_SIZE
getMaxSchemaNameLength	SQLGetInfo	fInfoType = SQL_MAX_OWNER_NAME_LEN
getMaxProcedureNameLength	SQLGetInfo	fInfoType = SQL_MAX_PROCEDURE_NAME_LEN
getMaxCatalogNameLength	SQLGetInfo	fInfoType = SQL_MAX_QUALIFIER_NAME_LEN
getMaxRowSize	SQLGetInfo	fInfoType = SQL_MAX_ROW_SIZE
doesMaxRowSizeIncludeBlobs	SQLGetInfo	fInfoType = SQL_MAX_ROW_SIZE_INCLUDES_LONG
getMaxStatementLength	SQLGetInfo	fInfoType = SQL_MAX_STATEMENT_LEN
getMaxStatements	SQLGetInfo	fInfoType = SQL_ACTIVE_STATEMENTS
getMaxTableNameLength	SQLGetInfo	fInfoType = SQL_MAX_TABLE_NAME_LEN
getMaxTablesInSelect	SQLGetInfo	fInfoType = SQL_MAX_TABLES_IN_SELECT
getMaxUserNameLength	SQLGetInfo	fInfoType = SQL_MAX_USER_NAME_LEN
getDefaultTransactionIsolation	SQLGetInfo	fInfoType = SQL_DEFAULT_TXN_ISOLATION
supportsTransactions	SQLGetInfo	fInfoType = SQL_TXN_CAPABLE; the result must not be SQL_TC_NONE

(continued)

TABLE 8.3

DatabaseMetaData ODBC calls (*continued*).

JDBC Interface Method	ODBC Call	Comments
supportsTransactionIsolation Level	SQLGetInfo	fInfoType = SQL_TXN_ISOLATION_ OPTION
supportsDataDefinitionAnd DataManipulationTransactions	SQLGetInfo	fInfoType = SQL_TXN_CAPABLE; the result must have the SQL_TC_ALL bit set
supportsDataManipulation TransactionsOnly	SQLGetInfo	fInfoType = SQL_TXN_CAPABLE; the result must have the SQL_TC_DML bit set
dataDefinitionCausesTransaction Commit	SQLGetInfo	fInfoType = SQL_TXN_CAPABLE; the result must have the SQL_TC_DDL_ COMMIT bit set
dataDefinitionIgnoredIn Transactions	SQLGetInfo	fInfoType = SQL_TXN_CAPABLE; the result must have the SQL_TC_DDL_ IGNORE bit set
getProcedures	SQLProcedures	Returns a list of procedure names
getProcedureColumns	SQLProcedure Columns	Returns a list of input and output parameters used for procedures
getTables	SQLTables	Returns a list of tables
getSchemas	SQLTables	Catalog = "", Schema = "%", Table = "", TableType = NULL; only the TABLE_SCHEM column is returned
getCatalogs	SQLTables	Catalog = "%", Schema = "", Table = "", TableType = NULL; only the TABLE_CAT column is returned
getTableTypes	SQLTables	Catalog = "", Schema = "", Table = "", TableType = "%"
getColumns	SQLColumns	Returns a list of column names in specified tables
getColumnPrivileges	SQLColumn Privileges	Returns a list of columns and associated privileges for the specified table
getTablePrivileges	SQLTable Privileges	Returns a list of tables and the privileges associated with each table

(continued)

TABLE 8.3

DATABASEMETADATA **ODBC** CALLS (*CONTINUED*).

JDBC Interface Method	ODBC Call	Comments
getBestRowIdentifier	SQLSpecial Columns	fColType = SQL_BEST_ROWID
getVersionColumns	SQLSpecial Columns	fColType = SQL_ROWVER
getPrimaryKeys	SQLPrimaryKeys	Returns a list of column names that comprise the primary key for a table
getImportedKeys	SQLForeignKeys	PKTableCatalog = NULL, PKTableSchema = NULL, PKTableName = NULL
getExportedKeys	SQLForeignKeys	FKTableCatalog = NULL, FKTableSchema = NULL, FKTableName = NULL
getCrossReference	SQLForeignKeys	Returns a list of foreign keys in the specified table
getTypeInfo	SQLGetTypeInfo	fSqlType = SQL_ALL_TYPES
getIndexInfo	SQLStatistics	Returns a list of statistics about the specified table and the indexes associated with the table

TABLE 8.4

STATEMENT **ODBC** CALLS.

JDBC Interface Method	ODBC Call	Comments
close	SQLFreeStmt	fOption = SQL_CLOSE
getMaxFieldSize	SQLGetStmtOption	fOption = SQL_MAX_LENGTH
setMaxFieldSize	SQLSetStmtOption	fOption = SQL_MAX_LENGTH
getMaxRows	SQLGetStmtOption	fOption = SQL_MAX_ROWS
setMaxRows	SQLSetStmtOption	fOption = SQL_MAX_ROWS
setEscapeProcessing	SQLSetStmtOption	fOption = SQL_NOSCAN
getQueryTimeout	SQLGetStmtOption	fOption = SQL_QUERY_TIMEOUT
setQueryTimeout	SQLSetStmtOption	fOption = SQL_QUERY_TIMEOUT

(continued)

TABLE 8.4

STATEMENT ODBC CALLS (*CONTINUED*).

JDBC Interface Method	ODBC Call	Comments
cancel	SQLCancel	Cancels the processing on a statement
setCursorName	SQLSetCursorName	Associates a cursor name with a statement
execute	SQLExecDirect	The Bridge checks for a SQL statement containing a 'FOR UPDATE' clause; if present, the cursor concurrency level for the statement is changed to SQL_CONCUR_LOCK
getUpdateCount	SQLRowCount	Returns the number of rows affected by an UPDATE, INSERT, or DELETE statement
getMoreResults	SQLMoreResults	Determines whether there are more results available on a statement and, if so, initializes processing for those results

TABLE 8.5

PREPAREDSTATEMENT ODBC CALLS.

JDBC Interface Method	ODBC Call	Comments
setNull	SQLBindParameter	fParamType = SQL_PARAM_INPUT; fSqlType = sqlType passed as parameter
setBoolean		
setByte		
setShort		
setInt		
setLong		
setFloat		
setDouble		

(continued)

TABLE 8.5

PREPAREDSTATEMENT **ODBC** CALLS (*CONTINUED*).

JDBC Interface Method	ODBC Call	Comments
setNumeric		
setString		
setBytes		
setDate		
setTime		
setTimestamp	SQLBindParameter	fParamType = SQL_PARAM_INPUT; fSqlType is derived by the type of get method
setAsciiStream		
setUnicodeStream		
setBinaryStream	SQLBindParameter	fParamType = SQL_PARAM_INPUT, pcbValue = SQL_DATA_AT_EXEC
execute	SQLExecute	May return SQL_NEED_DATA (because of setAsciiStream, setUnicodeStream, or setBinary Stream); in this case, the Bridge will call SQLParamData and SQLPutData until no more data is needed

TABLE 8.6

CALLABLESTATEMENT **ODBC** CALLS.

JDBC Interface Method	ODBC Call	Comments
registerOutParameter	SQLBindParameter	fParamType = SQL_PARAM_OUTPUT; rgbValue is a buffer that has been allocated in Java; when using the getXXX methods, this buffer is used to retrieve the data

TABLE **8.7**

RESULTSET ODBC CALLS.

JDBC Interface Method	ODBC Call	Comments
next	SQLFetch	Fetches a row of data from a ResultSet
close	SqlFreeStmt	fOption = SQL_CLOSE
getString		
getBoolean		
getByte		
getShort		
getInt		
getLong		
getFloat		
getDouble		
getNumeric		
getBytes		
getTime		
getTimestamp	SQLGetData	fCType is derived by the type of get method
getAsciiStream		
getUnicodeStream		
getBinaryStream	SQLGetData	An InputStream object is created to provide a wrapper around the SQLGetData call; data is read from the data source as needed
getCursorName	SQLGetCursorName	Returns the cursor name associated with the statement

TABLE 8.8

RESULTSETMETADATA ODBC CALLS.

JDBC Interface Method	ODBC Call	Comments
getColumnCount	SQLNumResultCols	Returns the number of columns in a ResultSet
isAutoIncrement	SQLColAttributes	fDescType = SQL_COLUMN_ AUTO_INCREMENT
isCaseSensitive	SQLColAttributes	fDescType = SQL_COLUMN_ CASE_SENSITIVE
isSearchable	SQLColAttributes	fDescType = SQL_COLUMN_ SEARCHABLE
isCurrency	SQLColAttributes	fDescType = SQL_COLUMN_MONEY
isNullable	SQLColAttributes	fDescType = SQL_COLUMN_ NULLABLE
isSigned	SQLColAttributes	fDescType = SQL_COLUMN_ UNSIGNED
getColumnDisplaySize	SQLColAttributes	fDescType = SQL_COLUMN_ DISPLAY_SIZE
getColumnLabel	SQLColAttributes	fDescType = SQL_COLUMN_LABEL
getColumnName	SQLColAttributes	fDescType = SQL_COLUMN_NAME
getSchemaName	SQLColAttributes	fDescType = SQL_COLUMN_ OWNER_NAME
getPrecision	SQLColAttributes	fDescType = SQL_COLUMN_ PRECISION
getScale	SQLColAttributes	fDescType = SQL_COLUMN_SCALE
getTableName	SQLColAttributes	fDescType = SQL_COLUMN_ TABLE_NAME
getCatalogName	SQLColAttributes	fDescType = SQL_COLUMN_ QUALIFIER_NAME
getColumnType	SQLColAttributes	fDescType = SQL_COLUMN_TYPE; the SQL type must be converted to the appropriate JDBC type
getColumnTypeName	SQLColAttributes	fDescType = SQL_COLUMN_ TYPE_NAME

(continued)

TABLE 8.8

RESULTSETMETADATA ODBC CALLS (*CONTINUED*).

JDBC Interface Method	ODBC Call	Comments
isReadOnly	SQLColAttributes	fDescType = SQL_COLUMN_ UPDATABLE; the value returned must be SQL_ATTR_READONLY
isWritable	SQLColAttributes	fDescType = SQL_COLUMN_ UPDATABLE; the value returned must be SQL_ATTR_READWRITE_ UNKNOWN
isDefinitelyWritable	SQLColAttributes	fDescType = SQL_COLUMN_ UPDATABLE; the value returned must be SQL_ATTR_WRITE

Coming Up Next

In the next chapter, we'll take a quick look at SQL data types and how they must be mapped into Java, which you will learn is really quite simple. In addition, a brief introduction of the Object Relation Model (ORM) will also be covered.

Part

MISCELLANEOUS

3

SQL DATA TYPES
IN JAVA

9

M any standard SQL-92 data types, such as Date, do not have a native Java equivalent. To overcome this deficiency, you must map SQL data types into Java. This process involves using JDBC classes to access SQL data types. In this chapter, we'll take a look at the classes in the JDBC used to access SQL data types. In addition, we'll briefly discuss the Object Relation Model (ORM), an interesting area in database development that attempts to map relational models into objects.

You need to know how to properly retrieve equivalent Java data types—like int, long, and string—from their SQL counterparts and store them in your database. This can be especially important if you are working with numeric data (which requires careful handling of decimal precision) and SQL timestamps (which have a well-defined format). We touch on the mechanism for handling raw binary data in this chapter, but we'll cover it in more detail in Chapter 12.

Mapping SQL Data To Java

Mapping Java data types into SQL is really quite simple. Table 9.1 shows how Java data types map into equivalent SQL data

	TABLE 9.1

MAPPING JAVA DATA TYPES TO SQL DATA TYPES.

Java	SQL
String	VARCHAR
Boolean	BIT
Byte	TINYINT
Short	SMALLINT
Int	INTEGER
Long	BIGINT
Float	REAL
Double	DOUBLE
Byte[]—byte array: images, sounds, documents, and so on	VARBINARY (BLOBs)
Java.sql.Date	DATE
Java.sql.Time	TIME
Java.sql.Timestamp	TIMESTAMP
Java.math.BigDecimal	NUMERIC

types. Note that the types beginning with "Java." are not elemental data types, but classes that have methods for translating the data into usable formats. These classes are also necessary because there is no primitive data type that maps directly to its SQL counterpart. Create these classes whenever you need to store an SQL data type in your Java program. Then, you can simply get or put this data from the database. Again, we show you how to put items into a database in various chapters in the book; Chapter 12 works specifically with image, or BLOB, data, and Chapter 14 has several examples of inserting text data into a database.

The **byte**[] data type is a byte array of variable size. This data structure stores binary data, which is manifested in SQL as VARBINARY and LONG-VARBINARY. These types store images, raw document files, and so on. To store or retrieve this data from the database, you would use the stream methods available in the JDBC: **setBinaryStream** and **getBinaryStream**. In Chapter 12, we'll use these methods to build a multimedia Java/JDBC application.

Table 9.2 shows the mapping of SQL data types into Java. You will find that both tables will come in handy when you're attempting to decide which types need special treatment. You can also use the tables as a quick reference to make sure that you're properly casting data that you want to store or retrieve.

Now that you've seen how these data types translate from Java to SQL and vice versa, let's look at some of the methods you'll use to retrieve data from a database. Table 9.3 shows the methods the **ResultSet** class, the class that is passed back when you invoke a **Statement.executeQuery** function, contains. You'll find a complete reference of the **ResultSet** class methods in Chapter 16.

TABLE 9.2

MAPPING SQL DATA TYPES TO JAVA DATA TYPES.

SQL	Java
CHAR	String
VARCHAR	String
BIT	Boolean
TINYINT	Byte
SMALLINT	Short
INTEGER	Int
BIGINT	Long
REAL	Float
FLOAT	Double
DOUBLE	Double
BINARY	Byte[]
VARBINARY	BYTE[]
DATE	Java.sql.Date
TIME	Java.sql.Time
TIMESTAMP	Java.sql.Timestamp
DECIMAL	Java.math.BigDecimal
NUMERIC	Java.math.BigDecimal

TABLE 9.3

A FEW RESULTSET METHODS FOR GETTING DATA.

Method	Description
GetString(String), GetString(int)	Returns a column value as a String.
GetObject(String), GetObject(int) object	Returns a column value as a Java.
GetBoolean(String), GetBoolean(int)	Returns a column value as a Boolean.
GetBinaryStream(String), gGetBinaryStream(int)	Retrieves a column value as a stream of uninterpreted bytes.

The parameters **int** and **String** allow you to specify the column you want by column number or column name. Remember that each "get" method returns a different Java data type. The **getString** method returns a Java String type, for example. Look at the reference chapter or at the documentation provided with the JDK for this information.

ResultSetMetaData

One of the most useful classes you can use to retrieve data from a **ResultSet** is the **ResultSetMetaData** class. This class contains methods that allow you to obtain vital information about the query's result. After a query has been executed, you can call the **ResultSet.getMetaData** method to fetch a **ResultSetMetaData** object for the resulting data. Table 9.4 shows some of the

TABLE 9.4

A FEW RESULTSETMETADATA METHODS.

Method	Description
GetColumnCount()	Indicates the number of columns in a ResultSet.
GetColumnLabel(int)	Returns the database-assigned Label for the column at position int in the ResultSet.
GetColumnName(int)	Returns the specified column's name (useful for query reference).
GetColumnType(int)	Returns the specified column's SQL data type.

(continued)

	TABLE 9.4

A FEW RESULTSETMETADATA METHODS (*CONTINUED*).

Method	Description
IsNullable(int)	Tells you if the specified column can contain NULLs.
IsSearchable(int)	Indicates whether the specified column is searchable via a WHERE clause. Certain BLOB type columns (VARBINARY) may not be searchable.

methods you will most likely use. Again, we list more **ResultSetMetaData** methods in Chapter 16.

Understanding The Object Relation Model

The Object Relation Model (ORM) attempts to fuse object orientation with the relational database model. Because many of today's programming languages, such as Java, are object-oriented, a tighter integration between the two would provide easier abstraction for developers who program in object-oriented languages and also are required to "program" in SQL. Such integration would also relieve the necessity of constant translation between database tables and object-oriented data structures, which can be an arduous task.

Mapping A Table Into A Java Object

Let's look at a simple example to demonstrate the basics of ORM. Suppose we create the following table in a database:

First_Name	Last_Name	Phone_Number	Employee_Number
Pratik	Patel	800-555-1212	30122
Karl	Moss	800-555-1213	30124
Keith	Weiskamp	800-555-1214	09249
Michelle	Stroup	800-555-1215	10464

You can easily map this table into a Java object. Here's the Java code you would write to encapsulate the data the table contains:

```
class Employee {
int Key;
String First_Name;
String Last_Name;
String Phone_Number;
int Employee_Number;

Key=Employee_Number;
}
```

To retrieve this table from the database into Java, we simply assign the respective columns to the **Employee** object we created previously for each row we retrieve, as shown here:

```
Employee emp_object = new Employee();
emp_object.First_Name = resultset.getString("First_Name");
emp_object.Last_Name = resultset.getString("Last_Name");
emp_object.Phone_Number = resultset.getString("Phone_Number");
emp_object.Employee_Number = resultset.getInt("Employee_Number");
```

With a larger database model (with links between tables), a number of problems can arise, including scalability due to multiple JOINs in the data model and cross-linking of table keys. Fortunately, a number of products are already available that allow you to create these kinds of object-oriented/relational bridges. Moreover, there are several solutions being developed to work specifically with Java.

We've given you an idea of what ORM is all about. If you would like to investigate this topic further, check out The Coriolis Group Web site (**www.coriolis. com/jdbc-book**) for links to ORM vendors and some really informative ORM documents. The ODMG (Object Database Management Group) is a consortium that is working on a revised standard for object database technology and the incorporation of this concept into programming languages such as Java. You can find a link to the consortium's Web site on The Coriolis Group Web site as well.

Object Databases And The JDBC

Throughout this book, when we refer to databases, we are specifically speaking of relational databases. There is another entire spectrum of databases: object databases, which allow you to directly store objects created in an object-oriented language such as Java. While some of the object databases now have JDBC drivers, they may or may not support the SQL-92 query language standard. There is a specialized language, used for object databases, that is known as OQL, or object query language.

The JDBC was built around SQL-92, so there are some inherent dilemmas when one wishes to apply object-database technology to the JDBC. It makes more sense to have a separate API specifically to bind to object databases, and several object database vendors have their own set of Java classes for doing so. Check the book's Web site at **www.coriolis.com/jdbc-book** for links to object database vendors that support Java.

Coming Up Next

As you can see from this brief chapter, mapping SQL data types to Java is truly a snap. We covered a few of the more important methods you will use to retrieve data from a database. For a complete reference, see Chapter 16 and have a look at the Date, Time, TimeStamp, and BigDecimal classes.

The next chapter continues our exploration of JDBC with a discussion about security. We'll discuss the issues involved with deploying JDBC-aware applets, whether it's over your intranet to the next office or across the Internet to someone halfway around the world.

10

JAVA AND DATABASE SECURITY

Security is at the top of the list of concerns for people sharing databases on the Internet and large intranets. In this chapter, we'll have a look at security in Java and how Java/JDBC security relates to database security. We'll also have a peek at some prospective Java security features, which will incorporate encryption and authentication into the JDK 1.1.

Database Server Security

The first issue we'd like to tackle, and the first one you need to consider, is the security of your actual database server. If you are allowing direct connections to your database server from your Java/JDBC programs, you need to prepare for a number of potential security pitfalls. Although security breaks are few and far between, we advise you to cover all the angles so you don't get caught off-guard.

Packets On The Network

Information is sent over networks in packets, and packet sniffing happens because a computer's network adapter is configured to read all of the packets sent over the network instead of just packets meant for that computer. Therefore, anyone with access to a computer attached to your LAN can check out all transactions as they occur. Of course, the best methods of preventing an inside job are a well-managed network and users you can trust. Unfortunately, you must also consider another possibility: the outside threat. The possibility that someone from outside your LAN might break into a computer inside your LAN is another issue altogether; you must make sure that you properly secure all computers on your LAN. To prevent a break-in, a firewall is often the best remedy. Though firewalls are not completely foolproof, they do prevent indiscriminate outside access to any computers behind them. There are several good books on basic Internet security, and you can find a list of URLs that highlight several books on firewalls at this book's Web site (**www.coriolis.com/jdbc-book**).

Packet sniffing doesn't necessarily involve only your local network; it can occur on the route the packet takes from the remote client machine somewhere on the Internet to your server machine. Along one of the many "hops" a packet takes as it travels across the Internet, a hacker who has gained entry into one of these hop points could be monitoring the packets sent to and from your server. Although remote, this is a possibility. One solution is to limit the IP addresses from which connections to the database server can be made. However, IP authorization isn't bulletproof either—IP spoofing is a workaround for this method. For more information on these basic security issues, please see this book's Web site for references to security material.

Web Server CGI And Servlet Holes

If you only allow local direct access to your database server via pre-written software, like CGI scripts run from Web pages, you'll still find yourself with a possible security hole. Some folks with too much time on their hands take great pleasure in hacking through CGI scripts to seek out unauthorized information. Are you vulnerable to this type of attack? Consider this situation: You have a CGI script that searches a table. The HTML form that gives the CGI its search information uses a field containing a table name; if a hacker realizes that you are directly patching in the table name from the HTML page, it would be easy to modify the CGI parameters to point to a different table. Of course, the easy solution to this scenario is to check the CGI script so that these security holes do not exist.

For in-house distribution of Java programs that access database servers, many of these security considerations are minimal. But for Internet applications, such as a merchandising applet where a user enters a credit card number to purchase some goods, you not only want to send this data encrypted to the Web server, but you also want to protect the actual database server on which you store this sensitive data.

Finding A Solution

So how do we deal with these security holes? The most straightforward way is to use a database server that implements secure login encryption. Some database servers do this already, and with the proliferation of "Web databases," login encryption is likely to be incorporated into more popular database servers in the future. The other solution, which is more viable, is to use an application server in a three-tier system. First, the Java program uses encryption to send login information to the application server. Then, the application server decodes the information. And finally, the application server sends the decoded information to the database server, which is either running on the same machine or on a machine attached to a secure local network. We discussed application servers in more detail in Chapter 5.

Another solution involves using the Java Security API, currently under development at JavaSoft. This API, which provides classes that perform encryption and authentication, will be a standard part of the Java API and will allow you to use plug-in classes to perform encryption on a remote connection.

As a user, how do you know if the Java applet you're getting is part of a front for an illegitimate business? The Java Security API addresses the security issue of determining whether an applet is from a legitimate source by using digital signatures, authorization, and certification. The Java Security API will likely be incorporated into Web browsers' Java interpreters and will also be linked in heavily with the security features of the Web browser itself. As of this writing, however, these APIs were still under construction.

Applet Security: Can I Trust You?

As we've seen, setting up safe connections is quite possible. However, applet security is an entirely different issue. This aspect of security, in which an applet that has been downloaded to your computer is running in your Web browser, has been under scrutiny since Java-enabled Web browsers appeared.

The Applet Security Manager

Every Web browser's Java interpreter includes a security manager to determine what an applet can and can't do. For instance, the security manager does not allow applets downloaded from remote Web pages to access the local disk; it restricts network connections attempted by the applet to only the machine from which the applet came from, and it restricts applets from gaining control of local system devices. These restrictions are in place to protect users from rogue applets (or should I say rogue applet programmers) attempting to break into your computer. The user does not need to worry about the applet formatting the hard disk or reading password files. Of course, I'm simplifying the applet security scheme, but I want to point out the care programmers take to protect the user and the restrictions developers face when programming applets. So how does this relate to the JDBC? The immediate concern for you as the developer is that your JDBC applet can only connect to the same machine that served the applet initially (for example, your Web server). This means that you must run a Web server on the same machine as your database server. However, if you choose the application server route, which we will discuss in Chapter 11, you must run the application server alongside the Web server, but then you are free to run the database server on another machine. If the user installs the applet locally and runs it, these security restrictions do not apply. But, unfortunately, that defeats the purpose behind an applet: a program that comes over the network and begins running locally without installation.

I'm A Certified Applet

To account for these tight security restrictions, the Java Security API addresses easing security *if the applet comes from a "trusted" source.* This means that if the Web browser recognizes as genuine the certification of the Web page, applets on the page may also be considered "certified." To obtain such a status, you must apply for certification from the proper authority. When you receive certification, simply attach it to applets your Web site serves. The Security API allows for the fetching of trusted applets, so if the user uses a Java interpreter that incorporates the Java Security API, you (the developer) can serve applets that can connect to an application server or database server running on a different machine than the Web server. In fact, you can even attach to different database servers simultaneously if necessary. In addition, this approach may allow the applet to save the contents of a database session on the user's disk or read data from the user's disk to load previous session data.

The exact security restrictions of trusted applets are not set in stone, and they may differ depending on the Web browser the applet is run on. Also, the Java Security specifications and related APIs have not been finalized as of this writing, so the preliminary details of the security scheme may change by the time the APIs are released and implemented.

Coming Up Next

Security in data transactions is a top priority in the Internet community. In this chapter, we've discussed possible security holes and techniques to sew them up. We also took a look at Javasoft's approach to easing security restrictions for applets that come from a certified trusted source.

In the next chapter, we will discuss how to deploy your data-aware applet on your intranet or the Internet. We'll discuss issues related to sending an entire application manifest as an applet over the network. There are a number of issues, such as security, that we must consider before sending a JDBC-enabled applet over the network.

11

DEPLOYING DATA-AWARE APPLETS

This chapter takes a quick look at some of the issues involving deployment of your JDBC applets and applications over the Internet and your intranet. We'll divide our discussion into these two general categories, though some issues cross the outside/inside boundary. We've already talked about security, JDBC driver types, and a little about the difficulty of integrating relational databases into an object-oriented language. We'll discuss how these issues interact.

We'll also talks about applets and firewalls—or how to go through them securely. The purpose of this chapter is to round out the discussion of JDBC at a higher level. A key reason you're interested in Java is that you can send Java applets over a network to run on a remote computer with no pre-installation. Let's make sure you can actually do this.

Internet Issues

First, let's look at some points to keep in mind if you plan on sending users on the Internet an applet that employs JDBC. This would interest you if you wanted to send a Java program that lets users pick music CDs directly from your database, shows your sales force the latest data, or create any host of applets that would benefit from a database backend. Let's look at some of the issues involved when you deploy your JDBC applet over the global Internet.

Middleware—A Basic Solution

Middleware is a good idea when many people, especially from outside your corporate intranet, are accessing your databases. While adding a middleware server can slow transactions down a bit, well-designed middleware software can cache, which eases the load on your database servers. It also allows you to specify a separate access-control list, a list where you store user names and a password for entry into the system. You can extend this model to include which databases a user can access through middleware (so that only certain users can access certain databases) based on the privileges you give him or her.

ISOLATION

One of the best reasons to set up a middleware server is to isolate your actual database servers. Why is it good to do this? First, your database server can only handle a limited number of connections. A middleware server can have several clients on one side, while using only one connection to the actual database server. You can configure your database server to accept connections from only this middleware server, thereby reducing the likelihood of break-ins into your data repository. Also, moving the access-control list from the database server to the middleware server will further secure your database server.

MOVING OUTSIDE

Your company has a firewall. You want to deploy a JDBC applet. Your database server lives inside the firewall. Your targeted users operate outside the firewall. End of project? Absolutely not! You can put the middleware server on your firewall. This way, users on the outside can access the middleware server, and the middleware server can access your database servers.

Realize that you might be opening up a security hole if you're not careful. If you have some really sensitive data, your system administrators may not buy this solution. However, if you're careful to choose a middleware server that supports SSL and is solid in its security authentication module, this *is* a viable solution.

Proxy

You've talked with your systems administration people, and they say that this is just too big a risk to take. You're still not stuck; you can provide access the old-fashioned way: dial-in lines. Companies are already using dial-in SLIP or PPP lines to allow their employees to access their intranet. This way, you're almost certain that no one can break into your intranet from the Internet (assuming your firewall is solid).

You'll need to remember that bandwidth will limit what you can do—after all, the fastest you can go over a modem today is 56Kbps. The user can still receive Web pages from your Web server, and get those JDBC applets you've been working on in a reasonable amount of time. The applets can then connect over the SLIP/PPP connection to your middleware or database server.

Speed

Of course, we can't discuss an Internet system without talking about speed. While the Java applet may come down quickly, the constant data transactions that will take place when you use the JDBC to query and retrieve data from the server can make the system very slow. This can be a big problem if you plan on showing large result sets or multimedia data. It doesn't mean that you're restricted from doing such things; just keep in mind that the user may be on a slow connection.

Intranet Issues

If you're primarily concerned with creating JDBC applets just for your company, then read on. This section highlights some issues that might arise when you're ready to roll out your new system. The issues here overlap somewhat with those we discussed earlier.

Connect To The Database Directly?

We've already talked about using middleware when deploying over the Internet. Middleware can also be a necessary part of your intranet deployment plans. One of the top reasons for using middleware is to isolate your database server, as we mentioned already. This keeps access to the actual database server to a minimum. The middleware connects to the database server and makes the queries for your user (via your JDBC applet, of course).

The other compelling reason to use a middleware server in intranet applications is that your database server may only support a limited number of simultaneous connections. As we already mentioned, a middleware server can handle many clients on one side, while using only a few connections to the database server. If you expect many people inside your organization to utilize your JDBC applet, they may not be able to connect directly to the database server if the number of allowed connections is exhausted, or if the server if overloaded with connections.

"Pushing" Applets And JDBC Drivers

If you're deploying a Java applet that incorporates JDBC, your users will have to download the applet each time they restart their Web browser. While persistence, or caching of Java applets, is still in the works, this still means that you must download the applet each time a new version is created, along with the JDBC driver. If your users are using the JDBC applet frequently, you may want to investigate the use of a push client. A push client allows software and other computer data to be pre-loaded onto a machine on a regular schedule (every night at 1 a.m., for example). Of course, you'll need a push server that stores original copies of your Java applets and distributes them to push clients. This approach, where Java applets are updated on a regular basis, can save time because the applets are already on the user's hard drive. The user simply needs to know where the applet is located. Another option is to create a series of links (shortcuts) to the local copy of the Java applets.

MARIMBA'S CASTANET
Marimba makes a push server and push client that allow Java applets to be distributed when the user is not using the machine. Check out their Web page at **www.marimba.com** and look at the Castanet product.

The speed of the network even for an intranet may be less than spectacular. This is especially true if your organization is split between multiple sites that may be physically next to each other, or half-way around the world. Be sure to account for users whose connection may be slow. There's nothing worse than waiting for a Java applet to download, and then having to wait for the server to receive data every time an operation is performed.

Coming Up Next

The next section of the book dives into four chapters of examples. The Java programs that we will develop in the following section will help you see JDBC in action. We'll look at two hot areas in Java: Servlets and Java Beans. We'll quickly explain each, and show you how to integrate JDBC into these APIs to make data-aware Java servlets and beans. The other two chapters show you more examples of using JDBC, including working with BLOBs and showing graphs with data retrieved from the database.

Part **4**

PROJECTS WITH COMPLETE CODE

12

THE MULTIMEDIA JDBC APPLICATION: IconStore

In the previous chapter, we learned how to process query results with JDBC. In this chapter, we'll take these query results and put them to use in a multimedia application. The application we'll be developing, IconStore, will connect to a database, query for image data stored in database tables, and display the images on a canvas. It's all very simple, and it puts the JDBC to good use by building a dynamic application totally driven by data stored in tables.

IconStore Requirements

The IconStore application will utilize two database tables: ICONCATEGORY and ICONSTORE. The ICONCATEGORY table contains information about image categories, which can be items like printers, sports, and tools. The ICONSTORE table contains information about each image. Tables 12.1 and 12.2 show the database tables' underlying data structures.

Note that the CATEGORY column in the ICONSTORE is a foreign key into the ICONCATEGORY table. If the category

		TABLE 12.1

THE ICONCATEGORY TABLE.

Column Name	SQL Type	Description
CATEGORY	INTEGER	Category ID
DESCRIPTION	VARCHAR	Description of the image category

		TABLE 12.2

THE ICONSTORE TABLE.

Column Name	SQL Type	Description
ID	INTEGER	Image ID
DESCRIPTION	VARCHAR	Description of the image
CATEGORY	INTEGER	Category ID
ICON	VARBINARY	Binary image

ID for sports is "1", you can obtain a result set containing all of the sports images by using this statement:

```
SELECT ID, DESCRIPTION, ICON FROM ICONSTORE WHERE CATEGORY = 1
```

Now, let's take a look at what's going on in the application:

- An Icons menu, which is dynamically created by the ICONCATEGORY table, contains each of the image categories as an option. The user can select an image category from this menu to display the proper list of image descriptions in a list box. The ICONSTORE table is used to dynamically build the list.

- The user can select an image description from the list box to display the corresponding image.

- Once an image has been displayed, the user can select the Save As menu option to save the image to disk.

As you can see, IconStore will not be too complicated, but it will serve as a very good foundation for developing database-driven applications.

Building The Database

Now that we've established the application's requirements, we need to build the underlying database. We'll look at a simple JDBC application to accomplish this, although it may be created by any number of methods. Listing 12.1 shows the BuildDB.java source code. This application uses the SimpleText JDBC driver (covered in great detail in Chapter 7) to create the ICONCATEGORY and ICONSTORE tables, but any JDBC driver can be used in its place.

LISTING 12.1   BUILDING THE ICONSTORE DATABASE.

```java
import java.sql.*;
import java.io.*;

class BuildDB {
//- - - - - - -
// main
//- - - - - - -
public static void main(String args[]) {
    try {
        // Create an instance of the driver
        java.sql.Driver d = (java.sql.Driver) Class.forName (
                "jdbc.SimpleText.SimpleTextDriver").newInstance();

        // Properties for the driver
        java.util.Properties prop = new java.util.Properties();

        // URL to use to connect
        String url = "jdbc:SimpleText";

        // The only property supported by the SimpleText driver
        // is "Directory."
        prop.put("Directory", "/java/IconStore");

        // Connect to the SimpleText driver
        Connection con = DriverManager.getConnection(url, prop);

        // Create the category table
        buildCategory(con, "IconCategory");

        // Create the IconStore table
        buildIconStore(con, "IconStore");

        // Close the connection
        con.close();
    }
```

```
    catch (SQLException ex) {
        System.out.println("\n*** SQLException caught ***\n");
        while (ex != null) {
            System.out.println("SQLState: " + ex.getSQLState());
            System.out.println("Message:  " + ex.getMessage());
            System.out.println("Vendor:   " + ex.getErrorCode());
            ex = ex.getNextException ();
        }
        System.out.println("");
    }
    catch (java.lang.Exception ex) {
        ex.printStackTrace ();
    }
}


//- - - - - - - - - - - - - - - - - - - - - - - - - - - - - - -
// BuildCategory
// Given a connection object and a table name, create the IconStore
// category database table.
//- - - - - - - - - - - - - - - - - - - - - - - - - - - - - - -
protected static void buildCategory(
    Connection con,
    String table)
    throws SQLException
{
    System.out.println("Creating " + table);

    Statement stmt = con.createStatement();

    // Create the SQL statement
    String sql = "create table " + table +
            " (CATEGORY NUMBER, DESCRIPTION VARCHAR)";

    // Create the table
    stmt.executeUpdate(sql);

    // Create some data using the statement
    stmt.executeUpdate("INSERT INTO " + table + " VALUES (1,
      'Printers')");
    stmt.executeUpdate("INSERT INTO " + table + " VALUES (2, 'Sports')");
    stmt.executeUpdate("INSERT INTO " + table + " VALUES (3, 'Tools')");
}


//- - - - - - - - - - - - - - - - - - - - - - - - - - - - - - -
// BuildIconStore
// Given a connection object and a table name, create the IconStore
// icon database table.
//- - - - - - - - - - - - - - - - - - - - - - - - - - - - - - -
```

```java
protected static void buildIconStore(
    Connection con,
    String table)
    throws SQLException
{
    System.out.println("Creating " + table);
    Statement stmt = con.createStatement();

    // Create the SQL statement
    String sql = "create table " + table +
            " (ID NUMBER, DESCRIPTION VARCHAR, CATEGORY NUMBER, ICON
                BINARY)";

    // Create the table
    stmt.executeUpdate(sql);
    stmt.close();

    // Create some data using a prepared statement
    sql = "insert into " + table + " values(?,?,?,?)";

    FileInputStream file;
    PreparedStatement ps = con.prepareStatement(sql);

    int category;
    int id = 1;

    // Add the printer icons
    category = 1;

    addIconRecord(ps, id++, "Printer 1", category, "printers/print.gif");
    addIconRecord(ps, id++, "Printer 2", category, "printers/print0.gif");

    // Add the sports icons
    category = 2;

    addIconRecord(ps, id++, "Archery", category, "sports/
      sport_archery.gif");
    addIconRecord(ps, id++, "Baseball", category, "sports/
      sport_baseball.gif");

    // Add the tools
    category = 3;

    addIconRecord(ps, id++, "Toolbox 1", category, "tools/toolbox.gif");
    addIconRecord(ps, id++, "Toolbox 2", category, "tools/toolbox1.gif");
    ps.close();
}
```

```
//- - - - - - - - - - - - - - - - - - - - - - - - - - - - - -
// AddIconRecord
// Helper method to add an IconStore record. A PreparedStatement is
// provided, to which this method binds input parameters. Returns
// true if the record was added.
//- - - - - - - - - - - - - - - - - - - - - - - - - - - - - -
protected static boolean addIconRecord(
    PreparedStatement ps,
    int id,
    String desc,
    int category,
    String filename)
    throws SQLException
{
    // Create a file object for the icon
    File file = new File(filename);

    if (!file.exists()) {
        return false;
    }

    // Get the length of the file. This will be used when binding
    // the InputStream to the PreparedStatement.
    int len = (int) file.length();

    FileInputStream inputStream;

    try {

        // Attempt to create an InputStream from the File object
        inputStream = new FileInputStream (filename);
    }
    catch (Exception ex) {

            // Some type of failure. Convert it into a SQLException.
            throw new SQLException (ex.getMessage ());
    }

        // Set the parameters
        ps.setInt(1, id);
        ps.setString(2, desc);
        ps.setInt(3,category);
        ps.setBinaryStream(4, inputStream, len);

        // Now execute
        int rows = ps.executeUpdate();
        return (rows == 0) ? false : true;
    }
}
```

The BuildDB application connects to the SimpleText JDBC driver, creates the ICONCATEGORY table, adds some image category records, creates the ICONSTORE table, and adds some image records. Note that when the image records are added to the ICONSTORE table, a **PreparedStatement** object is used. Using **PreparedStatements** is an efficient way to execute the same SQL statement multiple times with different parameters values. Also note that the image data is coming out of GIF files stored on disk. An **InputStream** is created using these files, which is then passed to the JDBC driver for input. The JDBC driver reads the **InputStream** and stores the binary data in the database table. Simple, isn't it? Now that we've created the database, we can start writing our IconStore application.

Application Essentials

The source code for the IconStore application is shown throughout the rest of this chapter, broken across the various sections. As always, you can copy all the book's source code from the CD-ROM enclosed with this book. Remember, you need to have the SimpleText JDBC driver installed before using the IconStore application. See Chapter 3 if you have trouble getting the application to run.

Writing The main Method

Every JDBC application must have an entry point, or a place at which to start execution. This entry point is the **main** method, which is shown in Listing 12.2. For the IconStore application, **main** simply processes any command line arguments, creates a new instance of the **IconStore** class (which extends **Frame**, a top-level window class), and sets up the window attributes. The IconStore application accepts one command line argument: the location of the IconStore database. The default location is /IconStore.

LISTING 12.2   IconStore main method.

```
import java.awt.*;
import java.io.*;
import java.util.*;
import java.sql.*;

public class IconStore
        extends Frame
{
```

```
IconCanvas        imageCanvas;
List              iconList;
Panel             iconListPanel;
MenuBar           menuBar;
Menu              fileMenu;
Menu              sectionMenu;
List              lists[];

static String myHome = "/IconStore";
Connection        connection;
Hashtable         categories;
Hashtable         iconDesc[];
String            currentList;
String            currentFile = null;
FileDialog        fileDialog;

//- - - -
// main
//- - - -
public static void main (String[] args) {

    // If an argument was given, assume it is the location of the
    // database.
    if (args.length > 0) {
        myHome = args[0].trim();

        // If there is a trailing separator, remove it
        if (myHome.endsWith("/") ||
            myHome.endsWith("\\")) {
            myHome = myHome.substring(0, myHome.length() - 1);
        }
    }

    // Create our IconStore object
    IconStore frame = new IconStore();

    // Setup and display
    frame.setTitle("The IconStore");
    frame.init();

    frame.pack();
    frame.resize(300, 400);
    frame.show();
}
```

A lot of work is being performed in **IconStore.init**, such as establishing the database connection, reading the icon categories, creating the menus, and reading the icon descriptions. We'll take a look at each of these in greater detail in the following sections.

Establishing The Database Connection

Listing 12.3 shows the code used by the IconStore application to connect to the SimpleText JDBC driver.

LISTING 12.3   ESTABLISHING THE DATABASE CONNECTION.

```
public Connection establishConnection()
    {
        Connection con = null;
        try {
            // Create an instance of the driver
            java.sql.Driver d = (java.sql.Driver) Class.forName (
                    "jdbc.SimpleText.SimpleTextDriver").newInstance();

            // Properties for the driver
            java.util.Properties prop = new java.util.Properties();

            // URL to use to connect
            String url = "jdbc:SimpleText";

            // Set the location of the database tables
            prop.put("Directory", myHome);

            // Connect to the SimpleText driver
            con = DriverManager.getConnection(url, prop);
        }
        catch (SQLException ex) {

            // An SQLException was generated. Dump the exception
            // contents. Note that there may be multiple SQLExceptions
            // chained together.

            System.out.println("\n*** SQLException caught ***\n");
            while (ex != null) {
                System.out.println("SQLState: " + ex.getSQLState());
                System.out.println("Message:  " + ex.getMessage());
                System.out.println("Vendor:   " + ex.getErrorCode());
                ex = ex.getNextException();
            }
            System.exit(1);
        }
```

```
    catch (java.lang.Exception ex) {
        ex.printStackTrace();
        System.exit(1);
    }
    return con;
}
```

Note that we need to set a property for the SimpleText driver to specify the location of the database tables. In reality, the SimpleText driver stores each database table as a file, and the **Directory** property specifies the directory in which these files are kept. As I mentioned in the previous section, the default location is /IconStore (the IconStore directory of your current drive), but this can be overridden to be any location.

If successful, a JDBC **Connection** object is returned to the caller. If there is any reason a database connection cannot be established, the pertinent information will be displayed and the application will be terminated.

Creating The Menu

One of the requirements for the IconStore application is the ability to dynamically build the Icons menu. To do this, we'll need to query the ICON CATEGORY table and build the menu from the results. First, we need to read the database table and store the query results, as shown in Listing 12.4.

LISTING 12.4   READING THE ICONCATEGORY TABLE.

```
//- - - - - - - - - - - - - - - - - - - - - - - - - - - - - - - - - -
// getCategories
// Read the IconStore CATEGORY table and create a Hashtable containing
// a list of all the categories. The key is the category description and
// the data value is the category ID.
//- - - - - - - - - - - - - - - - - - - - - - - - - - - - - - - - - -
public Hashtable getCategories(
    Connection con)
{
    Hashtable table = new Hashtable();

    try {
        // Create a Statement object
        Statement stmt = con.createStatement();

        // Execute the query and process the results
        ResultSet rs = stmt.executeQuery(
```

```
                "SELECT DESCRIPTION,CATEGORY FROM .ICONCATEGORY");

        // Loop while more rows exist
        while (rs.next()) {
            // Put the description and id in the Hashtable
            table.put(rs.getString(1), rs.getString(2));
        }
        // Close the statement
        stmt.close();
    }
    catch (SQLException ex) {

        // An SQLException was generated. Dump the exception contents.
        // Note that there may be multiple SQLExceptions chained
        // together.

        System.out.println("\n*** SQLException caught ***\n");
        while (ex != null) {
            System.out.println("SQLState: " + ex.getSQLState());
            System.out.println("Message:  " + ex.getMessage());
            System.out.println("Vendor:   " + ex.getErrorCode());
            ex = ex.getNextException();
        }

            System.exit(1);
    }


    return table;
}
```

The flow of this routine is very basic, and we'll be using it throughout our
IconStore application. First, we create a **Statement** object. Then, we submit an
SQL statement to query the database. Next, we process each of the resulting
rows. And finally, we close the **Statement**. Note that a **Hashtable** object containing a list of all the categories is returned—the category description is the
key and the category ID is the element. In this way, we can easily cross-reference a category description to an ID. We'll see why this is necessary a bit later.

Now that all of the category information has been loaded, we can create our
menu. Listing 12.5 shows how this is done.

LISTING 12.5   CREATING THE ICONS MENU.

```
// Get a Hashtable containing an entry for each icon category.
// The key is the description and the data value is the
// category number.
```

```
categories = getCategories(connection);

// File menu
fileMenu = new Menu("File");
fileMenu.add(new MenuItem("Save As"));
fileMenu.add(new MenuItem("Exit"));
menuBar.add(fileMenu);

// Icons menu
sectionMenu = new Menu("Icons");

Enumeration e = categories.keys();
    int listNo = 0;
    String desc;

// Loop while there are more keys (category descriptions)

while (e.hasMoreElements()) {
    desc = (String) e.nextElement();

    // Add the description to the Icons menu
    sectionMenu.add(new MenuItem(desc));
}

// Add the Icons menu to the menu bar
menuBar.add(sectionMenu);

// Set the menu bar
setMenuBar(menuBar);
```

Notice that the **Hashtable** containing a list of the image categories is used to create our menu. The only way to examine the contents of a **Hashtable** without knowing each of the keys is to create an **Enumeration** object, which can be used to get the next key value of the **Hashtable**. Figure 12.1 shows our database-driven menu.

Creating The Lists

Next on our agenda: creating the list boxes containing the image descriptions. We'll create a list for each category, so when the user selects a category from the Icons menu, only a list of the images for the selected category will be shown. We'll use a **CardLayout** to do this, which is a nifty way to set up any number of lists and switch between them effortlessly. For each of the categories that we read from the ICONCATEGORY table, we also read each of the image

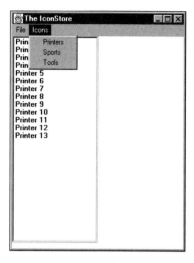

Figure 12.1
The IconStore menu.

descriptions for that category from the ICONSTORE table and store those descriptions in a **Hashtable** for use later. At the same time, we add each description to a list for the category. Listing 12.6 shows the code used to read the ICONSTORE table.

LISTING 12.6   READING THE ICONSTORE TABLE.

```
//- - - - - - - - - - - - - - - - - - - - - - - - - - - - - - - - -
// getIconDesc
// Read the IconStore ICONSTORE table and create a Hashtable that lists of
// all the icons for the given category. The key is the icon containing
// description and the data value is the icon ID. The description is also
// added to the List object given.
//- - - - - - - - - - - - - - - - - - - - - - - - - - - - - - - - -
public Hashtable getIconDesc(
    Connection con,
    String category,
    List list)
{
    Hashtable table = new Hashtable();
    String desc;

    try {
        // Create a Statement object
        Statement stmt = con.createStatement();
```

```java
        // Execute the query and process the results
        ResultSet rs = stmt.executeQuery(
                    "SELECT DESCRIPTION,ID FROM ICONSTORE WHERE CATEGORY=" +
                category);

        // Loop while more rows exist
        while (rs.next()) {
            desc = rs.getString(1);

            // Put the description and ID in the Hashtable
            table.put(desc, rs.getString(2));

            // Put the description in the list
            list.addItem(desc);
        }
        // Close the statement
        stmt.close();
    }
    catch (SQLException ex) {

        // An SQLException was generated. Dump the exception contents.
        // Note that there may be multiple SQLExceptions chained
        // together.
        System.out.println("\n*** SQLException caught ***\n");
        while (ex != null) {
            System.out.println("SQLState: " + ex.getSQLState());
            System.out.println("Message:  " + ex.getMessage());
            System.out.println("Vendor:   " + ex.getErrorCode());
            ex = ex.getNextException();
        }
        System.exit(1);
    }

    return table;
}
```

The process we used here is the same as we have seen before—creating a **Statement**, executing a query, processing the results, and closing the **Statement**. Listing 12.7 shows the entire code for the **IconStore.init** method. In addition to building the menu, we'll also build the **CardLayout**. It is important to note that the IconStore application is totally database-driven; no code will have to be modified to add or remove categories or images.

LISTING 12.7   ICONSTORE INIT METHOD.

```
//- - - - - - - - - - - - - - - - - - - - - - - - - - - - - - - - -
// init
// Initialize the IconStore object. This includes reading the
// IconStore database for the icon descriptions.
//- - - - - - - - - - - - - - - - - - - - - - - - - - - - - - - - -
public void init()
{
    // Create our canvas that will be used to display the icons
    imageCanvas = new IconCanvas();

    // Establish a connection to the JDBC driver
    connection = establishConnection();

    // Get a Hashtable containing an entry for each icon category.
    // The key is the description and the data value is the
    // category number.
    categories = getCategories(connection);

    // Setup the menu bar
    menuBar = new MenuBar();

    // File menu
    fileMenu = new Menu("File");
    fileMenu.add(new MenuItem("Save As"));
    fileMenu.add(new MenuItem("Exit"));
    menuBar.add(fileMenu);

    // Icons menu
    sectionMenu = new Menu("Icons");

    // Setup our category lists, list panel (using a CardLayout) and
    // icon menu.
    iconListPanel = new Panel();
    iconListPanel.setLayout(new CardLayout());

    lists = new List[categories.size()];
    iconDesc = new Hashtable[categories.size()];
    Enumeration e = categories.keys();
    int listNo = 0;
    String desc;

    // Loop while there are more keys (category descriptions)
    while (e.hasMoreElements()) {
            desc = (String) e.nextElement();
```

```
        // The first item in the list will be our default
        if (listNo == 0) {
            currentList = desc;
        }

        // Create a new list, with a display size of 20
        lists[listNo] = new List(20, false);

        // Create a new CardLayout panel
        iconListPanel.add(desc, lists[listNo]);

        // Add the description to the Icons menu
        sectionMenu.add(new MenuItem(desc));

        // Get a Hashtable containing an entry for each row found
        // for this category. The key is the icon description and
        // the data value is the ID.

        iconDesc[listNo] = getIconDesc(connection,
                (String) categories.get(desc), lists[listNo]);
        listNo++;
    }

    // Add the Icons menu to the menu bar
    menuBar.add(sectionMenu);

    // Set the menu bar
    setMenuBar(menuBar);

    // Create a Save As file dialog box
    fileDialog = new FileDialog(this, "Save File", FileDialog.SAVE);

    // Setup our layout
    setLayout(new GridLayout(1,2));
    add(iconListPanel);
    add(imageCanvas);
}
```

It is very important to note how the **CardLayout** has been set up. Each of the lists is added to the **CardLayout** with a descriptive title, which, in our case, is the name of the category. When the user selects a category from the Icons menu, we can use the category description to set the new **CardLayout** list. Figure 12.2 shows the initial screen after loading the database tables.

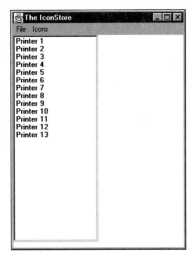

Figure 12.2
The IconStore main screen.

Handling Events

There are two types of events that we need to be aware of in the IconStore application: selecting menu options and clicking on the image list to select an icon. As with the Interactive SQL applet we discussed in Chapter 4, the event handling code is contained in the **handleEvent** method, as shown in Listing 12.8.

LISTING 12.8   ICONSTORE HANDLEEVENT.

```
//- - - - - - - - - - - - - -
// handleEvent
// Handle an event by the user.
//- - - - - - - - - - - - - -
public boolean handleEvent(
    Event evt)
{

    switch (evt.id) {
    case Event.ACTION_EVENT:

        // Determine the type of event that just occurred
        if (evt.target instanceof MenuItem) {

            // The user selected a menu item. Figure out what action
            // should be taken.
            String selection = (String) evt.arg;
```

```java
    // 'Save As' - Save the currently displayed icon to a file
    if (selection.equals("Save As")) {
        if (currentFile != null) {
            fileDialog.setFile("");
            fileDialog.pack();
            fileDialog.show();

            String saveFile = fileDialog.getFile();

            if (saveFile == null) {
                return true;
            }

            // If this is a new file, it will end with .*.*
            if (saveFile.endsWith(".*.*")) {
                saveFile = saveFile.substring(0,
                        saveFile.length() - 4);
                // If no extension is given, append .GIF
                if (saveFile.indexOf(".") < 0) {
                    saveFile += ".gif";
                }
            }

            // Copy the file. Returns true if successful.
            boolean rc = copyFile (currentFile, saveFile);
        }
        return true;
    }


    // 'Exit' - Exit the application
    else if (selection.equals("Exit")) {
        // If there was an image file, delete it
        if (currentFile != null) {
            (new File(currentFile)).delete();
        }

        System.exit(0);
    }

    // The user must have selected a different set of icons;
    // Display the proper list.
    else {
        currentList = selection;
        ((CardLayout) iconListPanel.getLayout()).show(
                        iconListPanel, currentList);

        // Display the icon, if one was previously selected
        displayIcon(connection);
```

```
                     return true;
                }
            }
            break;

        case Event.LIST_SELECT:
            displayIcon(connection);
            break;
        }

        return false;
}
```

Most of the code is very straightforward. Note how the **CardLayout** is managed. When a user makes a selection from the Icons menu, the selected item (which is the category description) is used to change the **CardLayout**. Remember that when the **CardLayout** was created, the title of each list was the category description. Also note that when the user selects an item from the list box (LIST_SELECT), the corresponding image can be displayed. Listing 12.9 shows how this is done.

When the user selects Exit from the menu, the temporary image file (which is discussed later in this chapter) is deleted from disk, and the application is terminated. This is the perfect time to close the **Connection** that was in use. I purposefully omitted this step to illustrate a point: The JDBC specification states that all close operations are purely optional. It is up to the JDBC driver to perform any necessary clean-up in the finalize methods for each object. I strongly recommend, though, that all JDBC applications close objects when it is proper to do so.

LISTING 12.9   LOADING AND DISPLAYING THE SELECTED IMAGE.

```
//- - - - - - - - - - - - - - - - - -
// displayIcon
// Display the currently selected icon.
//- - - - - - - - - - - - - - - - - - -
public void displayIcon(
    Connection con)
{
    // Get the proper list element
    int n = getCategoryElement(currentList);

    // Get the item selected
    String item = lists[n].getSelectedItem();
```

```
// Only continue if an item was selected
if (item == null) {
    return;
}

// Get the ID
String id = (String) iconDesc[n].get(item);

try {
    // Create a Statement object
    Statement stmt = con.createStatement();

    // Execute the query and process the results
    ResultSet rs = stmt.executeQuery(
            "SELECT ICON FROM ICONSTORE WHERE ID=" + id);

    // If no rows are returned, the icon was not found
    if (!rs.next()) {
        stmt.close();
        return;
    }

    // Get the data as an InputStream
    InputStream inputStream = rs.getBinaryStream(1);

    if (inputStream == null) {
        stmt.close();
        return;
    }

    // Here's where things get ugly. Currently, there is no way
    // to display an image from an InputStream. We'll create a
    // new file from the InputStream and load the Image from the
    // newly created file. We need to create a unique name for
    // each icon; the Java VM caches the image file.

    String name = myHome + "/IconStoreImageFile" + id + ".gif";

    FileOutputStream outputStream = new FileOutputStream(name);

    // Write the data
    int bytes = 0;
    byte b[] = new byte[1024];

    while (true) {
        // Read from the input. The number of bytes read is returned.
        bytes = inputStream.read(b);
```

```
                if (bytes == -1) {
                    break;
                }

                // Write the data
                outputStream.write(b, 0, bytes);
            }
            outputStream.close();
            inputStream.close();

            // Close the statement
            stmt.close();

            // Now, display the icon
            loadFile(name);

            // If there was an image file, delete it
            if (currentFile != null) {
                if (!currentFile.equals(name)) {
                    (new File(currentFile)).delete();
                }
            }

            // Save our current file name
            currentFile = name;
    }
    catch (SQLException ex) {

        // An SQLException was generated. Dump the exception contents.
        // Note that there may be multiple SQLExceptions chained
        // together.

        System.out.println("\n*** SQLException caught ***\n");
        while (ex != null) {
            System.out.println("SQLState: " + ex.getSQLState());
            System.out.println("Message:  " + ex.getMessage());
            System.out.println("Vendor:   " + ex.getErrorCode());
            ex = ex.getNextException();
        }
        System.exit(1);
    }
    catch (java.lang.Exception ex) {
        ex.printStackTrace();
        System.exit(1);
    }

}
```

Notice that each time an image is selected from the list, the image is read from the database. It could be very costly in terms of memory resources to save all of the images, so we'll just get the image from the database when needed. When the user selects an item from the list, we can get the image description. This description is used to get the icon ID from the image **Hashtable**. For the most part, we follow the same steps we have seen several times before to get results from a database. Unfortunately, we've had to use a very nasty workaround here. The image is retrieved from the database as a binary **InputStream**, and it is from this **InputStream** that we need to draw the image on our canvas. This technique seems like it should be a simple matter, but it turns out that JavaSoft did not supply a way to accomplish this with JDK 1.1. There are third-party classes that can accomplish this, such as **GifImage**. To get around this problem, the IconStore application uses the **InputStream** to create a temporary file on disk, from which an image can be loaded and drawn on the canvas. We'll see later that we'll use this approach to our advantage.

Figure 12.3 shows the IconStore screen after the user has selected an image from the initial category list. Figure 12.4 shows the IconStore screen after the user has changed the category (from the Icons menu) to sports and has made a selection.

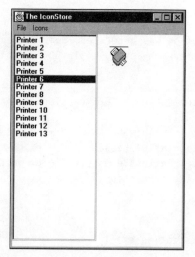

Figure 12.3
Selecting an image from the category list box.

Figure 12.4
Changing the image category.

Saving The Image

All that's left is to add the ability to save the image to disk. We saw earlier in this chapter how to handle the Save As menu event, so we just need to be able to create the disk file. Our workaround approach for drawing an image from an **InputStream** will now be an advantage. Because an image file has already been created, we can simply make a copy of the temporary file. Listing 12.10 shows the code used to copy a file.

LISTING 12.10 COPYING A FILE.

```
//- - - - - - - - - - - - - - - - - - - -
// copyFile
// Copy the source file to the target file.
//- - - - - - - - - - - - - - - - - - - -
public boolean copyFile(
    String source,
    String target)
{
    boolean rc = false;

    try {
        FileInputStream in = new FileInputStream(source);
        FileOutputStream out = new FileOutputStream(target);

        int bytes;
        byte b[] = new byte[1024];
```

```
            // Read chunks from the input stream and write to the output
            // stream.
            while (true) {
                bytes = in.read(b);
                if (bytes == -1) {
                    break;
                }
                out.write(b, 0, bytes);
            }
            in.close();
            out.close();
            rc = true;
        }
        catch (java.lang.Exception ex) {
            ex.printStackTrace();
        }

        return rc;
    }
```

Figure 12.5 shows the IconStore screen after the user has selected the Save As menu option.

That's all there is to it.

Coming Up Next

Let's recap the important details that we have covered in this chapter:

- Creating a basic GUI Java application

- Opening a connection to a data source

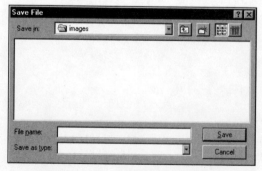

Figure 12.5
The IconStore Save As dialog box.

- Using database data to create dynamic GUI components (menus and lists)

- Handling user events

- Handling JDBC **InputStreams**

If you would like to take the IconStore application further, one possible enhancement would be to allow the user to add images to the database. I'll leave this as an exercise for you.

The next chapter covers additional ways of presenting your data in Java. Using Java packages available on the Net, we'll cover graphs, tables, and more. We'll also discuss some nifty methods in the JDBC that will help streamline your code for retrieving data from your database.

13

WORKING WITH QUERY RESULTS

So far, we've been concentrating on how to use the classes in the JDBC to perform SQL queries. That's great, but now we have to do something with the data we've retrieved. The end user of your JDBC applets or applications will want to see more than just rows and rows of data. In this chapter, we'll learn how to package the raw table data that is returned after a successful SQL query into a Java object, and then how to use this packaged data to produce easy-to-read graphs.

First, we'll create a Java object to store the results of a query. This object will provide a usable interface to the actual query results so that you can plug them into a Java graphics library. We'll create a simple data structure to hold the column results in a formatted way so that we can easily parse them and prepare them for display. Second, we will take these results in the Java object and set up the necessary code to plug the data into a pie chart and bar graph Java package.

In Chapter 12, we went one step further and worked with BLOB data types (like images). Between this and the previous chapter, I'll provide plenty of examples, complete with code, to help you work up your own JDBC programs. At the very least, these chapters will give you some ideas for dealing with raw table data and displaying it in an effective manner.

A Basic Java Object For Storing Results

Although the JDBC provides you with the **ResultSet** class to get the data from an SQL query, you will still need to store and format within your program the results for display. The smart way to do this is in a reusable fashion (by implementing a generic object or class), which allows you to reuse the same class you develop to retrieve data from a query in any of your JDBC programs. The code presented in Listing 13.1 is a method that will keep your results in a Java object until you are ready to parse and display the object.

Let's begin by defining the data we will be getting from the source, and determine how we want to structure it within our Java applet. Remember that the **ResultSet** allows us to retrieve data row by row, column by column; it simply gives us sequential access to the resulting table data. Table 13.1 shows the example table we will be using in this chapter.

The optimal way to store this data in our Java program is to put each column's data in its own structure and then link the different columns by using an index; this will allow us to keep the columnar relationship of the table intact. We will put each column's data in an array. To simplify matters, we'll use the **getString** method, which translates the different data types returned by a query into a String type. We'll then take the data in a column and delimit the instances with commas. We'll use an array of String to do this; each place in the array will represent a different column. The data object we will create is shown in the following code snippet.

TABLE **13.1**

EXAMPLE COMPANY EMPLOYEE TABLE.

emp_no	first_name	last_name	salary
10001	Keith	Weiskamp	95000.00
10002	Michelle	Stroup	75000.00
10003	Robert	Clarfield	65000.00
10010	Pratik	Patel	25000.00
10011	Karl	Moss	25000.00

```
table_data[0] => 01234,1235,0002,0045,0067
table_data[1] => Pratik,Karl,Keith,Robert,Michelle
table_data[2] => Patel,Moss,Weiskamp,Pronk,Friedel
table_data[3] => 8000,23000,90000,59999,53000
```

Listing 13.1 shows the method we'll use to query the database and return a String array that contains the resulting table data.

LISTING 13.1   THE GETDATA METHOD.

```
public String[] getData( String QueryLine ) {
// Run the QueryLine SQL query, and return the
// resulting columns in an array of String. The
// first column is at index [0], the second at [1}, etc.

  int columns, pos;
  String column[]=new String[4];
// We have to initialize the column String variable even though
// we declare it below, because the declaration below is in a try{}
// statement, and the compiler will complain that the variable may
// not be initialized.

  boolean more;

 try {

        Statement stmt = con.createStatement();
          // Create a Statement object from the
          // Connection.createStatement method.

        ResultSet rs = stmt.executeQuery(QueryLine);
          // Execute the passed-in query, and get
          // the ResultSet for the query.

        columns=(rs.getMetaData()).getColumnCount();
          // Get the number of columns in the resulting table so we
          // can declare the column String array, and so we can loop
          // through the results and retrieve them.

        column = new String[columns];
          // Create the column variable to be the exact number of
          // columns that are in the result table.

        // Initialize the column array to be blank, as we'll be
        // adding directly to them later.
```

```
for(pos=1; pos<=columns; pos++) {
      column[pos-1]="";
    }

    more=rs.next();
     // Get the first row of the ResultSet. Loop through the
     // ResultSet and get the data rowbyrow, columnbycolumn.
    while(more) {

       for (pos=1; pos<=columns; pos++) {
         column[pos-1]+=(rs.getString(pos));
       // Add each column to the respective column[] String array.
       }

       more=rs.next();
         // Get the next row of the result if it exists.

         // Now add a comma to each array element to delimit
         // that this row is done.
       for (pos=1; pos<=columns; pos++) {
         if(more) {
         // We only want to do this if this isn't the last row of
         // the table!
           column[pos-1]+=(",");
         }
       }
    }
    stmt.close();
      // All done. Close the statement object.
    }
    catch( Exception e ) {
      e.printStackTrace();
      System.out.println(e.getMessage());
    }
return column;
// Finally, return the entire column[] array.
}
```

Showing The Results

Now that we have the data nicely packaged into our Java object, how do we
show it? The code in Listing 13.2 dumps the data in the object to the screen.
We simply loop through the array and print the data.

LISTING 13.2   CODE TO PRINT RETRIEVED DATA TO
THE CONSOLE.

```
public void ShowFormattedData(String[] columnD ) {

int i;

for ( i=0; i< columnD.length; i++) {
  System.out.println(columnD[i]+"\n");
  }
}
```

Charting Your Data

Now that we've covered the preliminaries, we are ready to get to the fun stuff! Instead of creating a package that has graphics utilities, we're going to use the NetCharts library, which is stored on the CD-ROM enclosed with this book. The package on the CD is only an evaluation copy. Stop by **www.netcharts.com** to pick up the latest version (and some helpful documentation). We'll use the table in Table 13.1 and a bar chart to display the salary information for our fictional company. Figure 13.1 shows the applet that the code in Listing 13.3 generates.

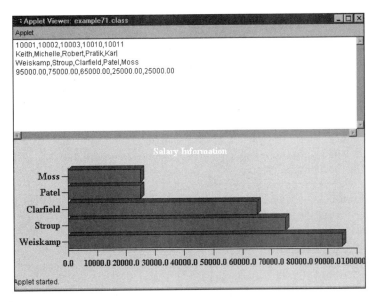

Figure 13.1
Screen shot of first example applet.

Remember that you can find the code for this example on the accompanying CD-ROM, or at The Coriolis Group Web site at **www.coriolis.com/jdbc-book**.

LISTING 13.3   DYNAMICALLY GENERATING A BAR CHART FROM A DATABASE QUERY—PART I.

```
/*
Example 13-1
*/
import java.awt.*;
import java.applet.Applet;
import java.sql.*;

public class example131 extends java.applet.Applet {
  String url;
  String Name;
  Connection con;
  TextArea OutputField = new TextArea(10,35);
  NFBarchartApp bar;
  // This is the bar chart class from the NetCharts package.

public void init() {
  setLayout(new BorderLayout());
  url="jdbc:mysql://president/company";
  // The URL for the database we wish to connect to.

ConnectToDB();
  // Connect to the database.

  add("North", OutputField);
  // Add the TextArea for showing the data to the user.
  String columnData[] = getData("select * from company");
  // Run a query that gets the complete table listing; we
  // can put any query here and would optimally want to get
  // only the columns we need.

  ShowFormattedData(columnData);
  // Show the data in the TextArea.
  ShowChartData(columnData[3],columnData[2]);
// Now, pass the two data sets and create a bar chart.
  add("Center", bar);
// And add the bar chart to the applet's panel.
}

public void ShowFormattedData(String[] columnD ) {
```

```
int i;

for ( i=0; i< columnD.length; i++) {
  OutputField.append(columnD[i]+"\n");
}


}

public void ConnectToDB() {


  try {
  Class.forName("gwe.sql.gweMysqlDriver");
 con = DriverManager.getConnection(url, "test", "test");
   }
  catch( Exception e ) {
    e.printStackTrace();
    System.out.println(e.getMessage());
  }
}

public void ShowChartData(String Data1, String Data2) {
try {
                bar = new NFBarchartApp(this);
                  // Instantiate the bar chart class.

                bar.init();
                bar.start();
                  // Initialize it, and start it running.

                  // Below is where we load the parameters for the
                  // chart. See the documentation at the NetCharts
                  // Web site, or on the CD-ROM enclosed with
                  // this book for details.
                bar.loadParams(
                       "Header      = ('Salary Information');"+
                       "DataSets    = ('Salary', red);"+
                       "DataSet1    = "+ Data1 + ";"+
                       "BarLabels   = "+ Data2 + ";"+
                       "GraphLayout= HORIZONTAL;"+
                       "BottomAxis = (black, 'TimesRoman', 14, 0,
                         0,100000)"
                       );

                bar.loadParams ("Update");
                  // Tell the bar chart class we've put
                  // some new parameters in.
```

```
        } catch (Exception e) {
                System.out.println (e.getMessage());
        }

} // More to come following some comments.
```

The bar chart class from the NetCharts package uses a method to load the values for the chart. We have to define the labels and corresponding values, but this is generally straightforward. Because we have delimited our data with commas, we don't have to parse the data again to prepare it for use. In the next example (the pie chart example), we do have to parse it to put it in the proper format for the charting class to recognize the data. Listing 13.4 picks up the code where we left off in Listing 13.3.

LISTING 13.4   DYNAMICALLY GENERATING A BAR CHART FROM A DATABASE QUERY—PART II.

```
public String[] getData( String QueryLine ) {

  int columns, pos;
  String column[]=new String[4];
  boolean more;

  try {

        Statement stmt = con.createStatement();
        ResultSet rs = stmt.executeQuery(QueryLine);
        columns=(rs.getMetaData()).getColumnCount();

        column = new String[columns];

        // Initialize the columns to be blank.
        for(pos=1; pos<=columns; pos++) {
          column[pos-1]="";
        }

        more=rs.next();

        while(more) {

            for (pos=1; pos<=columns; pos++) {
            column[pos-1]+=(rs.getString(pos));
            }
```

```
        more=rs.next();
        for (pos=1; pos<=columns; pos++) {
          if(more) {
            column[pos-1]+=(",");
          }
        }
      }
    }
    stmt.close();

  }
  catch( Exception e ) {
    e.printStackTrace();
    System.out.println(e.getMessage());
  }

return column;
}
```

That's it! We've successfully queried a database, formatted the resulting data, and created a bar chart to visually represent the results. Listing 13.5 shows the generation of a pie chart, and Figure 13.2 shows the pie chart applet.

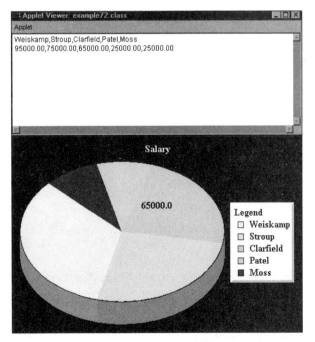

Figure 13.2
Screen shot of second example applet.

LISTING 13.5 DYNAMICALLY GENERATING A PIE CHART FROM A DATABASE QUERY.

```java
/*
Example 13-2: Pie chart
*/
import java.awt.*;
import java.applet.Applet;
import java.sql.*;
import java.util.StringTokenizer;

public class example132 extends java.applet.Applet {
  String url;
  String Name;
  Connection con;
  TextArea OutputField = new TextArea(10,35);
  NFPiechartApp pie;

public void init() {
  setLayout(new BorderLayout());
  url="jdbc:mysql://president/company";
  pie = new NFPiechartApp(this);

  ConnectToDB();

  add("North", OutputField);
  String columnData[] = getData("select last_name,
                                 salary from company");

  ShowFormattedData(columnData);
  ShowChartData(columnData[1],columnData[0]);
  add("Center", pie);

}


public void ConnectToDB() {


  try {
    Class.forName("gwe.sql.gweMysqlDriver");
    con = DriverManager.getConnection(url, "test", "test");
  }
  catch( Exception e ) {
    e.printStackTrace();
    System.out.println(e.getMessage());
  }


}
```

```java
public void ShowFormattedData(String[] columnD ) {

int i;

for ( i=0; i< columnD.length; i++) {
  OutputField.append(columnD[i]+"\n");
  }


}

public void ShowChartData(String dataNumber, String dataLabel) {

StringTokenizer nData, lData;
String SliceData = "";
ColorGenerator colorGen = new ColorGenerator();
// We need to assign colors to the pie slices automatically,
// so we use a class that cycles through colors. See this
// class defined below.

nData = new StringTokenizer(dataNumber, ",");
lData = new StringTokenizer(dataLabel, ",");
// We used our preformatted column data, and need to break it
// down to the elements. We use the StringTokenizer to break down
// the column string data individually by commas we inserted
// when we created the data.

// We assume that dataNumber and dataLabel have the same number of
// elements, as we just generated them from the getData method.

while(nData.hasMoreTokens()) {
// Loop through the dataNumber and dataLabel and build the slice
// data ( 1234, darkBlue, "Label" ). This is what the pie chart
// class expects, so we must parse our data and put it in this format.

SliceData += "("+nData.nextToken() + ", "
              + colorGen.next() + ", '"
              + lData.nextToken() + "')";

System.out.println(SliceData);
if (nData.hasMoreTokens()) {SliceData += ", ";}
}

try {

                // We already instantiated the pie chart
                // class(NFPieChartAPP) at the top of the applet.
```

```
                    pie.init();
                    pie.start();
                      // Initialize and start the pie chart class.

                    pie.loadParams(
                    "Background=(black, RAISED, 4);"+
                    "Header=('Cost Information (millions)');"+
                    "LabelPos=0.7;"+
                    "DwellLabel      = ('', black, 'TimesRoman', 16);"+
                    "Legend          = ('Legend', black);"+
                    "LegendBox       = (white, RAISED, 4);"+
                    "Slices="+SliceData);


                      // Above, we set the parameters for the pie chart,
                      // including the data and labels that we
                      // generated in the loop above ( SliceData ), and
                      // the Legend label position, header, and other
                      // properties. Again, have a look at the NetCharts
                      // documentation for all of the possible
                      // parameters.

                    pie.loadParams ("Update");
                      // Tell the pie chart class we've sent it new
                      // parameters to display.
            } catch (Exception e) {
                    System.out.println (e.getMessage());
            }
}


// Below is the same as before except for the new ColorGenerator
// class, which we needed to produce distinct colors.

public String[] getData( String QueryLine ) {

  int columns, pos;
  String column[]=new String[4];
  boolean more;

  try {

        Statement stmt = con.createStatement();
        ResultSet rs = stmt.executeQuery(QueryLine);
        columns=(rs.getMetaData()).getColumnCount();

        column = new String[columns];
```

```
      // Initialize the columns to be blank.
      for(pos=1; pos<=columns; pos++) {
        column[pos-1]="";
      }

      more=rs.next();

      while(more) {for (pos=1; pos<=columns; pos++) {
          column[pos-1]+=(rs.getString(pos));
        }

        more=rs.next();
        for (pos=1; pos<=columns; pos++) {
          if(more) {
            column[pos-1]+=(",");
          }
        }
      }
      stmt.close();
      // con.close();
    }
    catch( Exception e ) {
      e.printStackTrace();
      System.out.println(e.getMessage());
    }

return column;
}

public void destroy() {

  try {con.close();}
  catch( Exception e ) {
      e.printStackTrace();
      System.out.println(e.getMessage());
    }
}


}

class ColorGenerator {
// This class is needed to produce colors that the pie chart can
// use to color the slices properly. They are taken from the
// NetCharts color class, NFColor.
public ColorGenerator() {

}
```

```
int color_count = -1;
// Keep a running count of the colors we have used. We'll
// simply index the colors in a String array, and call up the
// incremented counter to get a new color. If you need more
// colors than those added below, you can add more by pulling
// them from the NFColor class found in the NetCharts package
// on the CD-ROM enclosed with this book, or the book's Web site.

String colors[] =
{"aliceblue","antiquewhite","aqua","aquamarine","azure","beige",
"bisque","black","blanchedalmond","blue","blue-violet","brown",
"chocolate","cadetblue","chartreuse","cornsilk","crimson","cyan"};


public String next() {

// Increment the color counter, and return a String that
// contains the color at this index.
  color_count += 1;
  return colors[color_count];

}

} // end example132.java
```

Coming Up Next

This chapter has shown you how to generate meaningful charts to represent data obtained from a query. We've seen how to create both bar and pie charts. You can use the properties of the NetCharts package to customize your charts as you wish. There are many more options in the package that you haven't seen in these examples.

In the next chapter, we will explore the world of servlets in the context of JDBC. We'll create a complete application using the Java Web server and its servlet API. The next chapter is a significantly different chapter in that it covers server-side programming. So far, we've been using the JDBC in a strict client-server sense—our JDBC applet runs on the user's machine. In the next chapter, we use JDBC on the server to generate HTML Web pages based on data in a database.

14

SERVER-SIDE DATABASES: SERVLETS AND JDBC

This chapter explores the world of server-side programming according to Java. If you're familiar with Common Gateway Interface (CGI) programming, you're in for a treat. Servlet programming is a far better way to generate Web pages dynamically. In this chapter, we'll look at how to use the Servlet API to generate Web pages using the Java Web Server's Servlet API—but with a special data-driven twist.

There are several reasons for using servlets instead of CGI. Speed, resource efficiency, and scalability are some of the issues we'll discuss. We'll begin with a crash course in servlet programming and will introduce the Servlet API that Javasoft developed. Then we'll move swiftly into an example servlet that hits a database to add and display information.

Servlet Architecture

First, let's look at the overall structure of servlets and the Java Web Server. If you're already familiar with this family of servers,

237

feel free to skip to the *JDBC And Servlets* section. The Java Web Server is built on the Javasoft's generic Server architecture. Hence, it is just a specialized servlet for the generic Server class.

Get The Java Web Server

You can get the Java Web Server from http://jeeves.javasoft.com. If you're not interested in running the Java Web Server, get the Java Servlet Development Kit—it allows you to write Java servlets that will work with your existing Web server. Be sure to read the installation instructions and set up your system properly to save yourself some trouble.

Other Java-based Web servers also support the Servlet API. One of them is Jigsaw, a free Web server from the W3 Consortium. You can download Jigsaw from its home page at http://www.w3.org/pub/WWW/Jigsaw.

The Java Web Server

The Java Web Server is an easily extensible software package that Javasoft offers. Let's look at a few reasons why the Java Web Server is a nice way of crafting a server. Remember that the Java Web Server runs as a Java application—hence you gain all of the advantages of Java, as well as the bad stuff. Speed is the major issue when running a server, and Java programs to date aren't nearly as speedy as their compiled C++ counterparts. Many software vendors are working on faster implementations of the Java Virtual Machine, or interpreter, so it may just be a matter of time before your Java applets and applications are within the speed range of compiled programs.

Extensible Servlets

The servlet architecture of the Java Web Server is very clean and logical. Let's have a look at how things are done. Figure 14.1 shows the overall flow of a request. We'll talk about the Javasoft Java Web Server in the context of an HTTP server, even though it can be crafted to be other types of servers.

There's an acceptor thread whose job it is to listen for requests on the configured port. This piece listens for a connection and grabs the incoming request. The acceptor also starts handler threads for processing requests. It manages the

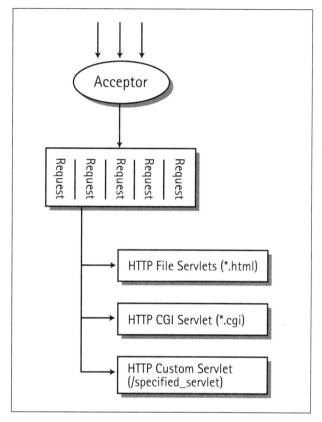

Figure 14.1
The architecture of the Java Web Server.

number of handlers running, starting up the number specified in the configuration. It will also start a new handler thread if one isn't available, in case multiple requests come in at once. You can also configure the maximum number of available handlers so that the machine the server is running on does not crash due to rapidly spawning handlers, or to maintain an acceptable level of performance on currently loaded handler threads.

The acceptor thread piles the requests on the handler queue. The HTTP server handler thread reads the request information and the connection from the queue. It then uses the configuration to map a request to a specific servlet. There are a number of servlets that are started automatically; the FileServlet and the CGIServlet are two of them. The FileServlet does exactly what you expect—it services requests for HTML files. The CGIServlet is used to activate CGI scripts and provide the necessary CGI interface. The CGIServlet is useful if you have existing CGI scripts that you may not wish to convert to Java servlets immediately.

Thread-Based Forking

Again, the HTTP server handler thread pops requests and items from the queue and determines which servlet can handle the request. This action of determining which servlet can handle the request is configured beforehand, as the HTTP handler can only service requests that it recognizes. The FileServlet and CGIServlet are configured to process their respective types of requests by default. You could write a servlet that is supposed to handle requests for URLs ending in *.DBX, for example. You would then need to enter into the Java Web Server's configuration and let the server know to start a specific servlet for these types of requests.

When the HTTP handler thread has determined which servlet will process the request, it calls the servlet's service method. This is an important efficiency advantage, as the only necessary function that needs to be performed to fulfill the request is a method call. Every servlet must implement this method, sensibly named *service*.

Additionally, each servlet runs in its own thread. When the number of currently available servlet threads for a specific request type is not enough, another *thread* of the same servlet is spawned. Hence, you avoid the overhead of forking another entire *process*.

Calling Your Own Servlets

A servlet can be configured for a specific file type, like *.HTML, which is what the FileServlet is dedicated to handle. You can also reference a servlet by pointing to the URL of the InvokerServlet. The HTTP server handler thread calls the InvokerServlet whenever a URL that includes /servlet/ is requested. The format for calling a specific servlet via the InvokerServlet is as follows:

```
http://your.webserver.com/servlet/your_servlet?request_arguments
```

Of course, your_servlet is the servlet you have created, and request_arguments are the parameters you plan on receiving. The InvokerServlet is a manager servlet;

it loads and calls the appropriate servlet when necessary. The HTTP server handler thread passes the connection and the request to the InvokerServlet, which in turn passes it to the proper servlet that falls under its command.

It's also possible to call a servlet that lives on a different machine. The servlet would be loaded across the network from another server and run as an untrusted servlet on the local server machine. Using this ability to call servlets across the network and HTTP redirects, it would be possible to perform smart load balancing.

Exploring The Servlet API

Now that you have been exposed to the overall architecture of servlets, let's take a look at some of the handy classes in the Servlet API. In the next section, we'll step through a complete example of a servlet that uses JDBC to hit a database to build HTML documents. Here we use a simple example to demonstrate the creation of an HTTP-specific servlet. You can find the API reference for servlets at **http://jeeves.javasoft.com**. Listing 14.1 shows our simple servlet. It prints out a friendly message and returns some data about the client.

LISTING 14.1   THE WELCOME SERVLET.

```
import java.servlet.http.*;
import java.servlet.*;
import java.io.*;

public class Welcome extends HttpServlet {
  public void service(HttpServletRequest req,
                      HttpServletResponse res)
    throws ServletException, IOException
  {
    res.setContentType("text/html");
    PrintWriter out = new PrintWriter(res.getOutputStream());
    // we'll use PrintWriter to send data back to the client.
    out.println("<html>");
    out.println("<head><title>Welcome to your first Servlet!
                </title></head>");
    out.println("<body>");
    out.println("<h1>Hi, here is who you are:</h1>");
    out.println("Your IP address:" + req.getRemoteAddr());
    out.println("Your hostname:  " + req.getRemoteHost());
    out.println("</body></html>");
    out.flush();
```

```
    //just print the information you want to send back,
    //and flush the stream.
  }

  public String getServletInfo() {
  //this is another method that needs to be overridden.
  //it simply returns information about the servlet.
    return "Example HttpServlet";
  }
}
```

First, be sure that the Java Web Server classes are in your CLASSPATH. This simple servlet extends the **HttpServlet** class, which is a subclass of the **GenericServlet** class. It is specialized in that it parses the HTTP header and packages client information into the **HttpServletRequest class**. The instance of this class above is req. We call several methods from the **ServletRequest** class—namely **getRemoteAddr** and **getRemoteHost**. Table 14.1 shows the methods for this **HttpServletRequest**. This class inherits from the **SerlvetRequest** class. Table 14.2 shows methods in this class.

No Need To Type The Code Examples

Remember that you can grab the code files from the CD-ROM enclosed with this book or this book's Web site: **http://www .coriolis.com/jdbc-book**.

There are more methods not listed in Table 14.1. See the API documentation for a complete listing. Below are some handy methods in the **ServletRequest** class, the superclass of **HttpServletRequest**, from which we pulled the client address and host name in the example servlet above.

TABLE **14.1**

USEFUL HTTPSERVLETREQUEST CLASS METHODS.

Method	Description
GetMethod()	Gives the method that was used to make the request.
GetQueryString()	Returns the query string if one exists for the request.
GetRemoteUser()	Returns the name of the user if known.
GetHeaderNames()	Returns an enumeration of the header names for the request.
GetHeader(string)	Returns the value of the specified header name.

TABLE 14.2

USEFUL SERVLETREQUEST CLASS METHODS.

Method	Description
GetParameterName()	Returns the parameters of this request as an enumeration.
GetParameter(String)	Returns the value of the specified parameter.
GetRemoteAddr()	Returns the client IP address.
GetRemoteHost()	Returns the client host name.
GetContentType()	Returns the client's supported MIME types.
GetInputStream()	Returns the input stream for the request. Useful if you wish to parse the request data yourself using a non-HTTP-specific method.

We also used the **HttpServletResponse** class, which inherits from the generic **ServletResponse** class. We used the **getOutputStream** method to get the stream handler for sending data to the client. We then assigned the stream to a **PrintWriter** class, which is what we used to pass the HTML text to the stream. Table 14.3 shows methods in the **HttpServletResponse** class, and Table 14.4 shows some methods in the **ServletResponse** class including the **getOutput Stream** method we used in our example servlet.

TABLE 14.3

USEFUL METHODS IN THE HTTPSERVLETRESPONSE CLASS.

Method	Description
SendError(int)	Reply with the specified integer response code.
SendError(int, String)	Reply with the specified integer response code and message.
SendRedirect(String)	Redirect the client to the specified URL using the redirect response code.
SetStatus(int)	Set the response code.
SetStatus(int, String)	Set the response code and give the specified message.
SetHeader(String, String)	Set the value for a header field.
SetIntHeader(String, int)	Set the value for the specified integer field with the specified string.
SetDateHeader(String, long)	Set the value for a specified date header field.

	TABLE 14.4

USEFUL METHODS IN THE SERVLETRESPONSE CLASS.

Method	Description
GetOutputStream()	Return the output stream for the client connection.
SetContentLength(int)	Set the content length for the response.
SetContentType(String)	Set the content type for the response.

So now you've seen how a basic servlet works. There are other methods that you need to implement for a more complex servlet, as we'll see in the next section. Though our example servlet was HTTP-specific, you could write a servlet that returns a binary type instead of an HTML page. For example, you could set the content type to "image/gif" and use the OutputStream handler to write a GIF that you construct on the fly to the Web browser client. This could be a way to pass images that you are storing in your database server to the Web browser. Let's begin building our data-aware servlet now.

JDBC And Servlets

The architecture of servlets makes writing data-driven server-side applications very simple and robust. A major advantage of using a servlet is that you can easily program into the servlet state information between client requests. This way, you can keep track of what the user has done in previous requests and implement functions like "rollback" or "cancel transaction" (assuming that your database server supports them). Also, each instance of a specific servlet runs within a Java thread, so you can control interactions between multiple instances. By using the **synchronized** identifier, you can tell servlets of the same type to wait for some transaction to occur before proceeding to fill a request. This can be especially useful if you have many people attempting to update the same database data at once, or if you have people trying to retrieve records from a database while they are being updated.

The News Wire Project

You've been tasked with developing a Web service that functions somewhat like a news wire. There are a number of people with authorization who can post news items to this wire, and another group of people can just read the news wire to see the latest news stories. Of course, everything has to be sorted by date and time, and possibly by category like sports, world events, local news, and so on.

You're a smart person, so you realize that storing this information in a database is the right thing to do. You could write a quick servlet that just piles this information into data files and holds submitted information, but managing these documents would become cumbersome, and searching and retrieving them would be slow, so a database is definitely the answer.

You want to store the passwords for accessing the news wire in the database rather than in the Web server configuration. You want to do this for two reasons: a large number of people plan to use this service, and you want to be able to associate a posting to the news wire to an individual. This will help you manage the large number of users (you plan on writing a JDBC applet that will aid in quickly adding and removing users and assigning privileges) and also track who has been posting to the news wire.

MYSQL: A SMALL AND FAST DATABASE SERVER FOR UNIX

Many of the sample JDBC programs we develop in this book use the MySQL database server. It's available for download at **http://www.tcx.se**. There are also links to the JDBC type four driver for MySQL at the above URL. MySQL runs under Linux, Solaris, and other popular Unix operating systems, and it's available for free download.

Database Tables

Figure 14.2 shows a diagram of the database. We also list the SQL statements for creating the tables below. You can create your own database on your server, or pick up the Access database file from this book's home page. If you plan on using the Access database, be sure to properly configure the ODBC alias in the ODBC manager under Windows. We developed this application using MySQL and its JDBC driver. If you're planning on using the provided Access database, recognize that you'll need to use the JDBC-ODBC bridge. If you plan on implementing this using another database engine, be sure that the JDBC drivers for it are available. You'll need to make changes to a few lines in the code. Don't worry, we'll point these out to you.

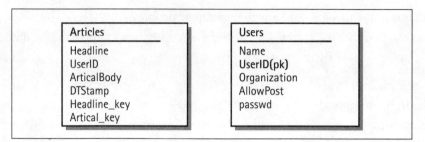

Figure 14.2
The database.

LISTING 14.2   THE SQL STATEMENTS FOR CREATING THE TABLES.

```
CREATE TABLE articles (
  headline varchar(255) NOT NULL,
  userID varchar(16) NOT NULL,
  articleBody blob,
  dTStamp timestamp(8) NOT NULL,
  KEY headline_key (headline(50),dTStamp),
  KEY article_key (userID)
);
CREATE TABLE users (
  userID varchar(16) NOT NULL,
  name varchar(60) NOT NULL,
  organization varchar(60) NOT NULL,
  allowPost char(1) NOT NULL DEFAULT 'N',
  passwd varchar(8) NOT NULL,
  PRIMARY KEY (userID)
);
```

As you can see, there are only two tables. If you were to implement categories, you'd need to add another table, or add a field in the articles tables. The primary key in the user's table is userID, and there is a composite key for the articles table (userID, headline, and dTStamp). We use a BLOB type to store the actual body of the news item. We also place a time stamp on each entry, so we know when it was added. This time stamp is used in the servlet to pull a specific day's news items when necessary.

Again, we store a user's password in the database table Users. Along with this we have a user ID, name, organization, and whether he or she is allowed to post to the news wire. If a user is not allowed to post to the news wire, we only allow read-only access. Of course, if someone doesn't appear in the user's table, he or she will have no access to the system.

Getting Form Data From A Servlet

The first thing we need to tackle is how we will process our form data. The first form page we use for the main page is shown in Figure 14.3. It's a simple HTML form, with two buttons. You don't need to enter the user information if you want to post to the news wire. Another page is called, as you'll see, to process information for posting to the news wire.

LISTING 14.3   THE HTML FOR THE MAIN NEWSWIRE PAGE.

```
<HTML>
<HEAD>
  <TITLE>NewsWire Home</TITLE>
</HEAD>
<BODY>

<FORM ACTION="/NewsWire" ENCTYPE="ENCTYPE=x-www-form-encoded"
                                                METHOD="POST">

<H2><CENTER>MetaLab NewsWire</CENTER></H2>

<P><CENTER><B>this project currently under construction!<BR>
</B></CENTER></P>

<P>Enter Your UserID for the NewsWire system: <BR>
<INPUT NAME="name" TYPE="text" SIZE="16" MAXLENGTH="16"><BR>
Enter your PASSWORD: <BR>
<INPUT NAME="passwd" TYPE="password" SIZE="8" MAXLENGTH="8"></P>

<P><INPUT NAME="action" TYPE="submit" VALUE="Read NewsWire"></P>
<hr>
<P><INPUT NAME="action" TYPE="submit" VALUE="Post to NewsWire">
</FORM>
</BODY>
</HTML>
```

You'll need to remember the names of the input fields so you can call **getParameter** and pull out the completed information. Here's the code we use to get this data into the servlet:

```
String userid = req.getParameter("name");
String passwd = req.getParameter("passwd");
```

The parameters designated as "name" and "passwd" in the form are put into variables **userID** and **passwd** in our Java servlet. We use these variables to authorize the user against the database. There will be more on this in the next section.

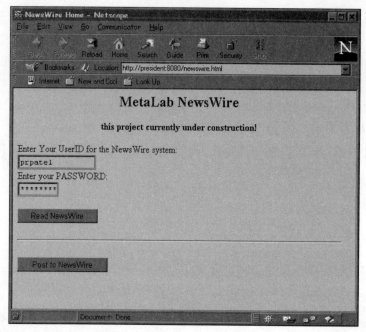

Figure 14.3
The NewsWire HTML form page.

We also need a page specifically for posting to the news wire. The HTML for
the page is shown in Listing 14.4. This page is shown in Figure 14.4, to give you
an idea of what it looks like.

LISTING 14.4   HTML FORM PAGE FOR POSTING DATA.

```
<HTML>
<HEAD>
  <TITLE>Post to NewsWire</TITLE>
</HEAD>
<BODY>

<FORM  ACTION="/NewsWire" ENCTYPE="ENCTYPE=x-www-form-encoded"
                                                METHOD="POST">
<H2>Post to NewsWire</H2>

<P><I>You don't need to enter your name and organization
in either of the inputs below.<BR>
They will automatically be added based on your login info!</I></P>
<P>Enter Your UserID for the NewsWire system: <BR>
<INPUT NAME="name" TYPE="text" SIZE="16" MAXLENGTH="16"><BR>
```

```
Enter your PASSWORD: <BR>
<INPUT NAME="passwd" TYPE="password" SIZE="8" MAXLENGTH="8"></P>
<H3>Article HeadLine:</H3>
<P><INPUT NAME="headline" TYPE="text" SIZE="25" MAXLENGTH="50"></P>
<H3>Article Body</H3>
<P><TEXTAREA NAME="body" ROWS="10" COLS="50"></TEXTAREA></P>
<P><INPUT NAME="action" TYPE="submit" VALUE="Ready to Post"></FORM>
</BODY>
</HTML>
```

As you can see, there are a few more fields here: the headline and body field for the user to enter the news item. Let's move on and look at some more of the servlet's elements before we list the entire code.

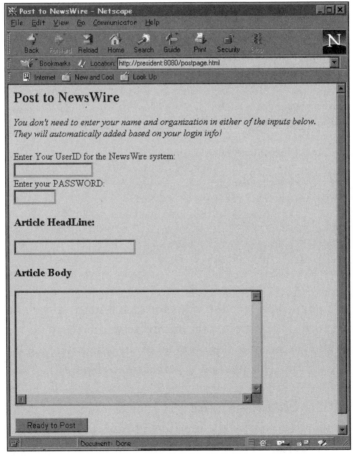

Figure 14.4
The HTML page for posting to the news wire.

Handy Methods

One thing we want to do is let the Web browser know that the request has been properly received. We use this code to let it know that everything is working properly:

```
res.setStatus(res.SC_OK);
```

We also want to set the content type to be HTML because we plan on sending this back to the Web browser:

```
res.setContentType("text/html");
```

But what about those buttons we had on the first page? How do we know which button the user clicked? Simple. We just do a **getParameter** on the button name (action), look at the values for the button that we assigned in the HTML in Listing 14.4, and process which button was clicked based on the values ("Read NewsWire" or "Post to NewsWire"):

```
String action = req.getParameter("action");
  authorization = authorize(req);

  if(action.equals("Read NewsWire")
                        && !authorization.equals("NOACCESS")) {
    readWire(req, res, dateReq);
  } else if(action.equals("Ready to Post")
                        && authorization.equals("POST") ){
    postWire(req, res);
  } else if(action.equals("Post to NewsWire")) {
    res.sendRedirect("/postpage.html");
  }
```

We specified in our form page the value for each button, so we know what to look for and process. We'll discuss the **authorize(req)** method next. Remember that you can also get an enumeration of all of the parameters the Web browser passes in from a form. This method is **getParameterNames()**.

Authorization From A Form

Now that we know how to get the userID and password from a form, how do we check this data against what's in the database? We use a query to see if the user exists in the user's table. By constructing our query carefully, we can also check the plain text password. The query looks for the userID *and* the password, so if the username is found, but the password doesn't match, the query returns nothing. The code for is shown in Listing 14.5.

LISTING 14.5   THE AUTHORIZATION ROUTINE.

```
public String authorize (HttpServletRequest req)throws
                         SQLException {
    Statement stmt = con.createStatement();
    String query;
    ResultSet rs;
    String validate="";
    String userid = req.getParameter("name");
    String passwd = req.getParameter("passwd");
 // get the data out of the form.
    String auth_result="";

    query="select allowPost from users where userID = '" + userid;
    query+="' AND passwd ='"+passwd+"'";
     // look for the userID and password in the same record!
    rs=stmt.executeQuery(query);
    //run the query
    while(rs.next()) {
      validate=rs.getString(1);
      }
    rs.close();
    stmt.close();
    if (validate.equals("")) {
    auth_result="NOACCESS";
    } else {
     // now check to see if the person can post to the list,
     // because he or she exists in the table
      if (validate.equals("N")) {
       auth_result="READ";
      }
      else if (validate.equals("Y")) {
      auth_result="POST";
      }
     }
    return auth_result;
  }
```

Creating A Connection

We need to create a connection so that these queries can take place. We use the **init()** method of the **HttpServlet** (actually, it's in the superclass **Servlet**) to instantiate the connection to the database server. We use the JDBC, of course, to interface with the database server. In the example we develop here, we use the JDBC driver for MySQL. This is a type four driver. Refer back to Chapter 6 for a detailed description of the different driver types. It's also possible to use any other type of driver because this servlet is running in the context of an application, so it's not bound by the sandbox security of an applet. As we discussed earlier, you could use the JDBC-ODBC bridge and an Access database if you don't have a real database server around. Here's the code for making the initial connection to the database:

```
DBurl="jdbc:mysql://president:3333/newswire";
    try {
        Class.forName("gwe.sql.gweMysqlDriver");
        con = DriverManager.getConnection(DBurl, username_poster,
                                                  passwd_poster);
        // continued.. see complete listing at the end of this chapter
```

If you're using the JDBC-ODBC bridge or other driver, you'll need to change the **Dburl** to have the proper JDBC URL. You'll also need to change the **Class.forName** method to call the driver you're using. Finally, you need to assign the proper values for accessing the database in the **username_poster** and **passwd_poster** variables.

There's more of this code necessary to connect, and it's mostly exception catching. Look at the complete code listing at the end of the chapter. There's one more thing to keep in mind: if your database server has a connection timeout setting, where the connection is dropped if there is no action for a set amount of time, you need to adjust your code to re-establish a connection. We'll discuss this more in the *TODO* section.

Reading From The Database

Now that we've created our connection, we want to make a query and read in some data. Listing 14.6 shows the core of the code for doing this. See the complete code listing (Listing 14.8) and look at the **readWire** method (shown in Listing 14.10) for the whole picture.

LISTING 14.6 READING THE DATA.

```
query="select articles.articleBody, articles.headline,
        articles.userid, users.organization, articles.dTStamp from
                articles, users where articles.userid=users.userid";
```

```
    rs = stmt.executeQuery(query);
   rsmd = rs.getMetaData();
 columns=rsmd.getColumnCount();

 PrintWriter out = new PrintWriter(res.getOutputStream());
 out.println("<html>");
   out.println("<head><title>Latest NewsWire</title></head>");
   out.println("<body>");

   while(rs.next()) {
   out.println("<h2>");
   out.println(rs.getString(1));
   out.println("</h2><p>");
   out.println("<i>Posted by: " + rs.getString(4) + "</i> ");

   //postDate = rs.getDate(5);
//out.println(" on " + date.format((java.util.Date)postDate));

   out.println("  on  " + rs.getString(5)+"<br>");
   out.println(rs.getString(2));
   out.println("<hr>");
 }
```

This code queries the database and pulls out all of the articles. We could easily modify the code and add a new field in the form to be able to pull news items sorted by date. We could also write another SQL query that allows users to search the news wire database for keywords, sort by who posted the item, and so on.

We call the **getString** method for each column in each row. This data is then formatted by row; each row is a news item. We can also enhance this by making hyperlinks to do canned searches or re-sorting. Figure 14.5 shows us some sample output.

Posting To The Database

Adding a new item is equally straightforward. Listing 14.7 shows the query and statements used to insert this data into the database. Because the authorization is done in another method, there are no other issues to consider.

LISTING 14.7   QUERYING THE DATABASE.

```
query="INSERT INTO articles VALUES ('";
query += req.getParameter("headline") + "','"+ userid +"','";
```

```
query += req.getParameter("body") + "', '')";
System.out.println(query);
  int result  = stmt.executeUpdate(query);

if (result == 0 ) {
  out.println("Your entry has been entered successfully.");
} else
  {
    out.println("There was a problem adding the entry to the database.
Please contact the administrator.");
  }
```

Look at the complete listing (in Listing 14.8) for the entire method named **postWire**, from which we took the above excerpt. There's more information we could add into the database if necessary, like a category. Be aware of characters in the submitted form data that are to be put into the database and need to be escaped; single or double quotation marks or extended characters may require you to pre-parse the data before INSERTing it into the database.

TODO

Before we show the complete code listing, let's talk about a few things to keep in mind and possible enhancements. One thing we discussed was that the

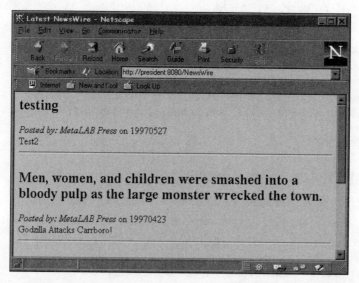

Figure 14.5
View the news wire.

connection between the servlet and the database server may be broken if a timeout occurs. We need to write some code to reside in the SQLException block that will attempt to re-establish the data connection if this happens.

We also might want to add categories to the database so posters to the news wire can select a category to post in. The news wire reader can then choose to only view news items in a category. This is also fairly straightforward. You'll need to change the queries to reflect that a new piece of information needs to be inserted into as well as extracted from the database. The complete code listing for the servlet is shown in Listing 14.8.

LISTING 14.8   COMPLETE NEWSWIRE SERVLET.

```
/*
NewsWire Servlet
This is a data-aware Java servlet that accesses an mysql
database. It uses the GWE JDBC driver to hit an mysql database.
 */

import java.io.*;
import java.net.*;
import java.sql.*;
import java.servlet.*;
import java.servlet.http.*;
import gwe.sql.*;

public class NewsWire extends HttpServlet {

    String DBurl="jdbc:mysql://president:3333/newswire";
    String username_reader="wireuser";
    String username_poster="wireposter";
    String passwd_reader="cancan";
    String passwd_poster="wrath";
    Connection con;
    DatabaseMetaData metaData;


    /**
     * Initializes the database
     */
    public void init(ServletConfig conf) throws ServletException {

      SQLWarning warn;
      Object timer = new Object();
```

```
     super.init(conf);

     DBurl="jdbc:mysql://president:3333/newswire";
     try {
       Class.forName("gwe.sql.gweMysqlDriver");

       con = DriverManager.getConnection(DBurl, username_poster,
                                                 passwd_poster);

           if ( (warn = con.getWarnings()) != null ) {
             while(warn != null) {
                 log("SQLWarning: " + warn.getSQLState() + '\t' +
                   warn.getMessage() + '\t' +
                   warn.getErrorCode() + '\t');
                 warn = warn.getNextWarning();
             }
           }

       } catch (ClassNotFoundException e) {
          throw new ServletException("init");
       } catch (SQLException e) {
          try {
            con = DriverManager.getConnection(DBurl,
                              username_reader, passwd_reader);

          } catch (SQLException ee) {
             ee.printStackTrace();
             while(e != null) {
               log("SQLException: " + e.getSQLState() + '\t' +
                 e.getMessage()  + '\t' +
                 e.getErrorCode());
               e = e.getNextException();
          }
          throw new ServletException("init");
          }
       }

     }


   public void service(HttpServletRequest req, HttpServletResponse res)
      throws ServletException, IOException
   {
     String action = req.getParameter("action");
     String dateReq="19970312";
     String authorization;
```

```java
    try {

      authorization = authorize(req);

      if(action.equals("Read NewsWire")
              && !authorization.equals("NOACCESS")) {
        readWire(req, res, dateReq);
      } else if(action.equals("Ready to Post")
                  && authorization.equals("POST") ){
        postWire(req, res);
      } else if(action.equals("Post to NewsWire")) {
        res.sendRedirect("/postpage.html");
      }
      else {
        PrintWriter out = new PrintWriter(res.getOutputStream());
        out.println("<html>");
        out.println("<head><title>No Access!</title></head>");
        out.println("<body>");
        out.println("There was an error:<br>");
      out.println("Your Login and Password are invalid or<br>");
        out.println("you do not have access to this function.");
        out.println("</body></html>");
        out.flush();
      }

    } catch (SQLException e) {
        while(e != null) {
        log("SQLException: " + e.getSQLState() + '\t' +
            e.getMessage() + '\t' +
            e.getErrorCode() + '\t');
        e = e.getNextException();
        }
      // insert connection re-establishing code here
      // call init() and re-call the service(req,res)
    }

}


/**
 * Cleans up database connection
 */
public void destroy() {
    try {
        con.close();
    } catch (SQLException e) {
        while(e != null) {
        log("SQLException: " + e.getSQLState() + '\t' +
```

```
                                e.getMessage() + '\t' +
                                e.getErrorCode() + '\t');
                        e = e.getNextException();
                        }
                } catch (Exception e) {
                    e.printStackTrace();
            }
        }


        /**
         * executes the given SQL query and returns the result
         */
        public void readWire(HttpServletRequest req,
                            HttpServletResponse res, String dateReq)
            throws IOException, SQLException {
            Statement stmt = con.createStatement();
            String query;
            ResultSet rs;
        ResultSetMetaData rsmd;
        int columns;
        String output;
        int pos;
        java.sql.Date postDate;

//java.text.DateFormat date=java.text.DateFormat.getDateInstance();

            res.setStatus(res.SC_OK);
            res.setContentType("text/html");


        query="select articles.articleBody, articles.headline,
            articles.userid, users.organization, articles.dTStamp from
            articles, users where articles.userid=users.userid";
            rs = stmt.executeQuery(query);
        rsmd = rs.getMetaData();
        columns=rsmd.getColumnCount();

        PrintWriter out = new PrintWriter(res.getOutputStream());
        out.println("<html>");
            out.println("<head><title>Latest NewsWire</title></head>");
            out.println("<body>");

        while(rs.next()) {
            out.println("<h2>");
            out.println(rs.getString(1));
            out.println("</h2><p>");
            out.println("<i>Posted by: " + rs.getString(4) + "</i> ");
```

```
        //postDate = rs.getDate(5);
        //out.println(" on " + date.format((java.util.Date)postDate));

        out.println("  on  " + rs.getString(5)+"<br>");
        out.println(rs.getString(2));
        out.println("<hr>");
    }

        out.println("</body></html>");
    out.flush();
    rs.close();
    stmt.close();
  }

public void postWire(HttpServletRequest req, HttpServletResponse res)
      throws IOException, SQLException {
      Statement stmt = con.createStatement();
      String query = "";
    String userid = req.getParameter("name");

    PrintWriter out = new PrintWriter(res.getOutputStream());
      res.setStatus(res.SC_OK);
      res.setContentType("text/html");
    out.println("<html>");
      out.println("<head><title>Posting to NewsWire</title></head>");
      out.println("<body>");

    query="INSERT INTO articles VALUES ('";
    query += req.getParameter("headline") + "','"+ userid +"','";
    query += req.getParameter("body") + "', '')";
    System.out.println(query);
      int result  = stmt.executeUpdate(query);

    if (result == 0 ) {
      out.println("Your entry has been entered successfully.");
    } else
      { out.println("There was a problem adding the entry to the
                    database. Please contact the administrator.");
      }

      out.println("</body></html>");
    out.flush();

    stmt.close();
  }
```

```java
public String getServletInfo() {
    return "The NewsWire servlet";
}

  public String authorize (HttpServletRequest req)
                                      throws SQLException {
    Statement stmt = con.createStatement();
    String query;
    ResultSet rs;
    String validate="";
    String userid = req.getParameter("name");
    String passwd = req.getParameter("passwd");
    String auth_result="";

    query="select allowPost from users where userID = '" + userid;
    query+="' AND passwd ='"+passwd+"'";
    //    System.out.println(query);
    rs=stmt.executeQuery(query);

    while(rs.next()) {
      validate=rs.getString(1);
      //    System.out.println(validate);
    }
    rs.close();
    stmt.close();
    if (validate.equals("")) {
    auth_result="NOACCESS";
    } else {
      if (validate.equals("N")) {
      auth_result="READ";
      }
      else if (validate.equals("Y")) {
      auth_result="POST";
      }
    }
    //    System.out.println(auth_result);
    return auth_result;
  }


}
```

Coming Up Next

In the next chapter, we begin our exploration of Java Beans, the component architecture specification based on Java. It's sure to be a big hit with developers like yourself because you will be able to use components seamlessly in your Java programs, and you will be able to craft your own beans for reuse. We'll take a look at the BDK—or Beans Developer Kit—and construct our own data-aware bean.

15

BUILDING DATA-AWARE COMPONENTS USING JAVA BEANS

One of the most powerful and exciting additions to the Java language is the Java Beans specification. In this chapter, we'll take a quick look at what Java Beans is all about and, in the process, develop some simple Java Beans of our own.

Java Beans: What's All The Hot Air About?

What is Java Beans and why is it so important? Let's take a look at how the Java Beans API specification defines Java Beans, "The goal of the Java Beans APIs is to define a software component model for Java, so that third party ISVs can create and ship Java components that can be composed together into applications by end users." This means that independent components (beans) can be developed by anyone, anywhere, and then dynamically assembled into useful applications. Each bean can be used and reused in any number of applications. So, turning to the Java

263

Beans specification again, "a Java Bean is a reusable software component that can be manipulated visually in a builder tool."

A builder tool is a software environment in which you can assemble Java Beans—for example, a visual application builder, a Web page builder, and document editors. What you find in these software environments is a palette of beans to choose from that can be visually manipulated on-screen to form some new functional application. The builder tool will be able to analyze how the bean works (introspection), customize the appearance, properties, and behavior of the bean (customization), save the customized bean for later use (persistence), and connect beans together via a standard communication process (events).

Hopefully, you are beginning to understand how important Java Beans is to the Java language. Coupled with Java's inherent platform independence, distribution, and security, Java Beans brings software reusability to a new level. We'll only just scratch the surface of Java Beans; entire books could (and will) be devoted to Java Beans alone.

The Beans Development Kit (BDK)

Before you get started writing Java Beans, you must first install the Beans Development Kit (BDK). But note that you only need the BDK if you are going to write beans. You will be able to assemble beans in builder tools (when they are available) and use beans in browsers (when they are enabled) without the need of the BDK. Also note that Java Beans is new with JDK 1.1. If your favorite builder or browser does not yet support JDK 1.1, it won't support Java Beans either.

You can get the BDK from the JavaSoft home page. The BDK provides:

- Support for the Java Beans APIs

- The BeanBox, which is a simple builder tool that allows you to test beans. The BeanBox is written completely in Java and the source code is included

- Sample beans with source code

Installing the BDK is very straightforward. Simply follow the installation instructions provided by JavaSoft and you should have no problems.

The BeanBox: A Test Drive

Because we'll be using the BeanBox as our builder tool to test all of our beans, let's give it a try. I'll assume that you installed the BDK in the bdk subdirectory off of the root (/bdk or \bdk, depending upon the operating system in use). For my convenience, I'll be using the forward-slash '/' to separate directories. If you are using an operating system that uses the back-slash '\', I'll leave it up to you to make this substitution. Note that the 'run' script sets the CLASSPATH for the BeanBox. You may need to add additional paths (like to a JDBC driver, for example). To start the BeanBox:

```
> cd /bdk/beanbox
```

For Win95/NT users:

```
> run
```

For Unix users:

```
> nmake run
```

The BeanBox will appear as shown in Figure 15.1. The BeanBox consists of three elements: the BeanBox, ToolBox, and PropertySheet.

The ToolBox contains a list of all of the beans known to the BeanBox (located in /bdk/jars of the Beans Developers Kit). The BeanBox is a free-form container that allows beans to be dropped in and manipulated. The BeanBox is also a bean, demonstrating that beans can contain nested beans. The PropertySheet shows all of the editable properties for the currently selected Bean. To get an idea of how easy it is to use beans, let's try out some of the sample beans provided with the BDK.

Juggling Beans

A good way to demonstrate the BeanBox is to use two sample beans included with the BDK: the Juggler bean and the ExplicitButton bean. The Juggler is a simple animation bean that can be started and stopped by connecting events to the Juggler's handler methods. The ExplicitButton is a simple GUI button bean that allows the button text to be changed. Each time the button is pressed, an event is fired.

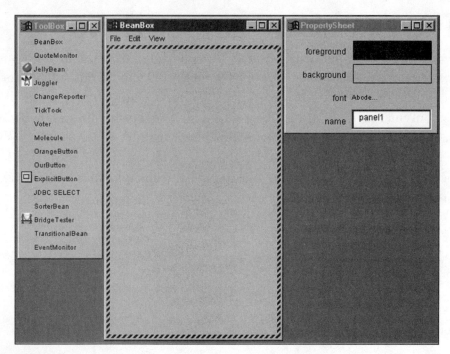

Figure 15.1
The BeanBox.

Before going much further, I think it would be helpful to graphically display the event capabilities of a bean. By this, I mean what events the bean can generate and what handler events are available. I am going to use an electronics analogy that has been used to describe other component architectures. Event handlers will be drawn as plug-in jacks that extend from the bean, as illustrated in Figure 15.2. Events will be drawn as plugs, as illustrated in Figure 15.3. Thus, figures drawn to represent a bean firing an event to another bean that exposes an event handler would include a plug fitting into a jack.

Now we can graphically illustrate the capabilities of the Juggler and ExplicitButton beans, as shown in Figure 15.4.

Now that the capabilities of both beans have been explored, let's use the BeanBox to connect them together. From the ToolBox, click on the ExplicitButton bean. Next, position your mouse pointer over the BeanBox and click at the position you would like to place an ExplicitButton. The ExplicitButton will then be instantiated inside the BeanBox, and the PropertySheet will show all of the

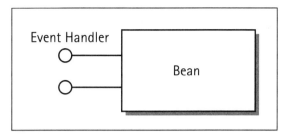

Figure 15.2
Event handlers are drawn as plug-in jacks extending from the bean.

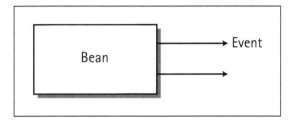

Figure 15.3
Events are drawn as outgoing arrows extending from the bean.

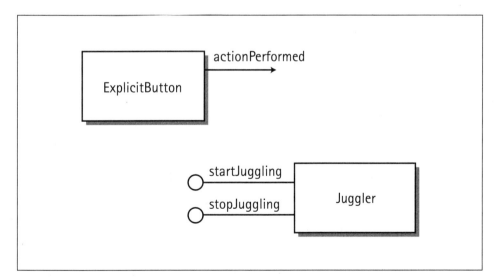

Figure 15.4
Juggler and ExplicitButton beans.

editable properties for the bean. One of the properties is the *label*. Go ahead and change it to Start. Perform the same steps with another ExplicitButton, changing the label to Stop. Now, click on the Juggler bean and place it in the BeanBox. Your BeanBox should look something like what is shown in Figure 15.5.

Now it's time to actually connect the beans together so the Start button will start the Juggler and the Stop button will stop it. Select the Start Explicit Button bean by clicking on it (a striped band should appear around the bean). Select the Edit|Events|button push|actionPerformed menu item (shown in Figure 15.6).

Once the actionPerformed menu item is selected, a rubber band will appear. One end of the band is anchored to the Start button and the other end is tied to the cursor. Place the cursor on top of the bean that will receive the **actionPerformed** event—in this case the Juggler bean—and click. The BeanBox will then display a list of all of the event handlers for the Juggler bean. Select the **startJuggling** method. The BeanBox will generate and compile an adapter class— code that will be executed when the actionPerformed event occurs. Go ahead and connect the Stop button **actionPerformed** event to the Juggler's **stopJuggling** event handler. Figure 15.7 shows the completed event diagram.

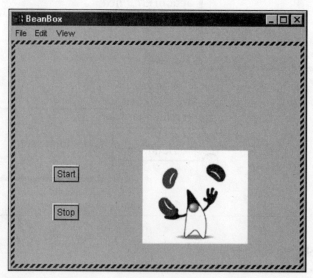

Figure 15.5
BeanBox with Juggler and two ExplicitButton beans.

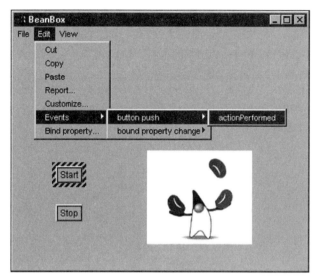

Figure 15.6
Selecting the actionPerformed event for the Start button.

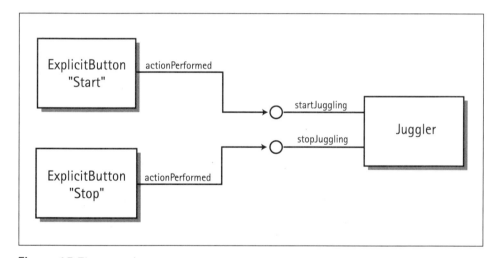

Figure 15.7
Completed event diagram for the Juggler example.

Now it's time to try it! Press the Stop button and the Juggler should stop. Pressing the Start button should start the Juggler again. Pretty easy, isn't it? That's the beauty of Java Beans. Someone has already written these components and you just need to put them together according to your particular need—without writing a single line of code.

Writing Your First Java Bean: The TrafficSignal

By now, I'm sure you are ready to start writing some Java Beans, so let's start by writing a very simple bean, which we'll call TrafficSignal. The TrafficSignal bean will have three event handlers, as shown in Figure 15.8.

The TrafficSignal bean will draw a traffic signal with a red, yellow, and green light. An event handler method will allow the state of the traffic signal to change. The complete code is shown in Listing 15.1. The complete source code can also be found on the CD-ROM enclosed with this book.

LISTING 15.1   TRAFFICSIGNAL.JAVA.

```java
package jdp.beans;

import java.awt.*;
import java.awt.event.*;
import java.beans.*;

public class TrafficSignal extends Canvas
{

    public TrafficSignal()
    {
        resize(width, height);
    }

    public void paint(Graphics g)
    {
        int x = spacing;
        int y = spacing;
        int wh = width - (spacing * 2);

        g.setColor(Color.orange);
        g.drawRect(0, 0, width - 1, height - 1);

        // Draw each light

        for (int i = 0; i < 3; i++) {

            switch(i) {
            case RED_LIGHT:
                g.setColor(Color.red);
                break;
```

```
            case YELLOW_LIGHT:
                g.setColor(Color.yellow);
                break;
            case GREEN_LIGHT:
                g.setColor(Color.green);
                break;
            }

            // If this is the light that is on, fill
            // it in

            if (i == lightOn) {
                g.fillArc(x, y, wh, wh, 0, 360);
            }
            else {
                g.drawArc(x, y, wh, wh, 0, 360);
            }
            y += (wh + spacing);
        }
}

// Event handling method to turn the light red

public void setRedLight(ActionEvent x)
{
    lightOn = RED_LIGHT;
    repaint();
}

// Event handling method to turn the light yellow

public void setYellowLight(ActionEvent x)
{
    lightOn = YELLOW_LIGHT;
    repaint();
}

// Event handling method to turn the light green

public void setGreenLight(ActionEvent x)
{
    lightOn = GREEN_LIGHT;
    repaint();
}


// Constants that describe the light that will be on
```

```
private final static int RED_LIGHT    = 0;
private final static int YELLOW_LIGHT = 1;
private final static int GREEN_LIGHT  = 2;

// Width and height of the traffic canvas.  The size of the canvas
// and lights can be controlled by changing the spacing (the space
// between the edge of the canvas and the light) and the total
// width of the canvas.

private int spacing = 5;
private int width   = 30;
private int height  = ((width - (spacing * 2)) * 3) +
                              (spacing * 4);

// Current light that is on

private int lightOn = GREEN_LIGHT;

}
```

In the TrafficSignal example, there is nothing in the code that distinguishes it as a JavaBean. It's a simple Java widget based on the **Canvas** object, and it has some public methods to change the state of the signal. How then, you might ask, do I turn this regular Java code into a bean? It's all in the packaging. Java Beans are packaged in a JAR file (Java ARchive). A JAR file is nothing more than a ZIP file that may optionally have a "table of contents" known as the manifest. The manifest describes the contents of the JAR file, informing you of

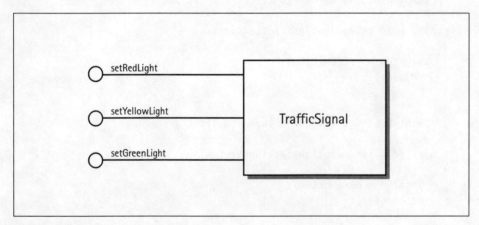

Figure 15.8
TrafficSignal event handlers.

which class files are beans. You don't necessarily have to include a manifest file in the JAR file because all class files in the JAR are considered to be beans. I personally prefer to always include a manifest file with each JAR since I don't want the tools using my JAR to have to make assumptions about the contents. You should also include any supporting files needed for your bean in the JAR file, including image and audio files.

Building The TrafficSignal JAR File

JavaSoft kindly included everything you need to build a JAR file in the Java Developer's Kit (JDK). The jar utility handles all of the JAR file maintenance and can create the manifest file for you as well. Listing 15.2 shows the jar utility arguments.

LISTING 15.2   JAR UTILITY ARGUMENTS.

```
Usage: jar {ctx}[vfmOM] [jar-file] [manifest-file] files ...
Options:
  -c  create new archive
  -t  list table of contents for archive
  -x  extract named (or all) files from archive
  -v  generate verbose output on standard error
  -f  specify archive file name
  -m  include manifest information from specified manifest file
  -0  store only; use no ZIP compression
  -M  Do not create a manifest file for the entries
```

If any file is a directory, then it is processed recursively.

Example: to archive two class files into an archive called classes.jar:

```
jar cvf classes.jar Foo.class Bar.class
```

Note: Use the '0' option to create a jar file that can be put in your CLASSPATH.

After compiling TrafficSignal.JAVA, you can create a JAR file using the following command:

```
jar cvfm TrafficSignal.jar manifest.txt jdp\beans\*.class
```

This will create a new JAR file named TrafficSignal.JAR, creating a manifest entry from the contents of manifest.TXT:

```
Name: jdp/beans/TrafficSignal.class
Java-Bean: True
```

It is extremely important to always include a blank line after each line containing 'Java-Bean: True', especially when placing multiple beans into one JAR file. While on the topic of important reminders, all Java Beans must also be part of a package (such as jdp.beans, as seen in our example).

Once you have created the JAR file, it must be copied to /bdk/jars, which is the JAR file repository for the BeanBox. After invoking the BeanBox, our TrafficSignal bean will be shown on the ToolBox, as shown in Figure 15.9.

Let's go ahead and try our bean out in the BeanBox. Instantiate three ExplicitButton beans (like you did in the Juggler example) and label them Stop, Caution, and Go. You also need to instantiate a TrafficSignal bean. Your BeanBox should look something like Figure 15.10.

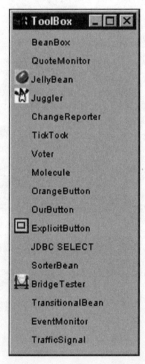

Figure 15.9
ToolBox with the TrafficSignal bean.

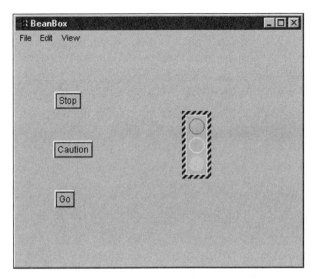

Figure 15.10
BeanBox with TrafficSignal.

Now, connect each actionPerformed event for the three ExplicitButton beans to the proper event handler in the TrafficSignal. Once complete, you will be able to press each button and have the TrafficSignal change to the corresponding signal state. Some of you may want to rename the Caution ExplicitButton to Speed Up.

The Java Beans Project: POSDatabase

We've seen how to take some simple Java code and "beanify" it, but now it's time to dive a little deeper. Let's see what it takes to generate events and tie some database activity (JDBC, of course) to some beans. It's really not that difficult. JavaSoft has worked hard to make the Java Beans specification fit seamlessly into the current Java specification.

The POSDatabase (Point Of Sale Database) project will consist of four beans:

- **POSDatabase.** This bean handles all of the database tasks using JDBC. It also displays status information about the current state of the system. Editable properties allow the JDBC driver and URL information to be specified.

- **POSSignOn.** This bean accepts a user name and password to sign on to the system. Once signed on, a SignOff button is enabled.

- **POSPriceInquiry.** This bean accepts an item code used to perform a data-base inquiry. Information about the item will be returned and displayed.

- **POSItemImage.** This bean displays an image of the price inquiry item.

Figures 15.11 through 15.14 show the events and event handlers for each of the **POSDatabase** beans.

Once the beans are connected together, the overall flow of the beans is quite simple (Figure 15.15). The user must first enter their user name and pass-word from the **POSSignOn** bean and press the Sign On button. This sends an event notification containing the user name and password to the **POSDatabase** bean, establishing a connection to the database specified in

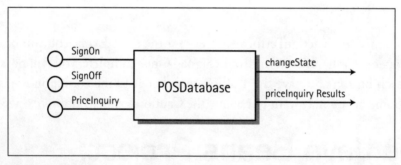

Figure 15.11
POSDatabase events and event handlers.

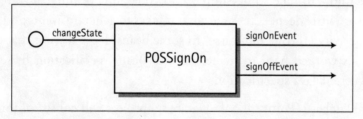

Figure 15.12
POSSignOn events and event handlers.

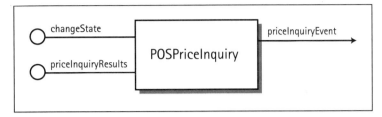

Figure 15.13
POSPriceInquiry events and event handlers.

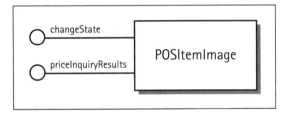

Figure 15.14
POSItemImage event handlers.

the **POSDatabase** property sheet. A successful sign on will result in a change of state (from signed off to signed on), and a change state event will be sent to all of the registered listeners—in our case, all of the other beans. This causes the **POSSignOn** bean to disable the Sign On button and enable the Sign Off button, and the **POSPriceInquiry** bean to enable the Price Inquiry button. The user can then enter an item code to query and press the Price Inquiry button. This will send a **priceInquiry** event to the **POSDatabase** bean, causing the database to be read for the item. If found, the **POSDatabase** bean sends a **priceInquiryResults** event to the event's *listeners:* the **POSPriceInquiry** and **POSItemImage** beans. The beans can then display the necessary information about the item. If the user presses the Sign Off button from the **POSSignOn** bean, the database connection will be closed, a state change event will be sent, and the system will be reset back to its original state. As you can see, there's a lot of interaction between these beans, but it is no more difficult to implement than our original TrafficSignal example. As always, the complete source code is on the CD along with the manifest file used to create the JAR.

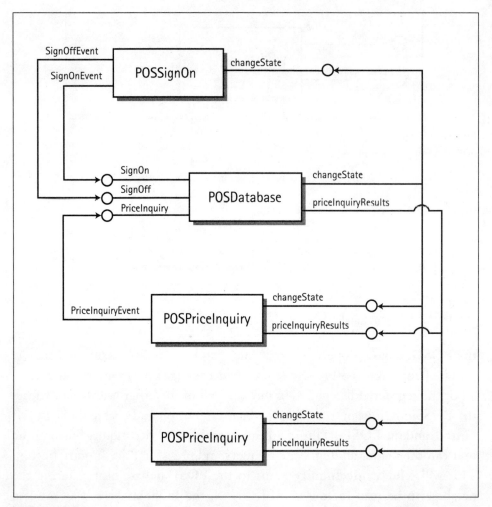

Figure 15.15
POSDatabase events and event handler connections.

Building The Database

The **POSDatabase** bean will utilize a single database table: ITEM. The ITEM table contains information about the store items that can be inquired. Table 15.1 delineates the ITEM table's underlying data structure.

Listing 15.3 shows the BuildItemFile.JAVA source code that can be used to build the ITEM file. It's a simple JDBC application that uses the SimpleText JDBC driver (covered in great detail in Chapter 7) to create the ITEM table and add rows with sample data. As always, the complete source code is included on the CD.

		TABLE 15.1

THE ITEM TABLE.

Column Name	SQL Type	Description
SKU	INTEGER	Item code or SKU (Stock Keeping Unit)
DESCRIPTION	VARCHAR	Description of the item
IMAGE	VARBINARY	Binary image of the item
PRICE	VARCHAR	Suggested retail price of the item

LISTING 15.3   BUILDING THE ITEM TABLE.

```java
import java.sql.*;
import java.io.*;

class BuildItemFile {

    //- - - -
    // main
    //- - - -
    public static void main(String args[]) {
        try {

            // Create an instance of the driver

            java.sql.Driver d = (java.sql.Driver) Class.forName (
                    "jdbc.SimpleText.SimpleTextDriver").newInstance();

            // Properties for the driver

            java.util.Properties prop = new java.util.Properties();

            // URL to use to connect

            String url = "jdbc:SimpleText";

            // The only property supported by the SimpleText driver
            // is 'Directory'.

            prop.put("Directory", "/jdp/beans/data");


            // Connect to the SimpleText driver

            Connection con = DriverManager.getConnection(url, prop);
```

```
        String tableName = "Item";

        if (exists(con, tableName)) {
            dropTable(con, tableName);
        }

        // Create the item file

        buildItemFile(con, tableName);


        // Close the connection

        con.close();

    }
    catch (SQLException ex) {
        System.out.println("\n*** SQLException caught ***\n");
        while (ex != null) {
            System.out.println("SQLState: " + ex.getSQLState());
            System.out.println("Message:  " + ex.getMessage());
            System.out.println("Vendor:   " + ex.getErrorCode());
            ex = ex.getNextException ();
        }
        System.out.println("");
    }
    catch (java.lang.Exception ex) {
        ex.printStackTrace ();
    }
}


//- - - - - - - - - - - - - - - - - - - - - - - - - - - - - - - - -
// exists
// Given a connection object and a table name, check to see if the
// table exists.  If it does, return true.
//- - - - - - - - - - - - - - - - - - - - - - - - - - - - - - - - -

protected static boolean exists(
    Connection con,
    String table)
    throws SQLException
{
    boolean rc = false;

    // Get the DatabaseMetaData object for the connection
```

```java
    DatabaseMetaData db = con.getMetaData();

    // Check if the table exists

    ResultSet rs = db.getTables(null, null, table, null);

    // If there is a row in the ResultSet, then the table must
    // exist

    if (rs.next()) {
        rc = true;
    }

    rs.close();

    return rc;
}

//- - - - - - - - - - - - - - - - - - - - - - - - - - - - - - - -
// dropTable
// Given a connection object and a table name, drops the given table
//- - - - - - - - - - - - - - - - - - - - - - - - - - - - - - - -

protected static void dropTable(
    Connection con,
    String table)
    throws SQLException
{
    Statement stmt = con.createStatement();

    System.out.println("Dropping table: " + table);

    stmt.execute("drop table " + table);
    stmt.close();
}

//- - - - - - - - - - - - - - - - - - - - - - - - - - - - - - - -
// buildItemFile
// Given a connection object and a table name, create the PriceInquiry
// 'item' database table
//- - - - - - - - - - - - - - - - - - - - - - - - - - - - - - - -

protected static void buildItemFile(
    Connection con,
    String table)
    throws SQLException
{
```

```java
System.out.println("Creating table: " + table);

Statement stmt = con.createStatement();

// Create the SQL statement


String sql = "create table " + table + "(" +
                "SKU NUMBER, " +
                "DESCRIPTION VARCHAR, " +
                "IMAGE BINARY, " +
                "PRICE VARCHAR" +
                ")";

// Create the table

stmt.executeUpdate(sql);
stmt.close();

// Create some data using a prepared statement

sql = "insert into " + table + " values(?,?,?,?)";


FileInputStream file;

PreparedStatement ps = con.prepareStatement(sql);


int sku = 1;

// Add the item records

addItemRecord(ps, sku++,
                "Java Database Programming with JDBC",
                "images/JavaDB_w_JDBC.gif", "39.99");
addItemRecord(ps, sku++,
                "Castanet & Bongo Programming",
                "images/Castanet&Bongo_FR.gif", "25.97");
addItemRecord(ps, sku++,
                "Developing ActiveX Controls with
                  Visual Basic 5",
                "images/DevActiveXCtrls_VB5.gif", "29.98");
addItemRecord(ps, sku++,
                "Digital Camera Companion",
                "images/DigCamCvr.gif", "24.50");
```

```
        addItemRecord(ps, sku++,
                        "High Performance ISAPI/NSAPI Web Programming",
                        "images/HP_ISAPI_rgb.gif", "32.25");
        addItemRecord(ps, sku++,
                        "Internet Protocols Handbook",
                        "images/Internet_ProtoHndbk.gif", "19.98");
        addItemRecord(ps, sku++,
                        "Java Programming EXplorer",
                        "images/JavaProg_Expl.gif", "27.77");
        addItemRecord(ps, sku++,
                        "Java Programming Language Handbook",
                        "images/JavaProg_Lang.gif", "32.22");
        addItemRecord(ps, sku++,
                        "Kick Ass Java Programming",
                        "images/KA_Java.gif", "39,98");
        addItemRecord(ps, sku++,
                        "Oracle Databases on the Web",
                        "images/OracleDB_on_Web.GIF", "44,99");
        addItemRecord(ps, sku++,
                        "VBScript & ActiveX Wizardry",
                        "images/VBScrpt&ActX_Wiz.gif", "36.66");
        addItemRecord(ps, sku++,
                        "Web Psycos, Stalkers, and Pranksters",
                        "images/WebPsychos_Stalkers.gif", "28.12");

    ps.close();
}


//- - - - - - - - - - - - - - - - - - - - - - - - - - - - - - - -
// addItemRecord
// Helper method to add an item record.  A PreparedStatement is
// provided to which this method binds input parameters.  Returns
// true if the record was added.
//- - - - - - - - - - - - - - - - - - - - - - - - - - - - - - - -

protected static boolean addItemRecord(
    PreparedStatement ps,
    int sku,
    String desc,
    String filename,
    String price)
    throws SQLException
{

    System.out.println(" Inserting '" + desc + "'");

    // Create a file object for the image
```

```
File file = new File(filename);

if (!file.exists()) {
    return false;
}

// Get the length of the file.  This will be used when binding
// the InputStream to the PreparedStatement

int len = (int) file.length();

FileInputStream inputStream;

try {

    // Attempt to create an InputStream from the File object

    inputStream = new FileInputStream (filename);
}
catch (Exception ex) {

    // Some type of failure.  Convert it into a SQLException

    throw new SQLException (ex.getMessage ());
}

// Set the parameters

ps.setInt(1, sku);
ps.setString(2, desc);
ps.setBinaryStream(3, inputStream, len);
ps.setString(4, price);

// Now execute

int rows = ps.executeUpdate();

return (rows == 0) ? false : true;
    }
}
```

This simple JDBC application is very similar to the BuildDB application used in Chapter 12. (In fact, if you look closely, you will notice that it is a complete hack!)

Writing The POSDatabase Bean

Creating the **POSDatabase** bean will be our first task. Some would argue that this bean should be an invisible bean: a bean with no GUI attributes. I chose to make it a visible bean for two reasons: I wanted to be able to display status and error information, and (at the time of writing) the BeanBox does not support invisible beans.

PROPERTIES

As mentioned before, the **POSDatabase** bean has editable properties that allow the JDBC driver name and connection URL to be set. The Java Beans specification states, "properties are always accessed via method calls on their owning object". Simply defining an attribute in a Java class as public will not do; a public method must be written to get and set the value of the property. In fact, Java Beans specifies a design pattern for the naming of these **get** and **set** methods in the form:

```
public <PropertyType> get<PropertyName>();
public void set<PropertyName>(<PropertyType>) a);
```

So for our **POSDatabase** bean, we need to create the editable properties required to define a **get** and **set** method, which is simple enough:

```
public void setDriverName(String newValue)
{
    driverName = newValue;
}

public String getDriverName()
{
    return driverName;
}

public void setConnectionURL(String newValue)
{
    connectionURL = newValue;
}

public String getConnectionURL()
{
    return connectionURL;
}
```

When our **POSDatabase** bean is loaded into a builder tool (such as the BeanBox), the tool will examine the bean for methods that match the property design pattern. If both a **get** and **set** method are found, the property is considered to be editable. If only the **get** method or **set** method is found, the property is considered to be read-only or write-only. When using the bean with the BeanBox, an editable property will be added to the PropertySheet. The **get** method is called to get the value and display it next to the property name (which was derived from the name of the **get** method). If the value is changed, the corresponding **set** method is called with the new value. The Java Beans specification calls this type of property a "simple" property. There are other types of properties (boolean and indexed) and advanced properties (bound and constrained) that we will not cover. Just be aware that we are examining only a small part of Java Beans' full power.

EVENTS AND EVENT LISTENERS

Events are one of the most fundamental features of the Java Beans architecture. As we have already seen, events enable one bean to be "plugged-in" to another bean, passing event information from the event source (the bean creating the event) to the event listener (the bean receiving the event notification). It is important to note that firing an event is meaningless unless there is someone listening (my wife tried to come up with an analogy here, but I don't remember what she said). Remember how we stretched the rubber band from an event source to the event target in the BeanBox? The BeanBox was actually registering an event listener with the event source. The event source keeps track of the event listeners internally by a *vector*:

```
// Event listener handling

    public synchronized void addListener(POSDatabaseEventListener l)
    {
        listeners.addElement(l);
    }

    public synchronized void removeListener(POSDatabaseEventListener l)
    {
        listeners.removeElement(l);
    }

// Utility objects

    private Vector listeners = new Vector();
```

To fire an event, it's a simple matter of going through the vector and making the appropriate method call of each **EventListener** object:

```java
// Tell whoever is listening that a state change has occurred

    public void changeState(int newState)
    {
        Vector clonedListeners;
        synchronized(this)
        {
            clonedListeners = (Vector) listeners.clone();
        }

        // If the state is not changing, no need to send out an event

        if (state != newState) {
            state = newState;
            Integer s = new Integer(state);
            for (int i = 0; i < clonedListeners.size(); i++) {

                // Get the listener
                POSDatabaseEventListener l =
                    (POSDatabaseEventListener)
clonedListeners.elementAt(i);
                l.changeState(s);
            }
        }
    }
```

Note that the first thing we do is to clone the vector. We wouldn't want the vector to change when a listener is added or removed while we are in the middle of firing an event, so we make a copy of it first. How exactly does the BeanBox keep track of the appropriate method to call in the event listener? An adapter class is created to tie them together. Here's a sample adapter class:

```java
// Automatically generated event hookup file.

package tmp.sun.beanbox;

public class ___Hookup_13fce80237
        implements jdp.POS.POSDatabaseEventListener, java.io.Serializable {

    public void setTarget(jdp.POS.POSSignOn t) {
        target = t;
    }
```

```
    public void changeState(java.lang.Integer arg0) {
        target.changeState(arg0);
    }

private jdp.POS.POSSignOn target;
}
```

When the event listener is registered, the adapter class **setTarget** method is called with the listener object (**POSSignOn**). When **POSDatabase** fires a **changeState** event, each registered listeners' **changeState** method is called indirectly by using the adapter class. The **changeEvent** method of the **POSDatabaseEventListener** object is called, and then, in turn, calls the appropriate method of the registered listener. In our case, the method name is the same (**changeState**). The adapter class serves an important, yet simple, role of keeping the beans tied together in a generic way. It might seem somewhat magical at first, but it's really quite simple once you understand the mechanics going on behind the scene.

EXPLICIT INFORMATION VIA BEANINFO

Through introspection, you can derive a lot of information from your bean using the design patterns described in the Java Beans specification. We touched upon this earlier when we discussed properties. There are cases, though, in which you may want to explicitly describe some facet of your bean. You can accomplish this by providing a BeanInfo class. The BeanInfo class name is derived by adding "BeanInfo" to the end of the bean's class name. You may have noticed in the BeanBox ToolBox that some of the beans have nice little icons beside them and some don't. The icon is one of the things you can specify in the BeanInfo class. We'll be using the BeanInfo class to specify the bean's fireable events. By doing so, the BeanBox can query the BeanInfo class for the event information and modify the Edit menu appropriately. Here's the BeanInfo class for **POSDatabase**:

```
package jdp.POS;

import java.beans.*;


public class POSDatabaseBeanInfo extends SimpleBeanInfo
{
```

```java
// Set the event descriptors for the POSDatabase bean

public EventSetDescriptor[] getEventSetDescriptors()
{
    String[] listenerMethods = { "changeState", "priceInquiryResults"
};
    EventSetDescriptor event;
    try {
        event = new EventSetDescriptor(POSDatabase.class,
                    "Event", POSDatabaseEventListener.class,
                    listenerMethods,
                    "addListener", "removeListener");

    } catch (IntrospectionException e) {
        throw new Error(e.toString());
    }

    EventSetDescriptor[] events = {event};
    return events;
}

}
```

Putting It All Together

Now that we've seen some of the more important parts of our JavaBean, let's put some of it together. We'll start out by creating the **POSSignOn** bean, which will collect a user name and password and allow a Sign On button to be clicked. When clicked, this button will send a **SignOnEvent** to our **POSDatabase** bean. The **POSDatabase** bean will then connect to the database using the sign on information. Remember that the JDBC driver and connection URL are editable properties and can be specified in the PropertySheet. If the database connection is successful, a changeState event is fired back to the POSSignOn bean. This event will cause the Sign On button to be disabled and the Sign Off button to be enabled. Thus, if you are signed on, you can only sign off—you can't sign on twice. Listing 15.3 shows the complete code for **POSSignOn**.

LISTING 15.3 POSSIGNON.JAVA SOURCE CODE.

```java
package jdp.POS;

import java.awt.*;
import java.awt.event.*;
import java.beans.*;
import java.util.*;
```

```java
public class POSSignOn extends Panel
    implements ActionListener
{

    public POSSignOn()
    {
        // Setup our layout manager with 3 rows and 2 columns

        setLayout(new GridLayout(3, 2, 10, 10));

        // Setup the operator ID

        add(new Label("Operator : "));
        operatorField = new TextField();
        add(operatorField);

        // Setup the password

        add(new Label("Password : "));
        passwordField = new TextField();
        add(passwordField);

        // Setup the signon button

        signOnButton = new Button("Sign On");
        signOnButton.addActionListener(this);
        add(signOnButton);

        // Setup the signoff button

        signOffButton = new Button("Sign Off");
        signOffButton.addActionListener(this);
        add(signOffButton);

        // Set the initial state to offline

        changeState(new Integer(POSDefine.OFFLINE));
    }

    public java.awt.Dimension preferredSize()
    {
        return new java.awt.Dimension(150, 90);
    }


    // Receive an internal state change notification
```

```
public void changeState(Integer newState)
{
    int state = newState.intValue();

    if (state == POSDefine.OFFLINE) {
        signOnButton.setEnabled(true);
        signOffButton.setEnabled(false);
        operatorField.setText("");
        operatorField.setEditable(true);
        passwordField.setText("");
        passwordField.setEditable(true);
    }
    else {
        signOnButton.setEnabled(false);
        signOffButton.setEnabled(true);
        operatorField.setEditable(false);
        passwordField.setText("");
        passwordField.setEditable(false);
    }

}


// Event listener handling

public synchronized void addListener(POSSignOnEventListener l)
{
    listeners.addElement(l);
}

public synchronized void removeListener(POSSignOnEventListener l)
{
    listeners.removeElement(l);
}


// ActionListener implementation

public void actionPerformed(ActionEvent e)
{
    // Get the source of the action

    Object source = e.getSource();

    // Perform some action depending upon the source

    if (source == signOnButton) {
        Vector clonedListeners;
```

```
        synchronized(this) {
            clonedListeners = (Vector) listeners.clone();
        }

        POSSignOnObject signOnObject = new POSSignOnObject();
        signOnObject.setOperator(operatorField.getText());
        signOnObject.setPassword(passwordField.getText());

        for (int i = 0; i < clonedListeners.size(); i++) {

            // Get the listener
            POSSignOnEventListener l =
                (POSSignOnEventListener)
                clonedListeners.elementAt(i);
            l.signOnEvent(signOnObject);

        }
    }

    if (source == signOffButton) {
        Vector clonedListeners;
        synchronized(this) {
            clonedListeners = (Vector) listeners.clone();
        }

        for (int i = 0; i < clonedListeners.size(); i++) {

            // Get the listener
            POSSignOnEventListener l =
                (POSSignOnEventListener)
                clonedListeners.elementAt(i);
            l.signOffEvent(null);

        }
    }

}


// Layout fields

private TextField operatorField;
private TextField passwordField;
private Button    signOnButton;
private Button    signOffButton;
```

```
// Utility objects

private Vector listeners = new Vector();
}
```

The code here is simple enough. The **POSSignOn** bean extends Panel, and we're using a GridLayout to position our GUI components. The signOnButton and signOffButton are tied to the **actionPerformed** method when they are pressed. From the **actionPerformed** method, we fire the appropriate event depending upon which button is pressed. We also have the **changeState** method, which is an event listener. The **changeState** method will take care of enabling and disabling components when we sign on or sign off.

So what happens when the Sign On button is clicked? Remember, a **SignOnEvent** is fired to whoever is listening, so in this case, the **POSDatabase** bean's **signOn** method will be called:

```
public void SignOn(POSSignOnObject signOnObject)
    {
        boolean failed = false;

        // No action if we're already online

        if (state == POSDefine.ONLINE) {
            return;
        }

        try {

            // Connect to the driver

            Driver d = (Driver) Class.forName(driverName).newInstance();
            con = DriverManager.getConnection(connectionURL,
                            signOnObject.getOperator(),
                            signOnObject.getPassword());


        }
        catch (Exception ex) {
            setError(ex.getMessage());

            // Dump the stack for debugging purposes
            ex.printStackTrace();
```

```
        failed = true;
    }


    // If everything went OK, change our internal
    // state to ONLINE, also notifying all other
    // beans who are listening

    if (!failed) {

        // Set the operator name

        operatorLabel.setText(POSDefine.OPERATOR +
                    signOnObject.getOperator());
        operatorLabel.repaint();
        setOnline();
    }

    repaint();

}
```

We connect to the JDBC driver specified in our editable property using the connection URL property as well. The user name and password are included when the event is received via the **POSSignOnObject** object. It is a simple matter to create a connection object using the information given. If the connection fails, the status line on the **POSDatabase** bean will display the error. If the connection succeeds, a **changeState** event is fired to notify our listening objects that we are now signed on.

Figure 15.16 shows the BeanBox with the **POSSignOn** and **POSDatabase** beans. The **SignOnEvent** event from the **POSSignOn** bean has been connected to the **signOn** method of the **POSDatabase** bean, the **SignOffEvent** event from the **POSSignOn** bean has been connected to the **signOff** method of the **POSDatabase** bean, and the **changeState** event from the **POSDatabase** bean has been connected to the **changeState** method of the **POSSignOn** bean.

Figure 15.17 shows the BeanBox after a successful sign on, after setting the **driverName** and **connectionURL** properties. Notice that the Sign On button has been disabled and the Sign Off button has been enabled.

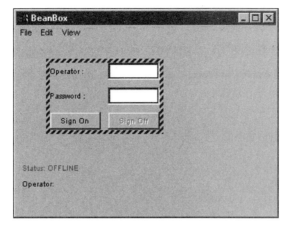

Figure 15.16
POSSignOn and POSDatabase.

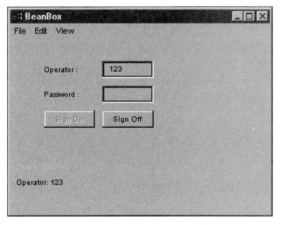

Figure 15.17
POSDatabase after sign on.

Signing off the database is a simple matter of closing the connection and firing an event to notify all of the listeners we are now signed off:

```
public void SignOff()
    {
        boolean failed = false;

        try {
            if (con != null) {
                con.close();
                con = null;
```

```
        }
    }
    catch (Exception ex) {
        setError(ex.getMessage());
        failed = true;
    }


    // Log off the database

    setOffline();
    repaint();

}
```

Adding More: Price Inquiry

Now that we can sign on to the database, let's add more functionality. The
POSPriceInquiry bean allows an item code to be entered and a **PriceInquiry**
event to be fired with the item code. The **POSDatabase** bean will be listening
for this event, and the **PriceInquiry** method will be called:

```
public void PriceInquiry(POSItemObject itemObject)
    {
        boolean failed = false;
        java.sql.Statement stmt = null;
        ResultSet rs = null;
        String item;
        POSItemObject o = null;

        item = itemObject.getItemCode();

        if ((item == null) ||
            (item.length() == 0)) {
            setError("Item code required for price inquiry");
            repaint();
            return;
        }

        try {

            // Create a statement object

            stmt = con.createStatement();

            // Execute the query
```

```
            rs = stmt.executeQuery("select SKU,DESCRIPTION,PRICE,IMAGE " +
                                    "from ITEM " +
                                    "where SKU=" + item);

        // Get the results

        if (!rs.next()) {
            setError("Item '" + item + "' not found");
            failed = true;
        }
        else {
            o = new POSItemObject();
            o.setItemCode(rs.getString(1));
            o.setItemDescription(rs.getString(2));
            o.setItemPrice(rs.getString(3));

            // We'll handle the image by getting the column as
            // an InputStream then reading it into a byte array.

            java.io.InputStream is = rs.getBinaryStream(4);
            byte b[] = new byte[is.available()];
            is.read(b);
            o.setItemImage(b);
        }

    }
    catch (Exception ex) {
        setError(ex.getMessage());

        // Dump the stack for debugging purposes
        ex.printStackTrace();

        failed = true;
    }


    // If everything went OK, send the item information
    // out to whoever is expecting it.

    if (!failed) {
        priceInquiryResults(o);
        setOnline();
    }

    repaint();


}
```

After some initial sanity checks to ensure an item code was entered, a new **Statement** object is created and a **SQL SELECT** statement is formed. If the **SQL** statement is executed and a ResultSet is returned, the first row's data is gathered. This data is sent along with a **priceInquiryResult** event. It would be much more efficient to create a **PreparedStatement** and use parameters to set the item code, because a price inquiry may be performed many times. I'll leave that to you as an exercise. Figure 15.18 shows the BeanBox after all of the beans have been connected and item code 1 has been queried.

Adding Even More: Images

When we built the ITEM table earlier, we added a VARBINARY column containing an image of the item. Since we are already including the binary data with the **PriceInquiryResults** event (as a byte array), it is a very simple matter to create a new bean to display the image. **POSItemImage** does just that. The one drawback, however, is the lack of Java support for displaying an

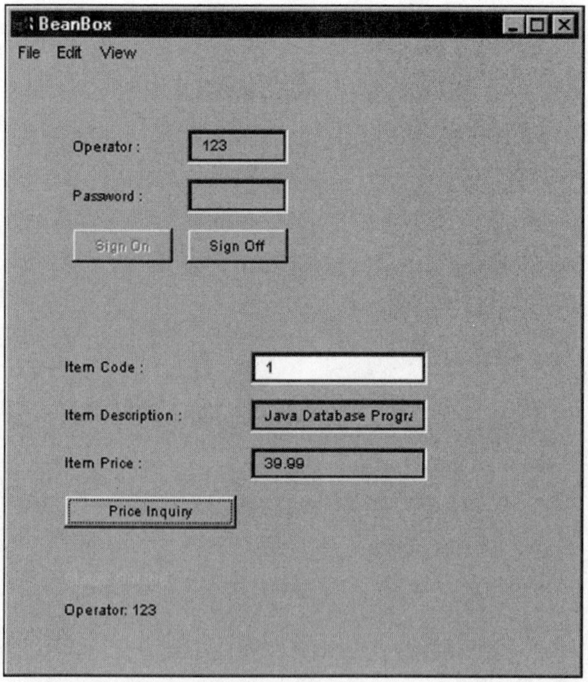

Figure 15.18
Price Inquiry.

image directly from a byte array, as we also saw in Chapter 12. I will mention again that although you can't do this using classes included with the JDK, there are third party classes that can (such as GifImage). For now, we'll just use the same ugly workaround we used in Chapter 12. We'll write the binary data out to a file and then use the JDK classes that load an image from disk and display it on a canvas:

```
// Receive a price inquiry result notification

    public void priceInquiryResults(POSItemObject o)
    {

        // Here's where things get ugly. Currently, there is no way
        // (using the JDK) to display an image from a byte array.
        // Note that there are vendors who supply classes that perform
        // task, as well as 'freeware' classes, such as GifImage.  We'll
        // create a new file from the InputStream and load the image from
        // the newly created file.

        String loadName = null;

        deleteFile(lastFileName);

        try {
            lastFileName = tempFileName + "-" + o.getItemCode();
            FileOutputStream outputStream = new
            FileOutputStream(lastFileName);
            byte b[] = o.getItemImage();
            outputStream.write(b, 0, b.length);
            outputStream.close();

            // If we got here, everything worked okay.  Set the name
            // of the file to load.

            loadName = lastFileName;
        }
        catch (Exception ex) {
            // Dump the stack for debugging purposes
            ex.printStackTrace();
        }

        loadFile(loadName);
        repaint();
    }
```

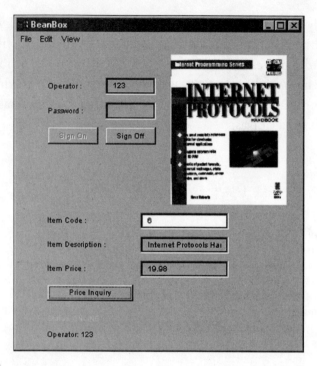

Figure 15.19
POSItemImage.

Figure 15.19 shows the BeanBox with the **POSItemImage** bean connected.

Coming Up Next

We've just taken a whirlwind tour of the Java Beans specification. While we have only just scratched the surface of Java Beans, we have covered some of the more important aspects, such as

- The BDK

- The BeanBox

- Properties

- Events

- Event notification

- Connecting beans

- BeanInfo
- JAR files
- Manifests

We've also implemented a simple database server as a JavaBean, including GUI components that

- Sign on the database
- Sign off the database
- Perform a price inquiry
- Display item information
- Display an item image

These examples will serve you well in building a foundation for understanding the Java Beans environment. Happy beaning!

Next in line is a reference chapter of the JDBC API. It contains documentation on the JDBC methods used in the writing of this book, as well as methods that we didn't explicitly cover. You may want to browse through the package tree to get an idea of how the various classes and methods fit together, as well as their relation to one another.

Part **5**

REFERENCE

16

THE JDBC API

This chapter ends our journey through the JDBC. I've provided a summary of the class interfaces and exceptions that are available in JDBC API version 1.2.2, which was the most current version at the time of this writing. This is also packaged as the java.sql.* classes in the new Java API, 1.1.2. If you're using this version of the Java API, or higher, then you already have the JDBC. Although this chapter primarily serves as a reference, you should still read through the sections completely so that you are aware of all the available constructors, variables, and methods.

Classes

We'll begin with the class listings. Each class listing includes a description and the class' constructors, methods, and variables. Remember that each class falls under the java.sql.* hierarchy.

public class Date

This class extends the **java.util.Date** object. But unlike the **java.util.Date**, which also stores time, day, year, and month, the **java.sql.Date** class supports the SQL Date type directly. This class exists for strict matching with the SQL Date type.

CONSTRUCTORS

Constructor	Additional Description
Date(int Year, int Month, int Day)	Constructs a java.sql.Date object with the appropriate parameters
Date(long millisec)	Constructs a java.sql.Date object with the number of milliseconds elapsed since Jan. 1, 1970, 00:00:00

METHODS

Method Name	Additional Description
public void **setTime** (long date)	Sets the date with the number of milliseconds elapsed since Jan. 1, 1970, 00:00:00
public int **getHours**()	Returns the hour of this Date object
public int **getMinutes**()	Returns the minutes past the hour of this Date object
public int **getSeconds**()	Returns the seconds past the minute of this Date object
public void **setHours**(int i)	Sets the hour of this Date object
public void **setMinutes**(int i)	Sets the minutes of this Date object
public void **setSeconds**(int i)	Sets the seconds of this Date object
public String **toString**()	Formats a Date object as YYYY-MM-DD
public static Date **valueOf** (String str)	Converts a String str to an sql.Date object

public class DriverManager

You use this class to load a JDBC driver and establish it as an available driver. It is usually not instantiated, but is called by the JDBC driver.

CONSTRUCTORS

DriverManager()

METHODS

Method Name	Additional Description
public static void **deregisterDriver** (Driver JDBCdriver) throws SQLException	Drops a driver from the available drivers list
public static synchronized Connection **getConnection** (String URL) throws SQLException	Creates a connection to the given JDBC with the specified parameters
public static synchronized Connection **getConnection**(String URL, String LoginName, String LoginPassword) throws SQLException	Creates a connection to the given JDBC with the specified parameters
public static synchronized Connection **getConnection**(String URL, Properties LoginInfo) throws SQLException	Creates a connection to the given JDBC with the specified parameters
public static Driver **getDriver** (String URL) throws SQLException	Finds a driver that understands the JDBC URL from the registered driver list
public static Enumeration **getDrivers**()	Gets an enumeration of the available JDBC drivers
public static int **getLoginTimeout**()	Indicates the maximum time (seconds) that a driver will wait when logging into a database
public static PrintStream **getLogStream**()	Gets the logging PrintStream that the DriverManager and JDBC drivers use
public static void **println**(String msg)	Sends msg to the current JDBC logging stream (fetched from getLogStream method)
public static synchronized void **registerDriver**(Driver JDBCdriver) throws SQLException	Specifies that a new driver class should call registerDriver when loading to "register" with the DriverManager
public static void **setLoginTimeout**(int sec)	Indicates the time (in seconds) that all drivers will wait when logging into a database
public static void **setLogStream** (PrintStream log)	Defines the PrintStream that logging messages are sent to via the println method

public class DriverPropertyInfo

This class is for developers who want to obtain and set properties for a loaded JDBC driver. It's not necessary to use this class, but it is useful for debugging JDBC drivers and advanced development.

CONSTRUCTORS

Constructor	Additional Description
public DriverPropertyInfo (String propName, String propValue)	The propName is the name of the property, and propValue is the current value; if it has not been set it may be null

VARIABLES

Variable Name	Additional Description
Choices	If the property value is part of a set of values, then **Choices** is an array of the possible values
description	The property's description
Name	The property's name
Required	This is true if this property is required to be set during Driver.connect
value	The current value of the property

public class Time

The public class **Time** is another SQL-JDBC data conversion class. This class extends **java.util.Date**, and implements the time-storing functions that are not present in the **java.sql.Date** class shown earlier.

CONSTRUCTORS

Constructor	Additional Description
public **Time**(int hour, int minute, int second)	Makes a Time object with the specified hour, minute, and second
public **Time**(long millisec)	Constructs a java.sql.Time object with the number of milliseconds elapsed since Jan. 1, 1970, 00:00:00

METHODS

Method Name	Additional Description
public int **getYear**()	Returns the year since 1900 (1997 = 97)
public int **getMonth**()	Returns the month for this Time object
public int **getDay**()	Returns the day of the week for this Time object
public int **getDate**()	Returns the day of the month for this Time object
public void **setYear**(int i)	Sets the year of this Time object to be the parameter since 1900 (1997 = 97)
public void **setMonth**(int i)	Sets the month of this Time object to the parameter
public void **setDate**(int i)	Sets the day of the month of this Time object to the parameter
public void **setTime**(long date)	Sets the date with the number of milliseconds elapsed since Jan. 1, 1970, 00:00:00
public String **toString**()	Returns a String with the Time formatted this way: HH:MM:SS
public static Time **valueOf** (String numStr)	Returns a Numeric object from the String numStr parameter that is in the format HH:MM:SS

public class TimeStamp

This class is used to map the SQL data type TIMESTAMP. This class extends **java.util.Date**, and has nanosecond precision for time-stamping purposes.

CONSTRUCTORS

Constructor	Additional Description
public **TimeStamp**(int year, int month, int date, int hour, int minute, int second, parameters: year, month, date, hour, minute, int nano)	Builds a TimeStamp object using int second and nanosecond
public **TimeStamp**(long millisec)	Constructs a java.sql.TimeStamp object with the number of milliseconds elapsed since Jan. 1, 1970, 00:00:00

METHODS

Method Name	Additional Description
public boolean **after** (TimeStamp stamp)	Compares the argument TimeStamp object against this one and returns true if this TimeStamp is chronologically after the parameter TimeStamp stamp
public boolean **before** (TimeStamp stamp)	Compares the argument TimeStamp object against this one and returns true if this TimeStamp is chronologically before the parameter TimeStamp stamp
public boolean **equals** (TimeStamp stamp)	Compares the TimeStamp object with the TimeStamp parameter tstamp; returns true if they match
public int **getNanos**()	Returns the TimeStamp object's nanoseconds
public void **setNanos**(int n)	Sets the TimeStamp object's nanosecond value
public String **toString**()	Returns a formatted String object with the value of the TimeStamp object in the format YYYY-MM-DD HH:MM:SS.F
public static TimeStamp **valueOf**(String strts)	Returns a TimeStamp object converted from the strts parameter that is in the previous format

public class Types

This class contains the SQL data types as constants. Other classes use it as the standard constant for the data types.

CONSTRUCTORS

Constructor	Additional Description
public **Types**()	Builds a Types object; not usually necessary as the type variables can be accessed as Types.BIGINT

VARIABLES
BIGINT
BINARY
BIT
CHAR
DATE
DECIMAL
DOUBLE
FLOAT
INTEGER
LONGVARBINARY
LONGVARCHAR
NULL
NUMERIC
OTHER (for a database-specific data type, not a standard SQL-92 data type)
REAL
SMALLINT
TIME
TIMESTAMP
TINYINT
VARBINARY
VARCHAR

Interfaces

Next are the interface listings. As with the class listings, each interface listing includes a description and the interface's methods and variables.

public interface CallableStatement

This is the primary interface to access stored procedures on a database. If you specify OUT parameters and a query is executed via this class, its results are fetched from this class, not the **ResultSet** class. This class extends the **Prepared Statement** class and thus inherits many of its methods.

The first 14 methods (the **get** methods) are identical in functionality to those in the **ResultSet** class, but they are necessary if you use OUT parameters. See the **ResultSet** class for a description of the methods.

METHODS

Method Name	Additional Description
public abstract boolean **getBoolean**(int parameterIndex) throws SQLException	
public abstract byte **getByte**(int parameterIndex) throws SQLException	
public abstract byte[] **getBytes**(int parameterIndex) throws SQLException	
public abstract Date **getDate**(int parameterIndex) throws SQLException	
public abstract double **getDouble**(int parameterIndex) throws SQLException	
public abstract float **getFloat**(int parameterIndex) throws SQLException	
public abstract int **getInt**(int parameterIndex) throws SQLException	
public abstract long **getLong**(int parameterIndex) throws SQLException	
public abstract BigDecimal **getBigDecimal**(int parameterIndex, int scale) throws SQLException	
public abstract Object **getObject**(int parameterIndex) throws SQLException	
public abstract short **getShort**(int parameterIndex) throws SQLException	
public abstract String **getString**(int parameterIndex) throws SQLException	
public abstract Time **getTime**(int parameterIndex) throws SQLException	
public abstract TimeStamp **getTimeStamp**(int parameterIndex) throws SQLException	

(continued)

Method Name	Additional Description
public abstract void **registerOutParameter** (int paramIndex, int sqlDataType) throws SQLException	You must register each parameter of the stored procedure before running the query. The stored procedure's parameter location in the output sequence is paramIndex. The data type of the parameter at the specified location is sqlDataType, which (should be set from the Type class using one of its variables, Types.BIGINT, for example
public abstract void **registerOutParameter** (int parameterIndex, int sqlDataType, int scale) throws SQLException	Specifies the number of places that you want to the right of the decimal
public abstract boolean **wasNull()** throws SQLException	Returns true if the stored procedure parameter had a NULL value

public interface Connection

This is the high-level class used to interact with a database. The object is established from the **DriverManager.getConnection** method, which returns this object (**Connection**). This class obtains information about the specific database connection via the instantiated JDBC driver. Primarily, it performs queries via the **createStatement**, **prepareCall**, and **prepareStatement** methods, which return **Statement**, **PreparedCall**, and **PreparedStatement** objects, respectively.

METHODS

Method Name	Additional Description
public abstract void **clearWarnings()** throws SQLException	Clears the warnings for the connection
public abstract void **close()** throws SQLException	Closes the connection to the database
public abstract void **commit()** throws SQLException	Functions as the JDBC equivalent of the standard database commit command; it applies all commands and changes made since the last commit or rollback, including releasing database locks; results from queries are closed when commit is invoked

(continued)

Method Name	Additional Description
public abstract Statement **createStatement()** throws SQLException	Returns a Statement object that can then be used to perform actual queries
public abstract boolean **getAutoClose()** throws SQLException	Returns true if automatic closing of the commit or rollback is performed
public abstract boolean **getAutoCommit()** throws SQLException	Returns true if automatic committing of the connection is on; automatic commit is on by default and means that the connection is committed on individual transactions; the actual commit occurs when the last row of a result set is fetched, or when the ResultSet is closed
public abstract String **getCatalog()** throws SQLException	Returns the current catalog name for the connection
public abstract DatabaseMetaData **getMetaData()** throws SQLException	Returns a DatabaseMetaData object for the current connection
public abstract int **getTransactionIsolation()** throws SQLException	Returns the transaction isolation mode of the connection
public abstract SQLWarning **getWarnings()** throws SQLException	Returns the SQLWarning object with the warnings for the connection
public abstract boolean **isClosed()** throws SQLException	Returns true if the connection has been closed
public abstract boolean **isReadOnly()** throws SQLException	Returns true if the connection is a read-only connection
public abstract String **nativeSQL**(String sqlQuery) throws SQLException	Returns the native SQL that the JDBC driver would send to the database for the specified sqlQuery parameter
public abstract CallableStatement **prepareCall**(String sqlQuery) throws SQLException	Returns a CallableStatement object used to perform stored procedures; note that the SQL query must be passed in as the sqlQuery parameter here
public abstract PreparedStatement **prepareStatement**(String sqlQuery) throws SQLException	Returns a PreparedStatement object used to perform the specified sqlQuery; this query can be executed repeatedly if desired by using the PreparedStatement. execute method

(continued)

Method Name	Additional Description
public abstract void **rollback()** throws SQLException	Drops changes made since the last commit or rollback, and closes respective results; database locks are also released
public abstract void **setAutoClose** (boolean auto) throws SQLException	Sets the connection to auto close mode if the auto parameter is true
public abstract void **setAutoCommit** (boolean auto) throws SQLException	Sets the connection to auto commit mode if the auto parameter is true
public abstract void **setCatalog** (String catalog) throws SQLException	You may change the catalog by specifying it
public abstract void **setReadOnly(** boolean readOnly) throws SQLException	Sets the connection to read-only mode
public abstract void **setTransactionIsolation** (int level) throws SQLException	Sets transaction isolation to the specified level

VARIABLES

The following constants are used in the **setTransactionIsolation** method as the level parameter:

TRANSACTION_NONE

TRANSACTION_READ_COMMITTED

TRANSACTION_READ_UNCOMMITTED

TRANSACTION_REPEATABLE_READ

TRANSACTION_SERIALIZABLE

public interface DatabaseMetaData

This class contains useful information about the open connection to the database. The **Connection.getMetaData** method returns a **Database-MetaData** object that is specific to the opened connection.

METHODS

Method Name	Additional Description
public abstract boolean **allProceduresAreCallable()** throws SQLException	Returns true if all the procedures available to the user are callable
public abstract boolean **allTablesAreSelectable()** throws SQLException	Returns true if all of the tables are accessible to the user on the open connection
public abstract boolean **dataDefinitionCausesTransactionCommit()** throws SQLException	Returns true if data definition causes the transaction to commit
public abstract boolean **dataDefinitionIgnoredInTransactions()** throws SQLException	Returns true if data definition is ignored in the transaction
public abstract boolean **doesMaxRowSizeIncludeBlobs()** throws SQLException	Returns true if the getMaxSize method does not account for the size of LONGVARCHAR and LONGVARBINARY SQL data types
public abstract ResultSet **getBestRowIdentifier**(String catalog, String schema, String table, int scope, boolean nullok) throws SQLException	Returns a ResultSet object for the specified parameters that get the specified table's key or the attributes that can be used to uniquely identify a row, which may be composite. The scope parameter is one of the following constants: bestRowTemporary, bestRowTransaction, or bestRowSession; the nullok parameter allows columns that may be null; the ResultSet is composed of the following columns: scope (of the same types as above scope parameter), column name, SQL data type, name of the data type dependent on the database, precision, buffer length, significant places if a Numeric type, and pseudo column (one of the constants bestRowUnknown, bestRowNotPseudo, or bestRowPseudo)
public abstract ResultSet **getCatalogs()** throws SQLException	Returns a ResultSet object that contains a column for the catalog names that are in the database
public abstract String **getCatalog Separator()** throws SQLException	Returns the separator between the catalog and the table name

(continued)

Method Name	Additional Description
public abstract String **getCatalogTerm**() throws SQLException	Returns the database-specific term for "catalog"
public abstract ResultSet **getColumnPrivileges** (String catalog, columnNamePattern) throws SQLException	Returns a ResultSet object that contains information about the specified table's matching columnNamePattern; the returned ResultSet object contains the following columns: the catalog name the table is in, the schema the table is in, the table name, the column name, owner of the table, grantee, type of access (SELECT, UPDATE, and so on), and, if the grantee can grant access to others, "YES," "NO," or null (if unknown)
public abstract ResultSet **getColumns** (String catalog, String schemaPattern, String tableNamePattern, String column NamePattern) throws SQLException	Returns a ResultSet object that contains information about the matching columns for the matching tables and schemas; the ResultSet contains the following columns: catalog name, schema name, table name, column name, SQL data type, name of the type specific to the database, the maximum number of characters or precision depending on the data type, buffer length (not used), the number of digits (if applicable), radix (if applicable), nullability (one of the constants columnNoNulls, columnNullable, or columnNullableUnknown), comments for the column, default value (if it exists, else null), empty column, empty column, maximum number of bytes in the column of type CHAR (if applicable), index number of column; the last column is set to "YES" if it can contain NULLS if not "NO" else it's empty if the status is unknown

(continued)

Method Name	Additional Description
public abstract ResultSet **getCrossReference** (String primaryCatalog, String primarySchema, ResultSet String primaryTable, String foreignCatalog, String foreignSchema, String foreignTable) throws SQLException	Returns a ResultSet object that describes the way a table imports foreign keys. The object returned by this method contains these columns: primary key's table catalog, primary key's table schema, primary key's table, primary key's column name, foreign key's table catalog, foreign key's table schema, foreign key's table, foreign key's column name, sequence number within foreign key, action to foreign key when primary key is updated (one of the constants importedKeyCascade, importedKeyRestrict, or importedKeySetNull), action to foreign key when primary key is deleted (one of the constants importedKeyCascade, importedKeyRestrict, or importedKeySetNull), foreign key identifier, and primary key indentifier
public abstract String **getDatabaseProductName()** throws SQLException	Returns the database product name
public abstract String **getDatabaseProductVersion()** throws SQLException	Returns the database product number
public abstract int **getDefaultTransactionIsolation()** throws SQLException	Returns the default transaction isolation level as defined by the applicable constants in the Connection class
public abstract int **getDriverMajorVersion()**	Gets the driver's major version
public abstract int **getDriverMinorVersion()**	Gets the driver's minor version
public abstract String **getDriverName()** throws SQLException	Returns the name of the JDBC driver
public abstract String **getDriverVersion()** throws SQLException	Returns the version of the JDBC driver

(continued)

Method Name	Additional Description
public abstract ResultSet **getExportedKeys**(String catalog, String schema, String table) throws SQLException	Returns a ResultSet object that describes the foreign key attributes that reference the specified table's primary key; the ResultSet object returns the following columns: primary key's table catalog, primary key's table schema, primary key's table, primary key's column name, foreign key's table catalog, foreign key's table schema, foreign key's table, foreign key's column name, sequence number within foreign key, action to foreign key when primary key is updated (one of the constants importedKeyCascade, importedKeyRestrict, or imported-KeySetNull), action to foreign key when primary key is deleted (one of the constants importedKeyCascade, importedKeyRestrict, or imported-KeySetNull), foreign key identifier, and primary key indentifier
public abstract String **getExtraNameCharacters**() throws SQLException	Returns characters that can be used in unquoted identifier names other than the standard A through Z, 0 through 9, and _
public abstract String **getIdentifierQuoteString**() throws SQLException	Returns the String used to quote SQL identifiers
public abstract ResultSet **getImportedKeys**(String String schema, String table) throws SQLException	Returns a ResultSet object that describes the primary key attributes that are referenced by the specified table's foreign key attributes; the ResultSet object contains the following columns: primary key's table catalog, primary key's table schema, primary key's table, primary key's column name, foreign key's table catalog, foreign key's table schema, foreign key's table, foreign key's column name, sequence number within foreign key, action to foreign key when primary key is updated (one of the constants importedKeyCascade, importedKey-Restrict, or importedKeySetNull), action

(continued)

Method Name	Additional Description
	to foreign key when primary key is deleted (one of the constants importedKey-Cascade, importedKeyRestrict, or importedKeySetNull), foreign key identifier, and primary key indentifier
public abstract ResultSet **getIndexInfo**-(String catalog, String schema, String table, boolean unique, boolean approximate) throws SQLException	Returns a ResultSet object that describes the specified table's indices and statistics. The ResultSet object contains the following columns: catalog name, schema name, table name, "false" boolean (if tableIndexStatic is the type), index catalog (or null if the type is tableIndexStatic), index type, sequence number, column name, column sort sequence, number of unique values in the table or number of rows (if tableIndexStatic), number of pages used for the index (or the number of pages used for the table if tableIndexStatic), and filter condition (if it exists)
public abstract int **getMaxBinaryLiteralLength**() throws SQLException	Returns the number of hex characters allowed in an inline binary literal
public abstract int **getMaxCatalogNameLength**() throws SQLException	Returns the maximum length for a catalog name
public abstract int **getMaxCharLiteralLength**() throws SQLException	Returns the maximum length for a character literal
public abstract int **getMaxColumnNameLength**() throws SQLException	Indicates the maximum length for a column name
public abstract int **getMaxColumnsInGroupBy**() throws SQLException	Indicates the maximum number of columns in a GROUP BY clause
public abstract int **getMaxColumnsInIndex**() throws SQLException	Indicates the maximum number of columns allowed in an index

(continued)

Method Name	Additional Description
public abstract int getMaxColumnsInOrderBy() throws SQLException	Indicates the maximum number of columns allowed in an ORDER BY clause
public abstract int getMaxColumnsInSelect() throws SQLException	Indicates the maximum number of columns allowed in a SELECT statement
public abstract int getMaxColumnsInTable() throws SQLException	Indicates the maximum number of columns allowed in a table
public abstract int getMaxConnections() throws SQLException	Indicates the maximum number of simultaneous connections allowed to the database
public abstract int getMaxCursorNameLength() throws SQLException	Returns the maximum allowed length of a cursor name
public abstract int getMaxIndexLength() throws SQLException	Returns the maximum allowed length of an index in bytes
public abstract int getMaxProcedureNameLength() throws SQLException	Returns the maximum allowed length of a procedure name
public abstract int getMaxRowSize() throws SQLException	Indicates the maximum allowed row size
public abstract int getMaxSchemaNameLength() throws SQLException	Returns the maximum allowed length of a schema name
public abstract int getMaxStatementLength() throws SQLException	Returns the maximum allowed length of an SQL statement
public abstract int getMaxStatements() throws SQLException	Returns the maximum number of statements allowed at one time
public abstract int getMaxTableNameLength() throws SQLException	Returns the maximum allowed length of a table name

(continued)

Method Name	Additional Description
public abstract int **getMaxTablesInSelect()** throws SQLException	Indicates the maximum number of tables allowed in a SELECT statement
public abstract int **getMaxUserNameLength()** throws SQLException	Returns the maximum allowed length of a user name
public abstract String **getNumericFunctions()** throws SQLException	Returns a comma-separated list of the available math functions
public abstract ResultSet **getPrimaryKeys**(String catalog, String schema, String table) throws SQLException	Returns a ResultSet object that contains the primary key's description for the specified table; the ResultSet object contains the following columns: catalog name, schema name, table name, column name, sequence number, primary key name, and, possibly, NULL
public abstract ResultSet **getProcedureColumns**(String catalog, String schemaPattern, String procedureNamePattern, String columnNamePattern) throws SQLException	Returns a ResultSet object that describes the catalog's stored procedures and result columns matching the specified procedureNamePattern and columnNamePattern; the ResultSet object contains the following columns: catalog name, schema name, procedure name, column or parameter name, column type, data type, data name, precision, length in bytes, scale, radix, nullability, and comments
public abstract ResultSet **getProcedures**(String catalogString String procedureNamePattern) throws SQLException	Returns a ResultSet object that describes the catalog's procedures; the ResultSet object contains the following columns: catalog name, schema name, procedure name, empty column, empty column, empty column, comments about the procedure, and kind of procedure
public abstract String **getProcedureTerm()** throws SQLException	Returns the database-specific term for procedure
public abstract ResultSet **getSchemas()** throws SQLException	Returns a ResultSet object that describes the schemas in a database; the ResultSet object contains one column that contains the schema names

(continued)

Method Name	Additional Description
public abstract String **getSchemaTerm**() throws SQLException	Returns the database-specific term for schema
public abstract String **getSearchStringEscape**() throws SQLException	Returns the escape characters for pattern searching
public abstract String **getSQLKeywords**() throws SQLException	Returns a comma-separated list of keywords that the database recognizes, but the keywords are not SQL-92 keywords
public abstract String **getStringFunctions**() throws SQLException	Returns a comma-separated list of string functions in the database
public abstract String **getSystemFunctions**() throws SQLException	Returns a comma-separated list of system functions in the database public abstract ResultSet
getTablePrivileges(String catalog, String schemaPattern, String tableNamePattern) throws SQLException	Returns a ResultSet object that describes the privileges for the matching schemaPattern and tableNamePattern; the ResultSet object contains the following columns: catalog name, schema name, table name, grantor, grantee, type of access, and "YES" if a grantee can grant other access
public abstract ResultSet **getTables**(String catalog, String schemaPattern, String tableNamePattern, String types[]) throws SQLException	Returns a ResultSet object that describes tables matching the schemaPattern and tableNamePattern; the ResultSet object contains the following columns: catalog name, schema name, table name, table type, and comments
public abstract ResultSet **getTableTypes**() throws SQLException	Returns a ResultSet object that describes the table types available in the database; the ResultSet object contains the column that is a list of the table types
public abstract String **getTimeDateFunctions**() throws SQLException	Returns the date and time functions for the database

(continued)

Method Name	Additional Description
public abstract ResultSet **getTypeInfo()** throws SQLException	Returns a ResultSet object that describes the SQL data types that the database; the ResultSet object contains the following columns: type name, SQL data type constants in the Types class, maximum precision, prefix used to quote a literal, suffix used to quote a literal, parameters used to create the type, nullability, case sensitivity, searchability, signed or unsigned (boolean), is it a currency, auto incrementable or not, local version of data type, minimum scale, maximum scale, empty column, empty column, and radix
public abstract String **getURL()** throws SQLException	Returns the URL for the database
public abstract String **getUserName()** throws SQLException	Returns the user name as known by the database
public abstract ResultSet **getVersionColumns**(String catalog, String String table) throws SQLException	Returns a ResultSet object that describes the specified table's columns that are updated when any column is updated in the table; the ResultSet object contains the following columns: empty columns, column name, SQL datatype, type name, precision, column value length in bytes, scale, and whether or not it's a pseudo column
public abstract boolean **isCatalogAtStart()** throws SQLException	Returns true if the catalog name appears at the start of a qualified table name
public abstract boolean **isReadOnly()** throws SQLException	Returns true if the database is in read-only mode
public abstract boolean **nullPlusNonNullIsNull()** throws SQLException	Returns true if a concatenation between a NULL and non-NULL is NULL

(continued)

Method Name	Additional Description
public abstract boolean **nullsAreSortedAtEnd()** throws SQLException	
public abstract boolean **nullsAreSortedAtStart()** throws SQLException	
public abstract boolean **nullsAreSortedHigh()** throws SQLException	
public abstract boolean **nullsAreSortedLow()** throws SQLException	
public abstract boolean **storesLowerCaseIdentifiers()** throws SQLException	
public abstract boolean **storesLowerCaseQuotedIdentifiers()** throws SQLException	
public abstract boolean **storesMixedCaseIdentifiers()** throws SQLException	
public abstract boolean **storesMixedCaseQuotedIdentifiers()** throws SQLException	
public abstract boolean **storesUpperCaseIdentifiers()** throws SQLException	
public abstract boolean **storesUpperCaseQuotedIdentifiers()** throws SQLException	
public abstract boolean **supportsAlterTableWithAddColumn()** throws SQLException	
public abstract boolean **supportsAlterTableWithDropColumn()** throws SQLException	

(continued)

Method Name	Additional Description
public abstract boolean **supportsAlterTableWithDropColumn()** throws SQLException	
public abstract boolean **supportsANSI92EntryLevelSQL()** throws SQLException	
public abstract boolean **supportsANSI92FullSQL()** throws SQLException	
public abstract boolean **supportsANSI92IntermediateSQL()** throws SQLException	
public abstract boolean **supportsANSI92FullSQL()** throws SQLException	
public abstract boolean **supportsCatalogsInDataManipulation()** throws SQLException	
public abstract boolean **supportsCatalogsInIndexDefinitions()** throws SQLException	
public abstract boolean **supportsCatalogsInPrivilegeDefinitions()** throws SQLException	
public abstract boolean **supportsCatalogsInProcedureCalls()** throws SQLException	
public abstract boolean **supportsCatalogsInTableDefinitions()** throws SQLException	
public abstract boolean **supportsColumnAliasing()** throws SQLException	
public abstract boolean **supportsConvert()** throws SQLException	

(continued)

Method Name	Additional Description
public abstract boolean supportsConvert(int fromType, int toType) throws SQLException	
public abstract boolean supportsCoreSQLGrammar() throws SQLException	
public abstract boolean supportsCorrelatedSubqueries() throws SQLException	
public abstract boolean supportsDataDefinitionAndDataManipulation- Transactions() throws SQLException	
public abstract boolean supportsDataManipulationTransactionsOnly() throws SQLException	
public abstract boolean supportsDifferentTableCorrelationNames() throws SQLException	
public abstract boolean supportsExpressionsInOrderBy() throws SQLException	
public abstract boolean supportsExtendedSQLGrammar() throws SQLException	
public abstract boolean supportsFullOuterJoins() throws SQLException	
public abstract boolean supportsGroupBy() throws SQLException	
public abstract boolean supportsGroupByBeyondSelect() throws SQLException	
public abstract boolean supportsGroupByUnrelated() throws SQLException	

(continued)

Method Name	Additional Description

public abstract boolean
supportsIntegrityEnhancementFacility()
throws SQLException

public abstract boolean
supportsLikeEscapeClause()
throws SQLException

public abstract boolean
supportsLimitedOuterJoins()
throws SQLException

public abstract boolean
supportsMinimumSQLGrammar()
throws SQLException

public abstract boolean
supportsMixedCaseIdentifiers()
throws SQLException

public abstract boolean
supportsMixedCaseQuotedIdentifiers()
throws SQLException

public abstract boolean
supportsMultipleResultSets()
throws SQLException

public abstract boolean
supportsMultipleTransactions()
throws SQLException

public abstract boolean
supportsNonNullableColumns()
throws SQLException

public abstract boolean
supportsOpenCursorsAcrossCommit()
throws SQLException

public abstract boolean
supportsOpenCursorsAcrossRollback()
throws SQLException

public abstract boolean
supportsOpenStatementsAcrossCommit()
throws SQLException

(continued)

Method Name	Additional Description
public abstract boolean **supportsOpenStatementsAcrossRollback()** throws SQLException	
public abstract boolean **supportsOrderByUnrelated()** throws SQLException	
public abstract boolean **supportsOuterJoins()** throws SQLException	
public abstract boolean **supportsPositionedDelete()** throws SQLException	
public abstract boolean **supportsPositionedUpdate()** throws SQLException	
public abstract boolean **supportsSchemasInDataManipulation()** throws SQLException	
public abstract boolean **supportsSchemasInProcedureCalls()** throws SQLException	
public abstract boolean **supportsSchemasInProcedureCalls()** throws SQLException	
public abstract boolean **supportsSchemasInTableDefinitions()** throws SQLException	
public abstract boolean **supportsSelectForUpdate()** throws SQLException	
public abstract boolean **supportsStoredProcedures()** throws SQLException	
public abstract boolean **supportsSubqueriesInComparisons()** throws SQLException	

(continued)

Method Name	Additional Description

public abstract boolean
supportsSubqueriesInExists()
throws SQLException

public abstract boolean
supportsSubqueriesInIns()
throws SQLException

public abstract boolean
supportsSubqueriesInQuantifieds()
throws SQLException

public abstract boolean
supportsTableCorrelationNames()
throws SQLException

public abstract boolean
supportsTransactionIsolationLevel(int level)
throws SQLException

public abstract boolean
supportsTransactions()
throws SQLException

public abstract boolean
supportsUnion()
throws SQLException

public abstract boolean
supportsUnionAll()
throws SQLException

public abstract boolean
usesLocalFilePerTable()
throws SQLException

public abstract boolean
usesLocalFiles()
throws SQLException

VARIABLES

public final static int bestRowNotPseudo
public final static int bestRowPseudo
public final static int versionColumnUnknown
public final static int versionColumnNotPseudo
public final static int versionColumnPseudo

public final static int importedKeyCascade

public final static int importedKeyRestrict

public final static int importedKeySetNull

public final static int public final static int importedKeyInitiallyDeferred

public final static int public final static int importedKeyInitiallyImmediate

public final static int importedKeyNotDeferrable

public final static int importedKeyNoAction

public final static int importedKeySetDefault

public final static int importedKeySetNull

public final static int procedureColumnIn

public final static int procedureColumnInOut

public final static int procedureColumnOut

public final static int procedureColumnResult public final static int procedure
  ColumnReturn

public final static int procedureColumnUnknown

public final static int procedureNoNulls

public final static int procedureNoResult

public final static int procedureNullable

public final static int procedureNullableUnknown

public final static int procedureResultUnknown

public final static int procedureReturnsResult

public final static int typeNoNulls

public final static int typeNullable

public final static int typeNullableUnknown

public final static int typePredNone

public final static int typePredChar

public final static int typePredBasic

public final static int typeSearchable

public final static short tableIndexStatistic

public final static short tableIndexClustered

public final static short tableIndexHashed

public final static short tableIndexOther

public interface Driver

The JDBC driver implements this interface. The JDBC driver must create an instance of itself and then register with the DriverManager.

METHODS

Method Name	Additional Description
public abstract boolean **acceptsURL**(String URL) throws SQLException	Returns true if the driver can connect to the specified database in the URL public abstract Connection **connect**(String URL, Properties props) throws SQLException
	Connects to the database specified in the URL with the specified Properties props
public abstract int **getMajorVersion**()	Returns the JDBC driver's major version number
public abstract int **getMinorVersion**()	Returns the JDBC driver's minor version number
public abstract DriverPropertyInfo[] **getPropertyInfo**(String URL, Properties props) throws SQLException	Returns an array of DriverPropertyInfo that contains possible properties based on the supplied URL and props
public abstract boolean **jdbcCompliant**()	Returns true if the JDBC driver can pass the JDBC compliance suite

public interface PreparedStatement

This object extends **Statement**, and is used to perform queries that will be repeated. This class exists primarily to optimize queries that will be executed repeatedly.

METHODS

Note: The **set** method sets the parameter at the **paramIndex** location in the prepared query to the specified **paramType** object.

Method Name	Additional Description
public abstract void **clearParameters**() throws SQLException	Resets all of the PreparedStatment's query parameters
public abstract boolean **execute**() throws SQLException	Runs the prepared query against the database; this method is used primarily if multiple ResultSets are expected
public abstract ResultSet **executeQuery**() throws SQLException	Executes the prepared query

(continued)

Method Name	Additional Description
public abstract int **executeUpdate**() throws SQLException	Executes the prepared query; this method is ResultSet (such as Update); returns the number or rows affected, or 0 if the SQL command returns nothingpublic abstract void
setAsciiStream(int paramIndex, InputStream paramType, int length) throws SQLException	
public abstract void **setBinaryStream**(int paramIndex, InputStream paramType, int length) throws SQLException	
public abstract void **setBoolean**(int paramIndex, boolean paramType) throws SQLException	
public abstract void **setByte**(int paramIndex, byte paramType) throws SQLException	
public abstract void **setBytes**(int paramIndex, byte paramType[]) throws SQLException	
public abstract void **setDate**(int paramIndex, Date paramType) throws SQLException	
public abstract void **setDouble**(int double paramType) throws SQLException	
public abstract void **setFloat**(int paramIndex, float paramType) throws SQLException	
public abstract void **setInt**(int paramIndex, int paramType) throws SQLException	
public abstract void **setLong**(int paramIndex, long paramType) throws SQLException	
public abstract void **setNull**(int paramIndex, int sqlType) throws SQLException	
public abstract void **setBigDecimal**(int paramIndex, BigDecimal paramType) throws SQLException	

(continued)

Method Name	Additional Description
public abstract void **setObject**(int paramIndex, Object paramType) throws SQLException	
public abstract void **setObject**(int paramIndex, Object paramType, int targetSqlType) throws SQLException	
public abstract void **setObject**(int paramIndex, Object paramType, int targetSqlType, int scale) throws SQLException	
public abstract void **setShort**(int paramIndex, short paramType) throws SQLException	
public abstract void **setString**(int paramIndex, String paramType) throws SQLException	
public abstract void **setTime**(int paramIndex, Time paramType) throws SQLException	
public abstract void **set TimeStamp**(int TimeStamp paramType) throws SQLException	
public abstract void **setUnicodeStream**(int paramIndexInputStream paramType, int length) throws SQLException	

public interface **ResultSet**

The results of a query are stored in this object, which is returned when the respective query execute method is run for the **Statement**, **PreparedStatement**, and **CallableStatement** methods. The **get** methods in this class fetch the result for the specified column, but the proper data type must be matched for the column. The **getMetaData** method in this class can facilitate the process of checking the data type in each column of the result set.

METHODS

Method Name	Additional Description
public abstract void **clearWarnings()** throws SQLException	Clears the warnings for the ResultSet
public abstract void **close()** throws SQLException	Closes the ResultSetpublic abstract int
findColumn(String columnName) throws SQLException	Gets the column number for the specified columnName in the ResultSet
public abstract **ResultSetMetaData** getMetaData() throws SQLException	Returns a ResultSetMetaData object that contains information about the query's resulting table
public abstract InputStream **getAsciiStream**(int columnIndex) throws SQLException	Fetches the result from the current row in the specified column (the column number columnIndex) in the resulting table
public abstract InputStream **getAsciiStream**(String columnName) throws SQLException	Fetches the result from the current row in the specified column (the column name— columnName) in the resulting table
public abstract InputStream **getBinaryStream**(int columnIndex) throws SQLException	Fetches the result from the current row in the specified column (the column number— columnIndex) in the resulting table
public abstract InputStream **getBinaryStream**(String columnName) throws SQLException	Fetches the result from the current row in the specified column (the column name— columnName) in the resulting table
public abstract boolean **getBoolean**(int columnIndex) throws SQLException	Fetches the result from the current row in the specified column (the column number— columnIndex) in the resulting table
public abstract boolean **getBoolean**(String columnName) throws SQLException	Fetches the result from the current row in the specified column (the column name— columnName) in the resulting table
public abstract byte **getByte**(int columnIndex) throws SQLException	Fetches the result from the current row in the specified column (the column number— columnIndex) in the resulting table
public abstract byte **getByte**(String columnName) throws SQLException	Fetches the result from the current row in the specified column (the column name— columnName) in the resulting table

(continued)

Method Name	Additional Description
public abstract byte[] **getBytes**(int columnIndex) throws SQLException	Fetches the result from the current row in the specified column (the column number—columnIndex) in the resulting table
public abstract byte[] **getBytes**(String columnName) throws SQLException	Fetches the result from the current row in the specified column (the column name—columnName) in the resulting table
public abstract String **getCursorName**() throws SQLException	Returns a String with this ResultSet's cursor name
public abstract Date **getDate**(int columnIndex) throws SQLException	Fetches the result from the current row in the specified column (the column number—columnIndex) in the resulting table
public abstract Date **getDate**(String columnName) throws SQLException	Fetches the result from the current row in the specified column (the column name—columnName) in the resulting table
public abstract double **getDouble**(int columnIndex) throws SQLException	Fetches the result from the current row in the specified column (the column number—columnIndex) in the resulting table
public abstract double **getDouble**(String columnName) throws SQLException	Fetches the result from the current row in the specified column (the column name—columnName) in the resulting table
public abstract float **getFloat**(int columnIndex) throws SQLException	Fetches the result from the current row in the specified column (the column number—columnIndex) in the resulting table
public abstract float **getFloat**(String columnName) throws SQLException	Fetches the result from the current row in the specified column (the column name—columnName) in the resulting table
public abstract int **getInt**(int columnIndex) throws SQLException	Fetches the result from the current row in the specified column (the column number—columnIndex) in the resulting table
public abstract int **getInt**(String columnName) throws SQLException	Fetches the result from the current row in the specified column (the column name—columnName) in the resulting table
public abstract long **getLong**(int columnIndex) throws SQLException	Fetches the result from the current row in the specified column (the column number—columnIndex) in the resulting table

(continued)

Method Name	Additional Description
public abstract long getLong(String columnName) throws SQLException	Fetches the result from the current row in the specified column (the column name—columnName) in the resulting table
public abstract Numeric getBigDecimal(int columnIndex, int scale) throws SQLException	Fetches the result from the current row in the specified column (the column number—columnIndex) in the resulting table
public abstract Numeric getBigDecimal(String columnName, int scale) throws SQLException	Fetches the result from the current row in the specified column (the column name—columnName) in the resulting table
public abstract Object getObject(int columnIndex) throws SQLException	Fetches the result from the current row in the specified column (the column number—columnIndex) in the resulting table
public abstract Object getObject(String columnName) throws SQLException	Fetches the result from the current row in the specified column (the column name—columnName) in the resulting table
public abstract short getShort(int columnIndex) throws SQLException	Fetches the result from the current row in the specified column (the column number—columnIndex) in the resulting table
public abstract short getShort (String columnName) throws SQLException	Fetches the result from the current row in the specified column (the column name—columnName) in the resulting table
public abstract String getString(int columnIndex) throws SQLException	Fetches the result from the current row in the specified column (the column number—columnIndex) in the resulting table
public abstract String getString (String columnName) throws SQLException	Fetches the result from the current row in the specified column (the column name—columnName) in the resulting table
public abstract Time getTime (int columnIndex) throws SQLException	Fetches the result from the current row in the specified column (the column number—columnIndex) in the resulting table
public abstract Time getTime (String columnName) throws SQLException	Fetches the result from the current row in the specified column (the column name—columnName) in the resulting table
public abstract TimeStamp get TimeStamp(int columnIndex) throws SQLException	Fetches the result from the current row in the specified column (the column number—columnIndex) in the resulting table

(continued)

Method Name	Additional Description
public abstract TimeStamp get TimeStamp(String columnName) throws SQLException	Fetches the result from the current row in the specified column (the column name—columnName) in the resulting table
public abstract InputStream getUnicodeStream(int columnIndex) throws SQLException	Fetches the result from the current row in the specified column (the column number—columnIndex) in the resulting table
public abstract InputStream getUnicodeStream(String columnName) throws SQLException	Fetches the result from the current row in the specified column (the column name—columnName) in the resulting table
public abstract SQLWarning getWarnings() throws SQLException	Returns the warnings for the ResultSet
public abstract boolean next() throws SQLException	Retrieves the next row of the resulting table
public abstract boolean wasNull() throws SQLException	Returns true if the last column read by one of the get methods was NULL

public interface ResultSetMetaData

This method allows access to information about a query's results, but not the results themselves. This object is created by the **ResultSet.getMetaData** method.

METHODS

Method Name	Additional Description
public abstract String getCatalogName(int column) throws SQLException	Returns the name of the catalog hit by the query
public abstract int getColumnCount() throws SQLException	Returns the number of columns in the resulting table
public abstract int getColumnDisplaySize (int column) throws SQLException	Returns the maximum size of the specified column
public abstract String getColumnLabel (int column) throws SQLException	Gets a label, if it exists, for the specified column in the result set
public abstract String getColumnName (int column) throws SQLException	Gets a name for the specified column number in the resulting table

(continued)

Method Name	Additional Description
public abstract int **getColumnType** (int column) throws SQLException	Returns a constant in the Type class that is the JDBC type of the specified column in the result set
public abstract String **getColumnTypeName**(int column) throws SQLException	Gets the name of the type of the specified column in the result set
public abstract int **getPrecision** (int column) throws SQLException	Returns the precision of the data in the specified column, if applicable
public abstract int **getScale**(int column) throws SQLException	Returns the scale of the data in the specified column, if applicable
public abstract String **getSchemaName**(int column) throws SQLException	Returns the name of the schema that was accessed in the query to produce the result set for the specified column
public abstract String **getTableName** (int column) throws SQLException	Returns the name of the table from which the specified column in the result set came
public abstract boolean **isAutoIncrement** (int column) throws SQLException	Returns true if the specified column is automatically numbered
public abstract boolean **isCaseSensitive** (int column) throws SQLException	Returns true if the specified column's contents are case sensitive, if applicable
public abstract boolean **isCurrency** (int column) throws SQLException	Returns true if the specified column in the result set contains currency
public abstract boolean **isDefinitelyWritable**(int column) throws SQLException	Returns true if a write operation in the specified column can be done for certain
public abstract int **isNullable**(int column) throws SQLException	Returns true if the specified column accepts NULL entries
public abstract boolean **isReadOnly** (int column) throws SQLException	Returns true if the specified column is read-only
public abstract boolean **isSearchable**(int column) throws SQLException	Returns true if the WHERE clause can be a part of the SQL query performed on the specified column
public abstract boolean **isSigned** (int column) throws SQLException	Returns true if the data contained in the specified column in the result set is signed, if applicable
public abstract boolean **isWritable** (int column) throws SQLException	Returns true if a write on the specified column is possible

VARIABLES

Variable Name	Additional Description
public final static int **columnNoNulls**	NULL values not allowed
public final static int **columnNullable**	NULL values allowed
public final static int **columnNullableUnknown**	NULL values may or may not be allowed, uncertain

public interface Statement

This class is used to execute an SQL query against the database via the **Connection** object. The **Connection.createStatement** returns a **Statement** object. Methods in the **Statement** class produce **ResultSet** objects that are used to fetch the result of a query executed in this class.

METHODS

Method Name	Additional Description
public abstract void **cancel**() throws SQLException	If a query is running in another thread, a foreign thread can cancel it by calling this method on the local Statement object's instantiation
public abstract void **clearWarnings**() throws SQLException	Clears the warnings for the Statement
public abstract void **close**() throws	Closes the Statement and frees its associated SQLException resources, including any ResultSets
public abstract boolean **execute**(String sql) throws SQLException	Executes the parameter sql, which is an SQL query; this method accounts for multiple ResultSets
public abstract ResultSet **executeQuery** (String sql) throws SQLException	Executes a query that returns a ResultSet object (produces some results) using the sql parameter as the SQL query
public abstract int **executeUpdate–** (String sql) throws SQLException	Executes a query that does not produce a resulting table; the method returns the number of rows affected, or 0 if no result is produced

(continued)

Method Name	Additional Description
public abstract int **getMaxFieldSize()** throws SQLException	Returns the maximum amount of data returned for a resulting column; applies only to the following SQL datatypes: BINARY, VARBINARY, LONGVARBINARY, CHAR, VARCHAR, and LONGVARCHAR
public abstract int **getMaxRows()** throws SQLException	Returns the maximum number of rows a ResultSet can contain
public abstract boolean **getMoreResults()** throws SQLException	Returns true if the next ResultSet of the query is present, and moves the ResultSet into the current result space
public abstract int **getQueryTimeout()** throws SQLException	Returns the number of seconds that the JDBC driver will wait for a query to execute
public abstract ResultSet **getResultSet()** throws SQLException	Returns a ResultSet object that is the current result of the query; only one of these is returned if only one ResultSet is the result of the query; if more ResultSets are present, the getMoreResults method is used to move to the next ResultSet
public abstract int **getUpdateCount()** throws SQLException	Returns the update count; if the result is a ResultSet, -1 is returned
public abstract SQLWarning **getWarnings()** throws SQLException	Returns the warnings encountered for the query of this Statement object
public abstract void **setCursorName** (String name) throws SQLException	Sets the name of a cursor for future reference and uses it in update statements
public abstract void **setEscapeProcessing** (boolean enable) throws SQLException	Sets escape substitution processing
public abstract void **setMaxFieldSize** (int max) throws SQLException	Sets the maximum amount of data that can be returned for a column of type BINARY, VARBINARY, LONGVARBINARY, CHAR, VARCHAR, and LONGVARCHAR
public abstract void **setMaxRows** (int max) throws SQLException	Sets the maximum number of rows that can be retrieved in a ResultSet
public abstract void **setQueryTimeout** (int seconds) throws SQLException	Sets the time a driver will wait for a query to execute

Exceptions

Finally, we get to the exceptions. As with the other sections, the exception listings include a description and the class' constructors and methods.

public class DataTruncation

This class extends **SQLWarning**. An exception is produced when data transfer is prematurely terminated on a write operation; a warning is generated when data transfer is prematurely terminated on a read operation. You can use the methods contained here to provide debugging information because the JDBC driver should throw this exception when it encounters a data transfer problem.

CONSTRUCTORS

Constructor	Additional Description
public **DataTruncation**(int index, boolean parameter, boolean read, int dataSize, int transferSize)	Builds a Throwable DataTruncation object with the specified propertiesMethods
public int **getDataSize**()	Returns the number of bytes that should have been transferred
public int **getIndex**()	Returns the index of the column or parameter that was interrupted
public boolean **getParameter**()	Returns true if the truncated value was a parameter, or false if it was a column
public boolean **getRead**()	Returns true if truncation occurred on a read; false means truncation occurred on a write
public int **getTransferSize**()	Returns the number of bytes actually transferred

public class SQLException

This class extends **java.lang.Exception**. It is the responsibility of the JDBC driver to throw this class when a problem occurs during an operation.

These constructors are used to create an **SQLException** with the specified information. It is normally not necessary to create an exception unless the developer is working on creating a driver or higher-level JDBC interface:

public **SQLException**()
public **SQLException**(String problem)
public **SQLException**(String problem, String SQLState)
public **SQLException**(String problem, String SQLState, int vendorCode)

METHODS

Method Name	Additional Description
public int **getErrorCode**()	Returns the error code that was part of the thrown exception
public SQLException **getNextException**()	Returns the next exception as an SQLException object
public String **getSQLState**()	Returns the SQL state that was part of the thrown exception
public synchronized void **setNextException** (SQLException excp) SQLException	Sets the next exception as excp for the object

public class SQLWarning

This class extends **SQLException**. It is the responsibility of the JDBC driver to throw this class when a problem occurs during an operation.

CONSTRUCTORS

These constructors build an **SQLWarning** object with the specified information. It is normally not necessary to create an **SQLWarning** unless the developer is working on creating a driver or higher-level JDBC interface:

public **SQLWarning**()
public **SQLWarning**(String problem)
public **SQLWarning**(String problem, String SQLState)
public **SQLWarning**(String problem, String SQLState, int vendorCode)

METHODS

Method Name	Additional Description
public SQLWarning getNextWarning()	Returns an SQLWarning object that contains the next warning
public void setNextWarning (SQLWarning warn)	Sets the next SQLWarning for the SQLWarning object

Java Language Fundamentals

I f you are already familiar with programming, especially C or C++ programming, this appendix should serve as a good hands-on review. As we discuss Java, we'll point out the areas in which Java differs from other languages. If you don't have much experience using structured programming languages, this appendix will give you a good overview of the basic components required to make programming languages like Java come alive.

The actual language components featured in this appendix include:

- Comments

- Identifiers

- Keywords

- Data types

- Variable declarations

This chapter, which originally appeared in the *Java Programming Language Handbook*, is reprinted with permission. David H. Friedel and Anthony Potts, *Java Programming Language Handbook*. The Coriolis Group: 1996

What Makes A Java Program?

Before we get into the details of each Java language component, let's stand back 10 steps and look at how many of the key language components are used in the context of a Java program. Figure A.1(shown later) presents a complete visual guide. Here, we've highlighted components such as variable declarations, Java keywords, operators, literals, expressions, and control structures.

In case you're wondering, the output for this program looks like this:

```
Hello John my name is Anthony
That's not my name!
Let's count to ten....
1 2 3 4 5 6 7 8 9 10
Now down to zero by two.
10 8 6 4 2 0
Finally, some arithmetic:
10 * 3.09 = 30.9
10 * 3.09 = 30 (integer cast)
10 / 3.09 = 3.23625
10 / 3.09 = 3 (integer cast)
```

Lexical Structure

The lexical structure of a language refers to the elements of code that make the code easy for us to understand, but have no effect on the compiled code. For example, all of the comments you place in a program to help you understand how it works are ignored by the Java compiler. You could have a thousand lines of comments for a 20-line program and the compiled *bytecodes* for the program would be the same size if you took out all the comments. This does not mean that *all* lexical structures are optional. It simply means that they do not effect the bytecodes.

The lexical structures we'll discuss include:

- Comments
- Identifiers
- Keywords
- Separators

Comments

Comments make your code easy to understand, modify, and use. But adding comments to an application only after it is finished is not a good practice. More often than not, you won't remember what the code you wrote actually does after you get away from it for a while. Unfortunately, many programmers follow this time-honored tradition. We suggest you try to get in the habit of adding comments as you write your code.

Java supports three different types of comment styles. The first two are taken directly from C and C++. The third type of comment is a new one that can be used to automatically create class and method documentation.

COMMENT STYLE #1

```
/* Comments here... */
```

This style of commenting comes to us directly from C. Everything between the initial slash-asterisk and ending asterisk-slash is ignored by the Java compiler. This style of commenting can be used anywhere in a program, even in the middle of code (not a good idea). This style of commenting is useful when you have multiple lines of comments because your comment lines can wrap from one line to the next, and you only need to use one set of the /* and */ symbols. Examples:

```
/*
This program was written by Joe Smith.
It is the greatest program ever written!
*/

while (i <= /* comments can be placed here */ maxnum)
{
    total += i;
    i++;
}
```

In the second example, the comment line is embedded within the program statement. The compiler skips over the comment text, and thus the actual line of code would be processed as:

```
while (i <= maxnum)
...
```

```
/**
 * Sample Java Application ——————— unique Java style comment
 * @author Anthony Potts
 * @version 1.0
 */                                    ┌— superclass
                                                        ┌—————— standard C++
class Test extends Object { // Begin Test class          style comment
    // Define class variables
    static int i = 10;        ————————— standard data type
                              ┌———————— variable
    static final double d = 3.09;
                              └————————— literal

    /*
    The main() method is automatically called when
    the program is run. Any words typed after the program
    name when it is run are placed in the args[] variable,
    which is an array of strings.
    For this program to work properly, at least one word must
    be typed after the program name or else an error will occur.
    */
    public static void main(String args[]) {
        Test thisTest = new Test(); // Create instance (object) of class
        String myName = "Anthony";  └——————— declaration and assignment
        boolean returnValue;        ————————— assignment operator

                                                        ┌— string data type
        System.out.println("Hello " + args[0] + " my name is " + myName);


        if(thisTest.sameName(args[0], myName)) {
            System.out.println("Your name is the same as mine!");
        } else {
            System.out.println("That's not my name!");
        }


        System.out.println("Let's count to ten....");    ┌—if-then-else
                                                          │ control structure
                              ┌————— increment operator
        for (int x = 1; x < 11; x++) {
            System.out.print(x + " ");
        }                     └——————————— expression
```

Figure A.1
A visual guide to the key Java language components.

```
        System.out.println("\nNow down to zero by two.");
                                          logical expression
        while ( i > -1) {
            System.out.print(i + " ");
            i -= 2;
        }


        System.out.println("\nFinally, some arithmetic:");

        thisTest.doArithmetic();    ——— method call
    }

    // This method compares the two names sent to it and
    // returns true if they are the same and false if they are not
    public boolean sameName(String firstName, String secondName) {
        if (firstName.equals(secondName)) {
            return true;
        } else {                                    returns value to calling class
            return false;
        }
    }


    // This method performs a few computations and prints the result
    public void doArithmetic(){
        i = 10;    ——————————— assignment expression
        System.out.println(i + " * " + d + " = " + (i * d));
        System.out.println(i + " * " + d + " = " +
                            (int)(i * d) + " (Integer)");
        System.out.println(i + " / " + d + " = " + (i / d));
        System.out.println(i + " / " + d + " = " +
                            (int)(i / d) + " (Integer)");
    }
} // End of class
```

while control statement — (points to while loop block)

method modifier — (points to public)

Figure A.1
Continued.

Programmers occasionally use this style of commenting while they are testing and debugging code. For example, you could comment out part of an equation or expression:

```
sum = i /* + (base - 10) */ + factor;
```

COMMENT STYLE #2

```
// Comment here ..
```

This style of commenting is borrowed from C++. Everything after the double slash marks is ignored by the Java compiler. The comment is terminated by a line return, so you can't use multiple comment lines unless you start each line with the double-slash. Examples:

```
// This program was written by Joe Smith.
// It is the greatest program ever written!

while (i <= // this won't work maxnum)
{
   total += i;
   i++;
}


base = 20;
// This comment example also won't work because the Java
   compiler will treat this second line as a line of code
value = 50;
```

The comment used in the second example won't work like you might intend because the remainder of the line of code would be commented out (everything after i <=). In the third example, the second comment line is missing the starting // symbols, and the Java compiler will get confused because it will try to process the comment line as if it were a line of code. Believe it or not, this type of commenting mistake occurs often—so watch out for it.

COMMENT STYLE #3

```
/** Doc Comment here... */
```

This comment structure may look very similar to the C style of commenting, but that extra asterisk at the beginning makes a huge difference. Of course, remember that only one asterisk must be used as the comment terminator. The Java compiler still ignores the comment, but another program called JAVADOC.EXE, which ships with the Java Development Kit, uses these comments to construct HTML documentation files that describe your packages, classes, and methods, as well as all the variables they use.

Let's look at the third style of commenting in more detail. If implemented correctly and consistently, this style of commenting can provide you with numerous benefits. Figure A.2 shows what the output of the JAVADOC program looks like when run on a typical Java source file.

If you have ever looked at the Java API documentation on Sun's Web site, Figure A.2 should look familiar to you. In fact, the entire API documentation was created this way.

JAVADOC will work if you have created comments or not. Figure A.3 shows the output from this simple application:

```java
class HelloWorld {
    public static void main(String args[]) {
        System.out.println("Hello World");
    }
}
```

To add a little more information to our documentation, all we have to do is add this third style of comments. If we change the little HelloWorld application and add a few key comments, the code will look like this:

```java
/**
 * Welcome to HelloWorld
 * @author Anthony Potts
 * @version 1.1
 * @see java.lang.System
 */
class helloworld {
    /**
     * Main method of helloworld
     */
    public static void main(String args[]) {
        System.out.println("Hello World!");
    }
}
```

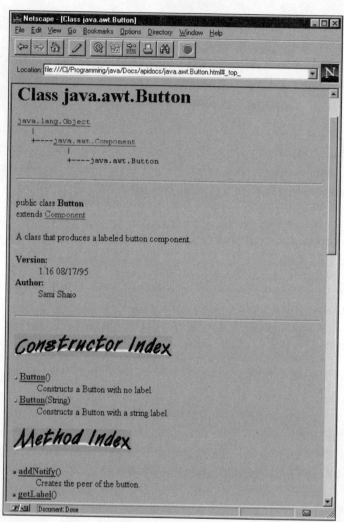

Figure A.2
Sample output from the JAVADOC program.

If you now run JAVADOC, the browser will display what you see in Figure A.4. As you can see, this gives us much more information. This system is great for producing documentation for public distribution. Just like all comments, though, it is up to you to make sure that the comments are accurate and plentiful enough to be helpful. Table A.1 lists the tags you can use in your class comments.

Figure A.3
Sample output from the JAVADOC program.

TABLE A.1

TAGS FOR CLASS COMMENTS.

Tag	Description
@see *classname*	Adds a hyperlinked "See Also" to your class; the *classname* can be any other class
@see *fully-qualified-classname*	Also adds a "See Also" to the class, but this time you need to use a fully qualified class name like "java.awt.window"
@see *fully-qualified-classname#methodname*	Also adds a "See Also" to the class, but now you are pointing to a specific method within that class
@version *version-text*	Adds a version number that you provide; the version number can be numbers or text
@author *author-name*	Adds an author entry; you can use multiple author tags

(continued)

	TABLE A.1

TAGS FOR CLASS COMMENTS (*CONTINUED*).

Tag	Description
The tags you can use in your method comments include all of the "@see" tags as well as the following:	
@param *paramter-name description...*	Used to show which parameters the method accepts; multiple "@param" tags are acceptable
@return *description...*	Used to describe what the method returns
@exception *fully-qualified-classname description...*	Used to add a "throw" entry that describes what type of exceptions this method can throw; multiple "@exception" tags are acceptable

Identifiers

Identifiers are the names used for variables, classes, methods, packages, and interfaces which allow the compiler to distinguish them. Identifiers in the Java language should always begin with a letter of the alphabet, either upper or lower case. The only exceptions to this rule are the underscore symbol (_) and the dollar sign ($), which may also be used. If you try to use any other symbol or a numeral as the initial character, you will receive an error.

After the initial character, you are allowed to use numbers, but not all symbols. You can also use almost all of the characters from the Unicode character set. If you are not familiar with the Unicode character set or you get errors, we suggest that you stick with the standard alphabetic characters.

The length of an identifier is basically unlimited. We managed to get up to a few thousand characters before we got bored. It's doubtful you will ever need that many characters, but it is nice to know that the Java compiler won't limit you if you want to create long descriptive names. The only limit you may encounter involves creating class names. Since class names are also used as file names, you need to create names that will not cause problems with your operating system or anyone who will be using your program.

You must also be careful not to use any of the special Java keywords listed in the next section. Here are some examples of valid identifiers:

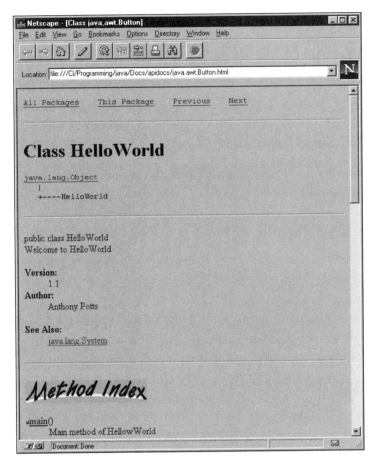

Figure A.4
The new JAVADOC output.

```
HelloWorld      $Money       TickerTape
_ME2            Chapter3     ABC123
```

And here are some examples of invalid identifiers:

```
3rdChapter      #Hello       -Main
```

COMMON ERRORS WHEN USING IDENTIFIERS

As you are defining and using identifiers in your Java programs, you are bound to encounter some errors from time to time. Let's look at some of the more common error messages that the Java compiler displays. Notice that we've included the part of the code that is responsible for generating the error, the error message, and a description of the message so that you can make sense of it.

Code Example:
```
public class 1test {
}
```

Error Message:
```
D:\java\lib\test.java:1: Identifier expected.
```

Description:
An invalid character has been used in the class identifier. You will see this error when the first character is invalid (especially when it is a number).

Code Example:
```
public class te?st {
}
```

Error Message:
```
D:\java\lib\test.java:1: '{' Expected
```

Description:
This is a common error that occurs when you have an invalid character in the middle of an identifier. In this case, the question mark is invalid, so the compiler gets confused where the class definition ends and its implementation begins.

Code Example:
```
public class #test {
}
```

Error Message:
```
D:\java\lib\test.java:1: Invalid character in input.
```

Description:
Here, the error stems from the fact that the initial character is invalid.

Code Example:
```
public class catch {
}
```

Error Message:
```
D:\java\lib\test.java:1: Identifier expected.
```

Description:
This error shows up when you use a protected keyword as an identifier.

Keywords

In Java, like other languages, there are certain *keywords* or "tokens" that are reserved for system use. These keywords can't be used as names for your classes, variables, packages, or anything else. The keywords are used for a number of tasks such as defining control structures (*if, while,* and *for*) and declaring data types (*int, char,* and *float*). Table A.2 provides the complete list of Java keywords.

The words marked with an asterisk (*) are not currently used in the Java language, but you still can't use them to create your own identifiers. More than likely, they will be used as keywords in future versions of the Java language.

Literals

Literals are the values that you assign when entering explicit values. For example, in an assignment statement like this

```
i = 10;
```

the value 10 is a literal. But do not get literals confused with types. Even though they usually go hand in hand, literals and types are not the same.

TABLE A.2

JAVA LANGUAGE KEYWORDS.

Keyword	Description
abstract	Class modifier
boolean	Used to define a boolean data type
break	Used to break out of loops
byte	Used to define a byte data type
byvalue *	Not implemented yet
cast	Used to translate from type to type
catch	Used with error handling
char	Used to define a character data type (16-bit)
class	Used to define a class structure
const *	Not implemented yet
continue	Used to continue an operation

(continued)

JAVA LANGUAGE KEYWORDS (*CONTINUED*).

Keyword	Description
default	Used with the switch statement
do	Used to create a do loop control structure
Double	Used to define a floating-point data type (64-bit)
else	Used to create an else clause for an if statement
extends	Used to subclass
final	Used to tell Java that this class can not be subclassed
finally	Used with exceptions to determine the last option before exiting; it guarantees that code gets called if an exception does or does not happen
float	Used to define a floating-point data type (32-bit)
for	Used to create a for loop control structure
future *	Not implemented yet
generic *	Not implemented yet
goto *	Not implemented yet
if	Used to create an if-then decision-making control structure
implements	Used to define which interfaces to use
import	Used to reference external Java packages
inner	Used to create control blocks
instanceof	Used to determine if an object is of a certain type
int	Used to define an integer data type (32-bit values)
interface	Used to tell Java that the code that follows is an interface
interfacelong	Used to define an integer data type (64-bit values)
native	Used when calling external code
new	Operator used when creating an instance of a class (an object)
null	Reference to a non-existent value
operator *	Not implemented yet
outer	Used to create control blocks
package	Used to tell Java what package the following code belongs to
private	Modifier for classes, methods, and variables
protected	Modifier for classes, methods, and variables

(continued)

JAVA LANGUAGE KEYWORDS (*CONTINUED*).

Keyword	Description
public	Modifier for classes, methods, and variables
rest *	Not implemented yet
return	Used to set the return value of a class or method
short	Used to define an integer data type (16-bit values)
static	Modifier for classes, methods, and variables
super	Used to reference the current class's parent class
switch	Block statement used to pick from a group of choices
synchronized	Modifier that tells Java that only one instance of a method can be run at one time; it keeps Java from running the method a second time before the first is finished; it is especially useful when dealing with files to avoid conflicts
this	Used to reference the current object
throw	Statement that tells Java what exception to pass on an error
transient	Modifier that can access future Java code
try	Operator that is used to test for exceptions in code
var *	Not implemented yet
void	Modifier for setting the return value of a class or method to nothing
volatile	Variable modifier
while	Used to create a while loop control structure

Types are used to define what type of data a variable can hold, while literals are the values that are actually assigned to those variables.

Literals come in three flavors: numeric, character, and boolean. Boolean literals are simply True and False.

NUMERIC LITERALS

Numeric literals are just what they sound like—numbers. We can further subdivide the numeric literals into *integers* and *floating-point* literals.

Integer literals are usually represented in *decimal* format, although you can use the *hexadecimal* and *octal* format in Java. If you want to use the hexadecimal format, your numbers need to begin with an 0x or 0X. Octal integers simply begin with a zero (0).

Integer literals are stored differently depending on their size. The **int** data type is used to store 32-bit integer values ranging from -2,147,483,648 to 2,147,483,648 (decimal). If you need to use even larger numbers, Java switches over to the **long** data type, which can store 64 bits of information for a range of - 9.223372036855e+18 to 9.223372036855e+18. This would give you a number a little larger than 9 million trillion—enough to take care of the national debt! To specify a **long** integer, you will need to place an "l" or "L" at the end of the number. Don't get confused by our use of the terms **int** and **long**. There are many other integer data types used by Java, but they all use **int** or **long** literals to assign values. Table A.3 provides a summary of the two integer literals.

Here are some examples of how integer literals can be used to assign values in Java statements:

```
int i;
i - 1;        // All of these literals are of the integer type
i= -9;
i - 1203131;

i - 0xA11;    // Using a hexadecimal literal
i - 07543;    // Using an octal literal

i - 4.5;      // This would be illegal because a floating-point
              // literal can't be assigned to an integer type
long lg;
lg - 1L;      // All of these literals are of the long
              // integer type
lg - -9e15;
lg - 7e12;
```

TABLE **A.3**

SUMMARY OF INTEGER LITERALS.

Integer Literals Ranges	Negative Minimum	Positive Maximum
int data type	-2,147,483,648	2,147,483,648
long data type	-9.223372036855e+18	9.223372036855e+18

The other type of numeric literal is the floating-point literal. Floating-point values are any numbers that have anything to the right of the decimal place. Similar to integers, floating-point values have 32-bit and 64-bit representations. Both data types conform to IEEE standards. Table A.4 provides a summary of the two floating-point literals.

Here are some examples of how floating-point literals can be used to assign values in Java statements:

```
float f;
f = 1.3;  // All of these literals are of the floating-point
          // type float (32-bit)
f = -9.0;
f = 1203131.1241234;


double d;
d = 1.0D;  // All of these literals are of the floating-
           // point type double(32-bit)
d = -9.3645e235;
d = 7.0001e52D;
```

CHARACTER LITERALS

The second type of literal that you need to know about is the *character literal*. Character literals include single characters and strings. Single character literals are enclosed in single quotation marks, while string literals are enclosed in double quotes.

Single characters can be any one character from the Unicode character set. There are also a few special two-character combinations that are non-printing characters but which perform important functions. Table A.5 shows these special combinations.

TABLE A.4

SUMMARY OF FLOATING–POINT LITERALS.

Floating–Point Ranges	Negative Minimum	Positive Maximum
float data type	1.40239846e-45	3.40282347e38
double data type	4.94065645841246544e-324	1.79769313486231570e308

	TABLE A.5

SPECIAL CHARACTER COMBINATIONS IN JAVA.

Character Combination	Standard Designation	Description
\	<newline>	Continuation
\n	NL or LF	New Line
\b	BS	Backspace
\r	CR	Carriage Return
\f	FF	Form Feed
\t	HT	Horizontal Tab
\\	\	Backslash
\'	'	Single Quote
\"	"	Double Quote
\xdd	0xdd	Hex Bit Pattern
\ddd	0ddd	Octal Bit Pattern
\uddd	0xdddd	Unicode Character

The character combinations from Table A.5 also apply to strings. Here are some examples of how character and string literals can be used in Java statements:

```
char ch;
ch = 'a';    // All of these literals are characters
ch = \n;     // Assign the newline character
ch = \';     // Assign a single quote
ch = \x30;   // Assign a hexadecimal character code

String str;
str = "Java string";
```

Operators

Operators are used to perform computations on one or more variables or objects. You use operators to add values, compare the size of two numbers, assign a value to a variable, increment the value of a variable, and so on. Table A.6 lists the operators used in Java. Later in this appendix, we'll explain in detail how each operator works, and we'll also explain operator precedence.

OPERATORS USED IN JAVA.

Operator	Description
+	Addition
-	Subtraction
*	Multiplication
/	Division
%	Modulo
++	Increment
—	Decrement
>	Greater than
>=	Greater than or equal to
<	Less than
<=	Less than or equal to
==	Equal to
!=	Not equal to
!	Logical NOT
&&	Logical AND
||	Logical OR
&	Bitwise AND
^	Bitwise exclusive OR
|	Bitwise OR
~	Bitwise complement
<<	Left shift
>>	Right shift
>>>	Zero fill right shift
=	Assignment
+=	Assignment with addition
-=	Assignment with subtraction
*=	Assignment with multiplication
/=	Assignment with division
%=	Assignment with modulo

(continued)

	TABLE A.6

OPERATORS USED IN JAVA (*CONTINUED*).

Operator	Description
&=	Assignment with bitwise AND
|=	Assignment with bitwise OR
^=	Assignment with bitwise exclusive OR
<<=	Assignment with left shift
>>=	Assignment with right shift
>>>=	Assignment with zero fill right shift

Separators

Separators are used in Java to delineate blocks of code. For example, you use curly brackets to enclose a method's implementation, and you use parentheses to enclose arguments being sent to a method. Table A.7 lists the seperators used in Java.

Types And Variables

Many people confuse the terms *types* and *variables*, and use them synonymously. They are, however, not the same. Variables are basically buckets that *hold information*, while types *describe what type of information* is in the bucket.

A variable must have both a type and an identifier. Later in this appendix we will cover the process of declaring variables. For now, we just want to guide you through the details of how to decide which types to use and how to use them properly.

	TABLE A.7

SEPARATORS USED IN JAVA.

Separator	Description
( )	Used to define blocks of arguments
[ ]	Used to define arrays
{ }	Used to hold blocks of code
,	Used to separate arguments or variables in a declaration
;	Used to terminate lines of contiguous code

Similar to literals, types can be split into several different categories, including the numeric types—**byte**, **short**, **int**, **long**, **float**, and **double**—and the **char** and **boolean** types. We will also discuss the string type. Technically, the string type is not a type—it is a class. However, it is used so commonly that we decided to include it here.

All of the integer numeric types use signed two's-complement integers for storing data. Table A.8 provides a summary of the ranges for each of the key Java data types.

byte

The **byte** type can be used for variables whose value falls between -256 and 255. **byte** types have an 8-bit length. Here are some examples of **byte** values:

`-7 5  238`

short

The **short** numeric type can store values ranging from -32768 to 32767. It has a 16-bit depth. Here are some examples:

`-7 256   -29524`

int

The **int** data type takes the **short** type to the next level. It uses a 32-bit signed integer value that takes our minimal and maximal value up to over 2 billion.

TABLE **A.8**

SUMMARY OF THE JAVA DATATYPES.

Data Type	Negative Minimal	Positive Maximal
byte	-256	255
short	-32768	32767
int	-2147483648	2147483647
long	-9223372036854775808	9223372036854775807
float	1.40239846e-45	3.40282347e38
double	4.94065645841246544e-324	1.79769313486231570e308
boolean	False	True

Because of this tremendous range, it is one of the most often used data types for integers.

Often, unskilled programmers will use the **int** data type even though they don't need the full resolution that this data type provides. If you are using smaller integers, you should consider using the **short** data type. The rule of thumb to follow is *if you know exactly the range of values a certain variable will store, use the smallest data type possible.* This will let your program use less memory and therefore run faster, especially on slower machines or machines with limited RAM.

Here are some examples of **int** values:

```
-7 256   -29523234 1321412422
```

long

The **long** data type is the mother of all integer types. It uses a full 64-bit data path to store values that reach up to over 9 million trillion. But be extremely careful when using variables of the **long** type. If you start using too many of them, or God forbid, an array of **long**s, you can quickly eat up a ton of resources.

The Danger Of Using Long

Java provides useful garbage collection tools, so when you are done with these large data types, they will be disposed of and their re-sources reclaimed. But if you are creating large arrays of **long** integers, you could really be asking for trouble. For example, if you created a two-dimensional array of **long** integers that had a 100×100 grid, you would be using up about 100 kilobytes of memory.

Here are some examples of **long** values:

```
-7 256   -29523234 1.835412e15  -3e18
```

float

The **float** data type is one of two types used to store floating-point values. The **float** type is compliant with the IEEE 754 conventions. The floating-point types of Java can store gargantuan numbers. We do not have enough room on the page to physically show you the minimal and maximal values the **float** data type can store, so we will use a little bit of tricky sounding lingo taken from the Java manual:

*The finite nonzero values of type **float** are of the form s * m * 2e, where s is +1 or -1, m is a positive integer less than 2^24 and e is an integer between -149 and 104, inclusive.*

Whew, that's a mouthful. Here are a few examples to show you what the **float** type might look like in actual use:

```
-7F   256.0   -23e34     23e100
```

double

As if the **float** type could not hold enough, the **double** data type gives you even bigger storage space. Let's look again at Sun's definition of the possible values for a **double**:

*The finite nonzero values of type **float** are of the form s * m * 2e, where s is +1 or -1, m is a positive integer less than 2^53 and e is an integer between -1045 and 1000, inclusive.*

Again, you can have some truly monstrous numbers here. But when you start dealing with hardcore programming, this type of number becomes necessary from time to time, so it is wise to understand its ranges. Here are a few examples:

```
-7.0D     256.0D     -23e424   23e1000
```

boolean

In other languages, the **boolean** data type has been designated by an integer with a nonzero or zero value to represent True and False, respectively. This method works well because it gives the user the ability to check for all kinds of values and perform expressions like this:

```
x=2;
if x then...
```

This can be handy when performing parsing operations or checking string lengths. In Java, however, the **boolean** data type has its own True and False literals that do not correspond to other values. In fact, as you will learn later in this appendix, Java does not even allow you to perform casts between the **boolean** data type and any others. There are ways around this limitation, and we will discuss them when we talk about conversion methods.

char

The **char** data type is used to store single characters. Since Java uses the Unicode character set, the **char** type needs to be able to store thousands of characters, so it uses a 16-bit signed integer. The **char** data type has the ability to be cast or converted to almost all of the others, as we will show you in the next section.

string

The **string** type is actually not a primitive data type; it is a class all its own. We decided to talk a little about it here because it is so commonly used that it might as well be considered a primitive. In C and C++, strings are stored in arrays of chars. Java does not use the **char** type for this, but instead has created its own class that handles strings.

One big advantage to using a class instead of an array of **char** types is that we are more or less unlimited in the amount of information we can place in a string variable. In C++, the array of chars was limited; now that limitation is taken care of within the class, where we do not care how it is handled.

Variable Declarations

Declaring variables in Java is very similar to declaring variables in C/C++, as long as you are using the primitive data types. As we said before, almost everything in Java is a class—except the primitive data types. Let's look at how primitive data types are declared.

Here is what a standard declaration for a primitive variable might look like:

```
int i;
```

We have just declared a variable "i" to be an integer. Here are a few more examples:

```
byte i, j;
int a=7, b = a;
```

```
float f = 1.06;
String name = "Tony";
```

These examples illustrate some of the things you can do while declaring variables. Let's look at each one individually.

```
int i;
```

This is the most basic declaration, with the data type followed by the variable you are declaring.

```
byte i, j;
```

In this example, we are declaring two byte variables at one time. There is no limit to the number of variables you can declare this way. All you have to do is add a comma between each variable you wish to declare of the given type, and Java takes care of it for you.

You also have the ability to assign values to variables as you declare them. You can even use a variable you are declaring as part of an expression for the declaration of another variable in the same line. Before we confuse you more, here is an example:

```
int i = 1;
int j = i, k= i + j;
```

Here we have first declared a variable **i** as **int** and assigned it a value of 1. In the next line, we start by declaring a variable **j** to be equal to **i**. This is perfectly legal. Next, on the same line, we declare a variable **k** to be equal to **i** plus **j**. Once again, Java handles this without a problem. We could even shorten these two statements to one line like this:

```
int i = 1, j = i, k= i + j;
```

One thing to watch out for is using variables *before* they have been declared. Here's an example:

```
int j = i, k= i + j;  // i is not defined yet
int i = 1;
```

This would cause an "undefined variable" error because Java does not know to look ahead for future declarations. Let's look at another example:

```
float f = 1.06;
```

Does this look correct? Yes, but it's not. This is a tricky one. By default, Java assumes that numbers with decimal points are of type **double**. So, when you try and declare a **float** to be equal to this number, you receive the following error:

```
Incompatible type for declaration. Explicit cast needed to convert double
to float.
```

Sounds complicated, but all this error message means is that you need to explicitly tell Java that the literal value 1.06 is a **float** and not a **double**. There are two ways to accomplish this. First, you can *cast* the value to a **float** like this:

```
float f = (float)1.06;
```

This works fine, but it can get confusing. Java also follows the convention used by other languages of placing an "f" at the end of the literal value to indicate explicitly that it is a **float**. This also works for the **double** data type, except that you would use a "d". (By the way, capitalization of the "f" and "d" does not make a difference.)

```
float f = 1.06f;
double d = 1.06d;
```

You should realize that the "d" is not needed in the **double** declaration because Java assumes it. However, it is better to label all of your variables when possible, especially if you are not sure.

Using Arrays

It's difficult to imagine creating any large application or applet without having an array or two. Java uses arrays in a much different manner than other languages. Instead of being a structure that holds variables, arrays in Java are actually objects that can be treated just like any other Java object.

The powerful thing to realize here is that because arrays are objects that are derived from a class, they have methods you can call to retrieve information about the array or to manipulate the array. The current version of the Java language only supports the **length** method, but you can expect that more methods will be added as the language evolves.

One of the drawbacks to the way Java implements arrays is that they are only one-dimensional. In most other languages, you can create a two-dimensional array by just adding a comma and a second array size. In Java, this does not work. The way around this limitation is to create an array of arrays. Because this is easy to do, the lack of built-in support for multi-dimensional arrays shouldn't hold you back.

Declaring Arrays

Since arrays are actually instances of classes (objects), we need to use constructors to create our arrays much like we did with strings. First, we need to pick a variable name, declare it as an array object, and specify which data type the array will hold. Note that an array can only hold a single data type—you can't mix strings and integers within a single array. Here are a few examples of how array variables are declared:

```
int intArray[];
String Names[];
```

As you can see, these look very similar to standard variable declarations, except for the brackets after the variable name. You could also put the brackets after the data type if you think this approach makes your declarations more readable:

```
int[] intArray;
String[] Names;
```

Sizing Arrays

There are three ways to set the size of arrays. Two of them require the use of the **new** operator. Using the **new** operator initializes all of the array elements to a default value. The third method involves filling in the array elements with values as you declare it.

The first method involves taking a previously declared variable and setting the size of the array. Here are a few examples:

```
int intArray[];                    // Declare the arrays
String Names[];

intArray[] - new int[10];          // Size each array
Names[] - new String[100];
```

Or, you can size the array object when you declare it:

```
int intArray[] - new int[10];
String Names[] - new String[100];
```

Finally, you can fill in the array with values at declaration time:

```
String Names[] - {"Tony", "Dave", "Jon", "Ricardo"};
int[] intArray - {1, 2, 3, 4, 5};
```

Accessing Array Elements

Now that you know how to initialize arrays, you'll need to learn how to fill them with data and then access the array elements to retrieve the data. We showed you a very simple way to add data to arrays when you initialize them, but often this just is not flexible enough for real-world programming tasks. To access an array value, you simply need to know its location. The indexing system used to access array elements is zero-based, which means that the first value is always located at position 0. Let's look at a little program that first fills in an array and then prints it out:

```
public class powersOf2 {

    public static void main(String args[]) {
        int intArray[] - new int[20];
        for (int i - 0; i < intArray.length; i++) {
            intArray[i] - 1;
            for(int p - 0; p <  i; p++) intArray[i] *- 2 ;
        }
        for (int i - 0; i < intArray.length; i++)
            System.out.println("2 to the power of " + i + " is " +
                intArray[i]);
    }
}
```

The output of this program looks like this:

```
2 to the power of 0 is 1
2 to the power of 1 is 2
2 to the power of 2 is 4
2 to the power of 3 is 8
2 to the power of 4 is 16
2 to the power of 5 is 32
2 to the power of 6 is 64
2 to the power of 7 is 128
2 to the power of 8 is 256
2 to the power of 9 is 512
2 to the power of 10 is 1024
2 to the power of 11 is 2048
2 to the power of 12 is 4096
2 to the power of 13 is 8192
2 to the power of 14 is 16384
2 to the power of 15 is 32768
2 to the power of 16 is 65536
2 to the power of 17 is 131072
2 to the power of 18 is 262144
2 to the power of 19 is 524288
```

So, how does the program work? We first create our array of integer values and assign it to the **intArray** variable. Next, we begin a loop that goes from zero to **intArray.length**. By calling the **length** method of our array, we find the number of indexes in the array. Then, we start another loop that does the calculation and stores the result in the index specified by the **i** variable from our initial loop.

Now that we have filled in all the values for our array, we need to step back through them and print out the result. We could have just put the **print** statement in the initial loop, but the approach we used gives us a chance to use another loop that references our array.

Here is the structure of an index call:

```
arrayName[index];
```

Pretty simple. If you try and use an index that is outside the boundaries of the array, a runtime error occurs. If we change the program to count to an index of 21, instead of the actual array length of 20, we would end up getting an error message like this:

```
java.lang.ArrayIndexOutOfBoundsException: 20
        at powersOf2.main(powersOf2.java:10)
```

This is a pretty common error in any programming language. You need to use some form of exception handling to watch for this problem, unless, of course, you are positive you can create code that never does this (in your dreams).

Multidimensional Arrays

Multidimensional arrays are created in Java by using arrays of arrays. Here are a few examples of how you can implement multidimensional arrays:

```
int intArray[][];
String Names[][];
```

We can even do the same things we did with a single dimension array. We can set the array sizes and even fill in values while we declare the arrays:

```
int intArray[][] = new int[10][5];
String Names[][] = new String[25][3];

int intArray[][] = {{2, 3, 4} {1, 2, 3}};
String Names[][] = {{"Jon", "Smith"}{"Tony", "Potts"}{"Dave",
  "Friedel"}};
```

We can also create arrays that are not "rectangular" in nature. That is, each array within the main array can have a different number of elements. Here are a few examples:

```
int intArray[][] = {{1, 2} {1, 2, 3} {1, 2, 3, 4}};
String Names[][] = {{"Jon", "Smith"} {"Tony","A", "Potts"} {"Dave", "H",
  "Friedel", "Jr."}};
```

Accessing the data in a multidimensional array is not much more difficult than accessing data in a single-dimensional array. You just need to track the values for each index. Be careful though—as you add dimensions, it becomes increasingly easy to create out of bounds errors. Here are a few examples of how you can declare multidimensional arrays, assign values, and access array elements:

```
int intArray[][] = new int[10][5];              // Declare the arrays
String Names[][] = new String[25][3];
```

```
intArray[0][0] = 5;       // Assign values
intArray[7][2] = 37;
intArray[7][9] = 37;      // This will cause an out of bounds error!
Names[0][0] = "Bill Gates";
// Access an array element in a Java statement
System.out.println(Names[0][0]);
```

Using Command-Line Arguments

Programming with command-line arguments is not a topic you'd typically expect to see in an appendix on basic data types and variable declarations. However, because we've been using command-line arguments with some of the sample programs we've been introducing, we thought it would be important to discuss how this feature works in a little more detail.

Command-line arguments are only used with Java applications. They provide a mechanism so that the user of an application can pass in information to be used by the program. Java applets, on the other hand, read in parameters using HTML tags. Command-line arguments are common with languages like C and C++, which were originally designed to work with command-line operating systems like Unix.

The advantage of using command-line arguments is that they are passed to a program when the program *first* starts, which keeps the program from having to query the user for more information. Command-line arguments are great for passing custom initialization data.

Passing Arguments

The syntax for passing arguments themselves to a program is extremely simple. Just start your programs as you usually would and then add any number of arguments to the end of the line, with each one separated by a space. Here is a sample call to a program named "myApp":

```
Java myApp open 640 480
```

In this case, we are calling the Java runtime interpreter and telling it to run the class file "myApp". We then are passing in three arguments: "open", "640", and "480".

If you wanted to pass in a longer string with spaces as an argument, you could. In this case, you enclose the string in quotation marks, and Java will treat it as a single argument. Here is an example:

```
Java myApp "Nice program!" "640x480"
```

Once again, the name of the program is "myApp". This time, however, we are only sending it two arguments: "Nice program!" and "640×480". Note that the quotes themselves are not passed, just the string between the quotes.

Reading In Arguments

Now that we know how to pass arguments, where are they stored? How can we see them in our application? If you'll recall, all applications have a **main**() method. You should also notice that this method has an interesting argument structure:

```
public static void main(String args[]) {
  ...
}
```

Here, **main**() indicates that it takes an array named **args**[] of type **String**. Java takes any command-line arguments and puts them into the **args**[] string array. The array is dynamically resized to hold just the number of arguments passed, or zero if none are passed. Note that the use of the **args** identifier is completely arbitrary. You can use any word you want as long as it conforms to the Java naming rules. You can even get a little more descriptive, like this:

```
public static void main(String commandLineArgumentsArray[]) { ...
```

That may be a bit much, but you will never get confused as to what is in the array.

Accessing Arguments

Once we've passed in the arguments to an application and we know where they are stored, how do we get to them? Since the arguments are stored in an array. we can access them just like we would access strings in any other array. Let's look at a simple application that takes two arguments and prints them out:

```
class testArgs {
   public static void main(String args[]) {
```

```
        System.out.println(args[0]);
        System.out.println(args[1]);
    }
}
```

If we use this command-line statement to run the application

```
java testArgs hello world
```

we'd get this output:

```
hello
world
```

Now, try this command line:

```
java testArgs onearg
```

Here is the result:

```
onearg
java.lang.ArrayIndexOutOfBoundsException: 1
        at testArgs.main(testArgs.java:4)
```

What happened? Since we were only passing a single argument, the reference to **args[1]** is illegal and produces an error.

So, how do we stop from getting an error? Instead of calling each argument in line, we can use a **for** loop to step through each argument. We can check the **args.length** variable to see if we have reached the last item. Our new code will also recognize if no arguments have been passed and will not try and access the array at all. Enough talking, here is the code:

```
class testArgs {
    public static void main(String args[]) {
        for (int i = 0; i < args.length; i++) {
            System.out.println(args[i]);
        }
    }
}
```

Now, no matter how many arguments are passed (or none), the application can handle it.

Indexing Command-line Arguments

Don't forget that Java arrays are zero-based, so the first command-line argument is stored at position 0, not position 1. This is different than some other languages, like C, where the first argument would be at position 1. In C, position 0 would store the name of the program.

Dealing With Numeric Arguments

One more thing we should cover here is how to deal with numeric arguments. If you remember, all arguments are passed into an array of strings, so we need to convert those values into numbers.

This is actually very simple. Each data type has an associated class that provides methods for dealing with that data type. Each of these classes has a method that creates a variable of that type from a string. Table A.9 presents a list of those methods.

Make sure you understand the difference between the **parse***() methods and the **valueOf**() methods. The parsing methods just return a value that can be plugged into a variable or used as part of an expression. The **valueOf**() methods return an *object* of the specified type that has an initial value equal to the value of the string.

TABLE A.9

CLASSES AND THEIR ASSOCIATED METHODS FOR HANDLING DATA TYPES.

Class	Method	Return
Integer	parseInt(String)	An integer value
Integer	valueOf(String)	An **Integer** object initialized to the value represented by the specified String
Long	parseLong(String)	A long value
Long	valueOf(String)	A **Long** object initialized to the value represented by the specified String
Double	valueOf(String)	A **Double** object initialized to the value represented by the specified String
Float	valueOf(String)	A **Float** object initialized to the value represented by the specified String

B
SIMPLETEXT JDBC DRIVER SOURCE CODE

Y
ou had a look at the SimpleText JDBC driver developed in Chapter 7. This appendix supplies you with the complete source code for three of its main classes: SimpleTextDriver, SimpleTextConnection, and SimpleTextStatement. The SimpleTextResultSet, SimpleText Object, and other SimpleText driver classes' source code can be found on the CD-ROM. The primary purpose of this appendix is to serve as a reference while you are reading or reviewing Chapter 7, as well as to detail the inner workings of a JDBC driver.

LISTING B.1   SIMPLETEXTDRIVER.JAVA.

```
//--------------------------------------------
// Module:       SimpleTextDriver.java
//
// Description: Implementation of the JDBC Driver interface
//
// Author:       Karl Moss
//
// Copyright:    (C) 1996,1997 Karl Moss.  All rights
// reserved.
//
//              You may study, use, modify and distribute
//              this example for any purpose, provided
//              that this copyright notice appears in all
//              copies.
```

```
//              This example is provided WITHOUT WARRANTY
//              either expressed or implied.
//----------------------------------------------------------


package jdbc.SimpleText;


//----------------------------------------------------------------
// The Java SQL framework allows for multiple database drivers.
//
// Each driver should supply a driver class that implements
// the Driver interface.
//
// The DriverManager will try to load as many drivers as it can
// find and then for any given connection request it will ask
// each driver in turn to try to connect to the target URL.
//
// It is strongly recommended that each Driver class should be
// small and standalone so that the Driver class can be loaded
// and queried without bringing in vast quantities of supporting
// code.
//
// When a Driver object is instantiated it should register itself
// with the SQL framework by calling DriverManager.registerDriver.
//
// Note: Each driver must support a null constructor so it can be
// instantiated by doing:
//
//     java.sql.Driver d =
//              Class.forName("foo.bah.Driver").newInstance();
//----------------------------------------------------------------
// NOTE - this is an implementation of the JDBC API version 1.20
//----------------------------------------------------------------


import java.sql.*;

public class SimpleTextDriver
    extends        SimpleTextObject
    implements     SimpleTextIDriver
{


    //----------------------------------------------------------------
    // SimpleTextDriver
    // Constructor.  Attempt to register the JDBC driver.
    //----------------------------------------------------------------
```

```java
public SimpleTextDriver()
   throws SQLException
{

   // Attempt to register this driver with the JDBC
   // DriverManager.  If it fails, an exception will be
   // thrown.

   DriverManager.registerDriver (this);
}


//----------------------------------------------------------
// connect - JDBC API
//
// Try to make a database connection to the given URL.
// The driver should return "null" if it realizes it is the
// wrong kind of driver to connect to the given URL.  This
// will be common, as when the JDBC driver manager is asked
// to connect to a given URL it passes the URL to each
// loaded driver in turn.
//
// The driver should raise a SQLException if it is the right
// driver to connect to the given URL, but has trouble
// connecting to the database.
//
// The java.util.Properties argument can be used to passed
// arbitrary string tag/value pairs as connection arguments.
// Normally at least a "user" and "password" properties
// should be included in the Properties.
//
//     url    The URL of the database to connect to.
//
//     info   a list of arbitrary string tag/value pairs as
//            connection arguments; normally at least a "user"
//            and "password" property should be included.
//
// Returns a Connection to the URL.
//----------------------------------------------------------

public Connection connect(
    String url,
    java.util.Properties info)
    throws SQLException
{
   if (traceOn()) {
      trace("@connect (url=" + url + ")");
   }
```

```
    // Ensure that we can understand the given url

    if (!acceptsURL(url)) {
       return null;
    }

    // Set the url for the driver

    driverURL = url;

    // For typical JDBC drivers, it would be appropriate to
    // check for a secure environment before connecting, and
    // deny access to the driver if it is deemed to be unsecure.
    // For the SimpleText driver, if the environment is not
    //secure we will turn into a read-only driver.


    // Create a new SimpleTextConnection object

    SimpleTextConnection con = new SimpleTextConnection();

    // Initialize the new object

    con.initialize (this, info);

    return con;
}

//-------------------------------------------------------------
// acceptsURL - JDBC API
//
// Returns true if the driver thinks that it can open a
// connection to the given URL.  Typically drivers will
// return true if they understand the subprotocol specified
// in the URL and false if they don't.
//
//    url        The URL of the database.
//
// Returns true if this driver can connect to the given URL.
//-------------------------------------------------------------

public boolean acceptsURL(
    String url)
    throws SQLException
{
    if (traceOn()) {
       trace("@acceptsURL (url=" + url + ")");
    }
```

```
      boolean rc = false;

      // Get the subname from the url.  If the url is not valid
      // for this driver, a null will be returned.

      if (getSubname(url) != null) {
         rc = true;
      }

      if (traceOn()) {
         trace(" " + rc);
      }
      return rc;
}


//-------------------------------------------------------------
// getPropertyInfo - JDBC API
//
// The getPropertyInfo method is intended to allow a generic
// GUI tool to discover what properties it should prompt a
// human for in order to get enough information to connect to
// a database.  Note that depending on the values the human
// has supplied so far, additional values may become
// necessary, so it may be necessary to iterate though
// several calls to getPropertyInfo.
//
//     url     The URL of the database to connect to.
//
//     info    A proposed list of tag/value pairs that will be
//             sent on connect open.
//
// Returns an array of DriverPropertyInfo objects describing
// possible properties.  This array may be an empty array if
// no properties are required.
//-------------------------------------------------------------

public DriverPropertyInfo[] getPropertyInfo(
   String url,
   java.util.Properties info)
   throws SQLException
{

   DriverPropertyInfo prop[];

   // Only one property required for the SimpleText driver;
   // the directory.  Check the property list coming in.  If
   // the directory is specified, return an empty list.

   if (info.getProperty("Directory") == null) {
```

```
        // Setup the DriverPropertyInfo entry

        prop = new DriverPropertyInfo[1];
        prop[0] = new DriverPropertyInfo("Directory", null);
        prop[0].description = "Initial text file directory";
        prop[0].required = false;
    }
    else {

        // Create an empty list

        prop = new DriverPropertyInfo[0];
    }

    return prop;
}


//----------------------------------------------------------
// getMajorVersion - JDBC API
//
// Get the driver's major version number. Initially this
// should be 1.
//----------------------------------------------------------

public int getMajorVersion()
{
    return SimpleTextDefine.MAJOR_VERSION;
}


//----------------------------------------------------------
// getMinorVersion - JDBC API
//
// Get the driver's minor version number. Initially this
// should be 0.
//----------------------------------------------------------

public int getMinorVersion()
{
    return SimpleTextDefine.MINOR_VERSION;
}


//----------------------------------------------------------
// jdbcCompliant - JDBC API
//
// Report whether the Driver is a genuine JDBC COMPLIANT (tm)
// driver.  A driver may only report "true" here if it passes
// the JDBC compliance tests, otherwise it is required to
// return false.
```

```
// JDBC compliance requires full support for the JDBC API and
// full support for SQL 92 Entry Level.  It is expected that
// JDBC compliant drivers will be available for all the major
// commercial databases.
//
// This method is not intended to encourage the development
// of non-JDBC compliant drivers, but is a recognition of
// the fact that some vendors are interested in using the
// JDBC API and framework for lightweight databases that do
// not support full database functionality, or for special
// databases such as document information retrieval where a
// SQL implementation may not be feasible.
//-------------------------------------------------------------

public boolean jdbcCompliant()
{

    // The SimpleText driver is not JDBC compliant

    return false;
}


//-----------------------------------------------------------
// getSubname
// Given a URL, return the subname.  Returns null if the
// protocol is not 'jdbc' or the subprotocol is not
// 'simpletext'.
//-----------------------------------------------------------

public String getSubname()
{
    return getSubname(driverURL);
}

public String getSubname(
    String url)
{
    String subname = null;
    String protocol = "JDBC";
    String subProtocol = "SIMPLETEXT";

    // Convert to upper case and trim all leading and trailing
    // blanks

    url = (url.toUpperCase()).trim();

    // Make sure the protocol is jdbc:
```

```
        if (url.startsWith(protocol)) {

            // Strip off the protocol
            url = url.substring (protocol.length());

            // Look for the colon

            if (url.startsWith(":")) {
                url = url.substring(1);

                // Check the subprotocol

                if (url.startsWith (subProtocol)) {

                    // Strip off the subprotocol, leaving the subname

                    url = url.substring(subProtocol.length());

                    // Look for the colon that separates the subname
                    // from the subprotocol (or the fact that there
                    // is no subprotocol at all)

                    if (url.startsWith(":")) {
                        subname = url.substring(1);
                    }
                    else if (url.length() == 0) {
                        subname = "";
                    }
                }
            }
        }
        return subname;
    }


    //---------------------------------------
    // getURL
    //
    // Get the URL specified for the driver.
    //---------------------------------------

    public String getURL()
    {
        return driverURL;
    }


    private String driverURL;
}
```

LISTING B.2   SIMPLETEXTCONNECTION.JAVA.

```java
//--------------------------------------------------------------
//
// Module:        SimpleTextConnection.java
//
// Description: Implementation of the JDBC Connection interface
//
// Author:        Karl Moss
//
// Copyright:     (C) 1996,1997 Karl Moss.  All rights reserved.
//                You may study, use, modify and distribute this
//                example for any purpose, provided that this
//                copyright notice appears in all copies.  This
//                example is provided WITHOUT WARRANTY either
//                expressed or implied.
//--------------------------------------------------------------

package jdbc.SimpleText;


//--------------------------------------------------------------
// A Connection represents a session with a specific
// database. Within the context of a Connection, SQL statements
// are executed and results are returned.
//
// A Connection's database is able to provide information
// describing its tables, its supported SQL grammar, its stored
// procedures, the capabilities of this connection, etc. This
// information is obtained with the getMetaData method.
//
// Note: By default the Connection automatically commits
// changes after executing each statement. If auto commit has
// been disabled an explicit commit must be done or database
// changes will not be saved.
//--------------------------------------------------------------
// NOTE - this is an implementation of the JDBC API version 1.20
//--------------------------------------------------------------

import java.sql.*;
import java.io.*;
import java.util.Hashtable;
import java.util.StringTokenizer;

public class SimpleTextConnection
    extends       SimpleTextObject
    implements    SimpleTextIConnection
{
```

```
//----------------------------------
// initialize
// Initialize the Connection object.
//----------------------------------

public void initialize (
   SimpleTextIDriver driver,
   java.util.Properties info)
   throws SQLException
{

   // Save the owning driver object

   ownerDriver = driver;

   // Get the security manager and see if we can write to a
   // file. If no security manager is present, assume that
   // we are a trusted application and have read/write
   // privileges.

   canWrite = false;

   SecurityManager securityManager =
               System.getSecurityManager ();

   if (securityManager != null) {
      try {
         // Use some arbitrary file to check for file write
         // privileges

         securityManager.checkWrite ("SimpleText_Foo");

         // Flag is set if no exception is thrown

         canWrite = true;
      }

      // If we can't write, an exception is thrown.  We'll
      // catch it and do nothing

      catch (SecurityException ex) {
      }
   }
   else {
      canWrite = true;
   }
```

```
    // Set our initial read-only flag

    setReadOnly(!canWrite);

    // Get the directory.  It will either be supplied with
    // the URL, in the property list, or we'll use our
    // current default.

    String s = ownerDriver.getSubname();
    int slen = 0;

    if (s != null) {
        slen = s.length();
    }

    if (slen == 0) {
        s = info.getProperty("Directory");
    }

    if (s == null) {
        s = System.getProperty("user.dir");
    }

    setCatalog(s);
}

//----------------------------------------------------------------
// createStatement - JDBC API
//
// SQL statements without parameters are normally executed
// using Statement objects. If the same SQL statement is
// executed many times it is more efficient to use a
// PreparedStatement.
//
// Returns a new Statement object.
//----------------------------------------------------------------

public Statement createStatement()
    throws SQLException
{
    if (traceOn()) {
        trace("Creating new SimpleTextStatement");
    }

    // Create a new Statement object

    SimpleTextStatement stmt = new SimpleTextStatement();
```

```
        // Initialize the statement

        stmt.initialize (this);

        return stmt;
    }


    //----------------------------------------------------------------
    // prepareStatement - JDBC API
    //
    // A SQL statement with or without IN parameters can be
    // pre-compiled and stored in a PreparedStatement object.
    // This object can then be used to efficiently execute this
    // statement multiple times.
    //
    // Note: This method is optimized for handling parametric SQL
    // statements that benefit from precompilation. If the driver
    // supports precompilation, prepareStatement will send the
    // statement to the database for precompilation. Some drivers
    // may not support precompilation. In this case, the statement
    // may not be sent to the database until the PreparedStatement
    // is executed.  This has no direct effect on users; however,
    // it does affect which method throws certain SQLExceptions.
    //
    //     sql     a SQL statement that may contain one or more
    //             '?' IN parameter placeholders.
    //
    // Returns a new PreparedStatement object containing the
    // pre-compiled statement.
    //----------------------------------------------------------------

    public PreparedStatement prepareStatement(
        String sql)
        throws SQLException
    {

        if (traceOn()) {
            trace("@prepareStatement (sql=" + sql + ")");
        }

        // Create a new PreparedStatement object

        SimpleTextPreparedStatement ps =
                        new SimpleTextPreparedStatement();

        // Initialize the PreparedStatement

        ps.initialize(this, sql);
```

```
    return ps;
}


//-----------------------------------------------------------
// prepareCall - JDBC API
//
// A SQL stored procedure call statement is handled by
// creating a CallableStatement for it. The CallableStatement
// provides methods for setting up its IN and OUT parameters,
// and methods for executing it.
//
// Note: This method is optimized for handling stored
// procedure call statements. Some drivers may send the call
// statement to the database when the prepareCall is done;
// others may wait until the CallableStatement is executed.
// This has no direct effect on users; however, it does
// affect which method throws certain SQLExceptions.
//
//    sql      a SQL statement that may contain one or more '?'
//             parameter placeholders.
//
// Returns a new CallableStatement object containing the
// pre-compiled SQL statement.
//-----------------------------------------------------------

public CallableStatement prepareCall(
    String sql)
    throws SQLException
{
    if (traceOn()) {
        trace("@prepareCall (sql=" + sql + ")");
    }

    // The SimpleText driver does not support callable statements

    throw new SQLException(
            "Driver does not support this function");
}


//-----------------------------------------------------------
// nativeSQL - JDBC API
//
// A driver may convert the JDBC sql grammar into its system's
// native SQL grammar prior to sending it; nativeSQL returns
// the native form of the statement that the driver would
// have sent.
```

```
//
//    sql      a SQL statement that may contain one or more '?'
//             parameter placeholders.
//
// Returns the native form of this statement.
//----------------------------------------------------------------

public String nativeSQL(
    String sql)
    throws SQLException
{

    // For the SimpleText driver, simply return the original
    // sql statement.  Other drivers will need to expand escape
    // sequences here.

    return sql;
}


//----------------------------------------------------------------
// setAutoCommit - JDBC API
//
// If a connection is in auto-commit mode, then all its SQL
// statements will be executed and committed as individual
// transactions.  Otherwise, its SQL statements are grouped
// into transactions that are terminated by either commit() or
// rollback().  By default, new connections are in auto-commit
// mode.
//
//    autoCommit  true enables auto-commit; false disables
//                auto-commit.
//----------------------------------------------------------------

public void setAutoCommit(
    boolean autoCommit)
    throws SQLException
{
    if (traceOn()) {
        trace("@setAutoCommit (autoCommit=" + autoCommit + ")");
    }

    // The SimpleText driver is always in auto-commit mode
    // (it does not support transactions).  Throw an
    // exception if an attempt is made to change the mode

    if (autoCommit == false) {
```

```
            throw DriverNotCapable();
        }
    }


    //-------------------------------------------------
    // getAutoCommit - JDBC API
    //
    // Get the current auto-commit state.
    // Returns the current state of auto-commit mode.
    //-------------------------------------------------

    public boolean getAutoCommit()
        throws SQLException
    {
        // The SimpleText driver is always in auto-commit mode (it
        // does not support transactions)

        return true;
    }


    //-------------------------------------------------------------
    // commit - JDBC API
    //
    // Commit makes all changes made since the previous
    // commit/rollback permanent and releases any database
    // locks currently held by the Connection.
    //-------------------------------------------------------------

    public void commit()
        throws SQLException
    {
        // No-op for the SimpleText driver
    }


    //-------------------------------------------------------------
    // rollback - JDBC API
    //
    // Rollback drops all changes made since the previous
    // commit/rollback and releases any database locks currently
    // held by the Connection.
    //-------------------------------------------------------------

    public void rollback()
        throws SQLException
    {
        // No-op for the SimpleText driver
    }
```

```
//----------------------------------------------------------------
// close - JDBC API
//
// In some cases, it is desirable to immediately release a
// Connection's database and JDBC resources instead of waiting
// for them to be automatically released; the close method
// provides this immediate release.
//----------------------------------------------------------------

public void close()
   throws SQLException
{
   connectionClosed = true;
}


//------------------------------------
// isClosed - JDBC API
//
// Check if a Connection is closed.
//------------------------------------

public boolean isClosed()
   throws SQLException
{
   return connectionClosed;
}


//----------------------------------------------------------------
// getMetaData - JDBC API
//
// A Connection's database is able to provide information
// describing its tables, its supported SQL grammar, its
// stored procedures, the capabilities of this connection,
// etc. This information is made available through a
// DatabaseMetaData object.
//
// Returns a DatabaseMetaData object for this Connection.
//----------------------------------------------------------------

public DatabaseMetaData getMetaData()
   throws SQLException
{
   SimpleTextDatabaseMetaData dbmd =
                    new SimpleTextDatabaseMetaData ();

   dbmd.initialize(this);
   return dbmd;
}
```

```
//------------------------------------------------------------
// setReadOnly - JDBC API
//
// You can put a connection in read-only mode as a hint to
// enable database optimizations.
//
// Note: setReadOnly cannot be called while in the
// middle of a transaction.
//------------------------------------------------------------

public void setReadOnly(
   boolean readOnly)
   throws SQLException
{

   // If we are trying to set the connection not read only
   // (allowing writes), and this connection does not allow
   // writes, throw an exception.

   if ((readOnly == false) &&
      (canWrite == false)) {
      throw DriverNotCapable();
   }

   // Set the readOnly attribute for the SimpleText driver.
   // If set, the driver will not allow updates or deletes
   // to any text file.

   this.readOnly = readOnly;
}


//------------------------------------------------
// isReadOnly - JDBC API
//
// Test if the connection is in read-only mode.
//------------------------------------------------

public boolean isReadOnly()
   throws SQLException
{
   return readOnly;
}


//------------------------------------------------------------
// setCatalog - JDBC API
//
```

```
// A sub-space of this Connection's database may be selected
// by setting a catalog name. If the driver does not support
// catalogs it will silently ignore this request.
//------------------------------------------------------------

public void setCatalog(String catalog)
    throws SQLException
{
    if (traceOn()) {
        trace("@setCatalog(" + catalog + ")");
    }

    // If the last character is a separator, remove it

    if (catalog.endsWith("/") ||
        catalog.endsWith("\\")) {
        catalog = catalog.substring(0, catalog.length());
    }

    // Make sure this is a directory

    File dir = new File(catalog);

    if (!dir.isDirectory()) {
        throw new SQLException("Invalid directory: " + catalog);
    }

    this.catalog = catalog;
}


//------------------------------------------------------------
// getCatalog
//
// Returns the Connection's current catalog name.
//------------------------------------------------------------

public String getCatalog()
    throws SQLException
{
    return catalog;
}


//------------------------------------------------------------
// setTransactionIsolation - JDBC API
//
// You can call this method to try to change the transaction
```

```
// isolation level on a newly opened connection, using one of
// the TRANSACTION_* values.
//
//    level   one of the TRANSACTION_* isolation values with
//            the exception of TRANSACTION_NONE; some
//            databases may not support other values.
//-------------------------------------------------------------

public void setTransactionIsolation(
   int level)
   throws SQLException
{
   if (traceOn()) {
      trace("@setTransactionIsolation (level=" + level + ")");
   }

   // Throw an exception if the transaction isolation is being
   // changed to something different

   if (level != TRANSACTION_NONE) {
      throw DriverNotCapable();
   }
}


//-------------------------------------------------------------
// getTransactionIsolation - JDBC API
//
// Get this Connection's current transaction isolation mode.
//-------------------------------------------------------------

public int getTransactionIsolation()
   throws SQLException
{
   // The SimpleText driver does not support transactions

   return TRANSACTION_NONE;
}


//-------------------------------------------------------------
// getWarnings - JDBC API
//
// The first warning reported by calls on this Connection is
// returned.
//
// Note: Subsequent warnings will be chained to this
// SQLWarning.
//-------------------------------------------------------------
```

```
public SQLWarning getWarnings()
   throws SQLException
{
   // No warnings exist for the SimpleText driver.  Always return
   // null

   return null;
}


//-------------------------------------------------------------
// clearWarnings - JDBC API
//
// After this call getWarnings returns null until a new
// warning is reported for this Connection.
//-------------------------------------------------------------

public void clearWarnings()
   throws SQLException
{
   // No-op
}


//-------------------------------------------------------------
// parseSQL
// Given a sql statement, parse it and return a String array
// with each keyword.  This is a VERY simple parser.
//-------------------------------------------------------------

public String[] parseSQL(
   String sql)
{
   String keywords[] = null;

   // Create a new Hashtable to keep our words in. This way,
   // we can build the Hashtable as we go, then create a
   // String array once we know how may words are present.

   java.util.Hashtable table = new java.util.Hashtable();
   int count = 0;

   // Current offset in the sql string

   int offset = 0;

   // Get the first word from the sql statement

   String word = parseWord(sql.substring(offset));
```

```
    // Loop while more words exist in the sql string

    while (word.length() > 0) {

        // Increment the offset pointer

        offset += word.length();

        // Trim all leading and trailing spaces

        word = word.trim();

        if (word.length() > 0) {

            // Put the word in our hashtable

            table.put(new Integer(count), word);
            count++;
        }

        // Get the next word

        word = parseWord(sql.substring(offset));
    }

    // Create our new String array with the proper number of
    // elements

    keywords = new String[count];

    // Copy the words from the Hashtable to the String array

    for (int i = 0; i < count; i++) {
        keywords[i] = (String) table.get(new Integer(i));
    }
    return keywords;
}

//------------------------------------------------------------
// getTables
// Given a directory and table pattern, return a Hashtable
// containing SimpleTextTable entries.
//------------------------------------------------------------

public Hashtable getTables(
    String dir,
    String table)
{
```

```
        Hashtable list = new Hashtable();

        // Create a FilenameFilter object. This object will only
        // allow files with the .SDF extension to be seen.

        FilenameFilter filter = new SimpleTextEndsWith(
                    SimpleTextDefine.DATA_FILE_EXT);

        File file = new File(dir);

        if (file.isDirectory()) {

            // List all of the files in the directory with the .SDF
            // extension

            String entries[] = file.list(filter);
            SimpleTextTable tableEntry;

            // Create a SimpleTextTable entry for each, and put in
            // the Hashtable

            for (int i = 0; i < entries.length; i++) {

                // A complete driver needs to further filter the
                // table name here

                tableEntry = new SimpleTextTable(dir, entries[i]);
                list.put(new Integer(i), tableEntry);
            }
        }

        return list;
    }

    //------------------------------------------------------------
    // getColumns
    // Given a directory and table name, return a Hashtable
    // containing SimpleTextColumn entries. Returns null if the
    // table is not found.
    //------------------------------------------------------------

    public Hashtable getColumns(
        String dir,
        String table)
    {
        Hashtable list = new Hashtable();
```

```java
// Create the full path to the table

String fullPath = dir + "/" + table +
                       SimpleTextDefine.DATA_FILE_EXT;

File f = new File (fullPath);

// If the file does not exist, return null

if (!f.exists()) {
   if (traceOn()) {
      trace("File does not exist: " + fullPath);
   }
   return null;
}

String line = "";

// Create a random access object and read the first line
// Create the table

try {
   RandomAccessFile raf = new RandomAccessFile(f, "r");

   // Read the first line, which is the column definitions

   line = raf.readLine();
   raf.close();
}
catch (IOException ex) {
   if (traceOn()) {
      trace("Unable to read file: " + fullPath);
   }
   return null;
}

// Now, parse the line. First, check for the branding

if (!line.startsWith(SimpleTextDefine.DATA_FILE_EXT)) {
   if (traceOn()) {
      trace("Invalid file format: " + fullPath);
   }
   return null;
}

line = line.substring(
         SimpleTextDefine.DATA_FILE_EXT.length());
```

```
// Now we can use the StringTokenizer, since we know
// that the column names can't contain data within quotes
// (this is why we can't use the StringTokenizer with
// SQL statements).0

StringTokenizer st = new StringTokenizer(line, ",");

String columnName;
int columnType;
int precision;
SimpleTextColumn column;
int count = 0;
boolean searchable;
int displaySize;
String typeName;

// Loop while more tokens exist

while (st.hasMoreTokens()) {
   columnName = (st.nextToken()).trim();

   if (columnName.length() == 0) {
      continue;
   }

   if (columnName.startsWith(
             SimpleTextDefine.COL_TYPE_NUMBER)) {
      columnType = Types.INTEGER;
      precision = SimpleTextDefine.MAX_INTEGER_LEN;
      columnName = columnName.substring(
             SimpleTextDefine.COL_TYPE_NUMBER.length());
      displaySize = precision;
      typeName = "VARCHAR";
      searchable = true;
   }
   else if (columnName.startsWith(
             SimpleTextDefine.COL_TYPE_BINARY)) {
      columnType = Types.VARBINARY;
      precision = SimpleTextDefine.MAX_VARBINARY_LEN;
      columnName = columnName.substring(
             SimpleTextDefine.COL_TYPE_BINARY.length());
      displaySize = precision * 2;
      typeName = "BINARY";
      searchable = false;
   } else {
      columnType = Types.VARCHAR;
```

```
            precision = SimpleTextDefine.MAX_VARCHAR_LEN;
            searchable = true;
            displaySize = precision;
            typeName = "NUMBER";
        }

        // Create a new column object and add to the Hashtable

        column = new SimpleTextColumn(columnName, columnType,
                                    precision);
        column.searchable = searchable;
        column.displaySize = displaySize;
        column.typeName = typeName;

        // The column number will be 1-based

        count++;

        // Save the absolute column number

        column.colNo = count;

        list.put(new Integer(count), column);
    }

    return list;
}

//------------------------------------------------------------
// getDirectory
// Given a directory filter (which may be null), format the
// directory to use in a search. The default connection
// directory may be returned.
//------------------------------------------------------------

public String getDirectory(
    String directory)
{
    String dir;

    if (directory == null) {
        dir = catalog;
    }
    else if (directory.length() == 0) {
        dir = catalog;
    }
    else {
```

```
            dir = directory;
            if (dir.endsWith("/") ||
               dir.endsWith("\\")) {
               dir = dir.substring(0, dir.length());
            }
         }

      return dir;
   }

   // Pointer to the owning Driver object
   protected SimpleTextIDriver ownerDriver;

   // true if the connection is currently closed
   protected boolean connectionClosed;

   // true if the connection is read-only
   protected boolean readOnly;

   // true if we are able to write to files
   protected boolean canWrite;

   // Current catalog (qualifier) for text files
   protected String catalog;

}


//-------------------------------------------------------------
// This class is a simple FilenameFilter.  It defines the
// required accept() method to determine whether a specified
// file should be listed.  A file will be listed if its name
// ends with the specified extension.
//-------------------------------------------------------------

class SimpleTextEndsWith
   implements FilenameFilter
{
   public SimpleTextEndsWith(
      String extension)
   {
      ext = extension;
   }

   public boolean accept(
      File dir,
      String name)
```

```
    {
        if (name.endsWith(ext)) {
            return true;
        }
        return false;
    }

    protected String ext;
}
```

LISTING B.3   SIMPLETEXTSTATEMENT.JAVA.

```
//-------------------------------------------------------------
//
// Module:      SimpleTextStatement.java
//
// Description: Implementation of the JDBC Statement interface
//
// Author:      Karl Moss
//
// Copyright:   (C) 1996,1997 Karl Moss. All rights reserved.
//              You may study, use, modify and distribute this
//              example for any purpose, provided that this
//              copyright notice appears in all copies. This
//              example is provided WITHOUT WARRANTY either
//              expressed or implied.
//-------------------------------------------------------------

package jdbc.SimpleText;

//-------------------------------------------------------------
// A Statement object is used for executing a static SQL
// statement and obtaining the results produced by it.
//
// Only one ResultSet per Statement can be open at any point
// in time. Therefore, if the reading of one ResultSet is
// interleaved with the reading of another, each must have
// been generated by different Statements.
//-------------------------------------------------------------
// NOTE - this is an implementation of the JDBC API version 1.20
//-------------------------------------------------------------

import java.sql.*;
import java.util.Hashtable;
import java.io.*;
```

```java
public class SimpleTextStatement
    extends        SimpleTextObject
    implements     SimpleTextIStatement
{

    //----------------------------------------
    // initialize
    //----------------------------------------

    public void initialize(
        SimpleTextIConnection con)
        throws SQLException
    {
        // Save the owning connection object

        ownerConnection = con;
    }


    //------------------------------------------------------------
    // executeQuery - JDBC API
    // Execute a SQL statement that returns a single ResultSet.
    //
    //   sql   typically this is a static SQL SELECT statement.
    //
    // Returns the table of data produced by the SQL statement.
    //------------------------------------------------------------

    public ResultSet executeQuery(
        String sql)
        throws SQLException
    {
        if (traceOn()) {
            trace("@executeQuery(" + sql + ")");
        }

        java.sql.ResultSet rs = null;

        // Execute the query.  If execute returns true, then a
        // result set exists

        if (execute(sql)) {
            rs = getResultSet();
        }

        return rs;
    }
```

```
//-----------------------------------------------------------
// executeUpdate - JDBC API
// Execute a SQL INSERT, UPDATE or DELETE statement. In
// addition, SQL statements that return nothing such as SQL
// DDL statements can be executed.
//
//    sql    a SQL INSERT, UPDATE or DELETE statement or a SQL
//           statement that returns nothing.
//
// Returns either the row count for INSERT, UPDATE or DELETE;
// or 0 for SQL statements that return nothing.
//-----------------------------------------------------------

public int executeUpdate(
    String sql)
    throws SQLException
{
    if (traceOn()) {
        trace("@executeUpdate(" + sql + ")");
    }

    int count = -1;

    // Execute the query.  If execute returns false, then an
    // update count exists.

    if (execute(sql) == false) {
        count = getUpdateCount();
    }

    return count;
}


//-----------------------------------------------------------------
// close - JDBC API
// In many cases, it is desirable to immediately release a
// Statements's database and JDBC resources instead of waiting
// for this to happen when it is automatically closed; the
// close method provides this immediate release.
//
// Note: A Statement is automatically closed when it is
// garbage collected. When a Statement is closed its current
// ResultSet, if one exists, is also closed.
//-----------------------------------------------------------------

public void close()
    throws SQLException
```

```
    {
        // If we have a current result set, close it

        if (currentResultSet != null) {
            currentResultSet.close();
            currentResultSet = null;
        }
    }


    //------------------------------------------------------------------
    // getMaxFieldSize - JDBC API
    // The maxFieldSize limit (in bytes) is the maximum amount of
    // data returned for any column value; it only applies to
    // BINARY, VARBINARY, LONGVARBINARY, CHAR, VARCHAR, and
    // LONGVARCHAR columns.  If the limit is exceeded, the excess
    // data is silently discarded.
    //
    // Returns the current max column size limit; zero means
    // unlimited.
    //------------------------------------------------------------------

    public int getMaxFieldSize()
        throws SQLException
    {
        // The SimpleText driver does not have a limit on size

        return 0;
    }


    //------------------------------------------------------------------
    // setMaxFieldSize - JDBC API
    // The maxFieldSize limit (in bytes) is set to limit the size
    // of data that can be returned for any column value; it only
    // applies to BINARY, VARBINARY, LONGVARBINARY, CHAR, VARCHAR,
    // and LONGVARCHAR fields.  If the limit is exceeded, the excess
    // data is silently discarded.
    //
    //     max     the new max column size limit; zero means
    //             unlimited.
    //------------------------------------------------------------------

    public void setMaxFieldSize(
        int max)
        throws SQLException
    {
```

```
    // The SimpleText driver does not allow the maximum field
    // size to be set

    if (max != 0) {
       throw DriverNotCapable();
    }
}


//------------------------------------------------------------------
// getMaxRows - JDBC API
// The maxRows limit is the maximum number of rows that a
// ResultSet can contain.  If the limit is exceeded, the
// excess rows are silently dropped.
//
// Returns the current max row limit; zero means unlimited.
//------------------------------------------------------------------

public int getMaxRows()
   throws SQLException
{
    // The SimpleText driver does not have a limit on the
    // number of rows that can be returned

    return 0;
}


//------------------------------------------------------------------
// setMaxRows - JDBC API
// The maxRows limit is set to limit the number of rows that
// any ResultSet can contain.  If the limit is exceeded,
// the excess rows are silently dropped.
//
//    max    the new max rows limit; zero means unlimited.
//------------------------------------------------------------------

public void setMaxRows(
   int max)
   throws SQLException
{
    // The SimpleText driver does not allow the maximum number of rows
    // to be set

    if (max != 0) {
       throw DriverNotCapable();
    }
}
```

```
//------------------------------------------------------------------
// setEscapeProcessing - JDBC API
// If escape scanning is on (the default) the driver will do
// escape substitution before sending the SQL to the
// database.
//
//     enable    true to enable; false to disable.
//------------------------------------------------------------------
public void setEscapeProcessing(
    boolean enable)
    throws SQLException
{
    // The SimpleText driver does not support escape sequence
    // expansion

    if (enable) {
        throw DriverNotCapable();
    }
}


//------------------------------------------------------------------
// getQueryTimeout - JDBC API
// The queryTimeout limit is the number of seconds the driver
// will wait for a Statement to execute. If the limit is
// exceeded a SQLException is thrown.
//
// Returns the current query timeout limit in seconds; zero
// means unlimited.
//------------------------------------------------------------------

public int getQueryTimeout()
    throws SQLException
{
    // The SimpleText driver does not have a query timeout

    return 0;
}


//------------------------------------------------------------------
// setQueryTimeout - JDBC API
// The queryTimeout limit is the number of seconds the driver
// will wait for a Statement to execute. If the limit is
// exceeded a SQLException is thrown.
//
//     seconds    the new query timeout limit in seconds; zero
//                means unlimited.
//------------------------------------------------------------------
```

```
public void setQueryTimeout(
   int seconds)
   throws SQLException
{
   // The SimpleText driver does not support query timeouts

   if (seconds != 0) {
      throw DriverNotCapable();
   }
}


//------------------------------------------------------------------
// cancel - JDBC API
// Cancel can be used by one thread to cancel a statement
// that is being executed by another thread.
//------------------------------------------------------------------

public void cancel()
   throws SQLException
{
   // No-op for the SimpleText driver
}


//------------------------------------------------------------------
// getWarnings - JDBC API
// The first warning reported by calls on this Statement is
// returned. A Statment's execute methods clear its
// SQLWarning chain. Subsequent Statement warnings will be
// chained to this SQLWarning.
//
// Note:  The warning chain is automatically cleared each time
// a statement is (re)executed.
//
// Note: If you are processing a ResultSet then any
// warnings associated with ResultSet reads will be chained
// on the ResultSet object.
//
// Returns the first SQLWarning or null.
//------------------------------------------------------------------

public SQLWarning getWarnings()
   throws SQLException
{
   return lastWarning;
}
```

```
//-----------------------------------------------------------
// clearWarnings - JDBC API
// After this call getWarnings returns null until a new
// warning is reported for this Statement.
//-----------------------------------------------------------

public void clearWarnings()
    throws SQLException
{
    setWarning(null);
}


//-----------------------------------------------------------
// setWarning
// Sets the given SQLWarning in the warning chain. If null,
// the chain is reset
//-----------------------------------------------------------

protected void setWarning(
    SQLWarning warning)
{
    if (warning == null) {
        lastWarning = null;
    }
    else {
        SQLWarning chain = lastWarning;

        // Find the end of the chain

        while (chain.getNextWarning() != null) {
            chain = chain.getNextWarning();
        }

        // We're at the end of the chain.  Add the new warning.

        chain.setNextWarning(warning);
    }
}


//-----------------------------------------------------------
// setCursorName - JDBC API
// setCursorname defines the SQL cursor name that will be
// used by subsequent Statement execute methods. This name
// can then be used in SQL positioned update/delete
// statements to identify the current row in the ResultSet
// generated by this statement. If the database doesn't
// support positioned update/delete, this method is a no-op.
```

```
//
// Note: By definition, positioned update/delete
// execution must be done by a different Statement than the
// one which generated the ResultSet being used for
// positioning. Also, cursor names must be unique within a
// Connection.
//
//     name    the new cursor name.
//------------------------------------------------------------

public void setCursorName(
    String name)
    throws SQLException
{
    // The SimpleText driver does not support positioned
    // updates.  Per the spec, this is a no-op.
}


//------------------------------------------------------------
// execute - JDBC API
// Execute a SQL statement that may return multiple results.
// Under some (uncommon) situations a single SQL statement
// may return multiple result sets and/or update counts.
// Normally you can ignore this, unless you're executing a
// stored procedure that you know may return multiple results,
// or unless you're dynamically executing an unknown SQL
// string. The "execute", "getMoreResults", "getResultSet"
// and "getUpdateCount" methods let you navigate through
// multiple results.
//
// The "execute" method executes a SQL statement and
// indicates the form of the first result. You can then
// use getResultSet or getUpdateCount to retrieve the
// result, and getMoreResults to move to any subsequent
// result(s).
//
//     sql    any SQL statement
//
// Returns true if the first result is a ResultSet; false
// if it is an count.
//------------------------------------------------------------

public boolean execute(
    String sql)
    throws SQLException
{
```

```
      resultSetColumns = null;

      // Convert the SQL statement into native syntax

      sql = ownerConnection.nativeSQL(sql);
      // Save the SQL statement

      sqlStatement = sql;

      // First, parse the sql statement into a String array

      parsedSQL = ownerConnection.parseSQL(sql);

      // Now validate the SQL statement and execute it.
      // Returns true if a result set exists.

      boolean rc = prepare(false);

      return rc;
   }


   //------------------------------------------------------------
   // getResultSet - JDBC API
   // Returns the current result as a ResultSet. It should
   // only be called once per result.
   //
   // Returns the current result as a ResultSet; null if it
   // is an integer.
   //------------------------------------------------------------

   public ResultSet getResultSet()
      throws SQLException
   {
      // If there are no column to be returned, return null

      if (resultSetColumns == null) {
         return null;
      }

      SimpleTextResultSet rs = new SimpleTextResultSet();

      rs.initialize(this, resultSetCatalog, resultSetTable,
                  resultSetColumns, resultSetFilter);

      // Save our current result set
```

```
        currentResultSet = rs;

        return rs;
    }


    //-----------------------------------------------------------
    // getUpdateCount - JDBC API
    // getUpdateCount returns the current result, which should
    // be an integer value.  It should only be called once per
    // result.
    //
    // The only way to tell for sure that the result is an update
    // count is to first test to see if it is a ResultSet. If it
    // is not a ResultSet it is an update count.
    //
    // Returns the current result as an integer; zero if it is
    // a ResultSet
    //-----------------------------------------------------------

    public int getUpdateCount()
        throws SQLException
    {
        return updateCount;
    }


    //-----------------------------------------------------------
    // getMoreResults - JDBC API
    // getMoreResults moves to a Statement's next result.  It
    // returns true if this result is a ResultSet.
    // getMoreResults also implicitly closes any current
    // ResultSet obtained with getResultSet.
    //
    // Returns true if the next result is a ResultSet; false if
    // it is an integer
    //-----------------------------------------------------------

    public boolean getMoreResults()
        throws SQLException
    {
        // The SimpleText driver does not support multiple result sets

        throw DriverNotCapable();
    }


    //-----------------------------------------------------------
    // getStatementType
    // Given a parsed SQL statement (in a String array),
```

```
    // determine the type of sql statement present.  If the sql
    // statement is not known, an exception is raised
    //----------------------------------------------------------------

    public int getStatementType(
        String sql[])
        throws SQLException
    {
        int type = 0;

        // There are no sql statements with less than 2 words

        if (sql.length < 2) {
            throw new SQLException("Invalid SQL statement");
        }

        if (sql[0].equalsIgnoreCase("SELECT")) {
            type = SimpleTextDefine.SQL_SELECT;
        }
        else if (sql[0].equalsIgnoreCase("INSERT")) {
            type = SimpleTextDefine.SQL_INSERT;
        }
        else if (sql[0].equalsIgnoreCase("CREATE")) {
            type = SimpleTextDefine.SQL_CREATE;
        }
        else if (sql[0].equalsIgnoreCase("DROP")) {
            type = SimpleTextDefine.SQL_DROP;
        }
        else {
            throw new SQLException("Invalid SQL statement: " +
                            sql[0]);
        }
        return type;
    }


    //----------------------------------------------------------------
    // prepare
    // Prepare the already parsed SQL statement.
    // Returns true if a result set exists.
    //----------------------------------------------------------------

    protected boolean prepare(
        boolean prepareOnly)
        throws SQLException
    {
        boolean resultSet = false;
```

```java
// Determine the type of statement present

statementType = getStatementType(parsedSQL);

// Perform action depending upon the SQL statement type

switch (statementType) {

// CREATE statement

case SimpleTextDefine.SQL_CREATE:

    // If attempting to prepare a DDL (Data Definition
    // Language) statement, raise an exception.

    if (prepareOnly) {
        throw new SQLException(
                "DDL statements cannot be prepared");
    }

    // Create the table

    createTable();

    updateCount = 0;
    break;

// DROP statement
case SimpleTextDefine.SQL_DROP:

    // If attempting to prepare a DDL (Data Definition
    // Language) statement, raise an exception.

    if (prepareOnly) {
        throw new SQLException(
                "DDL statements cannot be prepared");
    }

    // Drop the table

    dropTable();

    updateCount = 0;
    break;

// INSERT statement
```

```
        case SimpleTextDefine.SQL_INSERT:

            // Insert data into the table

            insert(prepareOnly);

            updateCount = 1;
            break;

        // SELECT statement

        case SimpleTextDefine.SQL_SELECT:

            // Select data from the table

            select(prepareOnly);

            resultSet = true;
            updateCount = -1;
            break;

        default:
            throw new SQLException("Unknown SQL statement type: " +
                    statementType);
        }

        return resultSet;
    }

    //-------------------------------------------------------------
    // createTable
    // Attempt to create the table from the parsed SQL statement.
    //
    // Grammar:
    //
    // create-statement ::= CREATE TABLE table-name
    //                      (column-element [,column-element] ...)
    //
    // column-element ::= column-identifier data-type
    //
    //-------------------------------------------------------------

    protected void createTable()
        throws SQLException
    {
        // The minimum SQL statement must have 7 elements:
        //
```

```
// CREATE TABLE foo (COL VARCHAR)

if (parsedSQL.length < 7) {
   throw new SQLException ("Invalid CREATE statement");
}

// The next word must be TABLE; this is the only type of
// CREATE that the SimpleText driver supports

if (!parsedSQL[1].equalsIgnoreCase("TABLE")) {
   throw new SQLException(
           "CREATE must be followed by TABLE");
}

// Make sure we are not in read-only mode

if (ownerConnection.isReadOnly()) {
   throw new SQLException(
       "Unable to CREATE TABLE: connection is read-only");
}

// The next word is the table name.  Verify that it does
// not contain any invalid characters

validateName(parsedSQL[2], "table");

// The next word should be an open paren

if (!parsedSQL[3].equals("(")) {
   throw new SQLException(
     "Invalid CREATE TABLE statement: missing paren '('");
}

// Now we can step through the other parameters.  The
// format should be:
//
//    ( column type [, column type] ... )
//
// We will build a text line that describes each of the
// columns. This line will be the first line in our
// simple text file.
//
//    Numeric column names start with '#'
//    Binary column names start with '@'
//    All other names are considered to be varchar

String line = "";
```

```
String columnName;
String typeName;
int word = 4;
boolean gotCloseParen = false;
int numCols = 0;
boolean hasBinary = false;

// Keep a Hashtable of all of the column names so we can
// check for duplicates.

Hashtable names = new Hashtable();

while ((word < parsedSQL.length) &&
       (!gotCloseParen)) {

    // Get the column name to create and validate

    columnName = parsedSQL[word].toUpperCase();
    validateName(columnName, "column");

    if (names.get(columnName) != null) {
        throw new SQLException("Duplicate column name: " +
                        columnName);
    }

    names.put(columnName, "");

    word++;

    // The next column should be the type

    if (word == parsedSQL.length) {
        throw new SQLException("Missing column type");
    }

    typeName = parsedSQL[word];

    if (numCols > 0) {
        line += ",";
    }

    numCols++;

    // Validate the type

    if (typeName.equalsIgnoreCase("VARCHAR")) {
        line += columnName;
```

```
      }
      else if (typeName.equalsIgnoreCase("NUMBER")) {
         line += SimpleTextDefine.COL_TYPE_NUMBER +
                        columnName;
      }
      else if (typeName.equalsIgnoreCase("BINARY")) {
         line += SimpleTextDefine.COL_TYPE_BINARY +
                        columnName;
         hasBinary = true;
      }
      else {
         throw new SQLException("Invalid column type: " +
                        typeName);
      }

      word++;

      if (word == parsedSQL.length) {
         throw new SQLException("Missing close paren");
      }

      // The next word must either be a comma, indicating more
      // columns, or the closing paren

      if (parsedSQL[word].equals(")")) {
         gotCloseParen = true;
         word++;
         break;
      }
      else if (!parsedSQL[word].equals(",")) {
         throw new SQLException("Invalid character near: " +
                        columnName + " " + typeName);
      }
      word++;
}

// If we got here and did not find a closing paren, raise an error

if (!gotCloseParen) {
   throw new SQLException("Missing close paren");
}

// We could check for extra junk at the end of the statement, but
// we'll just ignore it

// Verify that the file does not already exist
```

```
String fileName = parsedSQL[2].toUpperCase();
String fullFile = fileName +
                     SimpleTextDefine.DATA_FILE_EXT;
String fullPath = ownerConnection.getCatalog() + "/" +
                     fullFile;

File f = new File (fullPath);
if (f.exists()) {
    throw new SQLException("Table already exists: " +
                           fileName);
}

// Create the table

try {
    RandomAccessFile raf = new RandomAccessFile(f, "rw");

    // Brand the file

    raf.writeBytes(SimpleTextDefine.DATA_FILE_EXT);

    // Write the column info

    raf.writeBytes(line);
    raf.writeBytes("\n");
    raf.close();
}
catch (IOException ex) {
    throw new SQLException("Error accessing file " +
               fullPath + ": " + ex.getMessage());
}

// If a binary data type existed, create the binary data
// file now

fullFile = fileName + SimpleTextDefine.BINARY_FILE_EXT;
fullPath = ownerConnection.getCatalog() + "/" + fullFile;

f = new File (fullPath);

// Create the binary table

try {
    RandomAccessFile raf = new RandomAccessFile(f, "rw");
    raf.close();
}
catch (IOException ex) {
```

```
        throw new SQLException("Error accessing file " +
                fullPath + ": " + ex.getMessage());
    }
}

//------------------------------------------------------------
// dropTable
// Attempt to drop a table.
//
// Grammar:
//
// drop-statement ::= DROP TABLE table-name
//
//------------------------------------------------------------

protected void dropTable()
    throws SQLException
{
    // The SQL statement must have 3 elements:
    //
    // DROP TABLE table

    if (parsedSQL.length != 3) {
        throw new SQLException ("Invalid DROP statement");
    }

    // The next word must be TABLE; this is the only type of
    // DROP that the SimpleText driver supports

    if (!parsedSQL[1].equalsIgnoreCase("TABLE")) {
      throw new SQLException("DROP must be followed by TABLE");
    }

    // Make sure we are not in read-only mode

    if (ownerConnection.isReadOnly()) {
        throw new SQLException(
            "Unable to DROP TABLE: connection is read-only");
    }

    // The next word is the table name.  Verify that it does
    // not contain any invalid characters

    validateName(parsedSQL[2], "table");

    // Verify that the file exists
```

```
    String fileName = parsedSQL[2].toUpperCase();
    String fullFile = fileName +
                      SimpleTextDefine.DATA_FILE_EXT;
    String fullPath = ownerConnection.getCatalog() + "/" +
                      fullFile;

    File f = new File (fullPath);
    if (!f.exists()) {
        throw new SQLException("Table does not exist: " +
                      fileName);
    }

    // Delete the file

    f.delete();

    // If a binary data file exists, delete it now

    fullFile = fileName + SimpleTextDefine.BINARY_FILE_EXT;
    fullPath = ownerConnection.getCatalog() + "/" + fullFile;

    f = new File (fullPath);

    if (f.exists()) {
        f.delete();
    }
}


//------------------------------------------------------------
// insert
// Attempt to insert data into a table.
//
// Grammar:
//
// insert-statement ::= INSERT INTO table-name
//          [(column-identifier [,column-identifier]...)]
//          VALUES (insert-value [,insert-value]...)
//
//------------------------------------------------------------
synchronized protected void insert(
    boolean prepareOnly)
    throws SQLException
{
    // The SQL statement must have at least 7 elements:
    //
    // INSERT INTO table VALUES (value)
```

```
if (parsedSQL.length <= 7) {
   throw new SQLException ("Invalid INSERT statement");
}

// The next word must be INTO

if (!parsedSQL[1].equalsIgnoreCase("INTO")) {
 throw new SQLException("INSERT must be followed by INTO");
}

// Make sure we are not in read-only mode

if (ownerConnection.isReadOnly()) {
   throw new SQLException(
         "Unable to INSERT: connection is read-only");
}

// The next word is the table name. Verify that it does
// not contain any invalid characters.

String tableName = parsedSQL[2];
validateName(tableName, "table");

// Verify that the file exists. If getColumns returns null,
// the table does not exist.

Hashtable columnList = ownerConnection.getColumns(
          ownerConnection.getCatalog(), tableName);

if (columnList == null) {
   throw new SQLException("Table does not exist: " +
             tableName);
}

int pos = 3;
Hashtable insertList = null;
Hashtable valueList = null;
int colNo = 1;
SimpleTextColumn column;
SimpleTextColumn column2;
String name;

// If the next word is a paren '(', the column names are
// being specified.  Build a list of columns that will
// have data inserted.
```

```
   if (parsedSQL[pos].equals("(")) {
      insertList = new Hashtable();
      pos++;

      if (pos >= parsedSQL.length) {
         throw new SQLException ("Invalid INSERT statement");
      }

      // Build our insert list. Get each comma separated
      // name until we read a close paren.

      pos = buildList(parsedSQL, pos, ")", insertList);

      // Make sure at least one column was given

      if (insertList.size() == 0) {
         throw new SQLException ("No columns given");
      }

      // Now that we have the insert list, verify each name is
      // in our target table and get the type and precision.

      for (int i = 1; i <= insertList.size(); i++) {
         column = (SimpleTextColumn)
                       insertList.get(new Integer(i));
         column2 = findColumn(columnList, column.name);
         if (column2 == null) {
            throw new SQLException("Column does not exist: " +
                          column.name);
         }
         column.type = column2.type;
         column.precision = column2.precision;
      }

      // Position to the next word after the closing paren

      pos++;
      if (pos >= parsedSQL.length) {
         throw new SQLException(
           "Invalid INSERT statement; missing VALUES clause");
      }
   }

   // The next word is VALUES; no column list was given, so
   // assume all columns in the table.

   else if (parsedSQL[pos].equalsIgnoreCase("VALUES")) {
      insertList = new Hashtable();
```

```java
        // Build the insertList with all columns in the table

        for (colNo = 1; colNo <= columnList.size(); colNo++) {
            column2 = (SimpleTextColumn)
                            columnList.get(new Integer(colNo));

            if (column2 == null) {
                throw new SQLException("Invalid column number: " +
                            colNo);
            }
            column = new SimpleTextColumn(column2.name);
            column.type = column2.type;
            column.precision = column2.precision;
            insertList.put(new Integer(colNo), column);
        }
    }
    else {
        // Invalid SQL statement

        throw new SQLException(
            "Invalid INSERT statement, no VALUES clause");

    }

    // The next word must be VALUES.  If there was an insert
    // list, we have positioned past it.

    if (!parsedSQL[pos].equalsIgnoreCase("VALUES")) {
        throw new SQLException(
            "Invalid INSERT statement; missing VALUES clause");
    }

    pos++;
    if (pos >= parsedSQL.length) {
        throw new SQLException (
                "Invalid INSERT statement, missing values");
    }

    // The next word must be the open paren that starts the values

    if (!parsedSQL[pos].equals("(")) {
        throw new SQLException (
                "Invalid INSERT statement, missing values");
    }

    pos++;
    if (pos >= parsedSQL.length) {
        throw new SQLException (
```

```
                "Invalid INSERT statement, missing values");
}

// Build our value list. Get each comma separated value until
// we read a close paren.

valueList = new Hashtable();

pos = buildList(parsedSQL, pos, ")", valueList);

// We could check for junk after the INSERT statement, but we
// won't.

// Verify the the number of insert items matches the number
// of data items

if (insertList.size() != valueList.size()) {
   throw new SQLException(
      "Number of values does not equal the number " +
      "of items in the insert list");
}

// Verify the data is correct

validateData(insertList, valueList, prepareOnly);

// If we are just preparing the statement, exit now

if (prepareOnly) {
   return;
}

// Now we can build the line that will get written to the
// simple text file. If there is any binary data, write
// it first so that we know what the offset will be.

String sdfPath = ownerConnection.getCatalog() + "/" +
                  tableName +
                  SimpleTextDefine.DATA_FILE_EXT;
String sbfPath = ownerConnection.getCatalog() + "/" +
                  tableName +
                  SimpleTextDefine.BINARY_FILE_EXT;

File sdf = new File(sdfPath);
File sbf = new File(sbfPath);
RandomAccessFile rafsdf = null;
RandomAccessFile rafsbf = null;
```

```java
if (!sdf.exists()) {
    throw new SQLException("Text file does not exist: " +
                           sdfPath);
}

String line = "";
long binaryPos = 0;

for (int i = 1; i <= columnList.size(); i++) {
    column2 = (SimpleTextColumn)
                  columnList.get(new Integer(i));

    // Separate the data by a comma

    if (i > 1) {
        line += ",";
    }

    // If there is no data for this column, skip it

    colNo = findColumnNumber(insertList, column2.name);

    if (colNo == 0) {

        // No data, put in defaults

        switch(column2.type) {
        case Types.VARCHAR:
            line += "''";
            break;
        case Types.VARBINARY:
            line += "-1";
            break;
        default:
            line += "0";
            break;
        }
        continue;
    }

    column = (SimpleTextColumn)
                  valueList.get(new Integer(colNo));

    if (column2.type == Types.VARBINARY) {
        if (rafsbf == null) {
            if (!sbf.exists()) {
```

```
            throw new SQLException(
                    "Binary file does not exist: " +
                    sbfPath);
        }
        try {
            rafsbf = new RandomAccessFile(sbf, "rw");

            // Position to the end of file

            rafsbf.seek(rafsbf.length());

        }
        catch (Exception ex) {
            throw new SQLException("Unable to access " +
                    sbfPath + ": " + ex.getMessage());
        }
    }

    try {

        // Get the current position

        binaryPos = rafsbf.getFilePointer();

        // Create a new CommonValue with the hex
        // digits (remove the quotes).

        CommonValue value = new CommonValue(
                column.name.substring(1,
                    column.name.length() - 1));

        // Now let CommonValue convert the hex string into
        // a byte array.

        byte b[] = value.getBytes();

        // Write the length first

        rafsbf.writeInt(b.length);

        // Write the data

        rafsbf.write(b);

    }
    catch (Exception ex) {
        throw new SQLException("Unable to access " +
```

```
                            sbfPath + " for column " + i +
                            ": " + ex.getMessage());
            }

            // Put the offset pointer in the line

            line += binaryPos;
        }

        // Else some kind of text data, put directly in the
        // line.

        else {
            line += column.name;
        }
    }


    // If the binary file was opened, close it now

    if (rafsbf != null) {
        try {
            rafsbf.close();
        }
        catch (Exception ex) {
            throw new SQLException("Unable to close " +
                    sbfPath + ": " + ex.getMessage());
        }
    }


    // Now that we have the data line, write it out to the text
    // file.

    long seekPos;
    String msg = "";
    try {
        msg = "open";
        rafsdf = new RandomAccessFile(sdf, "rw");
        msg = "get length";
        seekPos = rafsdf.length();

        // Position to the end of file

        msg = "seek";
        rafsdf.seek(seekPos);
```

```
      // Write the data

      msg = "write";
      rafsdf.writeBytes(line);
      rafsdf.writeBytes("\n");
      msg = "close";
      rafsdf.close();

   }
   catch (Exception ex) {
      ex.printStackTrace();
      throw new SQLException("Unable to " + msg + " " +
            sdfPath + ": " + ex.getMessage());
   }
}


//----------------------------------------------------------------
// select
// Select data from a table
//
// Grammar:
//
// select-statement ::= SELECT select-list FROM table-name
//                            [WHERE search-condition]
//
// select-list ::= * | column-identifier
//                        [,column-identifier]...
// search-condition ::= column-identifier comparison-operator
//                            literal
// comparison-operator ::= < | > | = | <>
//
//----------------------------------------------------------------

protected void select(
   boolean prepareOnly)
   throws SQLException
{

   // Initialize the filter object

   resultSetFilter = null;

   // The SQL statement must have at least 4 elements:
   //
   // SELECT * FROM table

   if (parsedSQL.length < 4) {
```

```
      throw new SQLException ("Invalid SELECT statement");
   }

Hashtable selectList = new Hashtable();
int pos = 1;

// Build our select list. Get each comma separated name
// until we read a 'FROM'.

pos = buildList(parsedSQL, pos, "FROM", selectList);

// There must be at least one column

if (selectList.size() == 0) {
   throw new SQLException("Select list must be specified");
}

// Increment past the 'FROM' word. This is the table name

pos++;

if (pos >= parsedSQL.length) {
   throw new SQLException("Missing table name");
}

// The next word is the table name. Verify that it does
// not contain any invalid characters.

String tableName = parsedSQL[pos];
validateName(tableName, "table");

// Verify that the file exists. If getColumns returns
// null, the table does not exist.

Hashtable columnList = ownerConnection.getColumns(
            ownerConnection.getCatalog(), tableName);

if (columnList == null) {
   throw new SQLException("Table does not exist: " +
                          tableName);
}

// No go back through the select list and verify that each
// column specified is contained in the table. Also expand
// any * to be all columns.

Hashtable validList = new Hashtable();
int validCount = 0;
```

```
SimpleTextColumn column;
SimpleTextColumn column2;

for (int i = 1; i <= selectList.size(); i++) {

   // Get the next column from the select list

   column = (SimpleTextColumn)
                    selectList.get(new Integer(i));

   // If it's an *, expand it to all columns in the table

   if (column.name.equals("*")) {
      for (int j = 1; j <= columnList.size(); j++) {
         column2 = (SimpleTextColumn)
                    columnList.get(new Integer(j));

         validCount++;
         validList.put(new Integer(validCount), column2);
      }
   }
   else {

      // Make sure the column exists in the table

      column2 = findColumn(columnList, column.name);

      if (column2 == null) {
         throw new SQLException("Column not found: " +
                    column.name);
      }

      // Put column on our valid list

      validCount++;
      validList.put(new Integer(validCount), column2);
   }
}

// Now we know the table exists and have a list of valid
// columns. Process the WHERE clause if one exists.

pos++;

if (pos < parsedSQL.length) {

   // The next word should be WHERE
```

```
if (!parsedSQL[pos].equalsIgnoreCase ("WHERE")) {
   throw new SQLException("WHERE clause expected");
}

// Create a filter object

resultSetFilter = new SimpleTextFilter();

pos++;

if (pos >= parsedSQL.length) {
   throw new SQLException(
        "Column name expected after WHERE clause");
}

// The next word is a column name. Make sure it exists in
// the table.

resultSetFilter.column = findColumn(columnList,
                    parsedSQL[pos]);

if (resultSetFilter.column == null) {
   throw new SQLException("Column not found: " +
                    parsedSQL[pos]);

}

// Make sure the column is searchable

if (!resultSetFilter.column.searchable) {
   throw new SQLException(
      "Column is not searchable: " + parsedSQL[pos]);
}

pos++;

// The next word is the operator. Some operators may
// take 2 words (i.e <>).

if (pos >= parsedSQL.length) {
   throw new SQLException(
                "Operator expected in WHERE clause");
}

if (parsedSQL[pos].equals("=")) {
   resultSetFilter.operator = SimpleTextFilter.OP_EQ;
}
```

```
else if (parsedSQL[pos].equals("<")) {
   resultSetFilter.operator = SimpleTextFilter.OP_LT;
}
else if (parsedSQL[pos].equals(">")) {
   resultSetFilter.operator = SimpleTextFilter.OP_GT;
}
else {
   throw new SQLException("Invalid operator: " +
                  parsedSQL[pos]);
}

// The next word may be our value, or it may be the
// second part of an operator.

pos++;

if (pos >= parsedSQL.length) {
   throw new SQLException(
              "Value expected in WHERE clause");
}

if ((resultSetFilter.operator ==
                  SimpleTextFilter.OP_LT) &&
   (parsedSQL[pos].equals(">"))) {
   resultSetFilter.operator = SimpleTextFilter.OP_NE;
   pos++;
   if (pos >= parsedSQL.length) {
      throw new SQLException(
              "Value expected in WHERE clause");
   }
}

// Get the data value and validate

Hashtable whereList = new Hashtable();
Hashtable dataList = new Hashtable();
column = new SimpleTextColumn(parsedSQL[pos]);

whereList.put(new Integer(1), resultSetFilter.column);
dataList.put(new Integer(1), column);

validateData(whereList, dataList, prepareOnly);

String s = parsedSQL[pos];

// validateData could have massaged the data value
// (such as in executing a prepared statement with
// parameters).  Get the value back
```

```
        s = ((SimpleTextColumn)
                    dataList.get(new Integer(1))).name;

    // Strip off any quotes

    if (s.startsWith("'") &&
        s.endsWith("'")) {
      s = s.substring(1,s.length() - 1);
    }

    resultSetFilter.value = new CommonValue(s);

    pos++;

    // Check for extra junk at the end of the statement

    if (pos < parsedSQL.length) {
      throw new SQLException(
          "Invalid characters following WHERE clause");
    }
  }

  // Set the catalog name, table name, and column Hashtable
  // for the result set

  resultSetCatalog = ownerConnection.getCatalog();
  resultSetTable = tableName;
  resultSetColumns = validList;
}

//---------------------------------------------------------------
// findColumn
// Given a SimpleTextColumn Hashtable and a column name,
// return the SimpleTextColumn that matches. Null if no
// match. The column numbers are 1-based.
//---------------------------------------------------------------

protected SimpleTextColumn findColumn(
    Hashtable list,
    String name)
{
  SimpleTextColumn column;

  for (int i = 1; i <= list.size(); i++) {
    column = (SimpleTextColumn) list.get(new Integer(i));
    if (column != null) {
      if (column.name.equalsIgnoreCase(name)) {
```

```
                return column;
            }
        }
    }
    return null;
}


//----------------------------------------------------------------
// findColumnNumber
// Given a SimpleTextColumn Hashtable and a column name,
// return the column number that matches. 0 if no match.
// The column numbers are 1-based.
//----------------------------------------------------------------

protected int findColumnNumber(
    Hashtable list,
    String name)
{
    SimpleTextColumn column;

    for (int i = 1; i <= list.size(); i++) {
        column = (SimpleTextColumn) list.get(new Integer(i));
        if (column != null) {
            if (column.name.equalsIgnoreCase(name)) {
                return i;
            }
        }
    }
    return 0;
}


//----------------------------------------------------------------
// buildList
// Given a parsed SQL statement, the current position, and
// the ending word, build a list of the comma separated
// words from the SQL statement.  This is used for the insert
// column list, insert values, and select list. Returns the
// new position in the parsed SQL.
//----------------------------------------------------------------

public int buildList(
    String sql[],
    int pos,
    String endWord,
    Hashtable list)
    throws SQLException
{
```

```java
SimpleTextColumn column;
boolean done = false;
String name;
int colNo = 1;

// Loop while more data is present

while (!done) {

   // Get the next column
   name = sql[pos];

   column = new SimpleTextColumn(name);
   list.put(new Integer(colNo), column);
   colNo++;

   pos++;
   if (pos >= sql.length) {
      if (endWord.length() > 0) {
         throw new SQLException (
             "Invalid statement after " + name);
      }
      else {
         done = true;
         break;
      }
   }

   // If the next word is not a comma, it must be our
   // ending word.

   if (!sql[pos].equals(",")) {

      // Found the ending word?  exit the loop

      if (sql[pos].equalsIgnoreCase(endWord)) {
         done = true;
         break;
      }
      if (endWord.length() == 0) {
         throw new SQLException("Invalid data format");
      }

      throw new SQLException (
             "Invalid statement after " + name);
   }
```

```
            pos++;
            if (pos >= sql.length) {
                if (endWord.length() > 0) {
                    throw new SQLException (
                        "Invalid statement after " + name);
                }
                else {
                    done = true;
                    break;
                }
            }
        }
    }
    return pos;
}


//------------------------------------------------------------
// validateData
// Given an insert list and a data list, verify the each data
// element is proper for the given type and precision.
//------------------------------------------------------------

protected void validateData(
    Hashtable insertList,
    Hashtable dataList,
    boolean prepareOnly)
    throws SQLException
{
    SimpleTextColumn insert;
    SimpleTextColumn data;
    int precision = 0;
    int paramNum = 0;

    // Init number of parameters if we are preparing

    if (prepareOnly) {
        paramCount = 0;
    }

    for (int i = 1; i <= insertList.size(); i++) {
        insert = (SimpleTextColumn)
                        insertList.get(new Integer(i));
        data = (SimpleTextColumn) dataList.get(new Integer(i));

        // If a parameter marker is found, either continue
        // to the next list item because we are preparing, or
        // replace it with a bound parameter value.
```

```
if (data.name.equals("?")) {

   if (prepareOnly) {

      // Increment number of parameter markers

      paramCount++;
      continue;
   }

   // Increment current parameter number

   paramNum++;

   // Get String value for the bound parameter from the
   // boundParams Hashtable. If it is not found, throw
   // an exception indicating that not all of the
   // parameters have been set.

   if (boundParams != null) {
      String s = (String)
               boundParams.get(new Integer(paramNum));

      if (s == null) {
         throw new SQLException(
                 "Not all parameters have been set");
      }

      // Set the value into the SimpleTextColumn entry
      // If the data is a string or binary type,
      // enclose it in quotes.

      switch(insert.type) {
      case Types.VARCHAR:
      case Types.VARBINARY:
         data.name = "'" + s + "'";
         break;
      default:
         data.name = s;
         break;
      }

   }
}
```

```
          switch(insert.type) {
          case Types.VARCHAR:
             if (!data.name.startsWith("'") ||
                 (data.name.length() < 2) ||
                 !data.name.endsWith("'")) {
               throw new SQLException(
              "String data must be enclosed in single quotes: " +
                             data.name);
             }
             precision = data.name.length() - 2;
             break;
          case Types.INTEGER:
             try {
                Integer.valueOf(data.name);
             }
             catch (Exception ex) {
               throw new SQLException("Invalid numeric data: " +
                             data.name);
             }
             precision = data.name.length();
             break;
          case Types.BINARY:
             if (!data.name.startsWith("'") ||
                 (data.name.length() < 2) ||
                 !data.name.endsWith("'")) {
               throw new SQLException(
              "Binary data must be enclosed in single quotes: " +
                             data.name);
             }
             if ((data.name.length() % 2) != 0) {
                throw new SQLException(
              "Binary data must have even number of hex digits:" +
                             data.name);
             }
             precision = (data.name.length() - 2) / 2;
             break;
          }

          if (precision > insert.precision) {
             throw new SQLException("Invalid data precision for "+
                          insert.name);
          }
       }
    }
  }
```

```
//--------------------------------------------------------------
// validateName
// Verify that the given name does not contain any invalid
// characters. This will be used for both table names and
// column names.
//--------------------------------------------------------------

protected void validateName(
    String name,
    String type)
    throws SQLException
{
    // Invalid characters other than a-z, 0-9, and A-Z

    String invalid = "@#./\\()";

    char c;
    int j;

    for (int i = 0; i < name.length(); i++) {
        c = name.charAt(i);

        // If it's not an alpha numeric or numeric character,
        // check the list of invalid characters

        if (!((c >= 'a') && (c <= 'z')) &&
            !((c >= '0') && (c <= '9')) &&
            !((c >= 'A') && (c <= 'Z'))) {
            for (j = 0; j < invalid.length(); j++) {
                if (c == invalid.charAt(j)) {
                    throw new SQLException("Invalid " + type +
                                " name: " + name);
                }
            }
        }
    }
}


//-----------------------------------------------
// getConnection
// Returns the owner connection object.
//-----------------------------------------------

public SimpleTextIConnection getConnection()
{
    return ownerConnection;
}
```

```
// Owning connection object
protected SimpleTextIConnection ownerConnection;

// SQLWarning chain
protected SQLWarning lastWarning;

// The current SQL statement
protected String sqlStatement;

// The String array of parsed SQL words
protected String parsedSQL[];

// The current SQL statement type (i.e. SQL_SELECT,
// SQL_CREATE, etc.)
protected int statementType;

// Update count for the last statement that executed
protected int updateCount;

// Attributes used for creating a result set
String resultSetCatalog;
String resultSetTable;
Hashtable resultSetColumns;

// If a filter exists for a select statement, a
// SimpleTextFilter object will be created
SimpleTextFilter resultSetFilter;

// Our current result set
ResultSet currentResultSet;

// A Hashtable for each bound parameter.  Only valid
// for PreparedStatements
Hashtable boundParams;

// The count of parameter markers.  Only valid for
// PreparedStatements
int paramCount;
}
```

This sample chapter from the *Web Developer's Guide to Java Beans*, useful especially to AWT programmers, focuses on the advantages of the JDK 1.1 delegation-based event model. It covers using event listeners to connect event observers to event sources, delivering events to registered listeners, and utilizing an adapter to interpose between an event source and a listener.

This chapter, which originally appeared in the Web Developer's Guide to Java Beans, *is reprinted with permission. Jalal Feghhi,* Web Developer's Guide to Java Beans. *The Coriolis Group:1997.*

Chapter 7

The JDK 1.1 Event Model

Events are a general-purpose programming paradigm; they are used to transfer state-change information from one subsystem to another. One of the key applications of events is to model and design systems whose state changes may not be predictable. System failure is a good example of a behavior whose exact time of occurrence cannot be known in advance. If you are trying to design a system that responds to failures in a unit, you may want to use events to notify another unit that can take corrective actions.

Windowing environments utilize events to route user interactions (such as mouse clicks or keystrokes) with GUI widgets to appropriate branches of code that can respond to the interactions. A windowing application usually consists of two distinct but related parts: the GUI and the application logic. The GUI has a root window, which usually contains other windowing widgets organized in a hierarchy. When a user interacts with the root window, the windowing environment generates an event, determines the gadget in the hierarchy that should be receiving it, and sends it to that gadget. In response, the target GUI component executes a chunk of programming logic code to handle the event.

A good event model must be scaleable, have a fast response time, and separate the GUI portion of an application from the programming logic. These features allow new event handling units to be added to a system without distributing the system or degrading the performance.

In this chapter, we will present an overview of the JDK 1.0 event model. Although it is now obsolete, it provides a good example of an event model with flawed characteristics. This overview is followed by a discussion of the JDK 1.1 delegation-based event model.

We will discuss in detail the fundamentals of the event paradigm and show you its performance and scalability characteristics. We will precisely define events, event sources, event listeners, and event observers, as well as illustrate the life cycle of events (starting from their generation in event sources and their consumption in event observers). We will employ all the concepts and theory of the delegation-based event model to create an event-driven failure-recovery prototype system, which we call Failure Command System (FCM).

The JDK 1.0 Event Model

Although the Java Beans delegation-based event model is not based on the JDK 1.0 model, knowledge of the latter model can help you gain a better understanding of the Java Beans approach. This section presents an overview of the JDK 1.0 model and delineates its shortcomings.

Overview Of The JDK 1.0 Event Model

JDK 1.0 provides two entry points into its windowing event environment: **action()** and **handleEvent()** methods. You can override either of these two methods and insert your own programming logic for event handling. If you return **true** from either method, you signal the Java windowing system that you have consumed the event and it should not do any further processing. If you return **false**, Java propagates the event up through the hierarchy of GUI widgets until it is either consumed by a widget or the root window of the hierarchy is reached.

You can override the root container's **action()** or **handleEvent()** method and insert the event handling code for all your GUI components in the overridden method. This case requires a complex conditional statement to first determine the GUI widget that generated the event and then invoke an appropriate method to handle the event. All the event handling methods belong to the container and usually reside in the same source file that creates the front-end GUI.

Alternatively, you can use inheritance to subclass an AWT component and add the component-specific event handling code in the subclass. Even though this approach distributes the event handling code across many different subcomponents and does not have the complex conditional block of code, it results in a proliferation of AWT components whose sole purpose is to capture component-specific event handling logic.

Shortcomings Of The JDK 1.0 Event Model

The JDK 1.0 event model suffers from a lack of scaleability and performance, and it violates some software engineering design principles. Neither of the above approaches can result in a clean separation between the GUI code and the application logic code; you must integrate your event handling methods with the code that creates the GUI. For an application that has a large number of AWT components, you end up with a code that is difficult to maintain and is bug-prone. Using subclassing just to implement event handling code is cumbersome and violates object-oriented design principles (you should subclass only when you are extending the class in some functional or visual manner).

The JDK 1.0 event model does not scale up to applications with a large number of GUI components. The conditional statement in the first approach gets overly complicated and becomes a source of logical errors. (It is easy for a programmer to forget to handle an event within the conditional block.) The second approach is not scaleable due to the sheer number of derived classes that it produces. The Java AWT package itself cannot be scaled to add new event types without potentially breaking user applications in very unpredictable ways.

The 1.0 event model also suffers from a lack of performance because there is no event filtering—that is, events are always delivered to components whether or not the components are interested in them. The performance degradation is especially prominent for high-frequency event types, such as mouse moves or clicks. Furthermore, the conditional block in the first approach usually performs costly string comparisons in order to identify the method that should handle the event. These comparisons degrade the performance, particularly for high-frequency events, and are unwieldy to localize.

The JDK 1.0 event model has been completely revamped in JDK 1.1 in favor of a *delegation-based* model. This model addresses the shortcomings of its predecessor and supports Java Beans and different propagation models, as described below.

The 1.0 model provides a framework to define an extensible set of low-level and semantic events, and it supports different delivery semantics. The delegation model separates the application code from the GUI code, and facilitates the creation of more robust, maintainable, and extensible event handling systems. The new model supports dynamic discovery of the events that a subsystem generates, as well as dynamic discovery of events that it can observe. It also allows for the registration of event listeners and dynamic manipulation of relationships between event sources and event listeners. The delegation model supports the visual builder tools, and it results in high-performance, scaleable, robust systems. In the rest of this section, we will introduce you to all of the aspects of this new event model.

 The new delegation-based event model in JDK 1.1 has been introduced to resolve the inherent problems with the JDK 1.0 model and support the Java Beans technology.

The JDK 1.1 Event-Related Objects

There are two different processes necessary to designing an event-driven system in JDK 1.1: relationship creation and event processing. You create a relationship between an *event source* and an *event observer* through an *event listener*, and you add component-specific code to an event observer to process events.

Registering an event listener with an event source creates this relationship. An object identifies itself as an event source by defining a pair of registration methods that conform to a specific design pattern and associate a listener object with an event type. An object takes the role of a listener by implementing a listener interface inherited from **java.util.EventListener**.

An event listener acts as a bridge between an object that generates events and an object that observes events. The relationship between an event source and an event listener is one-to-many, which means that there can be any number of listeners associated with a source. Similarly, there is a one-to-many relationship between a listener and an observer, although in practice you usually call only one observer from within a listener. Figure 1 graphs these relationships.

 Registering event listeners with an event source creates a directed graph between an event source, event listeners, and event observers.

An event source generates event objects, which flow through listeners and *sink* in event observers (as determined by relationship graphs). An event object is a subclass of **java.util.EventObject** and has all the necessary information to recover the change of state that transpired in an event source. Event objects are *immutable*—an observer takes whatever action necessary to respond to an event, but it can neither alter the event nor recycle it back into the event system. This behavior is different from the JDK 1.0 event model, in which you can propagate the event upward in the chain of AWT components.

 The life cycle of an event object begins in an event source, transits through an event listener, and ends in an event observer.

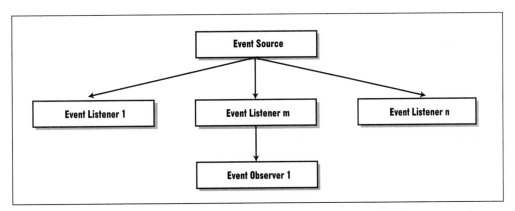

Figure 1   The relationships among an event source, event listeners, and an event observer.

You integrate your component-specific code with an observer. This code determines your component's response when an event occurs in another component. For example, if you are designing a fault-tolerant system, an observer subsystem might respond to a failure elsewhere by shutting down that subsystem and rerouting the internal messages through a redundant subsystem. The logic that performs this task should be in your observer class, cleanly separated from the classes that trigger events. Again, this characteristic is quite different than the 1.0 model, which essentially bundles up the event handling code with the GUI code.

The JDK 1.1 event model separates the code that sources an event, such as the GUI code, from the code that responds to an event.

In the JDK 1.1 event model, you need to explicitly express your interest in receiving events by registering your listeners with an event source. Because only the relevant objects receive events, this approach speeds up the overall performance of the system and creates a robust system that can be easily scaled up.

The 1.1 event model results in robust, high-performance, scaleable event-driven systems.

Event State Objects

An event state object represents a change in the state of an object and contains all the necessary information to identify the change. For example, the **PropertyChangeEvent** object can convey the change of value in a property because it holds the object whose property has changed, the name of the property, the old value, and the new value.

An event represents the old state of an object and a change that has occurred in that state, such as PropertyChangeEvent. An event also contains the object whose state has changed.

In JDK 1.1, events are no longer represented by the single **java.awt.Event** class with numeric IDs. The new event model defines the root **java.util.EventObject** event class and requires programmers to extend this class or any of its subclasses to create more specific event types. This approach is fundamentally different from that of the JDK 1.0 model because it uses a class to identify an event instead of a numeric ID. The **EventObject** class has one instance variable that keeps track of the object that has fired an event, as well as a constructor of the form **EventObject(Object)**.

The **java.awt.Event** class in JDK 1.0 is now superseded with **java.awt.AWTEvent**, which is extended from **java.util.EventObject** and is the parent class for all the windowing-related events. This class defines a number of constants, such as FOCUS_EVENT_MASK, KEY_EVENT_MASK, that are used to determine the event types that should be delivered to AWT components. These masks are automatically set when a component expresses its interest in an event through the process of registration. The **AWTEvent** class also defines an internal variable that keeps track of the ID of an event, which is used to identify an event within a small set of related events and is accessed via **AWTEvent.getId()**. You can create an object of this class through the **AWTEvent(Object, int)** constructor, where you need to provide the object that has generated the event and the event ID.

Because some event classes may represent more than one event type, however, they may contain an ID that identifies one member of a set of possible event types. **MouseEvent**, for instance, uses this approach to designate all the possible set of mouse-related events (mouse-drag, mouse-enter, mouse-exit, mouse-move, mouse-press, and mouse-release). In this case, you need to call **MouseEvent.getId()** and compare the returned value with the list of constant values defined in **MouseEvent** to determine the exact event type.

If you create beans or use the JDK 1.1 event model to design event-driven systems, you may need to define your own event types. If you find yourself in this situation, look over all the standard event types defined in the **java.awt.event** package to ensure that the event you need is not already defined there and to determine whether you can extend any of the standard classes. As a last resort, extend your new event type from **java.awt.AWTEvent** (if you are creating an AWT event) or **java.util.EventObject** (for non-AWT events). The code segment in Listing 1 shows the definition of a custom event of type **FailureEvent**.

The **FailureEvent** class represents a general failure event in FCM. This class identifies two types of system failure events: total and partial. A system cannot recover from a total failure; in such cases, it notifies any registered listeners and powers down. A system may continue operation if it fails partially. The class **Failure**, used in **FailureEvent**, contains more detailed information about a failure. You should observe that **FailureEvent** encapsulates these two event types by defining two constants and defining the internal variable **m_id**.

You should use the word "Event" to end the name of your event type. For example, if you are defining an event to represent a general failure in a system, name your event FailureEvent. If you are defining a set of closely related events, you may want to bundle them up in one class and use a numeric ID to distinguish between the sub-events. Always remember to call the superclass constructor.

Listing 1 Defining FailureEvent.

```
import java.util.*;

/**
 * This class implements a very simple event object
 * that represents a module failure in a system.
 * The FailureEvent class defines two event types,
 * representing total and partial failures.
 */
public class FailureEvent extends EventObject
{
  private Failure m_failure;
  private int m_id; // event type id (total/partial)

  /**
   * Total failure event type.
   */
  public final static int TOTAL_FAILURE = 0;

  /**
   * Partial failure event type.
   */
  public final static int PARTIAL_FAILURE = 1;

  public
  FailureEvent(Module module, int id, Failure failure)
```

```
{
  super(module);
  m_id = id;
  m_failure = failure;
}

public Failure getFailure()
{
  return m_failure;
}
}
```

Event state objects are immutable because an event captures a single change of state for an object. Of course, the object can go through more state changes, but these changes are captured by additional event objects.

Because events are immutable, you should not define any of their data members as **public**. You can expose these internal fields through getter accessor methods. Make sure that you adhere to the design patterns set forth for accessor methods in Chapter 6. There are circumstances, however, in which you must modify an event, for example, when translating view-relative coordinates when propagating a windowing event through a view hierarchy. In these cases, you should provide methods for your events that perform the appropriate modifications, instead of allowing a user to directly manipulate an event's internal states.

An event is immutable and does not usually change as it propagates from an event source to an event sink. (Note: the term "event sink" is interchangeable with "event observer." We will use both throughout this chapter, as they are both commonly used.)

Low-Level Vs. Semantic Events

AWT defines two types of events: low-level and semantic. A *low-level event* represents a low-level, uninterpreted user interaction with a visual component on the screen that corresponds to some input device. For example, **java.awt.event.KeyEvent** represents a raw, component-level keyboard event that a user has triggered by interacting with the keyboard input device. The JDK 1.1 AWT package currently defines nine such events, as shown in Figure 2.

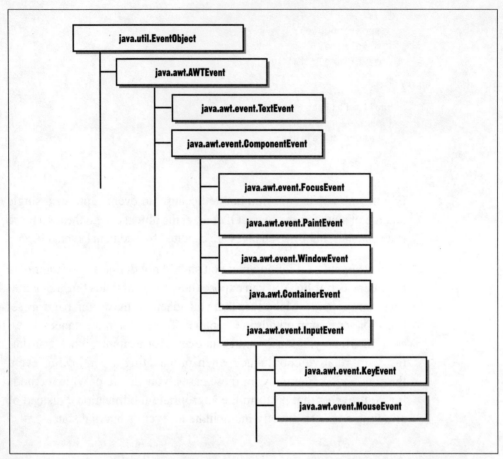

Figure 2 The hierarchy of low-level events defined in the JDK 1.1 AWT.

Semantic events are higher-level events that represent the intentions of a user when he or she interacts with a windowing component. These semantic events do not directly correspond to any specific component; they are higher-level events that may apply across a set of components that share a similar semantic model. For example, **java.awt.event.ActionEvent** is triggered by a button when it is pressed, by a list when one of its items is double-clicked, or by a menu when one of its items is selected. The AWT package in the JDK 1.1 identifies three semantic events, as depicted in Figure 3.

 A semantic event represents the user's intention interacting with a bean, whereas a low-level event corresponds to a raw, uninterpreted interaction.

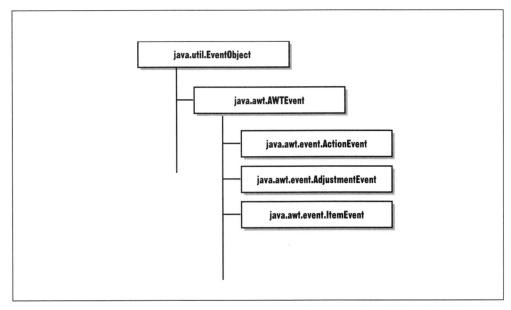

Figure 3 The hierarchy of semantic events defined in the JDK 1.1 AWT.

Event Listeners

Event listeners create relationships between event sources and event sinks (refer to Figure 1). They allow event state objects to flow from a source bean to a target bean. An event listener is essentially a callback object—a target bean creates a listener callback object and gives it to a source bean; the source calls back the listener when an event transpires that is significant to the target bean.

A listener encapsulates one or more related methods. For example, **java.awt.event.MouseListener** defines **mouseClicked()**, **mouse-Entered()**, **mouseExited()**, **mousePressed()**, and **mouseReleased()**. The grouping of a number of methods under one listener object is useful for maintaining a balance between the number and the granularity of listener objects. All of the methods, however, must be conceptually related and have the same signature. All of the methods in **MouseListener**, for example, take one argument of **MouseEvent** type.

An event listener is a callback object and serves as a bridge between a source and a consumer of events. A listener may encapsulate a number of semantically related methods.

The JDK 1.1 Event Model

In general, you use interfaces in Java to implement a callback object in the following manner. First, you define an interface with one or more methods (recall that an interface merely identifies a method without actually implementing it). You then define a trigger class that takes an instance of the interface and, based on certain conditions, invokes a method of the interface. Finally, you create an implementation of the interface and pass an instance of it to the trigger class. You are now ready to apply the above procedure to create a very simple event-driven timer system.

Create an interface called **ICallback** that declares a **wakeup()** method, as shown in Listing 2. This interface has the **ICallback** type, and any class that implements this interface acquires this type and can be used wherever the interface can be used.

Listing 2   ICallback interface.

```
/**
 * This interface defines a callback method.
 */
public interface ICallback
{
  public void wakeup();
}
```

Define a **Timer** class that extends **java.lang.Thread**. The constructor of this class takes an object of **ICallback** type and assigns it to an internal data member; the **run()** method of **Timer** sleeps for one second and then calls back to the callback object by invoking **wakeup()**. The **Timer** class is presented in Listing 3.

Listing 3   The Timer trigger class.

```
/**
 * This class implements a very simple timer class.
 * The timer sleeps for 1 second and then invokes the
 * wakeup() method of the callback object.
 */
public class Timer extends java.lang.Thread
{
  ICallback m_cb;

  public Timer(ICallback cb)
  {
    m_cb = cb;
  }
```

```
    public void run()
    {
      while (true)
      {
        try
        {
          sleep(1000);
          m_cb.wakeup();
        }
        catch (java.lang.InterruptedException e)
        {
          System.out.println(e);
        }
      }
    }
}
```

The **ICallback** and **Timer** objects conceptually represent general-purpose utility classes. You now need to provide some application-specific behavior by creating a class that implements **ICallback**. A simple such class, shown in Listing 4, prints a message when its **wakeup()** method is called.

Listing 4   CallbackImp implements ICallback.

```
/**
 * This class provides a simple implementation of
 * ICallback.
 * It defines the wakeup() method to print a message
 * on the screen.
 */
public class CallbackImp implements ICallback
{
  public void wakeup()
  {
    System.out.println("wakeup is called");
  }
}
```

Proceed to connect **CallbackImp** with **Timer** by simply creating an instance of **CallbackImp**, instantiating **Timer** with a reference to the **CallbackImp** instance, and starting the timer thread, as shown in Listing 5. Run the **Main** class; you will see the message "wakeup is called" printed on your screen approximately every one second.

Listing 5 Connecting CallbackImp and Timer.

```java
/**
 * This class tests the timer.
 */
public class Main
{
  public static void main(String[] argv)
  {
    // Create an instance of the callback object.
    //
    CallbackImp cb = new CallbackImp();

    // Create the timer.
    //
    Timer timer = new Timer(cb);

    // Start the timer.
    //
    timer.start();
  }
}
```

The **ICallback** interface is important because it allows you to separate the code specific to your application (in this case, **CallbackImp**) cleanly from the rest of the event-driven system. You can also extend the logic of your application simply by defining another implementation of **ICallback** (such as **CallbackImp1**) and using it instead of or in addition to **CallbackImp**. Another advantage of **ICallback** is that it defines a common type for all classes that implement it—for example, **CallbackImp** and **CallbackImp1** can be used in conjunction with **Timer** without causing any compile-time errors.

The usage of an event listener and its relationship with an event source and an event observer parallel the above description of **ICallback**, **Timer**, and **CallbackImp**. Like **ICallback**, an event listener is a Java interface that is used to separate the application-specific logic from the rest of any event-driven system (such as the Java windowing system). It also allows the creation of many applications in the form of event observers that can seamlessly integrate with an existing event system. An event source has the role of **Timer**: it can maintain a list of listeners and invoke their callbacks when appropriate. There is only one subtle difference between **CallbackImp**, which acts as a listener, and a general event listener. **CallbackImp** processes and consumes the event, whereas a general listener usually delegates the event processing to an event observer by invoking a method of the observer.

 An event listener allows the application-specific code to be localized in an event observer.

All event listeners are interfaces rooted at **java.util.EventListener**. You create your own listeners by extending this class or of any of its subclasses. Your listeners can identify one or more methods; in general, you should group the conceptually related methods within one listener to avoid a proliferation of listener classes.

 By convention, the name of an event listener should end in "Listener". For example, the listener class name for FailureEvent event object is FailureListener.

Callback methods in listener interfaces should conform to a standard design pattern to facilitate the documentation of a system of events, programmatic introspection of callbacks, and automatic construction of generic event adapters (which are discussed in a later section). The general signature of the design pattern for callback methods is as follows (note that a callback method may throw exceptions):

```
void <eventOccurenceMethodName> (<EventStateObjectType> evt);
```

FCM, for example, defines **FailureListener** to handle events of type **FailureEvent**. This listener, shown in Listing 6, identifies two callback methods, **failureTotal()** and **failurePartial()**, each of which takes an argument of **FailureEvent** type. You should note that **FailureListener** provides two callbacks because **FailureEvent** encapsulates two types of events. Also note that **failurePartial()** may throw an **EContinueOperation** exception to indicate to a partially failed system that it should not power down. This exception is shown in Listing 7.

 As a rule of thumb, you should define one callback method for each subevent that an event object identifies.

Listing 6 FailureListener listener.

```
import java.util.*;

/**
 * This interface defines a simple listener with
 * two callback methods.
 * The method failureTotal() is called if there is
 * a total failure, while failurePartial() is invoked
 * if the failure is partial.
 *
 * Note: FailureListener defines one callback method
 *  for each event type in FailureEvent.
 */
public interface FailureListener extends EventListener
{
  public void failureTotal(FailureEvent evt);

  /**
   * This callback method may throw an
   * EContinueOperation exception to instruct a
   * partially failed system to continue operation.
   */
  public void failurePartial(FailureEvent evt)
  throws EContinueOperation;
}
```

Listing 7 EContinueOperation exception.

```
/**
 * This exception is thrown to signal a failed
 * system that it should continue operation and
 * must not power down.
 */
public class EContinueOperation extends Exception
{
  public EContinueOperation()
  {
    super ();
  }
}
```

If you are defining an interface with a group of methods, you should name the methods accordingly. For instance, **MouseListener** starts the names of all of its callback methods with "mouse" (**mouseClicked**(), **mouseEntered**(), **mouseExited**(), and so on). Similarly, **FailureListener** names its callback methods **failureTotal**() and **failurePartial**().

Low-Level Vs. Semantic Events

Similar to event state objects, AWT identifies two types of event listeners: low-level and semantic. A *low-level listener* corresponds to an uninterpreted user interaction with a visual component, while a *semantic listener* is a higher-level event that represents the intentions of a windowing component's user. For example, **java.awt.event.KeyListener** represents a low-level listener, whereas **java.awt.event.ActionListener** is a semantic one. The JDK 1.1 AWT package currently defines eight low-level and three semantic event listeners, as depicted in Figure 4 and Figure 5.

A semantic event listener is used in conjunction with a semantic event object, whereas a low-level listener is used with a low-level event object.

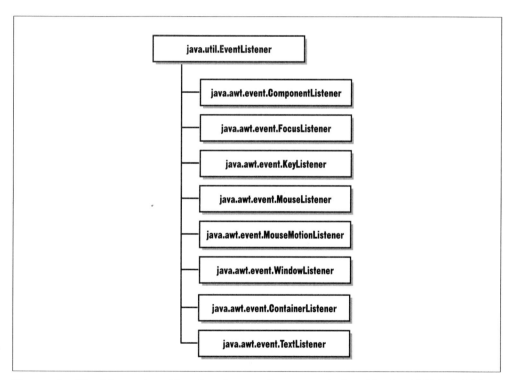

Figure 4   The hierarchy of low-level event listeners defined in the JDK 1.1 AWT.

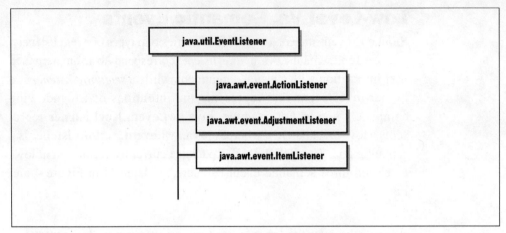

Figure 5 The hierarchy of semantic event listeners defined in the JDK 1.1 AWT.

Methods With Arbitrary Arguments

A callback method is usually required to take only one argument of **java.util.EventObject** type. Because an event is an object and can encapsulate an arbitrary number of data members, this restriction does not have any negative ramifications. There are cases, however, in which an event system needs to interface with another external event system that does not conform to this guideline (for example, this happens when bridging Java Beans events to other environments, such as ActiveX). In these cases, it is permissible to define callback methods that take one or more argument of any type, not just **EventObject**. These callbacks may throw exceptions and have the following general design pattern:

```
void <eventOccurenceMethodName> (...);
```

Visual builder tools should support both types of method signatures. In general, you should exercise restraint in defining callback methods with an arbitrary number of arguments.

  You should almost always define callback methods that take only one argument of EventObject type.

Event Sources

An event source generates an event, which flows through a listener to reach and sink in an event observer. An event source fires an event usually as a response to some external stimulus, which causes its internal state to change. A button, for example, triggers an **ActionEvent** when it is pressed.

You can always determine the types of events that a bean triggers by looking for a pair of add/remove functions that take an **EventListener** as an argument in either the bean's documentation or its source code (these functions are explained in the next section). Similarly, a framework can examine a bean and deduce the events it fires. You should keep in mind that a component can fire low-level or/and semantic events. For example, **java.awt.Dialog** generates a low-level **WindowEvent** because it supports **addWindowListener(WindowListener)** and **removeWindow-Listener(WindowListener)**, and **java.awt.Checkbox** fires a semantic **ItemEvent** because it defines **addItemListener(ItemListener)** and **removeItemListener(ItemListener)**.

An event source must call back all of the appropriate listeners when it triggers an event; we will discuss the delivery of events to listeners in much more detail in a later section. A listener is considered appropriate if it has registered its interest in events of the same type as that generated by the event source, as described in the next section.

 An event source triggers an event state object when its internal state changes, usually as a result of some external stimulus.

Registration

When you design an event source, you must provide a way for an event observer to register and deregister its interest in receiving events from the source. For each event type, you need to decide whether you want to support the multicast or unicast registration semantic.

The *multicast semantic* allows an arbitrary number of listeners to be associated with an event type, whereas the *unicast semantic* permits only one listener to be registered with an event type.

Multicast

So far, all of the examples of event registration in this book have the multicast semantic. A multicast event admits one or more event listeners, and it invokes their callbacks when an event interesting to the listeners transpires. The multicast registration has the following design pattern:

```
public void add<ListenerType>(< ListenerType> lis);
public void remove<ListenerType>(< ListenerType> lis);
```

 You should always define your registration methods as multicast unless you have a reason to believe this semantic is inappropriate.

You should normally synchronize the above two methods to guard against races in multithreaded code. The Java Beans specification does not specify the behavior of a bean if you attempt to register the same event listener more than once with the same event source, to delete a listener more than once, or to delete a listener that is not registered. All of the above behavior is implementation dependent and cannot be predicted. Moreover, passing a **null** to the registration methods is illegal and may result in an **IllegalArgumentException** or a **NullPointerException**.

The **Module** event source in the FCM application supports a multicast registration for **FailureListener**, as shown in Listing 8. This class defines an internal data member of type **Vector**, which keeps track of all the listeners registered to receive event notifications when **Module** triggers an **FailureEvent**. **Module** implements two methods for registration and deregistration (**addFailureListener()** and **removeFailureListener**, respectively).

Listing 8 A multicast event registration.

```
// List of all listeners who are interested in the
// FailureEvent generated by this module.
//
private Vector m_failureLs;

/**
 * Informs the module that this FailureListener
 * is interested in FailureEvents.
 *
 * @param l the FailureListener
 */
public synchronized void
addFailureListener(FailureListener l)
```

```
{
  m_failureLs.addElement(1);
}

/**
 * Informs the module that this FailureListener
 * is no longer interested in FailureEvents.
 *
 * @param l the FailureListener
 */
public synchronized void
removeFailureListener(FailureListener l)
{
  m_failureLs.removeElement(1);
}
```

 The multicast event registration allows any number of event listeners to be associated with an event source under the same event type.

Unicast

Although most events have a multicast semantic type, there might be cases where it is inappropriate or impractical to notify more than one listener when an event transpires. In such cases, you can use a unicast registration semantic, which permits only one listener to be associated with an event type. Any attempt to register a second listener for a unicast event fails. A unicast registration has the following naming convention:

```
public void add<ListenerType>(< ListenerType> lis)
throws java.util. TooManyListenersException;
public void remove<ListenerType>(< ListenerType> lis);
```

In the unicast semantic, the **add<ListenerType>** method may throw a **java.util.TooManyListenersException** if an attempt is made to associate more than one listener of the same type with an event source. As in the multicast model, the behavior of an event source is implementation dependent if you attempt to remove a listener that is not registered or pass a **null** argument to the registration methods.

The **Module** event source in FCM supports one unicast event—namely, **Failure1Event**. The internal variable **m_failure1L** (see Listing 9) holds only one **Failure1Listener**, as contrasted to **m_failureLs**, which has a

Vector type. The **addFailure1Listener()** throws an exception if a listener has already registered for **Failure1Event**.

Listing 9   A unicast event registration.

```
// The listener who is interested in the
// Failure1Event generated by this module.
//
private Failure1Listener m_failure1L;

/**
 * Informs the module that this Failure1Listener
 * is interested in Failure1Events.
 *
 * Note: This is a unicast event.
 *
 * @param l the Failure1Listener
 */
public synchronized void
addFailure1Listener(Failure1Listener l)
throws TooManyListenersException
{
  if (m_failure1L != null)
  {
    throw new TooManyListenersException();
  }

  m_failure1L = l;
}

/**
 * Informs the module that this FailureListener
 * is not longer interested in Failure1Events.
 *
 * @param l the Failure1Listener
 */
public synchronized void
removeFailure1Listener(Failure1Listener l)
{
  m_failure1L = null;
}
```

The unicast event registration allows a maximum of one event listener to be associated with an event type in an event source.

Delivery

After you have identified the events that an event source fires and provided the registration methods for those events, you need to deliver triggered events to all of the appropriate listeners. Typically, you deliver an event to listeners by going through the list of event listeners that you have maintained through the registration methods and invoking the listeners' callbacks, passing them the triggered event as an argument.

This section explains in detail all of the important issues related to event delivery. We use the **Module** event source to illustrate the concepts. As shown in Listing 10, **Module** simulates the occurrences of events in its **run** method, which calls **simulateFailureEvents()** and **simulateFailure1Events()** to deliver the events.

Event delivery is the process of flowing a triggered event from an event source to an event observer through a listener.

Listing 10　Event triggering in Module.

```
/**
 * Runs the hardware module in a system.
 * To illustrate the processing of events,
 * this method simulates the generation of
 * FailureEvents and Failure1Events.
 */
public void run()
{
  int counter = 0;

  while (true)
  {
    try
    {
      sleep(1000);

      if ((counter % 4) == 0)
      {
        simulateFailureEvents(true);
      }
      else if ((counter % 2) == 0)
      {
        simulateFailureEvents(false);
      }
      else
```

```
      {
        simulateFailure1Events();
      }

      ++counter;
    }
    catch (java.lang.InterruptedException e)
    {
      System.out.println(e);
    }
  }
}
```

Multicast

For multicast events, you have to deliver the fired event to all of the registered listeners. Listing 11 illustrates how **Module** delivers the multicast **FailureEvent** to registered listeners, which are kept in **m_failureLs**. We will dissect **simulateFailureEvents()** in the sections that follow the section on unicast event delivery.

Listing 11   Multicast event delivery.

```
/**
   * Calls all the listeners that have registered to
   * receive FailureEvents.
   *
   * Note: This is a multicast delivery.
   *
   * @param type the specific type of FailureEvent
   *   true: total
   *   false: partial
   */
private void simulateFailureEvents(boolean type)
{
  Vector ls;

  // All the listeners who have expressed their
  // interest at the time the module triggers
  // an event should get notified.
  // You should clone the listeners in a
  // synchronized block to ensure that the list
  // of listeners does not change until all the
  // listeners are informed.
  //
  synchronized (this)
  {
```

```
        ls = (Vector) m_failureLs.clone();
    }

    // Create a failure event.
    //
    FailureEvent evt;
    Failure fail = new Failure();
    if (type) // total failure
    {
      evt = new FailureEvent(this,
                 FailureEvent.TOTAL_FAILURE, fail);
    }
    else  // partial failure
    {
      evt = new FailureEvent(this,
                 FailureEvent.PARTIAL_FAILURE, fail);
    }

    // Invoke all the callbacks.
    //
    for (int i = 0; i < ls.size(); i++)
    {
      FailureListener l;
      l = (FailureListener)ls.elementAt(i);

      if (type) // total failure
      {
        l.failureTotal(evt);
      }

      // Callback the partial failure.
      // Note that this callback throws an exception,
      //  which must be caught.
      else
      {
        try
        {
          l.failurePartial(evt);
        }
        catch (EContinueOperation e)
        {
          System.out.println(e);
        }
      }
    }
}
```

Unicast

Because there is at most one listener associated with it, unicast event delivery is a more straightforward task than multicast delivery. When a unicast event is triggered, you need to determine whether there is a registered event listener for the event; if so, simply invoke the callback and pass the triggered event as an argument. Listing 12 shows you how **Module** delivers **Failure1Event**, which is a unicast event.

Listing 12   Unicast event delivery.

```
/**
   * Calls the listener that has registered to
   * receive Failure1Events.
   *
   * Note: This is a unicast delivery.
   */
  private void simulateFailure1Events()
  {
    if (m_failure1L != null)
    {
      Failure fail = new Failure();
      Failure1Event evt = new Failure1Event(this, fail);

      m_failure1L.failure1(evt);
    }
  }
}
```

Synchronous Delivery

The delivery of an event is synchronous with respect to an event source. When you call a listener's callback of an event observer, the call is executed in the same thread that is processing the triggered event in the event source, and the call does not return until the event is delivered to the event observer. Once the event is delivered, however, the event observer may process it asynchronously in a separate thread and return the control back to the event source.

An event source delivers an event to a list of listeners sequentially using its own thread.

Concurrency Control

Although the event delivery is synchronous with respect to an event source, an event-driven system as a whole has an asynchronous nature and operates in a multithreaded environment. To understand this behavior better, suppose that while an event source is in the process of delivering events, an event observer attempts to register a listener with the source. The registration call issued by the observer is executed in the observer's thread, which is most likely different than the thread in the event source that is delivering the event. This situation can cause a race between the source and the observer. If the observer manages to register its listener before the source finishes the delivery process, it receives an event from the in-progress delivery; otherwise, it does not.

To prevent races and deadlocks, you should synchronize access to the data members that contain event listeners, either by synchronizing your registration methods or by using synchronized blocks within the registration methods. Furthermore, you should not use a synchronized method to fire listeners' callback methods; instead, you should use a synchronized block to clone the list of the listeners and then invoke the callbacks from within unsynchronized code. The **simulateFailureEvents()** method, shown back in Listing 11, is a good example of an event delivery method that conforms to the rules we have laid out.

*An event-driven system runs in a multithreaded environment and has an asynchronous nature. Such environments are subject to races and deadlocks. To reduce the risk of races and deadlocks, define your registration methods as **synchronized** and call event listeners from within unsynchronized code.*

Handling Exceptions

When invoked by an event source, an event observer may raise an exception to inform the source about some unanticipated situation that it encountered when handling the event. The event source may take whatever action necessary to remedy the exceptional situation. This remedial action, however, is completely governed by the source, and the observer cannot dictate it.

To raise an exception, an observer creates and throws an exception to an event source; this exception should contain all of the information about the situation that is needed for the source to perform appropriate corrective actions. The **simulateFailureEvents()** method in **Module**, for example, must catch and handle **EContinueOperation** when it calls back **failurePartial()**. The **EContinueOperation** exception instructs

Module to continue operation despite its partial failure and must contain whatever information is necessary for **Module** to resume its operation.

An event source must catch and handle all the exceptions raised when it calls listeners. The handling of exceptions is completely determined by the event source.

Order Of Delivery

The Java Beans specification does not mandate any correlation between the order of listener registration and the order of event delivery for multicast events. An event source is free to deliver an event to a number of registered listeners in the order they were registered, in the opposite order, or in a random order. The **Module** event source in the FCM application, for example, delivers the events to listeners in the same order that they were registered (refer back to Listing 11).

You should not write event handling code that relies on a particular delivery order. If you need to control the event delivery to your listeners, register only one listener and then chain the other listeners through the registered listener. This technique allows you to have complete control over the order of event delivery to your listeners.

Java Beans does not specify the order of event delivery to event listeners. It permits event sources to define their own delivery-order semantics.

Updating Event Listeners During Delivery

The Java Beans specification does not define the handling of races when an event delivery is in progress and another thread concurrently updates the listeners in the delivery list. An event source may elect to use the updated list, whereas another may choose to make a copy of the listeners at the moment an event is triggered and deliver the event to only those listeners. The **simulateFailureEvents**() method in **Module**, for instance, clones the list of listeners in a synchronized block to ensure the delivery of an event to all of the listeners registered when the event occurred.

Even though Java Beans does not mandate it, we strongly urge you to copy the list of listeners before you proceed with the event delivery. Otherwise, the behavior of your bean is subject to race conditions.

Event Observers

An event observer is the part of an event-driven system that reacts to events triggered in an event source. The behavior of an observer when it receives an event is completely application specific. If you are creating an AWT application, for example, AWT components are already predefined for you as event sources, and your application deals with registering predefined listeners and responding to the events generated by AWT. In this example, you are designing only the event observer and the GUI code of the application, and you do not have any control over the event sources or the events they generate.

CmdModule is the event observer in the FCM application. As shown in Listing 13, this class implements listeners for the events defined by **Module** and uses them to receive failure events from the modules of a system. The **CmdModule** observer simply prints events of the **FailureEvent** type to the screen and raises an exception when it receives an event of the type **Failure1Event**. Obviously, a more sophisticated version of **CmdModule** would have to incorporate more application-logic code in order to control the modules of a system.

You should cleanly separate the GUI code of your application from the event handling code, which resides in your event observer.

Listing 13   The CmdModule event observer.

```
import java.util.*;

/**
 * This class defines the command module of a system.
 * Its function is to monitor the system and respond
 * to the failures that occur in different modules.
 * In a real-world application, this command module
 * would take a failed subsystem out of the system
 * and re-route the system through a redundant module.
 * Our simple implementation, however, only prints
```

```
 * the failures that it receives.
 */
public class CmdModule
{
  public static void main(String[] argv)
  {
    CmdModule cmd = new CmdModule();
    Module mod = new Module();

    // Register a FailureListener with the module.
    //
    FailureListenerImp l;
    l = new FailureListenerImp(cmd);
    mod.addFailureListener(l);

    // Register a Failure1Listener with the module.
    // Note: This is a unicast event, and you must
    // handle the TooManyListenersException.
    //
    Failure1ListenerImp l1;
    l1 = new Failure1ListenerImp(cmd);

    try
    {
      mod.addFailure1Listener(l1);
    }
    catch (TooManyListenersException e)
    {
      System.out.println(e);
    }

    // Start the module.
    //
    mod.start();
  }

  public void failureTotal(FailureEvent evt)
  {
    System.out.println(evt);
  }

  public void failurePartial(FailureEvent evt)
  throws EContinueOperation
  {
    System.out.println(evt);

    throw new EContinueOperation();
  }
```

```java
    public void failure1(Failure1Event evt)
    {
      System.out.println(evt);
    }
}

class FailureListenerImp implements FailureListener
{
  CmdModule m_cmd;

  FailureListenerImp(CmdModule cmd)
  {
    m_cmd = cmd;
  }

  public void failureTotal(FailureEvent evt)
  {
    m_cmd.failureTotal(evt);
  }

  public void failurePartial(FailureEvent evt)
  throws EContinueOperation
  {
    m_cmd.failurePartial(evt);
  }
}

class Failure1ListenerImp implements Failure1Listener
{
  CmdModule m_cmd;

  Failure1ListenerImp(CmdModule cmd)
  {
    m_cmd = cmd;
  }

  public void failure1(Failure1Event evt)
  {
    m_cmd.failure1(evt);
  }
}
```

You should compile and run the FCM application. The following shows the output of this program:

```
e:\coriolis\cdrom\chap7\failure>java CmdModule
FailureEvent[source=Thread[Thread-1,5,main]]
Failure1Event[source=Thread[Thread-1,5,main]]
FailureEvent[source=Thread[Thread-1,5,main]]
```

The JDK 1.1 Event Model

```
EContinueOperation
Failure1Event[source=Thread[Thread-1,5,main]]
FailureEvent[source=Thread[Thread-1,5,main]]
Failure1Event[source=Thread[Thread-1,5,main]]
FailureEvent[source=Thread[Thread-1,5,main]]
EContinueOperation
```

 An event observer contains application-specific event handling logic that responds to events triggered in an event source.

Event Adapters

Because some of the AWT event listeners define more than one callback, when you create one of these listener classes, you have to implement all of the callback methods—even the ones that you are not interested in. For example, **WindowListener** (which listens on window-related events) identifies **windowClosed()**, **windowClosing()**, **windowDeiconified()**, **windowIconified()**, and **windowOpened()**. Even if you are interested only in the closing of a window, you must provide an implementation of all the above methods, not just **windowClosing()**.

To remedy this situation, JDK 1.1 provides seven standard adapters for AWT, shown in Figure 6. The methods in these adapter classes are all empty; the adapter classes are provided solely as an easier way to create listeners by extending them and overriding only the methods of interest. For example, instead of implementing the **WindowListener** interface, you can simply extend **WindowAdapter** and override **windowClosing()**, if that is the method you are interested in.

 *JDK 1.1 does not provide any default adapters for the semantic listeners, because each of those identifies only a single method; as a result, an adapter does not provide any convenience.*

The notion of adapters can be generalized to any object that is placed between an event source and a listener to enforce a policy or provide supplementary functionality. The standard adapters packaged with JDK 1.1 provide a small amount of functionality by allowing you to implement only those methods of a listener that you are interested in. In a previous section, we showed you a chaining technique to control the

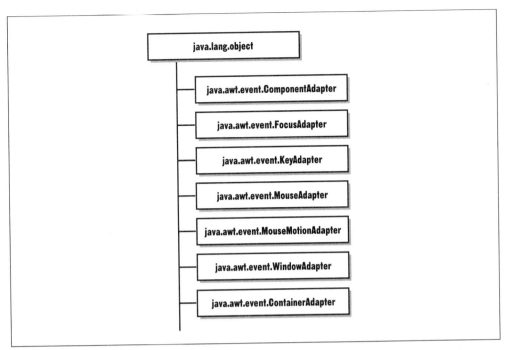

Figure 6   JDK 1.1 event adapters.

order of the event delivery to your listeners through one listener. This listener can be viewed as enforcing a policy on a set of listeners. You can use adapters to achieve a wide range of behaviors, such as implementing event queues for listeners, filtering events before they reach listeners, or demultiplexing multiple event sources into a single event listener.

An event adapter is interposed between an event source and an event listener to provide additional functionality or enforce a policy. An adapter essentially de-couples incoming event notifications from a listener.

Demultiplexing Adapters

When you use a listener to receive events from multiple event sources, you may want to target different methods on your event observer depending on the source of a particular event. To do this, of course, you will need to determine the source that actually generated a delivered event. Because an event always carries the source object that has triggered it, you may be able to make this determination based on the source information carried by the event. In some cases, however, this approach is impractical (for example, when possible event sources are instances of the same class).

Another approach is to use demultiplexing adapters, which can invoke different methods of a target event observer depending on the source of an event. You have already seen an example of such adapters in the HelloWorld applet in Chapter 5, which is shown again in Listing 14 for your convenience. This applet needs to invoke either the **on()** or **off()** method of the HelloDisplay bean, depending on whether the uses has clicked the "on" or "off" **PushButton**. Because these two buttons are instances of the same class, HelloDisplay uses two adapters, **OnButtonListener** and **OffButtonListener**, to accomplish the calling of different methods when a user presses a button. As you can see in Listing 14, these adapters are coded to call different methods on their target objects.

Listing 14 Demultiplexing adapters in the HelloWorld applet.

```
import java.awt.*;
import java.awt.event.*;

import mybeans.pushbutton.*;
import mybeans.hellodisplay.*;

/**
 * This class assembles three beans into an applet:
 * a display bean, an "on" button, and an "off" button.
 * The beans are hooked up so that the pushing of the
 * "on" button causes the message "Hello World" to
 * appear in the display bean. The "off" button turns
 * the display off.
 */
public class HelloWorld extends java.applet.Applet
{
  HelloDisplay hellodisp;

  public void init()
  {
    setLayout(new FlowLayout());

    // Add the display.
    //
    hellodisp = new HelloDisplay();
    add(hellodisp);
```

```
    // Add the "on" button.
    //
    PushButton btnOn = new PushButton("on");
    btnOn.addActionListener(new OnButtonListener());
    add(btnOn);

    // Add the "off" button.
    //
    PushButton btnOff = new PushButton("off");
    btnOff.addActionListener(new OffButtonListener());
    add(btnOff);
  }


/**
 * This class calls the "on" method of the display
 * bean.
 */
class OnButtonListener implements ActionListener
{
  public void actionPerformed(ActionEvent eve)
  {
    hellodisp.on(eve);
  }
}


/*
 * This class calls the "off" method of the display
 * bean.
 */
class OffButtonListener implements ActionListener
{
  public void actionPerformed(ActionEvent eve)
  {
    hellodisp.off(eve);
  }
}
}
```

 *Even though the above adapters are interposed directly between an event source and an observer (rather than between a source and a listener), they are still considered to be demultiplexing adapters.*

One drawback of simple demultiplexing adapters (such as the one presented in Listing 14) is that they can result in a proliferation of adapters if there are a large number of different event targets, because a different adapter class is required for each source-target hook-up. For such cases, you can automatically synthesize adapter classes that exploit the Java introspection APIs to map incoming events from multiple event sources into specific methods. This technique is accomplished by using the **invoke()** method of **java.lang.reflect.Method** class. This approach, however, is only suitable for frameworks and should not be used in manually generated code, as it bypasses the compile-time type checks of Java compilers and can cause fatal runtime errors.

Security Issues

The Java Virtual Machine (JVM) severely restricts untrusted applets by preventing them from accessing local files or performing any other operation that might otherwise compromise the security of the host machine. JVM concludes that an applet is untrusted by scanning backwards through the stack of the current thread and checking to determine if any stack frame belongs to an untrusted applet. Because an event source fires an event object synchronously within its thread, an event callback is as trustworthy as the event source that has triggered it. An untrusted applet, therefore, cannot breach the sandbox security model in Java by firing bogus events.

Event adapters that might be installed on the local disk, however, must not subvert the mechanism of checking the stack frame by allowing an event firing to look more trustworthy than the applet that has fired it. Failure to do so will allow a downloaded, untrusted applet to use a locally installed adapter and bypass the Java security model. The standard event adapters in the JDK 1.1 are simple utility classes supplied to make it easier to implement event listeners; these do not pose any security issues.

Conclusion

In this chapter, we presented an overview of the JDK 1.0 event model and cited its shortcomings (specifically, a lack of scaleability and performance). We then introduced you to the JDK 1.1 delegation-based event model and explained how this model results in a clean separation of an application's code into the GUI and event handling code. We discussed in detail the life cycle of an event state object—its creation in an event source, passage through an event listener, and consumption in an event observer.

We designed and implemented a simple timer example to introduce you to the underlying elements of an event-driven system. We used the ideas in this example to implement a more rigorous event system, the Failure Command Module (FCM) application. We purposely did not use AWT in FCM to emphasize that the delegation-based event model in JDK 1.1 is a general-purpose model that can be applied to a wide range of applications, not just programs with front-end GUIs. We used FCM to illustrate many concepts, such as low-level and semantic events, multicast and unicast registration, and event delivery.

By now, you know in detail the fundamentals of Java Beans: properties and events. What you don't know yet, however, is how to extend an AWT component and perform event handling in your subclass. Extended AWT widgets suffer from some of the shortcomings of the JDK 1.0 event model, and they result in complicated, error-prone logic code and a proliferation of classes. Therefore, you should subclass an AWT class only when you need to enhance an AWT class with a special look or behavior. You will learn much more about event handling in an extended AWT class in the next chapter.

INDEX

M